OCR
A LEVEL

2

ECONOMICS
FOR A LEVEL YEAR 2

Peter Smith

HODDER
EDUCATION
AN HACHETTE UK COMPANY

The Publishers would like to thank the following for permission to reproduce copyright material.

Photo credits
Cover Oleksiy Mark/Fotolia; **p4** Martinan/Fotolia; **p26** DragonImages/Fotolia; **p20** qaphotos.com/Alamy; **p26** Gem Photography/Fotolia; **p30** Dinodia Photos/Alamy; **p33** Stephen Brashear/Getty Images; **p45** txakel/Fotolia; **p49** Ana Malin/Fotolia; **p53** Mark Richardson /Alamy; **p63** British Airways; **p66** easyJet; **p73** Julio Etchart/Alamy; **p75** Vodolej/ Fotolia; **p81** Somkanokwan/Fotolia; **p84** Bloomberg/Getty Images; **p93** Wellphoto/ Fotolia; **p99** Frank Boston/Fotolia; **p104** Allstar Picture Library/Alamy; **p106** Nicefoto/ Fotolia; **p119** Monkey Business/Fotolia; **p123** Gregory Wrona/Alamy; **p129** Jeffrey Blackler/ Alamy; **p137** Monkey Business/Fotolia; **p142** The Final Miracle/Fotolia; **p146** rob245/ Fotolia; **p155** Stagecoach Group plc; **p158** Pornchai Kittiwongsakul/Getty Images; **p162** Željko Radojko/Fotolia; **p174** Kumar Sriskandan/Alamy; **p178** Lev/Fotolia; **p192** DB Images/ Alamy; **p206** Morane/Fotolia; **p211** Luis Apuccini/Fotolia; **p213** poco_bw/Fotolia; **p220** Tyler Olson/Fotolia; **p224** Thakala/Fotolia; **p228** Ace Stock Limited/Alamy; **p233** Lou Linwei/Alamy; **p248** David Levenson/Alamy; **p255** Tidchun/Fotolia; **p263** doble.d-/Fotolia; **p265** Andreaphoto/Fotolia; **p270** Popperfoto/Getty Images; **p281** Kadmy/Fotolia; **p289** Bloomberg/Getty Images; **p293** Clynt Garnham Business/Alamy; **p298** SC Photos/Alamy; **p305** VanderWolf Images/Fotolia; **p309** Robert Hoetink/Fotolia; **p315** Sonny Tumbelaka/ AFP/Getty Images; **p321** Sebastian Duda/Fotolia; **p329** Network Photographer/Alamy; **p336** asab974/Fotolia; **p340** Georg Kristiansen/Alamy; **p345** Alistair Cotton/Fotolia; **p349** Chris Dorney/Fotolia; **p359** Stephen Jaffe/IMF via Getty Images; **p361** Kostas Pikoulas/Alamy

Every effort has been made to trace all copyright holders, but if any have been inadvertently overlooked, the Publishers will be pleased to make the necessary arrangements at the first opportunity.

Although every effort has been made to ensure that website addresses are correct at time of going to press, Hodder Education cannot be held responsible for the content of any website mentioned in this book. It is sometimes possible to find a relocated web page by typing in the address of the home page for a website in the URL window of your browser.

Hachette UK's policy is to use papers that are natural, renewable and recyclable products and made from wood grown in sustainable forests. The logging and manufacturing processes are expected to conform to the environmental regulations of the country of origin.

Orders
Please contact Bookpoint Ltd, 130 Milton Park, Abingdon, Oxon OX14 4SB. Telephone: (44) 01235 827720. Fax: (44) 01235 400454. Email education@bookpoint.co.uk Lines are open from 9 a.m. to 5 p.m., Monday to Saturday, with a 24-hour message answering service. You can also order through our website: www.hoddereducation.co.uk

ISBN: 978 1 4718 2995 6

Typeset by Integra Software Services Pvt., Pondicherry, India. Printed in Dubai

A catalogue record for this title is available from the British Library.

Get the most from this book

In combination with Book 1, this textbook provides an introduction to economics. It has been tailored explicitly to cover the content of the OCR specification for the A Level qualification in Economics. The book is divided into sections, each covering one of the components that make up the OCR programme of study.

The text provides the foundation for studying OCR Economics, but you will no doubt wish to keep up to date by referring to additional topical sources of information about economic events. This can be done by reading the serious newspapers, visiting key sites on the internet, and reading such magazines as *Economic Review*.

Special features

Prior knowledge needed
The knowledge required for the course that you have already met in your first year of studies.

Learning objectives
A statement of the intended learning objectives for each chapter.

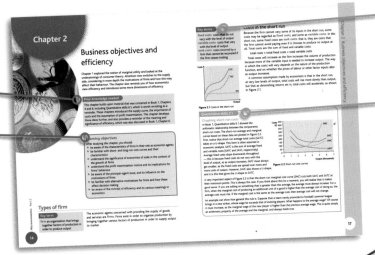

Key terms
Clear, concise definitions of essential key terms where they first appear and a list at the end of each section.

Quantitative skills
Worked examples of quantitative skills that you will need to develop.

Synoptic links
Synoptic links showing the connections between the themes.

Extension material
Extension points to stretch your understanding.

Study tips
Short pieces of advice to help you present your ideas effectively and avoid potential pitfalls.

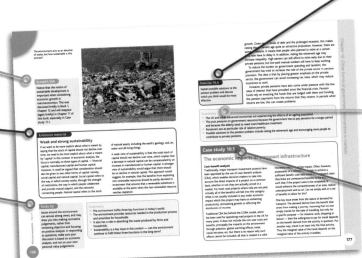

Exercises and questions
Exercises to provide active engagement with economic analysis and practice questions at the end of each section to check your knowledge and understanding.

Summaries
Bulleted summaries of each topic that can be used as a revision tool.

Case studies
Case studies to show economic concepts applied to real-world situations.

Contents

Section 2 Macroeconomics

Introduction

Prior learning, knowledge and progression

This book builds upon the material that was covered in Book 1. At key points during the text you will find references to particular chapters in Book 1 that will support your understanding.

Assessment objectives

In common with other economics specifications, OCR Economics entails four assessment objectives. Candidates will thus be expected to:

- demonstrate knowledge of terms/concepts and theories/models to show an understanding of the behaviour of economic agents and how they are affected by and respond to economic issues
- apply knowledge and understanding to various economic contexts to show how economic agents are affected by and respond to economic issues
- analyse issues within economics, showing an understanding of their impact on economic agents
- evaluate economic arguments and use qualitative and quantitative evidence to support informed judgements relating to economic issues.

The structure of assessment

The A Level assessment is based on three examinations at the end of the 2-year course, one in microeconomics, one in macroeconomics and one on themes in economics. Each is a written paper lasting 2 hours. The question papers contain a combination of multiple-choice questions, a data-response section and an essay (an extended writing question).

Further details are provided on the OCR website at **www.ocr.org.uk**.

Economics in this book

The study of economics also requires a familiarity with recent economic events in the UK and elsewhere, and candidates will be expected to show familiarity with 'recent historical data' — broadly defined as covering the last 25 years. The following websites will help you to keep up to date with recent trends and events:

- Recent and historical data about the UK economy can be found at the website of the Office for National Statistics (ONS) at: **www.ons.gov.uk**

- Also helpful is the site of HM Treasury at: **www.gov.uk/government/organisations/hm-treasury**. Especially useful is the Treasury's *Pocket Databank*, which is updated weekly, providing major economic indicators and series for both domestic and international economies: **www.gov.uk/government/statistics/weekly-economic-indicators**
- The Bank of England site is well worth a visit, especially the *Inflation Report* and the Minutes of the Monetary Policy Committee: **www.bankofengland.co.uk**
- The Institute for Fiscal Studies offers an independent view of a range of economic topics: **www.ifs.org.uk**

It is also important to be able to put the UK experience into an international context. There are many helpful websites that enable this. The World Bank offers an extensive array of indicators about almost every country at **http://data.worldbank.org/** or you can use their data visualiser at **http://devdata.worldbank.org/DataVisualizer/** which allows you to construct all sorts of interesting graphs to trace how countries have changed through time. You can also visit the UNDP at **http://hdr.undp.org/en/data-explorer**. Other data are available via OCED at **www.oecd.org** or via the European Commission at **http://ec.europa.eu/eurostat**.

Finally, for answers to case studies, exercises etc. featured in this book, please visit **https://www.hoddereducation.co.uk/Product?Product=9781471829956** and click 'Download answers'.

How to study economics

There are two crucial aspects of studying economics. The first stage is to study the theory, which helps us to explain economic behaviour. However, in studying A Level Economics it is equally important to be able to apply the theories and concepts that you meet, and to see just how these relate to the real world.

If you are to become competent at this, it is vital that you get plenty of practice. In part, this means carrying out the exercises that you will find in this text. However, it also means thinking about how economics helps us to explain news items and data that appear in the newspapers and on the television. Make sure that you practise as much as you can.

In economics, it is also important to be able to produce examples of economic phenomena. In reading this text, you will find some examples that help to illustrate ideas and concepts. Do not rely solely on the examples provided here, but look around the world to find your own examples, and keep a note of these ready for use in essays and exams. This will help to convince the examiners that you have understood economics. It will also help you to understand the theories.

Enjoy economics

Most important of all, I hope you will enjoy your study of economics. I have always been fascinated by the subject, and hope that you will capture something of the excitement and challenge of learning about how markets and the economy operate. I also wish you every success with your studies.

Acknowledgements

I would like to express my deep gratitude to Mark Russell, whose thorough reading of the book's precursor and insightful and helpful comments were invaluable in improving the scope and focus of this book. I am also grateful to the reviewer who commented on this edition, whose remarks and suggestions have enabled improvements in the content and style of this new edition. I would also like to thank the team at Hodder Education, especially Naomi Holdstock, Rachel Furse and Chris Bessant, for their efficiency in production of this book, and for their support and encouragement.

Many of the data series shown in figures in this book were drawn from the data obtained from the National Statistics website www.statistics.gov.uk and contain public sector information licensed under the Open Government Licence v3.0.

Other data were from various sources, including OECD, World Bank, United Nations Development Programme and other sources as specified.

While every effort has been made to trace the owners of copyright material, I would like to apologise to any copyright holders whose rights may have unwittingly been infringed.

Peter Smith

SECTION
1

MICROECONOMICS

Part 1
How competitive markets work

Chapter 1

Demand and marginal utility

Early on in your study of microeconomics, you were introduced to the demand and supply model, and to the way in which prices could be seen to act as a guide to resource allocation, providing signals and incentives to economic agents. Consumers represent one of the key economic agents in the analysis, and this chapter returns to the analysis of consumer behaviour, looking in more depth at the motivations of consumers and at how the demand curve can be derived and analysed. The chapter begins by introducing the important concept of the margin.

Learning objectives

After studying this chapter, you should:
- understand what is meant by the concept of the margin
- be able to evaluate the extent to which the marginal concept is useful to economic agents in decision making
- be familiar with the concepts of total and marginal utility
- understand the law of diminishing marginal utility and what this reveals about the nature of the demand curve
- be aware of the importance of the equi-marginal principle
- be familiar with the limitations of marginal utility theory
- understand the nature of a consumer's budget line
- be familiar with the income and substitution effects of a price change
- be able to evaluate the concept of rationality as a way of understanding the behaviour of economic agents

Prior knowledge needed

This chapter uses the concept of opportunity cost (first introduced in Chapter 1 of Book 1, and looks at the nature of demand (introduced in Chapter 3 of Book 1) in a new way.

The concept of the margin

Decisions, decisions...

How will you spend your evening? You have to read the chapter in your economics textbook that has been set for you, but there is a TV programme about to start that you would quite like to watch. Will the extra benefit that you gain from watching the TV programme compensate for the cost of not reading your chapter (or having to get up early tomorrow to read it)?

A firm finds that it is falling behind on its orders. Should it take on an extra worker to enable it to catch up? Would the additional benefit that the firm would gain by keeping its customers happy compensate for the extra wage costs incurred?

One of the first economic ideas that you met at the beginning of your study of economics was the notion of *opportunity cost*. This captures the

Key terms

marginal principle the idea that economic agents may take decisions by considering the effect of small changes from the existing situation

rational decision making a decision that allows an economic agent to maximise their objective, by setting the marginal benefit of an action equal to its marginal cost

idea that when you take a decision or make a choice, you will choose on the basis of comparing the benefit you gain from a choice with the benefit from the next best alternative choice. The two examples of decisions above illustrate this notion. If you choose to watch the TV programme, you incur an opportunity cost in terms of the cost of not reading your chapter. If the firm chooses not to hire the additional worker, it incurs an opportunity cost, by keeping its customers waiting and potentially losing orders.

The marginal principle

The decisions also illustrate another important notion in economics, as in both cases, the decision is taken on the basis of balancing two alternatives against each other by weighing up small changes. Economists rely heavily on the idea that firms, consumers and other economic agents can make good decisions by thinking in terms of the margin. This is known as the **marginal principle**.

You will meet this approach to decision making in a variety of situations as you study economics. At the heart of much of economic analysis is the notion that economic agents have clear objectives, and that they take decisions that allow them to do the best that they can to achieve those objectives. For example, to analyse the decisions taken by firms, it is often assumed that they set out to maximise profits. By taking decisions on the basis of small (marginal) changes, they can fine-tune their decisions, and home in on the best possible position. By assuming this, economists are able to model the decisions and analyse the consequences.

This approach is based on the assumption that economic agents are **rational**, in the sense that they always do what they expect to bring the best possible results. By balancing the marginal benefit against the marginal cost of an action, they can achieve this. In other words, if the marginal benefit of a particular choice exceeds its marginal cost, then a rational agent would choose to proceed, but if the marginal benefit is less than marginal cost, it would be better not to proceed. The cusp decision is where marginal benefit equals marginal cost, because there is no incentive to change the decision.

The marginal principle comes into play at the societal level as well. For example, you may recall that in the presence of externalities, the best position for society is reached when marginal social benefit is equal to marginal social cost. An example is where the firms in a market cause pollution as part of their production activities. This is an example of *market failure*, and in order to overcome this, it may be necessary to influence the behaviour of firms by bringing their marginal private costs into line with the marginal costs faced by society.

The marginal principle is thus seen to be important for the construction of economic models, and important for economic decision-makers in enabling them to take rational decisions. However, it also highlights an important criticism that has been levelled at economists and at economics. The assumption that economic agents behave rationally has been questioned by many critics. Do firms always act to maximise profits? Do consumers never take decisions on impulse or make choices that are not in their own best interests? It is important to be aware of these issues, and they will be considered as the course proceeds.

Exercise 1.1

a Think about some of the
  decisions that you take in your
  daily life. Can you think of
  examples where these illustrate
  the marginal principle?
b Do you consider that you take
  decisions rationally in order to
  maximise your satisfaction?

Summary

- Opportunity cost is an important element in making choices.
- Decisions are often taken by considering small changes to existing behaviour.
- This approach to decision making is known as the use of the marginal principle.
- The marginal principle underpins the notion of rational decision making.
- The assumption of rationality enables economists to model the behaviour of economic agents.
- There may be circumstances in which decisions do not reflect this rational approach.

Marginal utility theory

Key terms

utility the satisfaction received
from consuming a good or service
marginal utility the additional
utility gained from consuming an
extra unit of a good or service

Suppose you could measure the satisfaction that you derive from consuming a good. For example, consider the case of chocolate bars. Consuming a chocolate bar gives you a certain amount of satisfaction — which economists often refer to as **utility** in this context. Imagine that it is possible to put a numerical value on this utility, and for the sake of argument that the utility you get from consuming a chocolate bar is 30 'utils', this being the unit in which utility is measured.

Having consumed the chocolate bar, you are now offered a second, which you also consume, this time receiving 26 utils of utility. You probably get less utility from the second bar simply because you have already had some chocolate — and the more chocolate bars you eat, the less utility you are likely to get from the additional bar. Notice here that the valuation of the utility refers to the additional satisfaction that is gained from the second bar. This is therefore known as the **marginal utility** from consuming an additional chocolate bar. Indeed, there will come a time when you have eaten so much chocolate that you cannot face eating any more, as you know you would be ill. Table 1.1 shows the marginal utility that Emily gains from consuming chocolate bars.

Table 1.1 Utility from chocolate

Number of bars	Marginal utility (utils)
1	30
2	26
3	21
4	15
5	8
6	0

Economists refer to the utility of a good:
in this case, how much satisfaction you
receive from consuming a chocolate bar

Key term

law of diminishing marginal
utility states that the more
units of a good that are
consumed, the lower the
utility from consuming those
additional units

In this example, the sixth chocolate bar gives no satisfaction to Emily,
who has already had enough chocolate for the day.

This idea that the more of a good you consume, the less additional
pleasure you get from the extra unit of it is known as the **law of
diminishing marginal utility**. It is a 'law' because it has been found to
be universally true. If you keep consuming more of something, you get
less additional satisfaction from extra units. Figure 1.1 plots the marginal
utility values on a graph. The law of diminishing marginal utility ensures
that the *MU* curve is downward sloping.

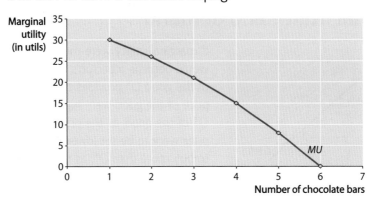

Figure 1.1 A marginal utility curve

If it were really possible to measure satisfaction in this way, it would
also be possible to calculate the total utility that Emily receives from
consuming chocolate bars. For instance, if she consumes two bars, she gets
30 + 26 = 56 utils. If she has a third bar, her *total utility* would be 77 utils.

The relationship between 'total' and 'marginal' appears in many areas
of economic analysis, and it is good to be clear about it. The 'marginal'
value is calculated as the change in the 'total'.

Quantitative skills 1.1

Calculating the marginal value from the total

Table 1.2 shows the total utility that Thomas obtains from consuming a good.

The second column of the table shows that Thomas
receives 10 utils from the first unit of the good
and 19 from the second, so the marginal utility of
the second is simply 19 − 10 = 9 utils. Similarly, he
receives 8 utils from consuming the third unit.

It is important to notice that the second column
in this particular example shows the total utility
of each and every unit of X. Full information
is not always available, so in the final column
only the alternate total utility values are shown.
This makes a difference to the calculation.

Table 1.2 Thomas's total utility from good X

Units of X	Total utility (utils)	Total utility (utils)
1	10	10
2	19	
3	27	27
4	34	
5	40	40
6	45	
7	49	49

To calculate marginal utility when moving from 3 to 5 units of X, the change in total utility (40 − 27 = 13 utils),
the result has to be expressed on a per unit basis, i.e. 13/2 = 6.5, this being the average increase in total utility as
consumption increases by 2 units.

Study tip

The relationship between the 'total' and the 'marginal' is not confined to this particular example of utility. It will also apply in the case of the costs faced by firms and the revenue that they receive from selling their products, and in many other contexts. It is a purely mathematical relationship, and you should watch out for it.

Marginal utility and demand

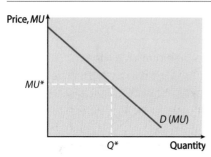

Figure 1.2 An individual's demand curve

If marginal utility were measured in terms of money, then the *MU* curve would become a person's demand curve. Consider Figure 1.2. The quantity of the good Q^* provides this individual with marginal utility of MU^*. If the price of the good were higher than MU^*, then the individual would not buy Q^* of the good, as the price exceeds his valuation. On the other hand, if price were to be set lower than MU^*, then the individual would be prepared to buy more than Q^*, as the marginal utility would be higher than the asking price. Another way of putting this is to say that the consumer will purchase the good up to the point where the price is equal to the marginal utility gained from consuming the good. Of course, a similar argument applies at each point along the *MU* curve, so this is indeed the individual's demand curve when utility is measured in money terms.

The previous discussion of the demand curve emphasised that the curve shows the relationship between the quantity demanded of a good and its price, *ceteris paribus*. In other words, it focused on the relationship between demand and price, holding other influences on demand constant. This argument also applies in this case. Changes in the price of other goods, in consumer incomes or in preferences would all affect the position of the D (*MU*) curve.

This highlights the fact that decisions about the consumption of one good are interconnected with decisions being made about other goods. If a consumer chooses to consume more of one good, that means there is less income available to be spent on other goods. Furthermore, a decision to consume more of one good will affect the consumption of complementary and substitute goods. So rather than focusing on a consumer's decisions about the demand for a single good, it is also necessary to consider the demand for a bundle of goods and services, and how a consumer can arrive at a joint decision.

The equi-marginal principle

To keep things simple, consider an individual choosing a combination of two goods, x and y. The individual gains utility from each good, and sets out to maximise the utility received from consumption of both. The quantity chosen of one good affects the demand for the other, given a limited budget to spend on the items. Therefore, it is not a simple question of setting marginal utility equal to price, because the decision about one good affects the position of the *MU* curve for the other good because of the linkage through the budget constraint.

equi-marginal principle that a consumer does best in utility terms by consuming at the point where the ratio of marginal utilities from two goods is equal to the ratio of their prices

It turns out that the best a consumer can do is to consume the two goods at the point where the ratio of the marginal utilities of the two goods is equal to the ratio of their prices. In other words, this is where:

$$\frac{MU_x}{MU_y} = \frac{P_x}{P_y}$$

This is known as the **equi-marginal principle**. It describes the conditions under which a consumer will maximise his or her utility. In principle, this can be extended to the case where consumers are choosing between many goods and services.

Limitations of marginal utility theory

The marginal utility approach provides insights into consumer behaviour, but it has its limitations. First, utility is not something that can be measured; there is no objective way of valuing utility, which will vary from individual to individual. In other words, because each consumer is different and has different preferences, it is impossible to compare utility between individuals. One person may gain different utility from £1 than another, and there is no way of comparing their utility values. This does not mean that the analysis is unhelpful — but it must be recognised that there are limitations when it comes to putting the theory into practice. For example, it may be difficult to think of aggregating across individual consumers in order to build a market demand curve from a good. However, it will be shown that there are some important insights to be gained from pushing this analysis a bit further.

It is also difficult to conceive of the marginal utility approach when the analysis needs to be extended to multiple goods and services, so that the many interactions between the demand for one good and another need to be taken into account. One way of making some sense of this would be to consider the consumer's choice as being between the utility gained from one good as compared with all other goods considered together. However, assume that a consumer is choosing between two goods.

The budget line

budget line shows the boundary of an individual's consumption set, given the amount available to spend and the prices of the goods

Suppose that Adam has £2.40 to spend, and wants to split his purchases between apples (which are 40p each) and cola (which is 80p per bottle). He can choose to spend the whole amount on apples, or on cola — or can buy some of each. Given these prices, he could buy 6 apples or 3 bottles of cola. The possibilities are shown as the **budget line** in Figure 1.3. This connects the combinations of apples and cola that Adam could purchase. For example, he could buy 4 apples and 1 bottle of cola, as marked on the figure. One way of interpreting the budget line is that it is the boundary that shows the combinations of apples and cola that Adam can afford — he could not choose to consume beyond the budget line.

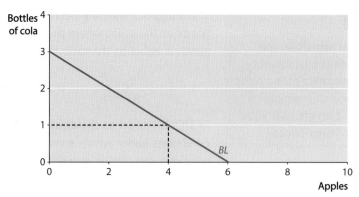

Figure 1.3 Adam's budget line

Figure 1.4 shows how the budget line would be affected if Adam found another £1.60 in his pocket so that he had £4 to spend on these two goods. The budget line shifts from BL_0 to BL_1, and Adam can now buy more of each of the goods. What combination of the two goods he will choose in the new situation is uncertain, as this will depend upon Adam's preferences. Notice that the slope of the budget line here does not change, as the relative price of the two goods remains the same.

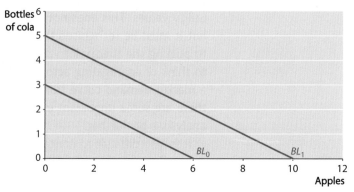

Figure 1.4 The effect of an increase in Adam's budget

The effect of a change in price

Consider the situation in which the price of apples changes. Perhaps there is a glut of apples, so that the price falls. If the price falls from 40p to 20p, Adam's (original) budget line will change. He can still buy a maximum of 3 bottles of cola, but could now buy 8 apples if he so wished. This is shown in Figure 1.5, where the budget line moves from BL_0 to BL_1.

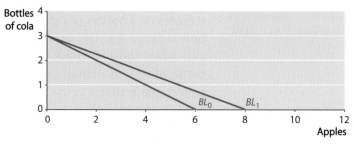

Figure 1.5 The effect of a change in the price of apples

income effect of a price change
reflects the way that a change
in the price of a good affects
purchasing power

substitution effect of a price
change reflects the way that
a change in the price of a good
affects relative prices

The choice set for Adam has expanded, as potentially he is now able to consume more of both goods. This is because the fall in price means that his budget is now worth more, in the sense that it allows him to expand his consumption set. This is known as the **income effect** of the price change. However, there is a second effect operating here, because the relative price of the two goods has changed. This is reflected in the slope of the budget line. From Adam's point of view, the relative price of apples has fallen, so *ceteris paribus* he will tend to shift towards consumption of apples. This is known as the **substitution effect** of the price change. Another way of looking at this is that Adam's opportunity cost of consuming cola has increased in terms of apples, so he will tend to substitute apples for cola.

The exact way in which Adam will change his consumption pattern between these goods as the relative price changes will depend upon his preferences. However, it is useful to realise that the change will be influenced by these two different effects. In real life, he would be choosing between a wider set of possible goods and services, but in principle the same effects will come into play.

Back to the demand curve

Notice that the analysis of the effect of a change in price on the demand for the two goods is providing information about the demand curve for the good whose price is changing. By tracking the way in which Adam's demand for apples changes as the price of apples varies, the shape of his individual demand curve is traced out. This is a reminder that the marginal utility analysis provides the underpinning for the demand curve.

Exercise 1.3

Suppose that Jennifer is allocating her available budget between two goods. Using a diagram, show how her budget line would shift:

a if the amount that she has to spend on these two goods falls

b if the price of one of the goods increases

Extension material

Modelling Adam's preferences

The indifference curve

In order to analyse Adam's choice between apples and cola, some way is needed to show his preferences on the diagram. This can be done using *indifference curves*. An indifference curve shows the various combinations of apples and cola that give Adam equal satisfaction — that is, equal utility. These are downward sloping because Adam can trade off the satisfaction received from one of the goods against that from the other. In other words, if he consumes fewer apples, he needs to consume more cola in order to maintain equal utility.

Figure 1.6 shows three such curves. Consider the curve IC_2. This shows that Adam would receive equal utility from consuming 2 bottles of cola and 2 apples as he would from 3 bottles of cola and 1 apple. Similarly, any point along this curve would be equally satisfactory to Adam (if he could consume fractions

of bottles or apples). The same argument applies to the other curves shown in the diagram, but because we assume that Adam would prefer more to less, he would maximise utility by reaching the highest possible curve that he can reach. In other words, he would prefer to be on IC_2 than on IC_1, but IC_3 would be better than both.

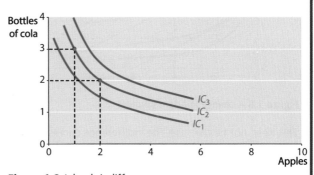

Figure 1.6 Adam's indifference curves

Adam's choice

Adam cannot choose to be on just any of the curves, as he is constrained by his budget line. However, if the budget line is superimposed on the map of indifference curves, his choice can be identified. This can be seen in Figure 1.7. The highest indifference curve that Adam can reach given his budget line (*BL*) is *IC₂*. The budget line just touches the indifference curve at one point, where Adam consumes 2 bottles of cola and 2 apples. At any other point along the budget line or below it, he would receive lower utility than this. The tangency point at *A* is his choice point.

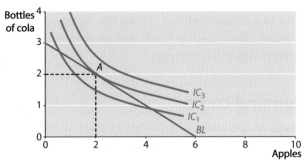

Figure 1.7 Adam's choice

The effect of a change in budget

Suppose that Adam receives an increase in his income, so that his budget for spending on these goods increases, as in the earlier discussion. This is shown in Figure 1.8, where the budget line moves from BL_0 to BL_1. As a result, Adam can now reach a higher indifference curve by moving from point *A* to point *B*. He now consumes 3 bottles of cola and 4 apples. In this example, Adam increases his consumption of both goods as income rises, indicating that they are both *normal goods*.

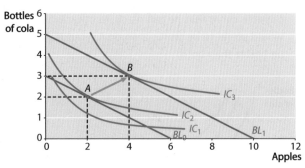

Figure 1.8 A change in Adam's budget

This need not be the case. The indifference curves could be such that the change in income causes Adam to consume less of one of the goods. In other words, one of the goods could be an *inferior good*. Figure 1.9

illustrates this on the assumption that Adam can consume fractions of bottles of cola and apples. In this example, Adam responds to the change in income by consuming more apples, but less cola.

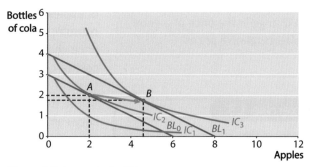

Figure 1.9 A marginal utility curve

A fall in the price of apples

If there is a fall in the price of apples, Adam's budget line is again affected. Figure 1.10 shows what happens to his budget line if the price of apples halves. With this set of indifference curves, his choice changes from point *A* to point *B*, and he continues to consume 2 bottles of cola, but now chooses 4 apples.

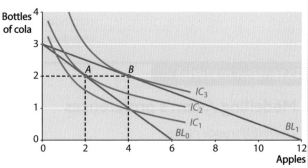

Figure 1.10 A fall in the price of apples

It is now possible to identify the income and substitution effects. Consider Figure 1.11. This time, suppose that there is an increase in the price of apples, shifting the budget line from BL_0 to BL_1. Adam's initial choice point is at *A*, and the increase in the price of apples means that he can no longer reach this point, and thus ends up at *B*. Given the new relative prices, the shadow budget line *BL** shows the level of income that would have left Adam at his original utility level — that is, this would have allowed him to reach *IC₂*. The impact of the price change is thus partly a substitution effect along the indifference curve from *A* to *C*, and partly an income effect from *C* to *B*.

Extension material (continued)

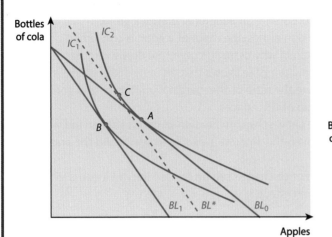

Figure 1.11 Income and substitution effects of a price change

Notice that in this example, both apples and cola are normal goods, and the substitution and income effects work in the same direction. In other words, when the price of apples increases, both income and substitution effects reduce the consumption of apples.

Figure 1.12 shows that when apples are an inferior good, the substitution and income effects work in opposite directions. Adam's tendency to substitute cola for apples (from A to C) is partly offset by the income effect from C to B: as income falls, Adam tends to consume more apples.

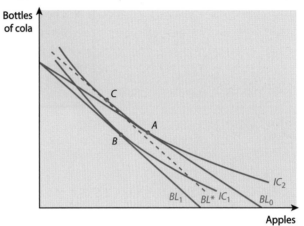

Figure 1.12 Income and substitution effects of a price change when apples are an inferior good

Do consumers always act rationally?

Key term

behavioural economics a branch of economics that builds on the psychology of human behaviour in decision making

Marginal utility theory rests on the crucial assumption that consumers act rationally in taking decisions about their spending and consumption by setting out to maximise their utility. Recent advances in **behavioural economics** suggest that this is not always the case.

This branch of economic analysis recognises that the psychology of human decision making is more complex than the simple desire to maximise utility. People do not always focus on purely economic influences, but may act on impulse, or in response to their feelings. This can lead them to take decisions about their spending that cannot be explained only by utility maximisation. For example, they may make charitable donations or may purchase more of some goods than would be dictated by rational economic behaviour, perhaps because there were seen to be special offers available.

Increasingly, behavioural economists are using experimental situations to discover more about how people react in situations of risk and how their spending behaviour is influenced by impulse and in response to stimuli. This analysis is potentially valuable to firms: if they can understand what induces people to behave in certain ways, they may be able to influence their spending.

Exercise 1.4

Do you ever give to charity, or buy a cake you don't really want to support Children in Need? Perhaps you engage in fund-raising activities when you could be having fun doing something else? Discuss the extent to which this represents a departure from rational behaviour.

Summary

- Marginal utility represents the additional satisfaction that a consumer receives from consuming an additional unit of a good.
- Marginal utility diminishes, the more of a good is consumed.
- This helps to explain why demand curves are downward sloping.
- The equi-marginal principle shows that an individual's utility is maximised where the ratio of the marginal utilities of two goods is equal to the ratio of their prices.
- The budget line shows the combination of goods that an individual can consume given the amount available to spend and the prices of the goods.
- The effects of a price change can be divided into an income effect and a substitution effect.

SECTION
1

MICROECONOMICS

Part 2
Competition and market power

Chapter 2

Business objectives and efficiency

Chapter 1 explored the notion of marginal utility and looked at the underpinnings of consumer theory. Attention now switches to the supply side, considering in more depth the motivations of firms and how this may affect their behaviour. The chapter also reminds you of how economists view efficiency and introduces some more dimensions of efficiency.

Prior knowledge needed

This chapter builds upon material that was contained in Book 1, Chapters 4 and 6, including Quantitative skills 6.1, which is worth revisiting as a reminder. These chapters introduced the supply curve, the importance of costs and the assumption of profit maximisation. This chapter develops these ideas further, and also provides a reminder of the meaning and significance of efficiency, which was also discussed in Book 1, Chapter 6.

Learning objectives

After studying this chapter, you should:
- be aware of the characteristics of firms in their role as economic agents
- be familiar with short- and long-run cost curves and their characteristics
- understand the significance of economies of scale in the context of the growth of firms
- understand the profit maximisation motive and its implications for firms' behaviour
- be aware of the principal–agent issue, and its influence on the motivations of firms
- be familiar with alternative motivations for firms and how these affect decision making
- be aware of the concept of efficiency and its various meanings in economics

Types of firm

Key term

firm an organisation that brings together factors of production in order to produce output

The economic agents concerned with providing the supply of goods and services are **firms**. Firms exist in order to organise production by bringing together various factors of production in order to supply output to market.

Internally, firms may be organised in various ways, from small sole proprietors (such as a corner shop) to mega-sized multinational corporations (such as Google). A key decision that all firms face concerns the scale of their operations. This decision turns partly on the nature of the market that they are serving, but it also depends upon the technology of the sector in which they operate and the structure of costs that they face.

Some firms may need to grow in order to compete with other large-scale competitors in global markets. There may be many reasons why firms wish to expand their operations. This chapter will begin to explain why this is so, and show how the decision about how much output to produce depends upon what it is that a firm is trying to achieve, and on the market environment in which it is operating.

In some sectors, there are examples of both large and small firms. For example, in the leisure sector, your local gymnasium may be a relatively small enterprise, but there are also some big players in the market, such as Chelsea FC and Sky. In the transport sector, there may be small local taxi firms, but there are also large firms such as British Airways.

Exercise 2.1

Identify firms that operate in the town or city where you live. Which of them would you classify as being relatively small-scale enterprises, and which operate on a more national basis?

Summary

- A firm is an organisation that exists to bring together factors of production in order to produce goods or services.
- Firms range, in the complexity of their organisation, from sole proprietors to public limited companies.
- Firms vary in size, from one-person concerns to large multinational corporations operating in global markets.

Firms and their costs

Key terms

short run the period over which a firm is free to vary its input of one factor of production (labour), but faces fixed inputs of the other factors of production

long run the period over which the firm is able to vary the inputs of all its factors of production

Firms have to make key decisions about the quantity of output that they wish to produce. This also involves taking decisions about the inputs of factors of production needed to produce this output, and the ways in which those factors are combined. An important element in taking these decisions concerns the way in which the costs of production vary with the level of output to be produced, which depends upon the prices of the factors of production and the way in which they are combined.

This section focuses on the relationship between costs and the level of output produced by a firm. For simplicity, assume that the firm produces a single product using two factors of production — labour and capital.

In exploring the firm's decisions, it is important to distinguish between the **short run** and the **long run**. In the short run the firm faces limited flexibility. Varying the quantity of labour input that the firm uses may be relatively straightforward — it can increase the use of overtime, or hire more workers, fairly quickly. However, varying the amount of capital that the firm has at its disposal may take longer. For example, it takes time to commission a new piece of machinery, or to build a new factory — or a Channel Tunnel! Hence labour is often regarded as a flexible factor and capital as a fixed factor. The short run is defined as the period over which the firm is free to vary the input of variable factors, but not of fixed factors. In the long run, the firm is able to vary inputs of both variable and fixed factors.

Additional computer programmers increase production provided they have machines to use

The nature of technology in an industry will determine the way in which output varies with the quantity of inputs. However, one thing is certain. If the firm increases the amount of inputs of the variable factor (labour) while holding constant the input of the other factor (capital), it will gradually derive less additional output per unit of labour for each further increase. This is known as the **law of diminishing returns**, and is one of the few 'laws' in economics. It is a *short-run* concept, as it relies on the assumption that capital is fixed.

It can readily be seen why this should be the case. Suppose a firm has 10 computer programmers working in an office, using 10 computers. The 11th worker may add some extra output, as the workers may be able to 'hot-desk' and take their coffee breaks at different times. The 12th worker may also add some extra output, perhaps by keeping the printers stocked with paper. However, if the firm keeps adding programmers without increasing the number of computers, each extra worker will be adding less additional output to the office. Indeed, the 20th worker may add nothing at all, being unable to get access to a computer.

Total, marginal and average costs

In talking about costs, economists distinguish between total, marginal and average costs. **Total cost** is the sum of all costs that are incurred in order to produce a given level of output. Total cost will always increase as the firm increases its level of production, as this will require more inputs of factors of production, materials and so on.

Average cost is simply the cost per unit of output — it is **total cost** divided by the level of output produced.

Economists rely heavily on the idea that firms, consumers and other economic actors can make good decisions by thinking in terms of the margin, as was explained in Chapter 1. This is known as the *marginal principle*. For example, a firm may examine whether a small change in its behaviour makes matters better or worse. In this context, **marginal cost** is important. It is defined as the change in total cost associated with a small change in output. In other words, it is the additional cost incurred by the firm if it increases output by 1 unit.

Costs in the short run

Because the firm cannot vary some of its inputs in the short run, some costs may be regarded as **fixed costs**, and some as **variable costs**. In this short run, some fixed costs are **sunk costs**: that is, they are costs that the firm cannot avoid paying even if it chooses to produce no output at all. Total costs are the sum of fixed and variable costs:

total costs = total fixed costs + total variable costs

Total costs will increase as the firm increases the volume of production because more of the variable input is needed to increase output. The way in which the costs will vary depends on the nature of the production function, and on whether the prices of labour or other factor inputs alter as output increases.

A common assumption made by economists is that in the short run, at very low levels of output, total costs will rise more slowly than output, but that as diminishing returns set in, total costs will accelerate, as shown in Figure 2.1.

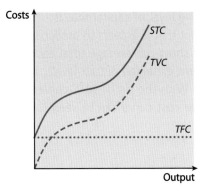

Figure 2.1 Costs in the short run

Quantitative skills 2.1

Graphing short-run costs

In Book 1, Quantitative skills 6.1 showed the arithmetic relationship between the components of short-run costs. The short-run average and marginal curves based on these data are plotted in Figure 2.2. First, notice that short-run average total costs (SATC) takes on a U-shape. This form is often assumed in economic analysis. SATC is the sum of average fixed and variable costs (SAFC and SAVC, respectively). Average fixed costs slope downwards throughout — this is because fixed costs do not vary with the level of output, so as output increases, SAFC must always get smaller, as the fixed costs are spread over more and more units of output. However, SAVC also shows a U-shape, and it is this that gives the U-shape to SATC.

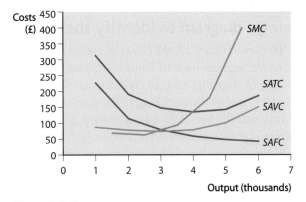

Figure 2.2 Short-run cost curves

A very important aspect of Figure 2.2 is that the short-run marginal cost curve (SMC) cuts both SAVC and SATC at their minimum points. This is always the case. If you think about this for a moment, you will realise that it makes good sense. If you are adding on something that is greater than the average, the average must always increase. For a firm, when the marginal cost of producing an additional unit of a good is higher than the average cost of doing so, the average cost must rise. If the marginal cost is the same as the average cost, then average cost will not change.

An example can show how general this rule is. Suppose that a team newly promoted to football's premier league brings in a new striker, whose wage far exceeds that of existing players. What happens to the average wage? Of course it must increase, as the marginal wage of the new player is higher than the previous average wage. This is quite simply an arithmetic property of the average and the marginal, and always holds true.

Remember that when you draw the average and marginal cost curves for a firm, the marginal cost curve will *always* cut average cost at the minimum point of average cost. Another way of viewing marginal cost is as the *slope* or gradient of the total cost curve.

Remember that the short-run cost curves show the relationship between the volume of production and costs under the assumption that the quantity of capital and other inputs are fixed, so that in order to change output the firm has to vary the amount of labour. The *position* of the cost curves thus depends on the quantity of capital. In other words, there is a short-run average total cost curve for each given level of other inputs.

Costs in the long run

In the long run, a firm is able to vary capital and labour (and other factor inputs). It is thus likely to choose the level of capital that is appropriate for the level of output that it expects to produce. Figure 2.3 shows a selection of short-run average total cost curves corresponding to different expected output levels, and thus different levels of capital. With the set of $SATC$ curves in Figure 2.3, the long-run average cost curve can be seen to take on a U-shape.

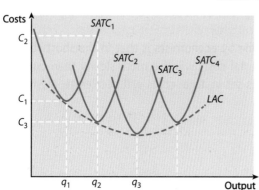

Figure 2.3 Short-run cost curves with different levels of capital input

Extension material

Using a diagram to identify the long-run average cost curve

For the firm in Figure 2.3, the choice of capital is important. Suppose the firm wants to produce the quantity of output q_1. It would choose to install the amount of capital corresponding to the short-run total cost curve $SATC_1$, and could then produce q_1 at an average cost of C_1 in the short run. However, if the firm finds that demand is more buoyant than expected, and so wants to increase output to q_2, in the short run it has no option but to increase labour input and expand output along $SATC_1$, taking cost per unit to C_2.

In the longer term, the firm will be able to adjust its capital stock and move on to $SATC_2$, reducing average

cost to C_3. Thus, as soon as the firm moves away from the output level for which capital stock is designed, it incurs higher average cost in the short run than is possible in the long run.

In this way a long-run average cost curve can be derived to illustrate how the firm chooses to vary its capital stock for any given level of output. The dashed line in Figure 2.3 shows what such a curve would look like for the firm. The long-run average cost curve (LAC) just touches each of the short-run average cost curves, and is known as the 'envelope' of the $SATC$ curves.

Economies of scale

One of the reasons why firms find it beneficial to be large is the existence of **economies of scale**. These occur when a firm finds that it is more efficient in cost terms to produce on a larger scale.

It is not difficult to imagine industries in which economies of scale are likely to arise. For example, recall the notion of the division of labour, which you encountered earlier. When a firm expands, it reaches a certain scale of production at which it becomes worthwhile to take advantage of division of labour. Workers begin to specialise in certain stages of the production process, and their productivity increases. Because this is only possible for

Key term

economies of scale occur for a firm when an increase in the scale of production leads to production at lower long-run average cost

relatively large-scale production, this is an example of economies of scale. It is the size of the firm (in terms of its output level) that enables it to produce more efficiently — that is, at lower average cost.

Although the division of labour is one source of economies of scale, it is by no means the only source, and there are several explanations of cost benefits from producing on a large scale. Some of these are industry-specific, and thus some sectors of the economy exhibit more significant economies of scale than others — it is in these activities that the larger firms tend to be found. There are no hairdressing salons in the top ten largest firms, but there are plenty of oil companies.

Technology

One source of economies of scale is in the technology of production. There are many activities in which the technology is such that large-scale production is more efficient.

Volume

One source of technical economies of scale arises from the physical properties of the universe. There is a physical relationship between the volume and surface area of an object, whereby the storage capacity of an object increases proportionately more than its surface area. Consider the volume of a cube. If the cube is 2 metres each way, its surface area is $6 \times 2 \times 2 = 24$ square metres, while its volume is $2 \times 2 \times 2 = 8$ cubic metres. If the dimension of the cube is 3 metres, the surface area is 54 square metres (more than double the surface area of the smaller cube), but the volume is 27 cubic metres (more than three times the volume of the smaller cube). Thus the larger the cube, the lower the average cost of storage. A similar relationship applies to other shapes of storage containers, whether they be barrels or ships.

What this means in practice is that a large ship can transport proportionally more than a small ship, and that large barrels hold more wine relative to the surface area of the barrel than small barrels. Hence there may be benefits in operating on a large scale.

Furthermore, some capital equipment is designed for large-scale production, and would only be viable for a firm operating at a high volume of production. Combine harvesters cannot be used in small fields; a production line for car production would not be viable for small levels of output. In other words, there may be *indivisibilities* in the production process.

Overheads

In addition to indivisibilities, there are many economic activities in which there are high *overhead* expenditures. Such components of a firm's costs do not vary directly with the scale of production. For example, having built a factory, the cost of that factory is the same regardless of the amount of output that is produced in it. Expenditure on research and development could be seen as such an overhead, which may be viable only when a firm reaches a certain size.

Notice that there are some economic activities in which these overhead costs are highly significant. For example, think about the Channel Tunnel. The construction (overhead) costs were enormous

The Channel Tunnel — the construction costs were enormous compared to the costs of running trains through the tunnel

Microeconomics Part 2

Key terms

natural monopoly monopoly that arises in an industry in which there are such substantial economies of scale that only one firm is viable

diseconomies of scale occur for a firm when an increase in the scale of production leads to higher long-run average costs

compared to the costs of running trains through the tunnel. Thus the overhead cost element is substantial — and the economies of scale will also be significant for such an industry.

There are other examples of this sort of cost structure, such as railway networks and electricity supply. The largest firm in such a market will always be able to produce at a lower average cost than smaller firms. This could prove such a competitive advantage that no other firms will be able to become established in that market, which may therefore constitute what is known as a **natural monopoly**. Intuitively, this makes sense. Imagine having several underground railway systems operating in a single city, all competing against each other on the same routes!

Management and marketing

A second source of economies of scale pertains to the management of firms. One of the key factors of production is managerial input. A certain number of managers are required to oversee the production process. As the firm expands, there is a range of volumes of output over which the management team does not need to grow as rapidly as the overall volume of the firm, as a large firm can be managed more efficiently. Notice that there are likely to be limits to this process. At some point, the organisation begins to get so large and complex that management finds it more difficult to manage. At this point **diseconomies of scale** are likely to cut in — in other words, average costs may begin to rise with an increase in output at some volume of production.

Similarly, the cost of marketing a product may not rise as rapidly as the volume of production, leading to further scale economies. One interpretation of this is that we might see marketing expenses as a component of fixed costs — or at least as having a substantial fixed cost element.

Finance and procurement

Large firms may have advantages in a number of other areas. For example, a large firm with a strong reputation may be able to raise finance for further expansion on more favourable terms than a small firm. This, of course, reinforces the market position of the largest firms in a sector and makes it more difficult for relative newcomers to become established.

Key terms

internal economies of scale
economies of scale that arise from the expansion of a firm

external economies of scale
economies of scale that arise from the expansion of the industry in which a firm is operating

economies of scope economies arising when average cost falls as a firm increases output across a range of different products

Once a firm has grown to the point where it is operating on a relatively large scale, it will also be purchasing its inputs in relatively large volumes. In particular, this relates to raw materials, energy and transport services. When buying in bulk in this way, firms may be able to negotiate good deals with their suppliers, and thus again reduce average cost as output increases.

It may even be the case that some of the firm's suppliers will find it beneficial to locate in proximity to the firm's factory, which would reduce costs even more.

External economies of scale

The factors listed so far that may lead to economies of scale arise from the internal expansion of a firm. If the firm is in an industry that is itself expanding, there may also be **external economies of scale**.

Some of the most successful firms of recent years have been involved in activities that require high levels of technology and skills. The computer industry is one example of an economic activity that has expanded rapidly. As the sector expands, a pool of skilled labour is built up that all the firms can draw upon. The very success of the sector encourages people to acquire the skills needed to enter it, colleges may begin to find it viable to provide courses and so on. Each individual firm benefits in this way from the overall expansion of the sector. The greater availability of skilled workers reduces the amount that individual firms need to spend on training.

Computer engineering is by no means the only example of this. Formula 1 development teams, pharmaceutical companies and others similarly enjoy external economies of scale.

Economies of scope

There are various ways in which firms expand their scale of operations. Some do so within a relatively focused market, but others are multi-product firms that produce a range of different products, sometimes in quite different markets.

For example, look at Nestlé. You may immediately think of instant coffee, and indeed Nestlé produces 200 different brands of instant coffee worldwide. However, Nestlé also produces baby milk powder, mineral water, ice cream and pet food, and has diversified into hotels and restaurants.

Such conglomerate companies can benefit from **economies of scope**, whereby there may be benefits of size across a range of different products. These economies may arise because there are activities that can be shared across the product range. For example, a company may not need a finance or accounting section for each different product, nor human resource or marketing departments. There is thus scope for economies to be made as the firm expands.

Exercise 2.2

Which of the following reflects a movement *along* a long-run average cost curve, and which would cause a *shift* of a long-run average cost curve?

a A firm becomes established in a market, learning the best ways of utilising its factors of production.
b A firm observes that average cost falls as it expands its scale of production.
c The larger a firm becomes, the more difficult it becomes to manage, causing average cost to rise.
d A firm operating in the financial sector installs new, faster computers, enabling its average cost to fall for any given level of service that it provides.

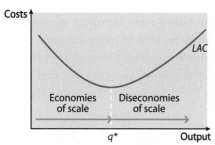

Costs

LAC

Economies   Diseconomies
of scale   of scale

q*   Output

Figure 2.4 Economies and diseconomies of scale

Returns to scale

In Figure 2.4, if the firm expands its output up to q^*, long-run average cost falls. Up to q^* of output is the range over which there are economies of scale. To the right of q^*, however, long-run average cost rises as output continues to be increased, and the firm experiences diseconomies of scale. The output q^* itself is at the intermediate state of **constant returns to scale.**

It is important not to confuse the notion of returns to scale with the idea introduced earlier of diminishing marginal returns to a factor. The two concepts arise in different circumstances. The law of diminishing returns to a factor applies in the *short run*, when a firm increases its inputs of one factor of production while facing fixed amounts of other factors. It is thus solely a short-run phenomenon. Diseconomies of scale (sometimes known as *decreasing returns to scale*) can occur in the *long run*, and the term refers to how output changes as a firm varies the quantities of *all* factors.

The point at which long-run average cost stops falling is known as the **minimum efficient scale**. This is the smallest level of output that a firm can produce at the minimum level of long-run average cost.

The long-run average cost curve (LAC) is drawn as a U-shape because of the assumptions that were made about the technology of production. The underlying assumption here is that the firm faces economies of scale at relatively low levels of output, so that LAC slopes downwards. However, at some point decreasing returns to scale set in, and LAC then begins to slope upwards.

Will the LAC curve always take this shape? It turns out to be a convenient representation, but in practice the LAC curve can take on a variety of shapes. Figure 2.5 shows some of these. LAC_1 is the typical U-shape, which has been discussed. LAC_2 shows an example of a situation in which there are economies of scale up to a point, after which long-run average cost levels out and there is a long flat range over which the firm faces constant returns to scale. LAC_3 is a bit similar, except that the constant returns to scale (flat) segment eventually runs out and diseconomies of scale set in. In LAC_4 the economies of scale continue over the whole range of output shown. This could occur in a market where the fixed costs are substantial, dominating the influence of variable costs.

It transpires that the size of the minimum efficient scale relative to market demand has an important influence on the way in which a market will develop, and this has implications for the market power held by firms. This will be explored in the following chapters.

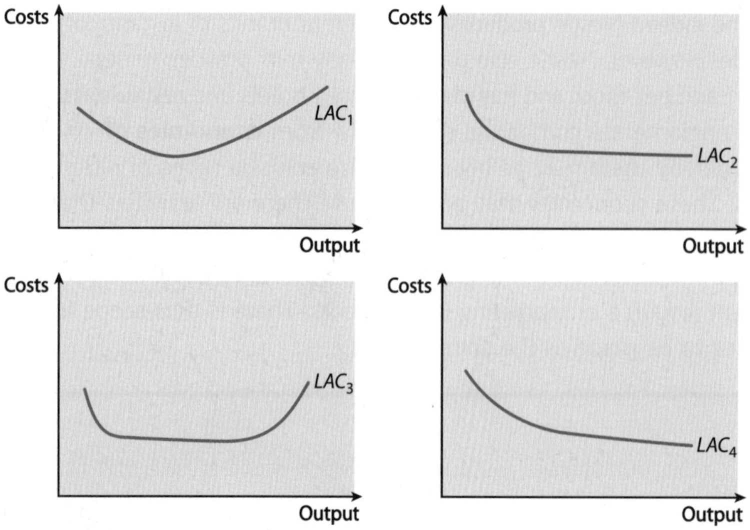

Costs

LAC₁

Output

Costs

LAC₂

Output

Costs

LAC₃

Output

Costs

LAC₄

Output

Figure 2.5 Possible shapes of the LAC curve

Summary

- A firm may face inflexibility in the short run, with some factors being fixed in quantity and only some being variable.
- The short run is defined in this context as the period over which a firm is free to vary some factors, but not others.
- The long run is defined as the period over which the firm is able to vary the input of all of its factors of production.
- The law of diminishing returns states that, if a firm increases the input of a variable factor while holding input of the fixed factor constant, eventually the firm will get diminishing marginal returns from the variable factor.
- Short-run costs can be separated into fixed, sunk and variable costs.
- There is a clear and immutable relationship between total, average and marginal costs.
- For a U-shaped average cost curve, marginal cost always cuts the minimum point of average cost.

Exercise 2.3

A firm faces long-run total cost conditions as shown in Table 2.1.

Table 2.1 Output and long-run costs

Output (000 units per week)	Total cost (£000)
0	0
1	32
2	48
3	82
4	140
5	228
6	352

a Calculate long-run average cost and long-run marginal cost for each level of output.
b Plot long-run average cost and long-run marginal cost curves on a graph. (Hint: don't forget to plot *LMC* at points that are halfway between the corresponding output levels.)
c Identify the output level at which long-run average cost is at a minimum.
d Identify the output level at which *LAC = LMC*.
e Within what range of output does this firm enjoy economies of scale?
f Within what range of output does the firm experience diseconomies of scale?
g If you could measure the nature of returns to scale, what would characterise the point where *LAC* is at a minimum?

Revenue of firms

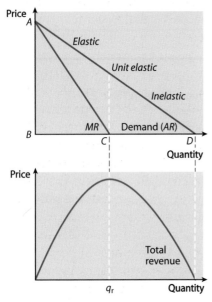

Key terms

total revenue the revenue received by a firm from its sales of a good or service; it is the quantity sold, multiplied by the price

average revenue the average revenue received by the firm per unit of output; it is total revenue divided by the quantity sold

marginal revenue the additional revenue received by the firm if it sells an additional unit of output

Figure 2.6 Elasticity and total revenue

Study tip

Whenever you have to draw this figure, remember that MR and AR have this relationship, meeting at A, and with the distance BC being the same as the distance CD. MR is zero (meets the horizontal axis) at the maximum point of the total revenue curve.

Key term

normal profit the return needed for a firm to stay in a market in the long run

In the first part of the course (Book 1, Chapter 5), you saw how the total revenue received by a firm varies along the demand curve, according to the price elasticity of demand. In the same way that there is a relationship between total, average and marginal cost, there is also a relationship between **total revenue**, **average revenue** and **marginal revenue**.

Figure 2.6 reminds you of the relationship between total revenue and the price elasticity of demand (PED). The marginal revenue (MR) curve has also been added to the figure, and has a fixed relationship with the average revenue (AR) curve. This is for similar mathematical reasons as the relationship between marginal and average costs explained earlier in this chapter. MR shares the intercept point on the vertical axis (at point A on Figure 2.6), and has exactly twice the slope of AR.

Motivations of firms

The opening section of this chapter stated that firms exist to organise production by bringing together the factors of production in order to produce output. This begs the question of what motivates them to produce particular *levels* of output, and at what price. This section considers alternative objectives that firms may set out to achieve.

Profit maximisation

Traditional economic analysis has tended to start from the premise that firms set out with the objective of maximising profits. In analysing this, economists define profits as the difference between the total revenue received by a firm and the total costs that it incurs in production:

profits = total revenue − total cost

Total revenue here is seen in terms of the quantity of the product that is sold multiplied by the price. Total cost includes the fixed and variable costs that have already been discussed, but also includes an element of opportunity cost.

Consider the case of a sole proprietor — a small local business such as a gym or a taxi firm. It seems reasonable to assume that such a firm will set out to maximise its profits. However, from the entrepreneur's perspective there is an *opportunity cost* of being in business, which may be seen in terms of the earnings that the proprietor could make in an alternative occupation. This required rate of return is regarded as a fixed cost, and is included in the total cost of production.

The same procedure applies to cost curves for other sorts of firm. In other words, when economists refer to costs, they include the rate of return that a firm needs to make it stay in a particular market in the long run. Accountants dislike this, as 'opportunity cost' cannot be identified as an explicit item in the accounts. This part of costs is known as **normal profit**.

abnormal, supernormal or economic profits profits above normal profits

principal–agent problem arises from conflict between the objectives of the principals and their agents, who take decisions on their behalf

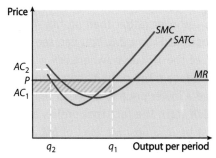

Figure 2.7 Maximising profit

The *MR* = *MC* rule for profit maximisation is an important one, as it applies in any market situation where a firm sets out to maximise profits, so make sure you understand and remember it.

Profits made by a firm above that level are known as **abnormal profits, supernormal profits or economic profits**.

In the short run, a firm may choose to remain in a market even if it is not covering its opportunity costs, provided its revenues are covering its variable costs. Since the firm has already incurred fixed costs, if it can cover its variable costs in the short run, it will be better off remaining in business and paying off part of the fixed costs than exiting the market and losing all of its fixed costs. Thus, the level of average variable costs represents the shut-down price, below which the firm will exit from the market in the short run. In situations where firms in a market are making abnormal profits, it is likely that other firms will be attracted to enter the market. The absence or existence of abnormal profits will thus be important in influencing the way in which a market may evolve over time.

How does a firm choose its output level if it wishes to maximise profits? An application of the marginal principle shows how. Suppose a firm realises that its marginal revenue is higher than its marginal cost of production. What does this mean for profits? If it were to sell an additional unit of its output, it would gain more in revenue than it would incur additional cost, so its profits would increase. Similarly, if it found that its marginal revenue was less than marginal cost, it would be making a loss on the marginal unit of output, and profits would increase if the firm sold less. This leads to the conclusion that profits will be maximised at the level of output at which marginal revenue (*MR*) is equal to marginal cost (*MC*). Figure 2.7 illustrates the situation. This shows a firm's short-run average and marginal costs curve (*SATC* and *SMC*). It is assumed that the firm is operating in a competitive market, accepting the market price (*P*). The price also represents the marginal revenue that the firm receives from selling an additional unit of output. By choosing the output (q_1) at which *MR* = *MC*, the firm makes profits given by the shaded area. At any other level of output the corresponding area of profit would be smaller. Indeed, the firm needs to be careful — notice that marginal revenue also equals marginal costs at q_2, but at this point, average cost exceeds the price, and the firm makes losses. Technically this means that profits are maximised at the level of output at which *MR* = *MC*, and with marginal cost cutting marginal revenue from below. Indeed, this *MR* = *MC* rule is a general rule that tells a firm how to maximise profits in any market situation.

The principal–agent problem

The discussion so far seems reasonable when considering a relatively small owner-managed firm. In this context, profit maximisation makes good sense as the firm's motivation.

However, for many larger firms — especially public limited companies — the owners may not be involved in running the business. This gives rise to the **principal–agent (or agency) problem**. In a public limited company, the shareholders delegate the day-to-day decisions concerning the operation of the firm to managers who act on their behalf. In this case the shareholders are the *principals*, and the managers are the *agents* who run things for them. In other words, there is a divorce of ownership from control. The principal–agent problem arises primarily from an information asymmetry. This is because the agents have better information about the effects of their decisions than the owners (the principals), who are not involved in the day-to-day running of the business. In order to overcome this, the owners need to overcome the information problem by improving their monitoring of the managers' actions, or to provide the managers with an incentive to take decisions that would align with the owners' objectives. For example, by offering bonuses related to profit, the managers would be more likely to try to maximise profits.

If the agents are in full sympathy with the objectives of the owners, there is no problem and the managers will take exactly the decisions that the owners would like. Problems arise in the presence of information asymmetry when there is conflict between the aims of the owners and those of the managers. There are various motivations that managers may pursue in this situation.

Revenue maximisation

The industrial economist William Baumol argued that managers may set out with the objective of maximising revenue. One reason is that in some firms managerial salaries are related to turnover rather than profits. The effects of this can be seen by looking back at Figure 2.6. You can see that total revenue is maximised at the peak of the *TR* curve (where $MR = 0$) at q_r. A revenue-maximising firm will produce more output than a profit-maximising one, and will need to charge a lower price in order to sell the extra output. This should be apparent from the fact that profits are maximised where $MR = MC$, which must be at a positive level of MR — and thus to the left of q_r in Figure 2.6.

Baumol pointed out that the shareholders might not be too pleased about this. The way the firm behaves then depends upon the degree of accountability that the agents (managers) have to the principals (shareholders). For example, the shareholders may have sufficient power over their agents to be able to insist on some minimum level of profits. The result may then be a compromise solution.

Sales maximisation

In some cases, managers may focus more on the volume of sales than on the resulting revenues. This could lead to output being set even higher, to the point at which total revenue only just covers total cost. Remember that total cost includes normal profit — the opportunity cost of the resources tied up in the firm. The firm would have to close down if it did not cover this opportunity cost.

Again, the extent to which the managers will be able to pursue this objective without endangering their positions with the shareholders depends on how accountable the managers are to the shareholders. Remember that the managers are likely to have much better information about the market conditions and the internal functioning of the firm than the shareholders, who view the firm only remotely. This may be to the managers' advantage.

Some managers may be pursuing other objectives than profit maximisation

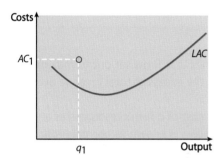

Figure 2.8 X-inefficiency

Utility maximisation

Oliver Williamson argued that managers would set out to maximise their utility. Just as consumers gain satisfaction from consuming goods, it is argued that managers gain satisfaction in various ways. For example, they may enjoy the status of having a large team of people working for them, or they may like to have discretion over the way in which profits made by the firm are used, perhaps allowing them to have a large and well-appointed office or a prestigious company car. Again, such activity would take the firm away from its profit-maximising position.

X-inefficiency

If managers are not fully accountable, they may become negligent, which may give rise to organisational slack. In other words, costs will not be minimised, as the firm is not operating as efficiently as it could. This is an example of what is called **X-inefficiency**. For example, in Figure 2.8 *LAC* represents the long-run average cost curve showing the most efficient cost positions for the firm at any output level. With X-inefficiency, a firm could end up producing output q_1 at average cost AC_1. Thus, in the presence of X-inefficiency the firm will be operating *above* its long-run average cost curve. It could be argued that X-inefficiency is also displayed when managers set out to maximise their utility.

Behavioural theories

Businesses may not set out to maximise anything, either consciously because they have other motivations, or as a result of the principal–agent issue. For example, it might be that managers simply prefer a quiet life, and therefore do not push for the absolute profit-maximising position, but do just enough to keep the shareholders off their backs. Herbert Simon referred to this as '**satisficing**' behaviour, where managers aim to produce satisfactory profits rather than maximum profits.

Firms may wish to develop a favourable reputation by demonstrating a commitment to acting in ways that benefit society at large, or that improve the welfare of their employees and the community in which they are located. This notion of **corporate social responsibility** (CSR) has become widespread, with firms devoting resources to promoting community programmes of various kinds and encouraging their employees to engage in volunteering activities.

Has this now become a prerequisite for firms' survival? If it is perceived that failure to engage with CSR has a major impact on firms' sales, then it becomes crucial for a firm to be able to demonstrate its commitment in order to compete with its rivals. Devoting resources to CSR then becomes part of a firm's strategy to safeguard its market position.

Why assume profit maximisation?

The discussion has revealed a range of reasons explaining why firms may depart from profit maximisation. Does this mean that it should be abandoned as an assumption?

It could be argued that some of the strategies adopted by firms may seem to diverge from profit maximisation in the short run, but may result in the maximisation of profits in the long run. For example, if all firms in a market are engaging in CSR in order to improve their credibility amongst their customers, then it could be argued that this expenditure becomes part of operating costs, and a necessary part of maintaining the market share needed to maximise profits in the long term.

From an economic modelling perspective, being able to assume that firms maximise profits allows the economist to come to an understanding of firms' behaviour under a simple and clear assumption. This offers much more straightforward insights into this behaviour than trying to implement some of the more complex assumptions that could be made about what motivates firms' decisions. Profit maximisation then provides a benchmark for other more complex models that enables an evaluation of how differently firms may behave under alternative assumptions. So even if it is not the case that firms always act to maximise profits, it is a useful starting point to ask how they would behave if they did maximise profits, and then explore alternative theories using profit maximisation as the benchmark against which to compare other models of behaviour.

Summary

- Traditional economic analysis assumes that firms set out to maximise profits, where profits are defined as the excess of total revenue over total cost.
- This analysis treats the opportunity cost of a firm's resources as a part of fixed costs. The opportunity cost is known as normal profit.
- Profits above this level are known as abnormal profits.
- A firm maximises profits by choosing a level of output such that marginal revenue is equal to marginal cost.
- For many larger firms, where day-to-day control is delegated to managers, a principal–agent problem may arise if there is conflict between the objectives of the owners (principals) and those of the managers (agents).
- This may lead to satisficing behaviour and to X-inefficiency.
- William Baumol suggested that managers may set out to maximise revenue rather than profits; others have suggested that sales or the growth of the firm may be the managers' objectives.

Efficiency

Book 1 introduced the ideas of productive and allocative efficiency. The extent to which markets will deliver efficiency will be explored in the following chapters, but it is also important to refine these notions further. Indeed, it has already been noted that the principal–agent problem can lead to X-inefficiency, which is one reason why the ideal combination of productive and allocative efficiency will not be achieved.

Productive efficiency

The notion of **productive efficiency** is closely tied to the costs faced by firms, particularly in relation to the average total cost of production. Productive efficiency can be seen in terms of the minimum average cost at which output can be produced, recognising that average cost is likely

Key term

productive efficiency when a firm operates at minimum average cost, choosing an appropriate combination of inputs and producing the maximum output possible from those inputs

to vary at different scales of output. For example, in Figure 2.4 the point q^* may be regarded as the optimum level of output, in the sense that it minimises average cost per unit of output.

From the firm's perspective, the decision process can be viewed as a three-stage procedure. First, the firm needs to decide how much output it wants to produce. Second, it chooses an appropriate combination of factors of production, given that intended scale of production. Third, it attempts to produce as much output as possible, given those inputs. Another way of expressing this is that, having chosen the intended scale of output, the firm tries to minimise its costs of production.

Notice that when the firm starts this decision process, it is likely to choose its desired output level on the basis of current or expected market conditions. However, remember the distinction between the short and the long run. Once the firm has chosen its desired scale of production, and installed the necessary capital, it is tied into that level of capital stock in the short run. If it needs to change its decision in the future, it will take time to implement the changes. In the short run, a firm may thus be in a situation of **static efficiency**, choosing the minimum average cost, given the market conditions at that time.

Allocative efficiency

The notion of **allocative efficiency** relates to the issue of whether an economy allocates its resources in such a way as to produce a balance of goods and services that matches consumer preferences. In an individual market, this would mean that firms were producing the ideal amount of a good that consumers wish to buy. This is related to the notion of equilibrium in the demand and supply model, in which prices act as signals to consumers and producers to bring demand and supply into equilibrium. However, Book 1 demonstrated that there are situations in which market failure can occur, thus preventing the best allocation of resources from society's point of view.

Dynamic efficiency

The discussion of efficiency so far has been conducted in terms of how to make the best use of existing resources, producing an appropriate mix of goods and services and using factor inputs as efficiently as possible, given existing knowledge and technology. This is good as far as it goes, but it does represent a relatively static view of efficiency.

Dynamic efficiency goes one step further, recognising that the state of knowledge and technology changes over time. For example, investment in research and development today means that production can be carried out more efficiently at some future date. Furthermore, the development of new products may also mean that a different mix of goods and services may serve consumers better in the long term.

The notion of dynamic efficiency stemmed from the work of Joseph Schumpeter, who argued that a preoccupation with static efficiency may sacrifice opportunities for greater efficiency in the long run. In other words, there may be a trade-off between achieving efficiency today and improving efficiency tomorrow.

Key terms

static efficiency efficiency at a particular point in time

allocative efficiency achieved when society is producing the appropriate bundle of goods and services relative to consumer preferences

dynamic efficiency a view of efficiency that takes into account the effect of innovation and technical progress on productive and allocative efficiency in the long run

Summary

- A society needs to find a way of using its limited resources as efficiently as possible.
- Productive efficiency occurs when firms have chosen appropriate combinations of factors of production, and produce the maximum output possible from those inputs.
- Allocative efficiency occurs when firms produce an appropriate bundle of goods and services, given consumer preferences.
- An individual market exhibits aspects of allocative efficiency when the marginal benefit received by society from consuming a good or service matches the marginal cost of producing it — that is, when price is equal to marginal cost.
- Dynamic efficiency recognises that there may be a trade-off between efficiency in the short run and in the long run.

Case study 2.1

Coke vs Pepsi in India

In the mid-2000s it was reported that Coca-Cola and PepsiCo were fighting to increase their sales in India. A pesticide scare in the previous year had caused sales to plummet, and the two firms were anxious to recover the situation.

The tactics they adopted were to reduce the size of the bottles for sale in order to appeal to consumers with low incomes, to cut prices, to increase the availability of the products in rural areas, and to encourage more at-home consumption in the urban areas.

It was seen that there was plenty of scope for growth in the market, as India showed one of the lowest average levels of consumption of fizzy drinks in the world, and was substantially below the Asian average. This may partly reflect the way that children have been discouraged from drinking colas by their teachers at school.

The prices being charged were rated as being the world's lowest prices for cola as the two firms battled to increase their market shares. However, in consequence the firms faced reductions in their profit margins, and continued to face competition from local producers. The logistics of supplying such a geographically large and diverse region, given the need to ensure refrigeration, added significantly to costs. Attempts were made to counter this by reducing the weight of the bottles and by making use of cheap transport in the form of bullock carts and cycle rickshaws in the rural areas.

Market analysts said that soft-drink companies should be able to improve profits, but executives remained bent on boosting volumes. The vice-president of Coca-Cola marketing in India was quoted as saying that 'any affordability strategy will put pressure on margins, but it is critical to build the market'.

The pesticide issue proved to be a long-lasting controversy, and the Kerala government filed a criminal complaint against PepsiCo over its environmental impact, although this was rejected by the Supreme Court of India in 2010. Indeed, the US Department of State named PepsiCo as one of the 12 multinationals that displayed 'the most impressive corporate social responsibility credentials in emerging markets'.

Coke and Pepsi compete for market share in India

Follow-up questions

a Given the statements in the passage, do you think that Coca-Cola and PepsiCo were trying to maximise short-run profits?

b Explain your answer to (a) and comment on what the firms were trying to achieve by their strategies.

c Identify ways in which the firms were seeking to influence their costs.

d How do you think PepsiCo's record on CSR will have affected its position in the market?

e Discuss what you think the firms would want to achieve in the long run.

Chapter 3

Market structure: perfect competition and monopoly

Book 1 introduced the notion of market failure — describing situations in which free markets may not produce the best outcome for society in terms of efficiency. One of the reasons given for this concerned what is termed 'imperfect competition'. It was argued that, if firms can achieve a position of market dominance, they may distort the pattern of resource allocation. It is now time to look at market structure more closely in order to evaluate the way in which markets work, and the significance of this for resource allocation. The fact that firms try to maximise profits is not in itself bad for society. However, the structure of a market has a strong influence on how well the market performs. 'Structure' here is seen in relation to a number of dimensions, but in particular to the number of firms operating in a market and the way in which they interact. This chapter considers two extreme forms of market structure: perfect competition and monopoly.

Learning objectives

After studying this chapter, you should:
- understand what is meant by market structure, and why it is important for firms
- appreciate the significance of barriers to entry in influencing the market structure
- be familiar with the assumptions of the model of perfect competition
- understand how a firm chooses profit-maximising output under perfect competition
- appreciate how a perfectly competitive market reaches long-run equilibrium
- understand how the characteristics of long-run equilibrium affect the performance of the market in terms of productive and allocative efficiency
- be familiar with the assumptions of the model of monopoly
- understand how the monopoly firm chooses output and sets price
- understand why a monopoly can arise in a market
- understand how the characteristics of equilibrium under monopoly affect the performance of the market in terms of productive and allocative efficiency
- be aware of the relative merits of perfect competition and monopoly in terms of market performance

Prior knowledge needed

Part 2 of Book 1 discussed market equilibrium under the assumption that firms operate in a competitive market. This chapter and the next build upon this, explaining more carefully what is meant by a 'competitive market', and examining markets that do not operate in this way.

Market structure

Firms cannot take decisions without having some awareness of the market in which they are operating. In some markets, firms find themselves to be such small players that they cannot influence the price at which they sell. In others, a firm may find itself to be the only firm, which clearly gives it much more discretion in devising a price and output strategy. There may also be many intermediate situations where the firm has some control over price, but needs to be aware of rival firms in the market.

Economists have devised a range of models that allow such different **market structures** to be analysed. Before looking carefully at the most important types of market structure, the key characteristics of alternative market structures will be introduced. The main models are summarised in Table 3.1. In many ways, we can regard these as a spectrum of markets with different characteristics.

Key term

market structure the market environment within which firms operate

Table 3.1 A spectrum of market structures

	Perfect competition	Monopolistic competition	Oligopoly	Monopoly
Number of firms	Many	Many	Few	One
Freedom of entry	Not restricted	Not restricted	Some barriers to entry	High barriers to entry
Firm's influence over price	None	Some	Some	Price maker, subject to the demand curve
Nature of product	Homogeneous	Differentiated	Varied	No close substitutes
Examples	Cauliflowers	Fast-food outlets	Cars	PC operating systems
	Carrots	Travel agents	Mobile phones	Local water supply

Perfect competition

At one extreme is *perfect competition*. This is a market in which each individual firm is a *price taker*. This means that no individual firm is large enough to be able to influence the price, which is set by the market as a whole. This situation would arise where there are many firms operating in a market, producing a product that is much the same whichever firm produces it. You might think of a market for a particular sort of vegetable, for example. One cauliflower is very much like another, and it would not be possible for a particular cauliflower-grower to set a premium price for its product.

Such markets are also typified by freedom of entry and exit. In other words, it is relatively easy for new firms to enter the market, or for existing firms to leave it to produce something else. The market price in such a market will be driven down to that at which the typical firm in the market just makes enough profit to stay in business. If firms make more than this, other firms will be attracted in, and thus abnormal profits will be competed away. If some firms in the market do not make sufficient profit to want to remain in the market, they will exit, allowing price to drift up until again the typical firm just makes enough to stay in business.

On trial in 1998, Microsoft was found to have a global monopoly on PC operating systems

Monopoly

At the other extreme of the spectrum of market structures is *monopoly*. This is a market where there is only one firm in operation. Such a firm has some influence over price, and can choose a combination of price and output in order to maximise its profits. The monopolist is not entirely free to set any price that it wants, as it must remain aware of the demand curve for its product. Nonetheless, it has the freedom to choose a point along its demand curve.

The nature of a monopolist's product is that it has no close substitutes — either actual or potential — so it faces no competition. An example might be Microsoft, which for a long time held a global monopoly for operating systems for PC computers. At the time of a famous trial in 1998, Microsoft was said to supply operating systems for about 95% of the world's PCs.

Another condition of a monopoly market is that there are barriers to the entry for new firms. This means that the firm is able to set its price such as to make profits that are above the minimum needed to keep the firm in business, without attracting new rivals into the market.

Monopolistic competition

Between the two extreme forms of market structure are many intermediate situations in which firms may have some influence over their selling price, but still have to take account of the fact that there are other firms in the market. One such market is known as *monopolistic competition*. This is a market in which there are many firms operating, each producing similar but not identical products, so that there is some scope for influencing price, perhaps because of brand loyalty. However, firms in such a market are likely to be relatively small. Such firms may find it profitable to make sure that their own product is differentiated from other goods, and may advertise in order to convince potential customers that this is the case. For example, small-scale local restaurants may offer different styles of cooking.

Oligopoly

Another intermediate form of market structure is *oligopoly*, which literally means 'few sellers'. This is a market in which there are just a few firms that supply the market. Each firm will take decisions in close awareness of how other firms in the market may react to their actions. In some cases, the firms may try to *collude* — to work together in order to behave as if they were a monopolist — thus making higher profits. In other cases, they may be intense rivals, which will tend to result in abnormal profits being competed away. The question of whether firms in an oligopoly collude or compete has a substantial impact on how the overall market performs in terms of resource allocation, and whether consumers will be disadvantaged as a result of the actions of the firms in the market.

Barriers to entry

It has been argued that if firms in a market are able to make abnormal profits, this will act as an inducement for new firms to try to gain entry into that market in order to share in those profits. A *barrier to entry* is a characteristic of a market that prevents new firms from joining the market. The existence of such barriers is thus of great importance in influencing the market structure that will evolve.

For example, if a firm holds a patent on a particular good, this means that no other firm is permitted by law to produce the product, and the patent-holding firm thus has a monopoly. The firm may then be able to set price such as to make abnormal profits without fear of rival firms competing away those profits. On the other hand, if there are no barriers to entry in a market, and if the existing firms set price to make abnormal profits, new firms will join the market, and the increase in market supply will push price down until no abnormal profits are being made.

Exercise 3.1

For each of the market situations listed below, select the form of market structure that is most likely to apply. In each case, comment on the way in which the firm's actions may be influenced by the market structure.

Forms of market structure:

A perfect competition
B monopoly
C monopolistic competition
D oligopoly

a A fairly large number of fast-food outlets in a city centre, offering various different styles of cooking (Indian, Chinese, fish and chips, burgers, etc.) at broadly similar prices.
b An island's only airport.
c A large number of farmers selling parsnips at the same price.
d A small number of large firms that between them supply most of the market for commercial vans.

Summary

- The decisions made by firms must be taken in the context of the market environment in which they operate.
- Under conditions of perfect competition, each firm must accept the market price as given, but can choose how much output to produce in order to maximise profits.
- In a monopoly market, where there is only one producer, the firm can choose output and price (subject to the demand curve).
- Monopolistic competition combines some features of perfect competition, and some characteristics of monopoly. Firms have some influence over price, and will produce a differentiated product in order to maintain this influence.
- Oligopoly exists where a market is occupied by just a few firms. In some cases, these few firms may work together to maximise their joint profits; in other cases, they may seek to outmanoeuvre each other.

The model of perfect competition

Key term

perfect competition a form of market structure that produces allocative and productive efficiency in long-run equilibrium

At one end of the spectrum of market structures is **perfect competition**. This model has a special place in economic analysis, because if all its assumptions were fulfilled, and if all markets operated according to its precepts, the best allocation of resources would be ensured for society as a whole. Although it may be argued that this ideal is not often achieved, perfect competition nonetheless provides a yardstick by which all other forms of market structure can be evaluated.

Assumptions

The assumptions of the model of perfect competition are as follows:
1   Firms aim to maximise profits.
2   There are many participants (both buyers and sellers).
3   The product is homogeneous.
4   There are no barriers to entry to or exit from the market.
5   There is perfect knowledge of market conditions.

Profit maximisation

The first assumption is that firms act to maximise their profits. You might think this means that firms, acting in their own self-interest, are unlikely to do consumers any favours. However, it transpires that this does not interfere with the operation of the market. Indeed, it is the pursuit of self-interest by firms and consumers which ensures that the market works effectively.

Many participants

This is an important assumption of the model: that there are so many buyers and so many sellers that no individual trader is able to influence the market price. The market price is thus determined by the operation of the market.

   On the sellers' side of the market, this assumption is tantamount to saying that there are limited economies of scale in the industry. If the minimum efficient scale is small relative to market demand, then no firm is likely to become so large that it will gain influence in the market.

A homogeneous product

This assumption means that buyers of the good see all products in the market as being identical, and will not favour one firm's product over another. If there were brand loyalty, such that one firm was more popular than others, then that firm would be able to charge a premium on its price. By ruling out this possibility the previous assumption is reinforced, and no individual seller is able to influence the selling price of the product.

No barriers to entry or exit

By this assumption, firms are able to join the market if they perceive it to be a profitable step, and they can exit from the market without hindrance. This assumption is important when it comes to considering the long-run equilibrium towards which the market will tend.

Perfect knowledge

It is assumed that all participants in the market have perfect information about trading conditions in the market. In particular, buyers always know the prices that firms are charging, and thus can buy the good at the cheapest possible price. Firms that try to charge a price above the market price will get no takers. At the same time, traders are aware of the product quality.

Perfect competition in the short run
The firm under perfect competition

With the above assumptions, it is possible to analyse how a firm will operate in the market. An important implication of these assumptions is that no individual trader can influence the price of the product. In particular, this means that the firm is a **price taker**, and has to accept whatever price is set in the market as a whole.

As the firm is a price taker, it faces a perfectly elastic demand curve for its product, as is shown in Figure 3.1. In this figure, P_1 is the price set in the market, and the firm cannot sell at any other price. If it tries to set a price above P_1 it will sell nothing, as buyers are fully aware of the market price and will not buy at a higher price, especially as they know that there is no quality difference between the products offered by different firms in the market. What this also implies is that the firm can sell as much output as it likes at that going price — which means there is no incentive for any firm to set a price below P_1. Thus, all firms charge the same price, P_1.

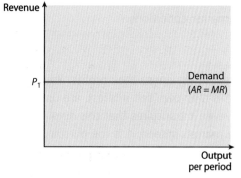

Figure 3.1 The firm's demand curve

The firm's short-run supply decision

If the firm can sell as much as it likes at the market price, how does it decide how much to produce?

Chapter 2 explained that to maximise profits a firm needs to set output at such a level that marginal revenue is equal to marginal cost. Figure 3.2 illustrates this rule by adding the short-run cost curves to the demand curve.

Remember from the previous chapter that *SMC* cuts the minimum points of *SAVC* and *SATC*. As the demand curve is horizontal, the firm faces constant average and marginal revenue and will choose to produce output q_1, where *MR* = *MC*.

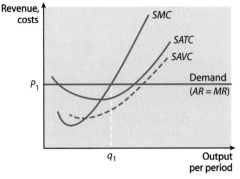

Figure 3.2 The firm's short-run supply decision

Key term

short-run supply curve for a firm operating under perfect competition, the curve given by its short-run marginal cost curve above the price at which *MC* = *SAVC*; for the industry, the horizontal sum of the supply curves of the individual firms

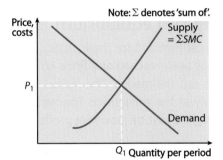

Figure 3.3 A perfectly competitive industry in short-run equilibrium

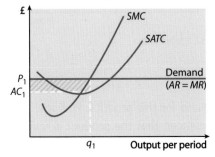

Figure 3.4 The firm in short-run equilibrium

If the market price were to change, the firm would react by changing output, but always choosing to supply output at the level at which *MR* = *MC*. This suggests that the short-run marginal cost curve represents the firm's short-run supply curve: in other words, it shows the quantity of output that the firm would supply at any given price.

However, there is one important proviso to this statement. If the price falls below short-run average variable cost, the firm's best decision will be to exit from the market, as it will be better off just incurring its fixed costs. So the firm's **short-run supply curve** is the *SMC* curve above the point where it cuts *SAVC* (at its minimum point).

Industry equilibrium in the short run

One crucial question not yet examined is how the market price comes to be determined. To answer this, it is necessary to consider the industry as a whole. In this case there is a conventional downward-sloping demand curve, of the sort met in Book 1. This is formed according to preferences of consumers in the market and is shown in Figure 3.3.

On the supply side, it has been shown that the individual firm's supply curve is its marginal cost curve above *SAVC*. If you add up the supply curves of each firm operating in the market, the result is the industry supply curve, also shown in Figure 3.3. The price will then adjust to P_1 at the intersection of demand and supply. The firms in the industry between them will supply Q_1 output, and the market will be in equilibrium.

The firm in short-run equilibrium revisited

As this seems to be a well-balanced situation, with price adjusting to equate market demand and supply, the only question is why it is described as just a *short-run equilibrium*. The clue to this is to be found back with the individual firm.

Figure 3.4 returns to the position facing an individual firm in the market. As before, the firm maximises profits by accepting the price P_1 as set in the market and producing up to the point where *MR* = *MC*, which is at q_1. However, now the firm's average revenue (which is equal to price) is greater than its average cost (which is given by AC_1 at this level of output). The firm is thus making supernormal profits at this price. (Remember that 'normal profits' are included in average cost.) Indeed, the amount of total profits being made is shown as the shaded area on the graph. Notice that average revenue minus average costs equals profit per unit, so multiplying this by the quantity sold determines total profit.

This is where the assumption about freedom of entry becomes important. If firms in this market are making profits above opportunity cost, the market is generating more profits than other markets in the economy. This will prove attractive to other firms, which will seek to enter the market — and the assumption is that there are no barriers to prevent them from doing so.

This process of entry will continue for as long as firms are making supernormal profits. However, as more firms join the market, the *position* of the industry supply curve, which is the sum of the supply curves of an ever-larger number of individual firms, will be affected. As the industrial supply curve shifts to the right, the market price will fall. At some point the price will have fallen to such an extent that firms are no longer making supernormal profits, and the market will then stabilise.

If the price were to fall even further, some firms would choose to exit from the market, and the process would go into reverse. Therefore price can be expected to stabilise such that the typical firm in the industry is just making normal profits.

Figure 3.5 shows a different situation. This firm also tries to maximise profits by setting $MC = MR$, but finds that its average cost exceeds the price. It makes losses shown by the shaded area, and in the long run will choose to leave the market. As this and other firms exit from the market, the market supply curve shifts to the left, and the equilibrium price will drift upwards until firms are again making normal profits.

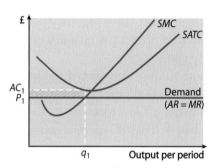

Figure 3.5 The firm in short-run equilibrium again

Perfect competition in long-run equilibrium

Figure 3.6 shows the situation for a typical firm and for the industry as a whole once long-run equilibrium has been reached and firms no longer have any incentive to enter or to exit the market. The market is in equilibrium, with demand equal to supply at the going price. The typical firm sets marginal revenue equal to marginal cost to maximise profits, and just makes normal profits.

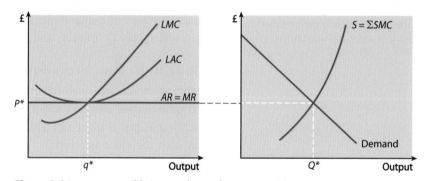

Figure 3.6 Long-run equilibrium under perfect competition

The long-run supply curve

Suppose there is an increase in the demand for this product. Perhaps, for some reason, everyone becomes convinced that the product is really health promoting, so demand increases at any given price. This disturbs the market equilibrium, and the question then is whether (and how) equilibrium can be restored.

Figure 3.7 reproduces the long-run equilibrium that was shown in Figure 3.6. Thus, in the initial position market price is at P^*, the typical firm is in long-run equilibrium producing q^*, and the industry is producing Q^*. Demand was initially at D_0, but with the increased popularity of the product it has shifted to D_1. In the short run this pushes the market price up to P_1 for the industry, because as market price increases existing firms have the incentive to supply more output: that is, they move along their short-run supply curves. So in the short run a typical firm starts to produce q_1 output. The combined supply of the firms then increases to Q_1.

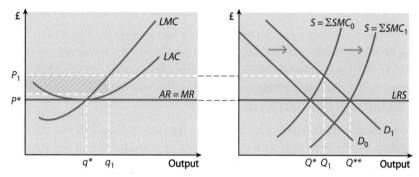

Figure 3.7 Adjusting to an increase in demand under perfect competition

However, at the higher price the firms start making supernormal profits (shown by the shaded area in Figure 3.7). Under the assumptions underpinning perfect competition, firms have perfect knowledge of market conditions, so the fact that firms in the market are making supernormal profits is known. Furthermore, there are no barriers to entry that prevent new firms joining the market. The fact that the product is homogeneous simplifies entry further. This means that in time more firms will be attracted into the market, pushing the short-run industry supply curve to the right. This process will continue until there is no further incentive for new firms to enter the market — which occurs when the price has returned to P^*, but with increased industry output at Q^{**}. In other words, the adjustment in the short run is borne by existing firms, but the long-run equilibrium is reached through the entry of new firms.

This suggests that the **industry long-run supply curve (LRS)** is horizontal at the price P^*, which is the minimum point of the long-run average cost curve for the typical firm in the industry.

Strictly speaking, the *LRS* is perfectly flat only if all firms face equal cost conditions, and if factor prices remain constant as the industry expands. For example, if there is a labour shortage, then industrial expansion may drive up labour costs, causing firms to face higher costs at any output level. In these sorts of circumstances, the *LRS* is slightly upward sloping.

Key term

industry long-run supply curve (LRS) under perfect competition, the curve that, for the typical firm in the industry, is horizontal at the minimum point of the long-run average cost curve

Extension material

Different cost conditions

If firms are not identical, but face different cost conditions, then the *LRS* may slope upwards. This could happen because some firms face a more favourable environment than others. Perhaps their location confers some advantage because they are closer to the market, or to some raw material. This would then allow some firms to survive for longer if the market price falls. In this case, as price falls, the least efficient firms would exit from the market until the marginal firm just makes normal profits. Notice that this also suggests that the most efficient firms in the market are able to make some abnormal profits even in long-run equilibrium, and it is only the marginal firm that just breaks even.

Interpreting points and areas on a diagram

Figure 3.8 shows the short-run cost curves for a firm that is operating in a perfectly competitive market. We can use a graph like this to analyse some key aspects of the firm's situation. Think carefully about what follows, and make sure you understand the points and areas mentioned.

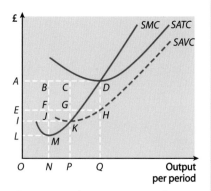

Figure 3.8 A firm operating under short-run perfect competition

A first question is to consider at what price the firm would just make 'normal' profits. This point would be where the price (average revenue) is just equal to average total costs, which would be at a price *OA* in the figure.

If the price were indeed at *OA*, then we could find areas of the figure to represent fixed and variable costs. With the price at *OA* the firm would produce *OQ* output (where *MC = MR*), so, average variable costs would be given by *OE*, and total variable costs would be the area *OEHQ*. We can then infer that total fixed costs are the area *EADH*.

Now consider the conditions under which a firm would choose to exit the market. In the short run, if the firm is getting a sufficiently high price to cover to its variable cost then it will stay in business, as it is at least covering a part of its fixed costs. However, if the price falls below average variable cost, this no longer applies. So the firm would exit if the price were to fall below *OI* (which is the minimum point of the *SAVC* curve. In other words, when the price is between *OI* and *OE* the firm makes a loss in the short run but continues in the market.

Notice that as the price varies, the firm effectively moves along its *SMC* curve, so we can interpret the *SMC* curve (above *OI*) as showing the short-run supply curve of the firm.

Notice also that if the price is above *OA*, the firm makes abnormal profits.

Starting from a diagram like Figure 3.6, track the response of a perfectly competitive market to a decrease in market demand for a good — in other words, explain how the market adjusts to a leftward shift of the demand curve.

These diagrams can be quite confusing until you get used to them, and you would be well advised to practise both interpreting and drawing them, so you can be confident in using them when you need to do so.

Efficiency under perfect competition

Having reviewed the characteristics of the long-run equilibrium of a perfectly competitive market, you may wonder what is so good about such a market in terms of productive and allocative efficiency.

Productive efficiency

For an individual market, productive efficiency is reached when a firm operates at the minimum point of its long-run average cost curve. Under perfect competition, this is indeed a feature of the long-run equilibrium position. So productive efficiency is achieved in the long run — but not in the short run, when a firm need not be operating at minimum average cost.

Allocative efficiency

For an individual market, allocative efficiency is achieved when price is set equal to marginal cost. Again, the process by which supernormal profits are competed away through the entry of new firms into the market ensures that price is equal to marginal cost within a perfectly competitive market in long-run equilibrium. So allocative efficiency is also achieved. Indeed, firms set price equal to marginal cost even in the short run, so allocative efficiency is a feature of perfect competition in both the short run and the long run.

Evaluation of perfect competition

A criticism sometimes levelled at the model of perfect competition is that it is merely a theoretical ideal, based on a sequence of assumptions that rarely holds in the real world. Perhaps you have some sympathy with that view.

It could be argued that the model does hold for some agricultural markets. One study in the USA estimated that the elasticity of demand for an individual farmer producing sweetcorn was −31,353, which is pretty close to perfect elasticity.

However, to argue that the model is useless because it is unrealistic is to miss a very important point. By allowing a glimpse of what the ideal market would look like, at least in terms of resource allocation, the model provides a measure against which alternative market structures can be compared. Furthermore, economic analysis can be used to investigate the effects of relaxing the assumptions of the model, which can be another valuable exercise. For example, it is possible to examine how the market is affected if firms can differentiate their products, or if traders in the market are acting with incomplete information.

So, although there may be relatively few markets that display all the characteristics of perfect competition, that does not destroy the usefulness of the model in economic theory. It will continue to be a reference point when examining alternative models of market structure.

Extension material

A word of warning

Some writers, such as Nobel prize winner Friedrich von Hayek (1899–1992), have disputed the idea that perfect competition is the best form of market structure. Hayek argued that supernormal profits can be seen as the basis for investment by firms in new technologies, research and development (R&D) and innovation. If supernormal profits are always competed away, as happens under perfect competition, such activity will not take place. Similarly, Joseph Schumpeter argued that only in monopoly or oligopoly markets can firms afford to undertake R&D. Under this sort of argument, it is not quite so clear that perfect competition is the most desirable market structure.

Summary

- The model of perfect competition describes an extreme form of market structure. It rests on a sequence of assumptions.
- Its key characteristics include the assumption that no individual trader can influence the market price of the good or service being traded, and that there is freedom of entry and exit.
- In such circumstances each firm faces a perfectly elastic demand curve for its product, and can sell as much as it likes at the going market price.
- A profit-maximising firm chooses to produce the level of output at which marginal revenue (MR) equals marginal cost (MC).
- The firm's short-run marginal cost curve, above its short-run average variable cost curve, represents its short-run supply curve.
- The industry's short-run supply curve is the horizontal summation of the supply curves of all firms in the market.
- Firms may make supernormal profits in the short run, but because there is freedom of entry these profits will be competed away in the long run by new firms joining the market.
- The long-run industry supply curve is horizontal, with price adjusting to the minimum level of the typical firm's long-run average cost curve.
- Under perfect competition in long-run equilibrium, both productive efficiency and allocative efficiency are achieved.

The model of monopoly

Key term

monopoly a form of market structure in which there is only one seller of a good or service

At the opposite end of the spectrum of market structures is **monopoly**, which is a market with a single seller of a good.

There is a bit more to it than that, and economic analysis of monopoly rests on some important assumptions. In the real world, the Competition and Markets Authority (CMA), the official body in the UK with responsibility for monitoring monopoly markets, is empowered to investigate a merger if it results in the combined firm having more than 25% of a market. The operations of the CMA will be discussed in Chapter 10.

Assumptions

The assumptions of the monopoly model are as follows:

1 There is a single seller of a good.
2 There are no substitutes for the good, either actual or potential.
3 There are barriers to entry into the market.

It is also assumed that the firm aims to maximise profits. You can see that these assumptions all have their counterparts in the assumptions of perfect competition, and that in one sense this model can be described as being at the opposite end of the market structure spectrum.

If there is a single seller of a good, and if there are no substitutes for the good, the monopoly firm is thereby insulated from competition. Furthermore, any barriers to entry into the market will ensure that the firm can sustain its market position into the future. The assumption that there are no potential substitutes for the good reinforces the situation. (Chapter 5 will explore what happens if this assumption does not hold.)

A monopoly in equilibrium

The first point to note is that a monopoly firm faces the market demand curve directly. Thus, unlike in perfect competition, the demand curve slopes downwards. For the monopolist, the demand curve may be regarded as showing average revenue. Unlike a firm under perfect competition, therefore, the monopolist has some influence over price, and can make decisions regarding price as well as output. This is not to say that the monopolist has complete freedom to set the price, as the firm is still constrained by market demand. However, the firm is a *price maker* and can choose a location *along* the demand curve.

As a preliminary piece of analysis, recall from Chapter 2 that there is a relationship between the own-price elasticity of demand along a straight-line demand curve and total revenue. The key graphs are reproduced here as Figure 3.9.

As with the firm under perfect competition, a monopolist aiming to maximise profits will choose to produce at the level of output at which marginal revenue equals marginal cost. This is at Q_m in Figure 3.10. Having selected output, the monopolist then identifies the price that will clear the market for that level of output — in Figure 3.10 this is P_m. Notice that a monopoly will always produce in the segment of the demand curve where *MR* is positive, which implies that demand is price elastic.

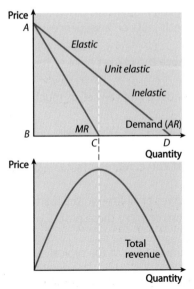

Figure 3.9 Elasticity and total revenue

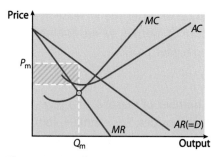

Figure 3.10 Profit maximisation and monopoly

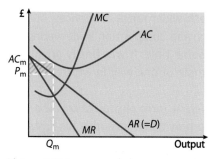

Figure 3.11 Losses made by a monopoly

This choice allows the monopolist to make supernormal profits, which can be identified as the shaded area in the figure. As before, this area is average revenue minus average cost, which gives profit per unit, multiplied by the quantity.

It is at this point that barriers to entry become important. Other firms may see that the monopoly firm is making healthy supernormal profits, but the existence of barriers to entry will prevent those profits from being competed away, as would happen in a perfectly competitive market.

It is important to notice that the monopolist cannot be guaranteed always to make such substantial profits as are shown in Figure 3.10. The size of the profits depends upon the relative position of the market demand curve and the position of the cost curves. For example, if the cost curves in the diagram were higher, as in Figure 3.11, the monopoly would actually incur losses, as if the monopoly tries to maximise profits by choosing the output at which $MR = MC$, it will charge a price (P_m) that is below average cost (AC_m).

Exercise 3.3

Table 3.2 shows the demand curve faced by a monopolist.

Table 3.2 Demand curve for a monopolist

Demand (000 per week)	Price (£)
0	80
1	70
2	60
3	50
4	40
5	30
6	20
7	10

a   Calculate total revenue and marginal revenue for each level of demand.
b   Plot the demand curve (*AR*) and marginal revenue on a graph.
c   Plot total revenue on a separate graph.
d   Identify the level of demand at which total revenue is at a maximum.
e   At what level of demand is marginal revenue equal to zero?
f   At what level of demand is there unit own-price elasticity of demand?
g   If the monopolist maximises profits, will the chosen level of output be higher or lower than the revenue-maximising level?
h   What does this imply for the price elasticity of demand when the monopolist maximises profits?

A monopoly and an increase in demand

If a monopoly experiences (or can induce) an increase in the demand for its product, it will benefit. In Figure 3.12, suppose that initially the monopoly faces the demand curve D_0. It maximises profits by setting $MR = MC$, producing Q_0 output and charging a price P_0. If the demand curve shifts to the right, notice that the *MR* curve will also shift, as this

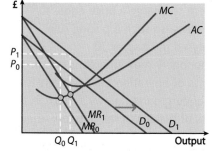

Figure 3.12 A monopoly and an increase in demand

has a fixed relationship with the demand curve. After the increase in demand, the monopoly chooses to produce Q_1 output, where $MR = MC$, and now sets a higher price at P_1, making higher profits.

How do monopolies arise?

Monopolies may arise in a market for a number of reasons. In a few instances, a monopoly is created by the authorities. For example, for 150 years the UK Post Office held a licence giving it a monopoly on delivering letters. This service is now open to some competition, although any company wanting to deliver packages weighing less than 350 grams and charging less than £1 can do so only by applying for a licence. The Post Office monopoly formerly covered a much wider range of services, but its coverage has been eroded over the years, and competition in delivering larger packages has been permitted for some time. It was finally privatised in 2013. Nonetheless, it remains an example of one way in which a monopoly can be created.

The patent system offers a rather different form of protection for a firm. The patent system was designed to provide an incentive for firms to innovate through the development of new techniques and products. By prohibiting other firms from copying the product for a period of time, a firm is given a temporary monopoly.

A natural monopoly

In some cases the technology of the industry may create a monopoly situation. In a market characterised by substantial economies of scale, there may not be room for more than one firm in the market. This could happen where there are substantial fixed costs of production but low marginal costs. For example, in establishing an underground railway in a city, a firm faces very high fixed costs in building the network of rails and stations, and buying the rolling stock. However, once in operation, the marginal cost of carrying an additional passenger is very low.

Figure 3.13 illustrates this point. The firm in this market enjoys economies of scale right up to the limit of market demand. Any new entrant into the market will be operating at a lower scale, so will inevitably face higher average costs. The existing firm will always be able to price such firms out of the market. Here the economies of scale act as an effective barrier to the entry of new firms and the market is a **natural monopoly**. A profit-maximising monopoly would thus set $MR = MC$, produce at quantity Q_m and charge a price P_m.

Such a market poses particular problems regarding allocative efficiency. Notice in the figure that marginal cost is below average cost over the entire range of output. If the firm were to charge a price equal to marginal cost, it would inevitably make a loss, so such a pricing rule would not be viable. This problem is analysed in Chapter 10.

The sort of market where a natural monopoly may emerge is one in which there may be substantial fixed costs of operation but relatively low marginal cost. An example might be an underground railway system in a city or a Channel Tunnel. The setup costs of building a rail network under a city or a tunnel under the Channel are enormous compared with the marginal cost of carrying an additional passenger. Some cities (e.g. Kuala Lumpur) do have more than one underground railway system, but they

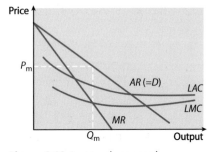

Figure 3.13 A natural monopoly

Key term

natural monopoly monopoly that arises in an industry in which there are such substantial economies of scale that only one firm is viable

The London Underground is an example of a natural monopoly

do not compete on the same routes. It would not make economic sense to have parallel rail systems competing for the same passengers on a particular route, any more than it would be sensible to have two Channel Tunnels close to each other. Notice that although the Channel Tunnel may seem an obvious natural monopoly, this does not mean that the firm operating it faces no competition. The tunnel has to compete with ferry companies and airlines.

Another example of a natural monopoly might seem to be the manufacture of passenger aircraft. Building a plane capable of carrying large numbers of passengers on long-haul routes has large economies of scale. There are indivisibilities in the production process, and any firm producing such aircraft has to make substantial investment in research and development upfront. Furthermore, the market is relatively small, in the sense that the number of aircraft sold in a year is modest. However, looking at the market, it is clear that it is not a monopoly as there are two firms operating in the market — Boeing and Airbus. These are the only effective global competitors.

Does this negate the natural monopoly theory? The answer is no. In fact, this market has aroused much transatlantic debate and contention. Boeing, the US producer, has accused European governments of unfairly subsidising Airbus's R&D programme. In return, Airbus has responded by pointing to the benefits that Boeing has received from the US military research programme. Without being drawn into this debate at this stage, the net effect of the interventions has been to create a duopoly situation (a market with just two firms) in which Boeing and Airbus compete for market share. Later discussion will examine why such competition is regarded as being more favourable for consumers than allowing an unregulated natural monopoly to develop.

There are markets in which firms have risen to become monopolies by their actions in the market. Such a market structure is sometimes known as a *competitive monopoly*. Firms may get into a monopoly position through effective marketing, through a process of merger and acquisition, or by establishing a new product as a widely accepted standard.

In the first Microsoft trial in 1998, it was argued that Microsoft had gained 95% of the world market for operating systems for PC computers. The firm claimed that this was because it is simply very good at what it does. However, part of the reason why Microsoft was on trial was that not everyone agreed with this claim, and they alleged unfair market tactics.

Exercise 3.4

In 2000, AOL merged with Time Warner, bringing together an internet service provider with an extensive network and a firm in the entertainment business.

One product that such a merged company might produce is a digitised music performance that could be distributed through the internet. Think about the sorts of cost entailed in producing and delivering such a product, and categorise them as fixed or variable costs. What does this imply for the economies of scale faced by the merged company?

Monopoly and efficiency

The characteristics of the monopoly market can be evaluated in relation to productive and allocative efficiency (see Figure 3.10).

Productive efficiency

A firm is said to be productively efficient if it produces at the minimum point of its long-run average cost curve. It is clear from the figure that this is extremely unlikely for a monopoly. The firm will produce at its minimum long-run average cost only if it so happens that the marginal *revenue* curve passes through this exact point — and this would happen only by coincidence.

Allocative efficiency

For an individual firm, allocative efficiency is achieved when price is set equal to marginal cost. It is clear from Figure 3.10 that this will not be the case for a profit-maximising monopoly firm. The firm chooses output where *MR* equals *MC*; however, given that *MR* is below *AR* (i.e. price), price will always be set above marginal cost.

Perfect competition and monopoly compared

It is possible to identify the extent to which a monopoly by its behaviour distorts resource allocation, by comparing the monopoly market with the perfectly competitive market. To do this, the situation can be simplified by setting aside the possibility of economies of scale. This is perhaps an artificial assumption to make, but it can be relaxed later.

Suppose that there is an industry with no economies of scale, which can be operated either as a perfectly competitive market with many small firms, or as a monopoly firm running a large number of small plants.

Figure 3.14 shows the market demand curve (*D* = *AR*), and the long-run supply curve under perfect competition (*LRS*). If the market is operating

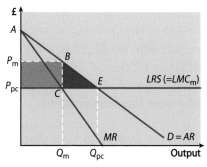

Figure 3.14 Comparing perfect competition and monopoly

under perfect competition, the long-run equilibrium will produce a price of P_{pc}, and the firms in the industry will together supply Q_{pc} output. Consumer surplus is given by the area $AP_{pc}E$, which represents the surplus that consumers gain from consuming this product. In other words, it is a measure of the welfare that society receives from consuming the good, as was explained in Book 1.

Now suppose that the industry is taken over by a profit-maximising monopolist. The firm can close down some of the plants to vary its output over the long run, and the *LRS* can be regarded as the monopolist's long-run marginal cost curve. As the monopoly firm faces the market demand curve directly, it will also face the *MR* curve shown, so will maximise profits at quantity Q_m and charge a price P_m.

Thus, the effect of this change in market structure is that the profit-maximising monopolist produces less output than a perfectly competitive industry and charges a higher price.

It is also apparent that consumer surplus is now very different, as in the new situation it is limited to the area AP_mB. Looking more carefully at Figure 3.14, you can see that the loss of consumer surplus has occurred for two reasons. First, the monopoly firm is now making profits shown by the shaded area P_mBCP_{pc}. This is a redistribution of welfare from consumers to the firm, but as the monopolist is also a member of society, this does not affect overall welfare. However, there is also a deadweight loss, which represents a loss to society resulting from the monopolisation of the industry. This is measured by the area of the triangle *BCE*.

Summary
- A monopoly market is one in which there is a single seller of a good.
- The model of monopoly used in economic analysis also assumes that there are no substitutes for the goods or services produced by the monopolist, and that there are barriers to the entry of new firms.
- The monopoly firm faces the market demand curve, and is able to choose a point along that demand curve in order to maximise profits.
- Such a firm may be able to make supernormal profits, and sustain them in the long run because of barriers to entry and the lack of substitutes.
- A monopoly may arise because of patent protection or from the nature of economies of scale in the industry (a 'natural monopoly').
- A profit-maximising monopolist does not achieve allocative efficiency, and is unlikely to achieve productive efficiency in the sense of producing at the minimum point of the long-run average cost curve.
- A comparison of perfect competition with monopoly reveals that a profit-maximising monopoly firm operating under the same cost conditions as a perfectly competitive industry will produce less output, charge a higher price and impose a deadweight loss on society.

Study tip

Remember that there are some key concepts (such as consumer surplus, mentioned in this section) that you will have learned in Book 1 which are likely to be important here as well. If you cannot recall the details, it is worth looking back to remind yourself.

Price discrimination

Are there any conditions in which a monopoly firm would produce the level of output that is consistent with allocative efficiency? Consider Figure 3.15. Suppose this market is operated by a monopolist that faces constant marginal cost *LMC*. What would induce the monopolist to produce at Q^*?

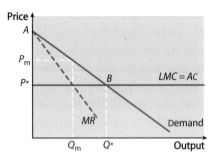

Figure 3.15 Perfect price discrimination

One of the assumptions made throughout the analysis so far is that all consumers in a market get to pay the same price for the product. This leads to the notion of consumer surplus. In Figure 3.15, if the market were operating under perfect competition and all consumers were paying the same price, consumer surplus would be given by the area AP^*B. If the market were operated by a monopolist, also charging the same price to all buyers, then profits would be maximised where $MC = MR$: that is, at quantity Q_m and price P_m.

But suppose this assumption is now relaxed? Suppose that the monopolist is able to charge a different price to each individual consumer. A monopolist is then able to charge each consumer a price that is equal to his or her willingness to pay for the good. In other words, the demand curve effectively becomes the marginal revenue curve, as it represents the amount that the monopolist will receive for each unit of the good. It will then maximise profits at point B in Figure 3.15, where MR (i.e. AR) is equal to *LMC*. The difference between this situation and that under perfect competition is that the area AP^*B is no longer consumer surplus, but producer surplus: that is, the monopolist's profits. The monopolist has hijacked the whole of the original consumer surplus as its profits.

From society's point of view, total welfare is the same as it is under perfect competition (but more than under monopoly without discrimination). However, now there has been a redistribution from consumers to the monopoly — and presumably to the shareholders of the firm. This situation is known as **perfect price discrimination** or **first-degree price discrimination**.

Perfect price discrimination is fairly rare in the real world, although it might be said to exist in the world of art or fashion, where customers may commission a painting, sculpture or item of designer jewellery and the price is a matter of negotiation between the buyer and supplier.

However, there are situations in which partial price discrimination is possible. For example, students or old-age pensioners may get discounted bus fares, the young and/or old may get cheaper access to sporting events or theatres, etc. In these instances, individual consumers are paying different prices for what is in fact the same product.

There are three conditions under which a firm may be able to price discriminate:

- The firm must have market power.
- The firm must have information about consumers and their willingness to pay — and there must be identifiable differences between consumers (or groups of consumers).
- The consumers must have limited ability to resell the product.

Perfect price discrimination exists in the art world

Market power

Clearly, price discrimination is not possible in a perfectly competitive market, where no seller has the power to charge other than the going market price. So price discrimination can take place only where firms have some ability to vary the price.

Information

From the firm's point of view, it needs to be able to identify different groups of consumers with different willingness to pay. What makes price discrimination profitable for firms is that different consumers display different sensitivities to price: that is, they have different price elasticities of demand.

Ability to resell

If consumers could resell the product easily, then price discrimination would not be possible, as consumers would engage in **arbitrage**. In other words, the group of consumers who qualified for the low price could buy up the product and then turn a profit by reselling to consumers in the other segment(s) of the market. This would mean that the firm would no longer be able to sell at the high price, and would no longer try to discriminate in pricing.

In the case of student discounts and old-age concessions, the firm can identify particular groups of consumers; and such 'products' as bus journeys and dental treatment cannot be resold. But why should a firm undertake this practice?

The simple answer is that, by undertaking price discrimination, the firm is able to increase its profits by switching sales from a market with relatively low marginal revenue to a market where it is higher.

An extreme form of price discrimination was used by NAPP Pharmaceutical Holdings, as a result of which the firm was fined £3.2 million by the Office of Fair Trading. NAPP sold sustained-release morphine tablets and capsules in the UK. These are drugs administered to patients with incurable cancer. NAPP realised that the market was segmented. The drugs were sold partly to the National Health Service

49

for use in hospitals, but were also prescribed by GPs. As these patients were terminally ill, they tended to spend a relatively short time in hospital before being sent home. NAPP realised that GPs tended to prescribe the same drugs as the patients had received in hospital. It therefore reduced its price to hospitals by 90%, thereby forcing all competitors out of the market and gaining a monopoly in that market segment. It was then able to increase the price of these drugs prescribed through GPs, and so maximise profits. The OFT investigated the firm, fined it and instructed it to stop its actions, thus saving the NHS £2 million per year.

Exercise 3.5

In which of the following products might price discrimination be possible? Explain your answers.

a hairdressing

b peak and off-peak rail travel

c apples

d air tickets

e newspapers

f plastic surgery

g beer

Summary
- In some markets a monopolist may be able to engage in price discrimination by selling its product at different prices to different consumers or groups of consumers.
- This enables the firm to increase its profits by absorbing some or all of the consumer surplus.
- Under first-degree price discrimination, the firm is able to charge a different price to each customer and absorb all of the consumer surplus.
- The firm can practise price discrimination only where it has market power, where consumers have differing elasticities of demand for the product, and where consumers have limited ability to resell the product.

Case study 3.1

Of cabbages and rings

Ted Greens has a farm on which he grows a variety of crops, including cabbages that grow well on his south field, which seems especially suited to the crop. When Ted takes his cabbage crop to market, hoping to make as much profit as possible, he finds that the price he can charge for cabbages depends on market conditions — after all, one cabbage is very much like any other. He thus has to accept the price that he can get, which is the same as that charged by his many rival producers. If he tries to set a higher price, he sells nothing as all traders in the market have good awareness of market conditions. But as he can sell as much as he likes at the going price, there is no need to drop price below that prevailing in the market. Price tends to fluctuate from one harvest season to the next,

and in some years when cabbages are plentiful, Ted finds that he barely covers his costs.

Edward de Vere owns a diamond mine — the only such mine in the country. His company cuts the stones and uses them to produce diamond rings. In selling the rings, Edward takes into account the strength of demand, choosing a price that will clear the market. He finds that by restricting the number of rings that he produces, he is able to charge a higher price. By doing so he is able to increase the profits that he makes. As he controls the only source of diamonds, Edward does not have to worry about other producers entering the market, and there are no acceptable substitutes for diamonds that people are prepared to accept.

Case study 3.1 (continued)

Follow-up questions

a Which of the two producers appears to operate under conditions of perfect competition, and which is a monopoly?

b Explain your answer to part (a), referring to the assumptions that underlie the two theories of market structure.

c Under what conditions would Ted Greens decide to give up growing cabbages?

d Can you think of steps that Ted Greens might take in order to improve his profits on cabbages?

e Draw a diagram to explain how Edward de Vere would react to an increase in the demand for diamond rings.

f Suppose that a foreign firm starts to import diamond rings into the country in competition with Edward de Vere. How would you expect him to react?

Chapter 4

Market structure: monopolistic competition and oligopoly

The previous chapter introduced the models of perfect competition and monopoly, and described them as being at the extreme ends of a spectrum of forms of market structure. In between those two extremes are other forms of market structure, which have some but not all of the characteristics of either perfect competition or monopoly. It is in this sense that there is a spectrum of structures. Attention in this chapter is focused on some of these intermediate forms of market structure, including a discussion of the sorts of pricing strategy that firms may adopt, and how they decide which to go for. This chapter also discusses ways in which firms may try to prevent new firms from joining a market, in terms of both pricing and non-price strategies. The theory of contestable markets completes the discussion.

Learning objectives

After studying this chapter, you should:
- be familiar with the range of market situations that exists between the extremes of perfect competition and monopoly
- understand the meaning of product differentiation and its role in the model of monopolistic competition
- understand the notion of oligopoly and be familiar with approaches to modelling firm behaviour in an oligopoly market
- understand the benefits that firms may gain from forming a cartel — and the tensions that may result
- be aware of the possible pricing rules that can be adopted by firms
- understand the notion of limit pricing, and how this may relate to profit maximisation
- be familiar with the idea of predatory pricing
- understand the notion of contestable markets and its implications for firms' behaviour

Prior knowledge needed

This chapter continues the discussion of market structure from Chapter 3.

Monopolistic competition

If you consider the characteristics of the markets that you frequent on a regular basis, you will find that few of them display all of the characteristics associated with perfect competition. However, there may be some that show a few of these features. In particular, you will find some

The monopolistic competition model describes the fast-food market in many cities

markets in which there appears to be intense competition among many sellers, but in which the products for sale are not identical. For example, think about restaurants. In many cities, you will find a wide range of restaurants, cafés and pubs that compete with each other for business, but do so by offering slightly different products.

The theory of **monopolistic competition** was devised by Edward Chamberlin, writing in the USA in the 1930s, and his name is often attached to the model, although Joan Robinson published her book on imperfect competition in the UK at the same time. The motivation for the analysis was to explain how markets worked when they were operating neither as monopolies nor under perfect competition.

The model describes a market in which there are many firms producing similar, but not identical, products: for example, package holidays, hairdressers and fast-food outlets. In the case of fast-food outlets, the high streets of many cities are characterised by large numbers of different types of takeaway — burgers, fish and chips, Indian, Chinese, fried chicken and so on.

Model characteristics

Three important characteristics of the model of monopolistic competition distinguish this sort of market from others.

Product differentiation

First, firms produce differentiated products, and face downward-sloping demand curves. In other words, each firm competes with the others by making its product slightly different. This allows the firms to build up brand loyalty among their regular customers, which gives them some influence over price. It is likely that firms will engage in advertising in order to maintain such brand loyalty, and heavy advertising is a common characteristic of a market operating under monopolistic competition.

Because other firms are producing similar goods, there are substitutes for each firm's product, which means that demand is relatively price elastic (although this does not mean that it is never inelastic). However, it is certainly not perfectly price elastic, as was the case with perfect competition. These features — that the product is not homogeneous and

Key terms

monopolistic competition
a market that shares some characteristics of monopoly and some of perfect competition
product differentiation
a strategy adopted by firms that marks their product as being different from their competitors'

53

demand is not perfectly price elastic — represent significant differences from the model of perfect competition.

Freedom of entry

Second, there are no barriers to entry into the market. Firms are able to join the market if they observe that existing firms are making supernormal profits. New entrants will be looking for some way to differentiate their product slightly from the others — perhaps the next fast-food restaurant will be Nepalese, or Peruvian.

This characteristic distinguishes the market from the monopoly model, as does the existence of fairly close substitutes.

Many firms

Third, there are many firms operating in the market. For this reason, a price change by one of the firms will have negligible effects on the demand for its rivals' products.

Overview

Taking these three characteristics together, it can be seen that a market of monopolistic competition has some of the characteristics of perfect competition and some features of monopoly; hence its name.

Short-run equilibrium

Figure 4.1 represents short-run equilibrium under monopolistic competition. D_s is the demand curve and MR_s is the corresponding marginal revenue curve. AC and MC are the average and marginal cost curves for a representative firm in the industry. If the firm is aiming to maximise profits, it will choose the level of output such that $MR_s = MC$. This occurs at output Q_s, and the firm will then choose the price that clears the market at P_s.

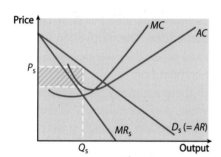

Figure 4.1 Short-run equilibrium under monopolistic competition

This closely resembles the standard monopoly diagram that was introduced in Chapter 3. As with monopoly, a firm under monopolistic competition faces a downward-sloping demand curve, as already noted. The difference is that now it is assumed that there is free entry into the market under monopolistic competition, so that Figure 4.1 represents equilibrium only in the short run. This is because the firm shown in the figure is making supernormal profits, shown by the shaded area (which is $AR - AC$ multiplied by output).

The importance of free entry

This is where the assumption of free entry into the market becomes important. In Figure 4.1 the supernormal profits being made by the representative firm will attract new firms into the market. The new firms will produce differentiated products, and this will affect the demand curve for the representative firm's product. In particular, the new firms will attract some customers away from this firm, so that its demand curve will tend to shift to the left. Its shape may also change as there are now more substitutes for the original product.

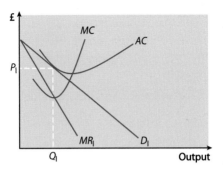

Figure 4.2 Long-run equilibrium under monopolistic competition

Long-run equilibrium

This process will continue as long as firms in the market continue to make profits that attract new firms into the activity. It may be accelerated if firms are persuaded to spend money on advertising in an attempt to defend their market shares. The advertising may help to keep the demand curve downward sloping, but it will also affect the position of the average cost curve, by pushing up average cost at all levels of output.

Figure 4.2 shows the final position for the market. The typical firm is now operating in such a way that it maximises profits (by setting output such that $MR = MC$); at the same time, the average cost curve (AC) at this level of output is at a tangent to the demand curve. This means that $AC = AR$, and the firm is just making normal profit (i.e. is just covering opportunity cost). There is thus no further incentive for more firms to join the market. In Figure 4.2 this occurs when output is at Q_l and price is set at P_l.

Efficiency

One way of evaluating the market outcome under this model is to examine the consequences for productive and allocative efficiency. It is clear from Figure 4.2 that neither of these conditions will be met. The representative firm does not reach the minimum point on the long-run average cost curve, and so does not attain productive efficiency; furthermore, the price charged is above marginal cost, so allocative efficiency is not achieved.

Evaluation

If the typical firm in the market is not fully exploiting the possible economies of scale that exist, it could be argued that product differentiation is damaging society's total welfare, in the sense that product differentiation allows firms to keep their demand curves downward sloping. In other words, too many different products are being produced. However, this argument could be countered by pointing out that consumers may enjoy having more freedom of choice. The very fact that they are prepared to pay a premium price for their chosen brand indicates that they have some preference for it. For example, some people may be prepared to pay more than £65 to watch Chelsea although they could watch 90 minutes of football at Wimbledon AFC for about £20.

Another crucial difference between monopolistic competition and perfect competition is that under monopolistic competition firms would like to sell more of their product at the going price, whereas under perfect competition they can sell as much as they like at the going price. This is because price under monopolistic competition is set above marginal cost. The use of advertising to attract more customers and to maintain consumer perception of product differences may be considered a problem with this market. It could be argued that excessive use of advertising to maintain product differentiation is wasteful, as it leads to higher average cost curves than needed. On the other hand, the need to compete in this way may result in less X-inefficiency than under a complacent monopolist.

Exercise 4.1

Figure 4.3 shows a firm under monopolistic competition.

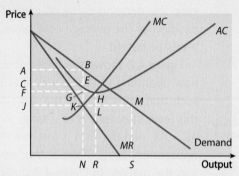

Figure 4.3 A firm under monopolistic competition

a Identify the profit-maximising level of output.

b At what price would the firm sell its product?

c What supernormal profits (if any) would be made by the firm?

d Is this a short-run or a long-run equilibrium? Explain your answer.

e Describe the subsequent adjustment that might take place in the market (if any).

f At what level of output would productive efficiency be achieved? (Assume that *AC* represents long-run average cost for this part of the question.)

Summary

- The theory of monopolistic competition has its origins in the 1930s, when economists such as Edward Chamberlin and Joan Robinson were writing about markets that did not conform to the models of perfect competition and monopoly.
- The model describes a market where there are many firms producing similar, but not identical, products.
- By differentiating their product from those of other firms, it is possible for firms to maintain some influence over price.
- To do this, firms engage in advertising to build brand loyalty.
- There are no barriers to entry into the market, and concentration ratios are low.
- Firms may be able to make supernormal profits in the short run.
- In response, new entrants join the market, shifting the demand curves of existing firms and affecting their shape.
- The process continues until supernormal profits have been competed away, and the typical firm has its average cost curve at a tangent to its demand curve.
- Neither productive nor allocative efficiency is achieved in long-run equilibrium.
- Consumers may benefit from the increased range of choice on offer in the market.

Oligopoly

Key term

oligopoly a market with a few sellers, in which each firm must take account of the behaviour and likely behaviour of rival firms in the industry

A number of markets seem to be dominated by relatively few firms — think of commercial banking in the UK, cinemas or the newspaper industry. A market with just a few sellers is known as an **oligopoly** market. An important characteristic of such markets is that when making economic decisions each firm must take account of its rivals' behaviour and reactions. The firms are therefore interdependent.

An important characteristic of oligopoly is that each firm has to act strategically, both in reacting to rival firms' decisions and in trying to anticipate their future actions and reactions.

There are many different ways in which a firm may take such strategic decisions, and this means that there are many ways in which an oligopoly market can be modelled, depending on how the firms are behaving. This chapter reviews just a few such models.

Oligopolies may come about for many reasons, but perhaps the most convincing concerns economies of scale. An oligopoly is likely to develop in a market where there are some economies of scale — economies that are not substantial enough to require a natural monopoly, but which are large enough to make it difficult for too many firms to operate at the minimum efficient scale.

Within an oligopoly market, firms may adopt rivalrous behaviour or they may choose to cooperate with each other. The two attitudes have implications for how markets operate. Cooperation will tend to take the market towards the monopoly end of the spectrum, whereas non-cooperation will take it towards the competitive end. In either scenario, it is likely that the market outcome will be somewhere between the two extremes.

The kinked demand curve model

One model of oligopoly revolves around how a firm perceives its demand curve. This is called the kinked demand curve model, and was developed by Paul Sweezy in the USA in the 1930s.

The model relates to an oligopoly in which firms try to anticipate the reactions of rivals to their actions. One problem that arises is that a firm cannot readily observe its demand curve with any degree of certainty, so it must form expectations about how consumers will react to a price change.

Figure 4.4 shows how this works. Suppose the price is currently set at P^*; the firm is selling Q^* and is trying to decide whether to alter price. The problem is that it knows for sure about only one point on the demand curve: that is, when price is P^*, the firm sells Q^*.

However, the firm is aware that the degree of sensitivity to its price change will depend upon whether or not the other firms in the market will follow its lead. In other words, if its rivals ignore the firm's price change, there will be more sensitivity to this change than if they all follow suit.

Figure 4.4 shows the two extreme possibilities for the demand curve which the firm perceives that it faces. If other firms *ignore* its action, D_{ig} will be the relevant demand curve, which is relatively elastic. On the other hand, if the other firms *copy* the firm's moves, D_{cop} will be the relevant demand curve.

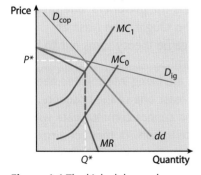

Figure 4.4 The kinked demand curve

The question then is: under what conditions will the other firms copy the price change, and when will they not? The firm may imagine that if it raises price, there is little likelihood that its rivals will copy. After all, this is a non-threatening move that gives market share to the other firms. So for a price *increase*, D_{ig} is the relevant section.

On the other hand, a price reduction is likely to be seen by the rivals as a threatening move, and they are likely to copy in order to preserve their market positions. For a price *decrease*, then, D_{cop} is relevant.

Putting these together, the firm perceives that it faces a kinked demand curve (*dd*). Furthermore, if the marginal revenue curve is added to the picture, it is seen to have a discontinuity at the kink. It thus transpires that Q^* is the profit-maximising level of output under a wide range of cost conditions from MC_0 to MC_1; so, even in the face of a change in marginal costs, the firm will not alter its behaviour.

Thus, the model predicts that if the firm perceives its demand curve to be of this shape, it has a strong incentive to do nothing, even in the face of changes in costs. However, it all depends upon the firm's perceptions. If there is a general increase in costs that affects all producers, this may affect the firm's perception of rival reaction, and thus encourage it to raise price. If other firms are reading the market in the same way, they are likely to follow suit. Notice that this model does not explain how the price reaches P^* in the first place.

Game theory

A more recent development in the economic theory of the firm has been in the application of **game theory**. This began as a branch of mathematics, but it became apparent that it had wide applications in explaining the behaviour of firms in an oligopoly.

Game theory itself has a long history, with some writers tracing it back to correspondence between Pascal and Fermat in the mid-seventeenth century. Early applications in economics were by Antoine Augustin Cournot in 1838, Francis Edgeworth in 1881 and J. Bertrand in 1883, but the key publication was the book by John von Neumann and Oskar Morgenstern, *Theory of Games and Economic Behaviour,* in 1944. Other famous names in game theory include John Nash (played by Russell Crowe in the film *A Beautiful Mind*), John Harsanyi and Reinhard Selton, who shared the 1994 Nobel prize for their work in this area.

Almost certainly, the most famous game is the **prisoners' dilemma**, introduced in a lecture by Albert Tucker (who taught John Nash at Princeton) in 1950. This simple example of game theory turns out to have a multitude of helpful applications in economics.

Two prisoners, Al Fresco and Des Jardins, are being interrogated about a major crime, and the police know that at least one of the prisoners is guilty. The two are kept in separate cells and cannot communicate with each other. The police have enough evidence to convict them of a minor offence, but not enough to convict them of the major one.

Each prisoner is offered a deal. If he turns state's evidence and provides evidence to convict the other prisoner, he will get off — *unless* the other prisoner also confesses. If both refuse to deal, they will just be charged with the minor offence. Table 4.1 summarises the sentences that each will receive in the various circumstances.

Table 4.1 The prisoners' dilemma: possible outcomes (years in jail)

		Des			
		Confess		Refuse	
Al	Confess	10	10	0	15
	Refuse	15	0	5	5

Quantitative skills 4.1

Reading a matrix of numerical data

In each case, Al's sentence (in years) is shown in orange and Des's in purple. How do we read the matrix? Think about this from Al's perspective. If Al confesses, we look at the orange entries in the first row of the table. This shows that the sentence that Al will receive depends upon what Des chooses to do. If Des also confesses, then Al gets a sentence of 10 years, but if Des refuses to deal, then Al gets away scot-free.

Suppose Al instead refuses to confess. We then read across the second row, and see that Al gets a heavy sentence if he refuses to confess but Des confesses (i.e. testifies against Al), but if they both refuse to confess they both get off relatively lightly.

If both Al and Des refuse to deal, they will be convicted of the minor offence, and each will go down for 5 years. However, if Al confesses and Des refuses to deal, Al will get off completely free, and Des will take the full rap of 15 years. If Des confesses and Al refuses, the reverse happens. However, if both confess, they will each get 10 years.

Think about this situation from Al's point of view, remembering that the prisoners cannot communicate, so Al does not know what Des will choose to do and vice versa. You can see from Table 4.1 that, whatever Des chooses to do, Al will be better off confessing. If Des confesses, Al is better off confessing also, going down for 10 years instead of 15; if Des refuses, Al is still better off confessing, going free instead of getting a 5-year term. John Nash referred to such a situation as a **dominant strategy**.

The dilemma is, of course, symmetric, so for Des too the dominant strategy is to confess. The inevitable result is that, if both prisoners are selfish, they will both confess — and both will then get 10 years in jail. If they had both refused to deal, they would both have been better off; but this is too risky a strategy for either of them to adopt. A refusal to deal might have led to 15 years in jail.

What has this to do with economics? Think about the market for DIY products. Suppose there are two firms (Diamond Tools and Better Spades) operating in a duopoly market (i.e. a market with only two firms). Each firm has a choice of producing 'high' output or 'low' output. The profit made by one firm depends upon two things: its own output and the output of the other firm.

Table 4.2 shows the range of possible outcomes for a particular time period. Consider Diamond Tools: if it chooses 'low' when Better Spades also chooses 'low', it will make £2 million profit (and so will Better Spades); but if Diamond Tools chooses 'low' when Better Spades chooses 'high', Diamond Tools will make zero profits and Better Spades will make £3 million.

Key term

dominant strategy a situation in game theory where a player's best strategy is independent of those chosen by others

Table 4.2 Diamond Tools and Better Spades: possible outcomes (profits in £m)

		Better Spades			
		High		Low	
Diamond Tools	High	1	1	3	0
	Low	0	3	2	2

The situation that maximises joint profits is for both firms to produce low; but suppose you were taking decisions for Diamond Tools — what would you choose?

If Better Spades produces 'low', you will maximise profits by producing 'high', whereas if Better Spades produces 'high', you will still maximise profits by producing high! So Diamond Tools has a dominant strategy to produce high — it is the profit-maximising action whatever Better Spades does, even though it means that joint profits will be lower.

Given that the table is symmetric, Better Spades faces the same decision process, and also has a dominant strategy to choose high, so they always end up in the northwest corner of the table, even though southeast would be better for each of them. Furthermore, after they have made their choices and seen what the other has chosen, each firm feels justified by its actions, and thinks that it took the right decision, given the rival's move. This is known as a **Nash equilibrium**, which has the characteristic that neither firm needs to amend its behaviour in any future period. This model can be used to investigate a wide range of decisions that firms need to take strategically.

Key term

Nash equilibrium situation occurring within a game when each player's chosen strategy maximises payoffs given the other player's choice, so no player has an incentive to alter behaviour

Exercise 4.2

Suppose there are two cinemas, X and Y, operating in a town; you are taking decisions for firm X. You cannot communicate with the other firm; both firms are considering only the next period. Each firm is choosing whether to set price 'high' or 'low'. Your expectation is that the payoffs (in terms of profits) to the two firms are as shown in Table 4.3 (firm X in orange, firm Y in purple):

Table 4.3 Cinemas X and Y: possible outcomes

		Firm Y chooses:			
		High price		Low price	
Firm X chooses:	High price	0	10	1	15
	Low price	15	1	4	4

a If firm Y sets price high, what strategy maximises profits for firm X?
b If firm Y sets price low, what strategy maximises profits for firm X?
c So what strategy will firm X adopt?
d What is the market outcome?
e What outcome would maximise the firms' joint profit?
f How might this outcome be achieved?
g Would the outcome be different if the game were played over repeated periods?

Cooperative games and cartels

Look back at the prisoners' dilemma game in Table 4.2. It is clear that the requirement that the firms are unable to communicate with each other is a serious impediment from the firms' point of view. If both firms could agree to produce 'low', they would maximise their joint profits, but they will not risk this strategy if they cannot communicate.

If they could join together in a **cartel**, the two firms could come to an agreement to adopt the low–low strategy. However, if they were to agree to this, each firm would have a strong incentive to cheat because, if each now knew that the other firm was going to produce low, they would also know that they could produce high and dominate the market — at least, given the payoffs in the table.

This is a common feature of cartels. Collusion can bring high joint profits, but there is always the temptation for each of the member firms to cheat and try to sneak some additional market share at the expense of the other firms in the cartel.

Extension material

The operation of a cartel

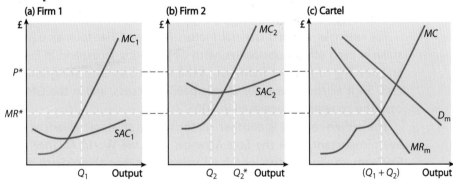

Figure 4.5 Market allocation in a two-firm cartel

You can see how a cartel might operate in Figure 4.5, which shows the situation facing a two-firm cartel (a duopoly). Panels (a) and (b) show the cost conditions for each of the firms, and panel (c) shows the whole market.

If the firms aim to maximise their joint profits, then they set $MR = MC$ at the level of the market (shown in panel (c)). This occurs at the joint level of output $Q_1 + Q_2$, with the price set at P^*. Notice that the joint marginal cost curve is the sum of the two firms' marginal cost curves.

The critical decision is how to divide the market up between the two firms. In the figure, the two firms have different cost conditions, with firm 1 operating at lower short-run average cost than firm 2. If the firms agree to set price at P^*, and each produces up to the point where marginal cost equals the level of (market) marginal revenue at MR^*, then the market

should work well. Firm 1 produces Q_1 and firm 2 produces Q_2. Joint profits are maximised, and there is a clear rule enabling the division of the market between the firms.

However, notice that firm 2 is very much the junior partner in this alliance, as it gets a much smaller market share. The temptation to cheat is obvious. If firm 2 accepts price P^*, it sees that its profits will be maximised at Q_2^*, so there is a temptation to try to steal an extra bit of market share.

Of course, the temptation is also there for firm 1, but as soon as either one of the firms begins to increase output, the market price will have to fall to maintain equilibrium, and the cartel will be broken: the market will move away from the joint profit-maximising position.

There is another downside to the formation of a cartel. In most countries around the world (with one or two exceptions, such as Hong Kong) they are illegal. For example, in the UK the operation of a cartel is illegal under the UK Competition Act, under which the Competition and Markets Authority (CMA) is empowered to fine firms up to 10% of their worldwide turnover for each year the cartel is found to have been in operation.

This means that overt collusion is rare. The most famous example is not between firms but between nations, in the form of the Organisation of the Petroleum Exporting Countries (OPEC), which over a long period of time has operated a cartel to control the price of oil.

Some conditions may favour the formation of cartels — or at least, some form of collusion between firms. The most important of these is the ability of each of the firms involved to monitor the actions of the other firms, and so ensure that they are keeping to the agreement.

Collusion in practice

Although cartels are illegal, the potential gains from collusion may tempt firms to find ways of working together. In some cases, firms have joined together in rather loose strategic alliances, in which they may work together on part of their business, perhaps in undertaking joint research and development or technology swaps.

For example, in 2000 General Motors (GM) and Fiat took an equity stake in each other's companies, with GM wanting to expand in Europe and needing to find out more about the technology of making smaller cars. Such alliances have not always been a success, and in the GM–Fiat case the companies separated in 2005.

The airline market is another sector where strategic alliances have been important, with the Star Alliance, the One World Alliance and SkyTeam carving up the long-haul routes between them. Such alliances offer benefits to passengers, who can get access to a wider range of destinations and business-class lounges and frequent-flier rewards, and to the airlines, which can economise on airport facilities by pooling their resources. However, the net effect is to reduce competition, and the regulators have interfered with some suggested alliances, such as that between British Airways and American Airlines in 2001, which was investigated by regulators on both sides of the Atlantic. The conditions under which the alliance would have been permitted were such that British Airways withdrew the proposal. This proposed alliance resurfaced in August 2008, when the European Commission opened a new anti-trust investigation into a revenue-sharing deal announced between British Airways, American Airlines and Iberia.

The alliance between British Airways, American Airlines and Iberia attracted the attention of the regulators in 2008

Key term

tacit collusion a situation occurring when firms refrain from competing on price, but without communication or formal agreement between them

Alternatively, firms may look for **tacit collusion**, in which the firms in a market observe each other's behaviour very closely and refrain from competing on price, even if they do not actually communicate with each other. Such collusion may emerge gradually over time in a market, as the firms become accustomed to market conditions and to each other's behaviour.

One way in which this may happen is through some form of *price leadership*. If one firm is a dominant producer in a market, then it may take the lead in setting the price, with the other firms following its example. It has been suggested that the OPEC cartel operated according to this model in some periods, with Saudi Arabia acting as the dominant country.

An alternative is *barometric price leadership*, in which one firm tries out a price increase and then waits to see whether other firms follow. If they do, a new higher price has been reached without the need for overt discussions between the firms. On the other hand, if the other firms do not feel the time is right for the change, they will keep their prices steady and the first firm will drop back into line or else lose market share. The initiating firm need not be the same one in each round. It has been argued that the domestic air travel market in the USA has operated in this way on some internal routes. The practice is facilitated by the ease with which prices can be checked via computerised ticketing systems, so that each firm knows what the other firms are doing.

The frequency of anti-cartel cases brought by regulators in recent years suggests that firms continue to be tempted by the gains from collusion. The operation of a cartel is now a criminal act in the UK, as it has been in the USA for some time.

Study tip

When talking about the various forms of market structure, it is often useful to be ready to illustrate the discussion by using examples. It is a good idea to build up a stock of examples so you are ready to use them.

Monopsony

The discussion of market structure so far has focused on the number of sellers in a market, and the interrelationships between them. However, it is also helpful to be aware of the number of traders who are potential *buyers* in a market. An extreme situation would be where there is a single buyer of a good or service. Such a market structure is known as a *monopsony*.

A single buyer may be able to exert substantial influence over the suppliers of the good when drawing up contracts on the price and quality of goods. This power may be especially strong when the sellers are relatively small and numerous. For example, think about the supermarkets in the UK. It is possible that the sheer buying power of the large chains would leave the relatively fragmented suppliers in a weak bargaining position. The supermarkets would then be able to keep their costs down by using their bargaining strength. Another example might occur in some labour markets. There may be towns in which there is a single large employer that employs a significant proportion of the local labour force. Again, such an employer might be seen to have market power within that local labour market. This could constitute another form of market failure, in which the buyer can exert influence in the market.

Exercise 4.3

For each of the following markets, identify the model that would most closely describe it (e.g. perfect competition, monopoly, monopolistic competition or oligopoly):

a a large number of firms selling branded varieties of toothpaste

b a sole supplier of postal services

c a large number of farmers producing cauliflowers, sold at a common price

d a situation in which a few large banks supply most of the market for retail banking services

e a sole supplier of rail transport

Summary

- An oligopoly is a market with a few sellers, each of which takes strategic decisions based on likely rival actions and reactions.
- As there are many ways in which firms may interact, there is no single way of modelling an oligopoly market.
- One model is the kinked demand curve model, which argues that firms' perceptions of the demand curve for their products are based on their views about whether or not rival firms will react to their own actions.
- This suggests that price is likely to remain stable over a wide range of market conditions.
- Game theory is a more recent and more flexible way of modelling interactions between firms.
- The prisoners' dilemma can demonstrate the potential benefits of collusion, but also shows that in some market situations each firm may have a dominant strategy to move the market away from the joint profit-maximising position.
- If firms could join together in a cartel, they could indeed maximise their joint profits — but there would still be a temptation for firms to cheat, and try to steal market share. Such action would break up the cartel, and move the market away from the joint profit-maximising position.
- However, cartels are illegal in most societies.
- Firms may thus look for covert ways of colluding in a market: for example, through some form of price leadership.

Pricing strategies and contestable markets

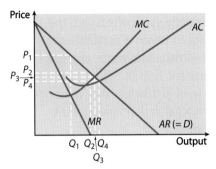

Figure 4.6 Possible pricing rules

Pricing rules

In the analysis of market structure, it was assumed that firms set out to maximise profits. However, Chapter 2 pointed out that sometimes they may set out to achieve other objectives. The price of a firm's product is a key strategic variable that must be manipulated in order to attain whatever objective the firm wishes to achieve.

Figure 4.6 illustrates the variety of pricing rules that are possible. The figure shows a firm operating under a form of market structure that is not perfect competition — because the firm faces a downward-sloping demand curve for its product shown by $AR (= D)$.

Profit maximisation

If the firm chooses to maximise profits, it will choose output such that marginal revenue is equal to marginal cost, and will then set the price to clear the market. In terms of the figure, it will set output at Q_1 and price at P_1.

Revenue maximisation

As mentioned in Chapter 2, the economist William Baumol argued that if there is a divorce of ownership from control in the organisation of a firm, whereby the shareholders have delegated day-to-day decision making to managers (a principal–agent situation), the managers may find themselves with some freedom to pursue other objectives, such as revenue maximisation. A revenue maximiser in Figure 4.6 would choose to produce the output level at which marginal revenue is zero. This occurs at Q_2 in the figure, with the price set at P_2.

Sales maximisation

If instead managers set out to maximise the volume of sales subject to covering opportunity cost, they will choose to set output at a level such that price equals average cost, which will clear the market. In Figure 4.6 this happens at Q_4 (with price at P_4).

Allocative efficiency

It has been argued that allocative efficiency in an individual market occurs at the point where price is equal to marginal cost. In Figure 4.6 this is at Q_3 (with price P_3). However, from the firm's perspective there is no obvious reason why this should become an objective of the firm, as it confers no particular advantage.

Exercise 4.4

For each of the following situations, identify the pricing rule most appropriate to achieve the firm's objectives, and comment on the implications that this has for efficiency.

a A firm producing DVD recorders tries to achieve as high a market share as possible, measured in value terms.

b A local gymnasium tries to make as high a surplus over costs as can be achieved.

c A national newspaper sets out to maximise circulation (subject to covering its costs), knowing that this will affect advertising revenues.

d A garden centre producing Christmas trees finds that it cannot influence the price of its product.

Predatory pricing

Perhaps the most common context in which price wars have broken out is where an existing firm or firms have reacted to defend the market against the entry of new firms.

One example occurred in 1996, in the early years of easyJet, the low-cost air carrier, which was then trying to become established. When easyJet started flying the London–Amsterdam route, charging its now well-known low prices, the incumbent firm (KLM) reacted very aggressively, driving its price down to a level just below that of easyJet. The response from easyJet was to launch legal action against KLM, claiming it was using unfair market tactics.

So-called **predatory pricing** is illegal under English, Dutch and EU law. It should be noted that, in order to declare an action illegal, it is necessary to define that action very carefully — otherwise it will not be possible to prove the case in the courts. In the case of predatory pricing, the legal definition is based on economic analysis.

Remember that if a firm fails to cover average variable costs, its strategy should be to close down immediately, as it would be better off doing so. The courts have backed this theory, and state that a pricing strategy should be interpreted as being predatory if the price is set below average variable costs, as the only motive for remaining in business while making such losses must be to drive competitors out of business and achieve market dominance. This is known as the *Areeda–Turner principle* (after the case in which it was first argued in the USA).

On the face of it, consumers have much to gain from such strategies through the resulting lower prices. However, a predator that is successful in driving out the opposition is likely to recoup its losses by putting prices back up to profit-maximising levels thereafter, so the benefit to consumers is short lived.

Having said that, the low-cost airlines survived the attempts of the established airlines to hold on to their market shares. Indeed, in the post-9/11 period, which was a tough one for the airlines for obvious reasons, the low-cost airlines flourished while the more conventional established airlines went through a very difficult period indeed.

The low-cost airlines survived the attempts of the established airlines to hold on to their market shares

In some cases, the very threat of predatory pricing may be sufficient to deter entry by new firms, if the threat is a credible one. In other words, the existing firms need to convince potential entrants that they, the existing firms, will find it in their best interests to fight a price war, otherwise the entrants will not believe the threat. The existing firms could do this by making it known that they have surplus capacity, so that they would be able to increase output very quickly in order to drive down the price.

Whether entry will be deterred by such means may depend in part on the characteristics of the potential entrant. After all, a new firm may reckon that, if the existing firm finds it worth sacrificing profits in the short run, the rewards of dominating the market must be worth fighting for. It may therefore decide to sacrifice short-term profit in order to enter the market — especially if it is diversifying from other markets and has resources at its disposal. The winner will then be the firm that can last the longest; but, clearly, this is potentially very damaging for all concerned.

Limit pricing

An associated but less extreme strategy is limit pricing. This assumes that the incumbent firm has some sort of cost advantage over potential entrants: for example, economies of scale.

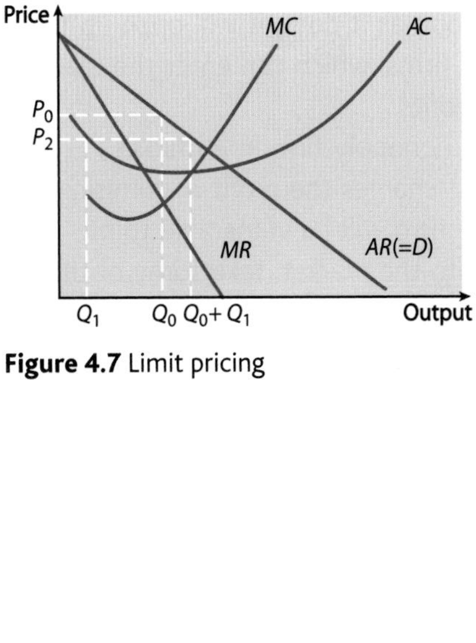

Figure 4.7 shows a firm facing a downward-sloping demand curve, and thus having some influence over the price of its product. If the firm is maximising profits, it is setting output at Q_0 and price at P_0. As average revenue is comfortably above average cost at this price, the firm is making healthy supernormal profits.

Suppose that the natural barriers to entry in this industry are weak. The supernormal profits will be attractive to potential entrants. Given the cost conditions, the incumbent firm is enjoying the benefit of economies of scale, although producing below the minimum efficient scale.

If a new firm joins the market, producing on a relatively small scale, say at Q_1, the impact on the market can be analysed as follows. The immediate effect is on price, as now the amount $Q_0 + Q_1$ is being produced, pushing price down to P_2. The new firm (producing Q_1) is just covering average cost, so is making normal profits and feeling justified in having joined the market. The original firm is still making supernormal profits, but at a lower level than before. The entry of the new firm has competed away part of the original firm's supernormal profits.

One way in which the firm could have guarded against entry is by charging a lower price than P_0 to begin with. For example, if it had set output at $Q_0 + Q_1$ and price at P_2, then a new entrant joining the market would have pushed the price down to a level below P_2, and without the benefit of economies of scale would have made losses and exited the market. In any case, if the existing firm has been in the market for some time, it will have gone through a process of learning by doing, and therefore will have a lower average cost curve than the potential entrant. This makes it more likely that limit pricing can be used.

Thus, by setting a price below the profit-maximising level, the original firm is able to maintain its market position in the longer run. This could be a reason for avoiding making too high a level of supernormal profits in the short run, in order to make profits in the longer term.

Exercise 4.5

Discuss the extent to which consumers benefit from a price war.

Figure 4.7 Limit pricing

Notice that such a strategy need not be carried out by a monopolist, but could also occur in an oligopoly, where existing firms may jointly seek to protect their market against potential entry.

Contestable markets

It has been argued that in some markets, in order to prevent the entry of new firms, the existing firm would have to charge such a low price that it would be unable to reap any supernormal profits at all.

This theory was developed by William Baumol and is known as the theory of **contestable markets**. It was in recognition of this theory that the monopoly model in Chapter 3 included the assumption that there must be no substitutes for the good, *either actual or potential*.

For a market to be contestable, it must have no barriers to entry or exit and no sunk costs. *Sunk costs* refer to costs that a firm incurs in setting up a business and which cannot be recovered if the firm exits the market. Furthermore, new firms in the market must have no competitive disadvantage compared with the incumbent firm(s): in other words, they must have access to the same technology, and there must be no significant learning-by-doing effects. Entry and exit must be rapid.

Under these conditions, the incumbent firm cannot set a price that is higher than average cost because, as soon as it does, it will open up the possibility of *hit-and-run entry* by new firms, which can enter the market and compete away the supernormal profits.

Consider Figure 4.8, which shows a monopoly firm in a market. The argument is that, if the monopolist charges the profit-maximising price, then in a contestable market the firm will be vulnerable to hit-and-run entry — a firm could come into the market, take some of the supernormal profits, then exit again. The only way the monopolist can avoid this happening is to set price equal to average cost, so that there are no supernormal profits to act as an incentive for entry.

On the face of it, the conditions for contestability sound pretty stringent. In particular, the firm in Figure 4.8 enjoys some economies of scale, so you would think that some sunk costs had been incurred.

However, suppose a firm has a monopoly on a domestic air route between two destinations. An airline with surplus capacity (i.e. a spare aircraft sitting in a hangar) could enter this route and exit again without incurring sunk costs in response to profits being made by the incumbent firm. This is an example of how contestability may limit the ability of the incumbent firm to use its market power.

Notice in this example that, although the firm only makes normal profits, neither productive nor allocative efficiency is achieved.

A moot point is whether the threat of entry will in fact persuade firms that they cannot set a price above average cost. Perhaps the firms can risk making some profit above normal profits and then respond to entry very aggressively if and when it happens. After all, it is difficult to think of an example in which there are absolutely no sunk costs. Almost any business is going to have to advertise in order to find customers, and such advertising expenditure cannot be recovered. Pricing is not the only strategy that firms adopt in order to deter entry by new firms. Barriers to entry are discussed in Chapter 5.

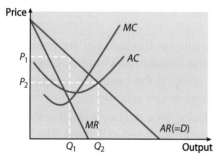

Figure 4.8 Contestability

Summary

- There are many pricing rules that a firm may choose to adopt, depending on the objectives it wishes to achieve.
- Although price wars are expected to be damaging for the firms involved, they do break out from time to time.
- This may occur when firms wish to increase their market shares, or when existing firms wish to deter the entry of new firms into the market.
- Predatory pricing is an extreme strategy that forces all firms to endure losses. It is normally invoked in an attempt to eliminate a competitor, and is illegal in many countries.
- Limit pricing occurs when a firm or firms choose to set price below the profit-maximising level in order to prevent entry. The limit price is the highest price that an existing firm can set without allowing entry.
- In contestable markets, the incumbent firm or firms may be able to make only normal profit.
- Contestability requires that there are no barriers to entry or exit and no sunk costs — and that the incumbent firm(s) have no cost advantage over hit-and-run entrants.

Case study 4.1

Competition in oligopolistic markets

An oligopolistic market is one in which firms engage in strategic competition. Strategic competition exists when the actions of one firm have an appreciable effect on its rival or rivals. Common textbook examples of oligopoly include the oil industry, motor manufacturing, soft drinks and airlines operating between particular pairs of cities. But oligopolists are not necessarily large firms. Close to the university campus in Southampton there is a road containing several small restaurants and takeaways. They are engaged in strategic competition because if one firm were to change its prices this would have an appreciable effect on the sales and thus profits of the others. So you can see that many firms will find themselves competing in oligopolistic markets and thus it is important that, as economists, we try to understand how such markets operate.

Modelling oligopoly

The defining characteristic of oligopoly is that the actions of one firm have an appreciable effect on its rival(s) and thus when modelling such a market it is natural to begin by assuming that each firm recognises this interdependence and takes it into account when formulating its strategy. To keep things simple, let's suppose there are just two firms in the market and each of them is thinking about what price to charge for its product. Again, just for simplicity, we will focus on two possibilities.

What is the highest price that they might conceivably choose? To answer this, consider the maximum aggregate profit that the two firms could theoretically generate.

Figure 4.9 depicts the case of two firms producing identical products with identical horizontal marginal cost (average cost) curves.

The market demand curve is D and MR shows the (joint) marginal revenue accruing to the firms if they set the same price. This is the same marginal revenue curve that would exist had the market been a monopoly.

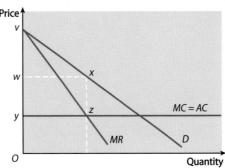

Figure 4.9 Maximising joint profit?

If the firms were producing different products (as is usually the case) then the analysis would be more complex but again we could take the monopoly price or prices to be the upper limit on possible choices.

An alternative option for each of our two firms would be to set a price below the monopoly level. If one firm were to choose the monopoly price and the other a lower price, then the latter would gain a larger market share and, provided the price was not too low, a larger profit. But if both chose the low price, each would earn less profit than if they had both chosen the monopoly price. The situation facing the firms is illustrated in Table 4.4.

The two firms, A and B, must choose either a high price or a low price and the decisions are assumed to be made simultaneously, in the sense that each firm makes its decision without knowledge of the other firm's choice. The figures represent the profits of the two firms, with the numbers in orange denoting the profit of firm A and the numbers in purple the profit of firm B. Thus, for example, if both opt for high (the monopoly price) then each will earn a profit of 2 (half the monopoly profit), but if, say, A chooses high and B chooses low, A will make a profit of 0 and B will make 3.

Table 4.4 Profits of two firms

		Firm B			
		High		Low	
Firm A	High	2	2	0	3
	Low	3	0	1	1

a What is the maximum joint profit that the firms could theoretically generate? Explain how this could be achieved.
b What prices will the two firms choose?
c The passage described the situation close to the campus at the University of Southampton, in which there are several restaurants operating in close proximity. Discuss whether they would be able to maximise their joint profits.

Chapter 5

Markets and resource allocation

The previous two chapters have explored different forms of market structure that arise in the real-world economy. The significance of these forms of market structure is that they have different implications for the way in which resources come to be allocated within society. This has been discussed through exploring the extent to which different market structures lead to allocative and productive efficiency. This chapter explores how market structure affects the behaviour of firms, examines the ways in which firms grow and introduces aspects of competition policy.

Learning objectives

After studying this chapter, you should:
- be aware of structure–conduct–performance analysis
- know what is meant by competition policy
- be familiar with reasons why firms grow
- understand the significance of concentration in a market and how to measure it
- be aware of the relationship between firm size and concentration
- understand what is meant by market dominance
- be familiar with factors that may give rise to natural and strategic barriers to entry
- be aware of some of the effects on a market if competition is limited

Prior knowledge needed

This chapter explores the extent to which the analysis in Chapters 3 and 4 suggests there is a need for policy intervention.

Economic analysis and competition policy

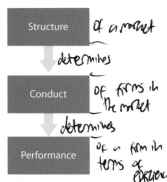

Figure 5.1 The structure–conduct–performance paradigm

Chapter 3 undertook a comparison of perfect competition and monopoly, showing that a monopoly would charge a higher price and produce less output than an industry operating under perfect competition. If this is the case, the question arises as to whether it is necessary to intervene to protect consumers from being exploited by monopoly producers.

Indeed, this thinking led to a belief in what became known in the economics literature as the *structure–conduct–performance paradigm*. At the core of this belief, illustrated in Figure 5.1, is the simple idea that the structure of a market, in terms of the number of firms, determines how firms in the market conduct themselves, which in turn determines how well the market performs in achieving productive and allocative efficiency.

Thus, under perfect competition firms cannot influence price, and all firms act competitively to maximise profits, thereby producing good overall performance of the market in allocating resources. On the other hand, under monopoly the single firm finds that it can extract consumer surplus by using its market power, and as a result the market performs less well.

This point of view leads to a distrust of monopoly — or, indeed, of any market structure in which firms might be seen to be conducting themselves in an anti-competitive manner. Moreover, it is the structure of the market itself that leads to this anti-competitive behaviour.

If this line of reasoning is accepted, then monopoly is always bad, and leads to allocative inefficiency in the market's performance. Thus, legislation in the USA tends to presume that a monopoly will work against the interests of society. However, there are some important issues to consider before pinning too much faith on this assumption. In particular, it is important to understand how a market can evolve to a situation in which it may become anti-competitive — and how this may be recognised.

Exercise 5.1

Figure 5.2 shows a market in which there are only two firms operating.

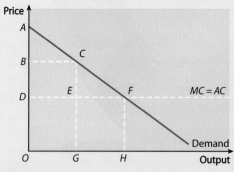

Figure 5.2 Anti-competitive behaviour

a The two firms competing in the market produce at constant marginal cost *OD*, which means that average cost is also constant and equal to marginal cost. Competing intensively, the price is driven down to a level at which no surplus above marginal cost is made. Identify the price charged, the quantity traded and consumer surplus.

b Suppose the two firms decide to collude to raise price to level *OB*. Identify the quantity traded and the consumer surplus.

c You should have found that consumer surplus is much smaller in the second situation than in the first. What has happened to the areas that were formerly part of consumer surplus?

The growth of firms

A feature of the economic environment in recent years has been the increasing size of firms. Some, such as Google, Microsoft, Walmart and Shell, have become giants. Why is this happening?

Firms may wish to increase their size in order to gain market power within the industry in which they are operating. A firm that can gain market share, and perhaps become dominant in the market, may be able to exercise some control over the price of its product, and thereby influence the market. However, firms may wish to grow for other reasons.

A Tesco store in China — diversifying into new markets is one way to maintain growth

Organic growth

Some firms grow simply by being successful. For example, a successful marketing campaign may increase a firm's market share, and provide it with a flow of profits that can be reinvested to expand the firm even more. Some firms may choose to borrow in order to finance their growth, perhaps by issuing shares (equity).

Such *organic growth* may encounter limits. A firm may find that its product market is saturated, so that it can grow further only at the expense of other firms in the market. If its competitors are able to maintain their own market shares, the firm may need to diversify its production activities by finding new markets for its existing product, or perhaps offering new products.

There are many examples of such activity. Tesco, the leading UK supermarket, has launched itself into new markets by opening branches overseas, and has also introduced a range of new products, including financial services, to its existing customers. Microsoft has famously used this strategy, by selling first its internet browser and later its media player as part of its Windows operating system, in an attempt to persuade existing customers to buy its new products.

Diversification may be a dangerous strategy: moving into a market in which the firm is inexperienced and existing rival firms already know the business may pose quite a challenge. In such circumstances, much may depend on the quality of the management team.

Mergers and acquisitions

Instead of growing organically — that is, based on the firm's own resources — many firms choose to grow by merging with, or acquiring, other firms. The distinction here is that an *acquisition* (or takeover) may be hostile, whereas a *merger* may be the coming together of equals, with each firm committed to forming a single entity.

Growth in this way has a number of advantages: for example, it may allow some rationalisation to take place within the organisation. On the other hand, firms tend to develop their own culture, or way of doing

horizontal merger a merger between two firms at the same stage of production in the same industry

vertical merger a merger between two firms in the same industry, but at different stages of the production process

conglomerate merger a merger between two firms operating in different markets

things, and some mergers have foundered because of an incompatibility of corporate cultures.

Mergers (or acquisitions) can be of three different types. A **horizontal merger** is a merger between firms operating in the same industry and at the same stage of the production process: for example, the merger of two car assembly firms. The car industry has been characterised by such mergers in the past, including the takeover of Rover by BMW in 1994 and the merger of Daimler-Benz with Chrysler in 1998. The Daimler-Benz merger with Chrysler ended in 2007, and Chrysler became bankrupt in 2009, after which it was acquired by Fiat.

A horizontal merger can affect the degree of market concentration, because after the merger takes place there are fewer independent firms operating in the market. This may increase the market power held by the new firm.

A car assembly plant merging with a tyre producer, on the other hand, is an example of a **vertical merger**. Vertical mergers may be either upstream or downstream. If a car company merges with a component supplier, that is known as *backward integration*, as it involves merging with a firm that is involved in an earlier part of the production process. *Forward integration* entails merging in the other direction, as for example if the car assembly plant decided to merge with a large distributor.

Vertical integration may allow rationalisation of the process of production. Car producers often work on a just-in-time basis, ordering components for the production line only as they are required. This creates a potential vulnerability because if the supply of components fails then production has to stop. If a firm's component supplier is part of the firm rather than an independent operator, this may improve the reliability of, and confidence in, the just-in-time process, and in consequence may make life more difficult for rival firms. However, vertical mergers have less impact on concentration and market power than horizontal mergers.

The third type of merger — **conglomerate merger** — involves the merging of two firms that are operating in quite different markets or industries. For example, companies like Unilever and Nestlé operate in a wide range of different markets, partly as a result of acquisitions.

One argument in favour of conglomerates is that they reduce the risks faced by firms. Many markets follow fluctuations that are in line with the business cycle but are not always fully synchronised. By operating in a number of markets that are on different cycles, the firm can even out its activity overall. However, this is not necessarily an efficient way of doing business, as the different activities undertaken may require different skills and specialisms.

Not all mergers turn out to be successful. In some cases it may be that the costs of integrating the managements of two different firms are underestimated before the event. Computer or production systems may not be compatible, and it may not be as easy as expected to make staff cuts. Corporate cultures may collide, especially where the merger takes place across national borders. This may mean that the expected gains in market share or profits do not materialise. Once two firms have merged, reversing the process by separating can turn out to be costly and acrimonious. Perhaps for these reasons, in recent years conglomerate mergers seem to have become less popular.

A car assembly plant merging with a tyre producer is an example of a vertical merger

Exercise 5.2

Categorise each of the following as a horizontal, vertical or conglomerate merger:

a the merger of a firm operating an instant coffee factory with a coffee plantation

b the merger of a brewer with a bakery

c the merger of a brewer with a crisp manufacturer

d the merger of a soft drinks manufacturer with a chain of fast-food outlets

e the merger of an internet service provider with a film studio

f a merger between two firms producing tyres for cars

Globalisation

Since the 1980s, advances in the technology of transport and communications and deregulation of international markets have led to a process known as *globalisation*. This has had a significant effect on the growth of firms. The whole process of marketing goods and services has been revolutionised with the spread of the internet and e-commerce.

Multinational corporations will make a number of appearances in later chapters of the book, and their increasing role in the global economy will be evaluated. One motive for mergers and acquisitions has been defensive — that is, to try to compete with other large firms in the global market. However, there are many firms that aspire to operate as a multinational in order to have access to larger international markets, to obtain competitively priced resources or to become more efficient by outsourcing parts of their production chain.

Summary

- Firms may undergo organic growth, building upon their own resources and past profits.
- If limited by the size of their markets, firms may diversify into new markets or products.
- Firms may also grow through horizontal, vertical or conglomerate mergers and acquisitions.
- Globalisation has enabled the growth of giant firms operating on a global scale.

Market concentration

As firms grow, markets may become more concentrated, especially if the growth takes place through mergers and acquisitions. With fewer firms in a market, the market may move closer to being an oligopoly, so an important question is whether such markets behave more like a competitive market or more like a monopoly. You have seen in Chapter 4 that there are many different ways in which markets with just a few firms operating can be modelled, because there are many ways in which the firms may interact.

It is helpful to have some way of gauging how close a particular market is to being a monopoly. One way of doing this is to examine the degree of concentration in the market. Later it will be seen that this is not all that is required to determine how efficiently a market will operate; but it is a start.

Concentration is normally measured by reference to the **concentration ratio**, which measures the market share of the largest firms in an industry. For example, the three-firm concentration ratio measures the market share of the largest three firms in the market; the five-firm concentration ratio calculates the share of the top five firms, and so on. Concentration can also be viewed in terms of employment, reflected in the proportion of workers in any industry that are employed in the largest firms.

> **Key term**
>
> **n-firm concentration ratio**
> a measure of the market share of the largest n firms in an industry

Quantitative skills 5.1

Calculating a concentration ratio

Consider the following example. Table 5.1 gives average circulation figures for firms that publish national newspapers in the UK (with a circulation of more than 100,000 per day). In the final column these are converted into market shares. Where one firm produces more than one newspaper, their circulations have been combined (e.g. News International publishes both the *Sun* and *The Times*).

Table 5.1 Concentration in the UK newspaper industry, January 2013

Firm	Average circulation	Market share (%)
News International Newspapers Ltd	2,809,150	30.7
Associated Newspapers Ltd	1,863,151	20.4
Express Newspapers Ltd	1,065,605	11.6
Trinity Mirror plc	1,058,488	11.6
Evening Standard	695,645	7.6
Telegraph Group Ltd	555,817	6.1
Independent Newspapers (UK) Ltd	307,748	4.1
Financial Times Ltd	275,375	3.0
Guardian Newspapers Ltd	204,440	2.2
Other	251,535	2.7
Total	**9,149,954**	**100.0**

Source: Audit Bureau of Circulations

The market shares are calculated by expressing the average circulation for a firm as a percentage of the total. For example, the market share of the *Financial Times* is 100 × 275,375/9,149,954 = 3%.

The three-firm concentration ratio is then calculated as the sum of the market shares of the biggest three firms: that is, 30.7 + 20.4 + 11.6 = 62.7%.

Concentration ratios may be calculated on the basis of either shares in output or shares in employment. In the above example, the calculation was on the basis of output (daily circulation). The two measures may give different results because the largest firms in an industry may be more capital-intensive in their production methods, which means that their share of employment in an industry will be smaller than their share of output. For the purposes of examining market structure, however, it is more helpful to base the analysis of market share on output.

This might seem an intuitively simple measure, but it is *too* simple to enable an evaluation of a market. For a start, it is important to define the market appropriately; for instance, in the above example are the *Financial Times* and the *Sun* really part of the same market?

There may be other difficulties too. Table 5.2 gives some hypothetical market shares for two markets. The five-firm concentration ratio is calculated as the sum of the market shares of the largest five firms. For markets A and B, the result is the same. In both cases the market is perceived to be highly concentrated, at 75%. However, the nature of likely interactions between the firms in these two markets is very different because the large relative size of firm 1 in market A is likely to give it substantially more market power than any of the largest five firms in market B. Nonetheless, the concentration ratio is useful for giving a first impression of how the market is likely to function.

Table 5.2 Market shares (% of output)

Largest firms in rank order	Market A	Market B
Firm 1	68	15
Firm 2	3	15
Firm 3	2	15
Firm 4	1	15
Firm 5	1	15

Figure 5.3 shows the five-firm concentration ratio for a number of industrial sectors in the UK. Concentration varies from 5% in construction and 12% in printing and publishing to 71% in cement and 99% in tobacco products. In part, the difference between sectors might be expected to reflect the extent of economies of scale, and this makes sense for many of the industries shown.

Summary

- It is important to be able to evaluate the degree of concentration in a market.
- While not a perfect measure, the concentration ratio is one way of doing this, by calculating the market share of the largest firms.

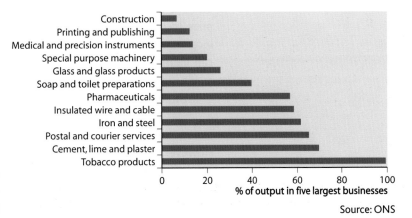

Source: ONS

Figure 5.3 Concentration in UK industry, 2004

Scale and market concentration

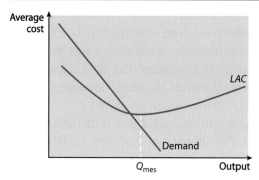

Figure 5.4 How many firms can a market support?

An important issue that arises as firms become larger concerns is the number of firms that a market can support. Suppose that economies of scale are available right up to the limit of market demand, as in Figure 5.4. If more than one firm were to try to supply this market, each producing at minimum average cost, there would be substantial excess supply, and the situation would not be viable.

In this situation, the largest firm in the market will come to dominate, as it will be able to produce at lower average costs than any potential competitor. This will be reinforced if there are significant learning-by-doing effects, which will further entrench the largest firm as the market leader. Such a market is likely to become a *natural monopoly*.

Such substantial economies of scale are not available in all sectors. It will depend upon the nature of technology and all the other factors that can give rise to economies of scale. In some activities there may be little scope at all for economies of scale. For example, there are no great fixed costs in setting up a restaurant or a hairdressing salon — at least, compared with those involved in setting up a steel plant or an underground railway. The level of output at which minimum average cost is reached for such activities may thus be relatively small compared with market demand, so there may be room for many firms in the market. This helps to explain the proliferation of bars, takeaway restaurants and hairdressing salons.

There may also be an intermediate position, where the economies of scale are not sufficient to bring about a monopoly situation, but only relatively few firms can operate efficiently. Such markets are known as *oligopolies*, which were investigated in Chapter 4.

How does this affect the way in which a market works? Is there any reason to believe that a monopoly or oligopoly will work against society's best interests? If market share is concentrated among a small number of firms, does this *inevitably* mean that consumers will suffer?

The answer to these questions depends upon the behaviour of firms within the market. There may be an incentive for a monopoly firm to use its market power to increase its profits. It can do this by restricting the amount of output that it releases on to the market, and by raising the price to consumers. In Chapter 3 it was shown that a monopoly has the incentive to act in this way, since by lowering output and raising price it can increase its overall profits. From the consumer's point of view, the result is a loss of consumer surplus.

If there is an incentive for a single firm to act in this way, there is a similar incentive for firms in an oligopoly to do the same, as they can increase their joint profits — with the same effects on consumers. However, the oligopoly case is more complicated, as there is always the possibility that individual firms will try to increase their own share of the market at the expense of others in the oligopoly.

Market dominance

A key issue is whether firms actually have the market power to exploit consumers in this way. Do firms have market dominance that can be exploited to bring higher profits? In other words, to what extent do firms have the freedom to set prices at their preferred levels, and to what extent do they have to take into account the actions of other firms or face other constraints?

Even monopoly firms have to accept the constraint of the demand curve. They are not free to set a price at any level they choose, otherwise consumers would simply not buy the product. The question is more one of whether firms are free to choose where to position themselves on their demand curve, rather than having to accept the market equilibrium price.

The fact that most countries have legislation in place to protect consumers from this sort of exploitation by firms recognises that firms might have market power and also have an incentive to use it. In the UK this monitoring is in the hands of the Competition and Markets Authority (CMA). For these purposes, a firm is said to have a dominant position if its market share exceeds 40%. The existence of the CMA helps to act as a restraint on anti-competitive practices by firms.

There may also be natural constraints that limit the extent to which a firm is able to achieve a position of dominance in a market. An important consideration is whether a firm (or firms) in a market needs to be aware of the possibility of new firms joining the market. Remember that in Chapter 3 a competitive market was seen to tend towards a long-run equilibrium. In response to an increase in consumer demand, a key part of the adjustment involved the entry of new firms, which would be attracted into the market when the incumbent firms were seen to be making abnormal profits. This had the effect of competing away those profits until the incentive for entry was removed. Can firms in a market prevent this from happening?

Barriers to entry

Another way of thinking about this is to examine what might constitute a **barrier to the entry** of new firms into a market. If such barriers are present, the existing firm or firms may be able to continue to make higher profits.

Economies of scale

One source of entry barriers is the existence of economies of scale. If the largest firm has a significant cost advantage over later entrants, it can adopt a pricing strategy that makes it very difficult for new firms to become established.

This advantage of the existing firm is likely to be reinforced by a learning-by-doing effect, by which a firm becomes more proficient as it gathers experience of operating in a particular industry. This could produce an even stronger cost advantage that would need to be overcome by new entrants.

> ### Key term
>
> **barrier to entry** a characteristic of a market that prevents new firms from readily joining the market

Ownership of raw materials

Suppose that the production of a commodity requires the input of a certain raw material, and that a firm in the market controls the supply of that raw material. You can readily see that this would be a substantial barrier to the entry of new firms. A key commodity in the fashion industry is that of diamonds. Until relatively recently, DeBeers controlled the world's supply of uncut diamonds, and there was no way that new firms could enter the market because of the agreements that DeBeers had with mining companies and governments in those parts of the world where diamonds are mined. This monopoly lasted for many years and only began to break down in the early years of the twenty-first century.

The patent system

The patent system exists to provide protection for firms developing new products or processes. The rationale for this is that, unless firms know that they will have ownership over innovative ideas, they will have no incentive to be innovative. The patent system ensures that, at least for a time, firms can be assured of gaining some benefit from their innovations. For the duration of the patent, they will be protected from competition. This therefore constitutes a legal barrier to the entry of new firms.

Advertising and publicity

Advertising can be regarded as a component of fixed costs because expenditure on it does not vary directly with the volume of output. If the firms in an industry typically spend heavily on advertising, it will be more difficult for new firms to become established, as they too will need to advertise widely in order to attract customers.

Similarly, firms may spend heavily on achieving a well-known brand image that will ensure customer loyalty. Hence they may invest a lot in the design and packaging of their merchandise. One example was the high-profile television campaign run by Sunny Delight when trying to gain entry into the soft drinks market in the early part of the twenty-first century.

Notice that such costs are also sunk costs, and cannot be recovered if the new firm fails to gain a foothold. It has sometimes been suggested that the cost of excessive advertising should be included in calculations of the social cost of monopoly.

Research and development

A characteristic of some industries is the heavy expenditure undertaken on research and development (R&D). A prominent example is the pharmaceutical industry, which spends large amounts on researching new drugs — and new cosmetics.

This is another component of fixed costs, as it does not vary with the volume of production. Again, new firms wanting to break into the market know that they will need to invest heavily in R&D if they are going to keep up with the new and better drugs and cosmetics always coming on to the market.

The high costs of R&D in the pharmaceutical industry can deter new firms entering the market

Strategic and innocent barriers to entry

In the case of economies of scale, it could be argued that the advantage of the largest firm in the industry is a purely natural barrier to entry that arises from the market position of the firm.

In other cases, it may be that firms can consciously erect barriers to entry in order to make entry into the market more difficult for potential new firms. In other words, firms may make strategic moves to protect their market position behind entry barriers.

One example of this might be the advertising undertaken by firms. Some firms have become (and remain) well known by dint of heavy advertising expenditures. In some cases these expenditures have very little impact on market shares, and merely serve to maintain the status quo. However, for potential entrants they make life very difficult. Any new firm coming into the market has to try to match the advertising levels of existing firms in order to gain a viable market share. Effectively, existing firms have increased the fixed costs of being in the market, making entry more difficult to achieve. For example, when the soft drink Sunny Delight was launched, it had to undertake a large-scale television advertising campaign to try to break into a market dominated by Coca-Cola and PepsiCo.

An alternative method is for an existing firm to operate with spare capacity, making it clear to potential entrants that entry will trigger a price war. The surplus capacity adds credibility to this threat, as the existing firm is seen to be able to increase output — and thus force down price — very quickly.

Extension material

Barriers to entry and the consumer

The existence or absence of barriers to entry is, of course, closely linked to the notion of contestable markets, which were discussed in Chapter 4. The absence of barriers to entry is a key requirement if a market is to be contestable. For a perfectly contestable market, it can be argued that the market outcome will be closer to that in a fully competitive market, as the firm will not be able to use its market power to exploit the consumers.

If barriers to entry are weak, so that a firm may be disciplined by the threat of entry, how does this affect consumers? Suppose barriers to entry are weak, but a firm decides to chance its arm and push up the price. This could then trigger a price war — but will consumers benefit from this? Clearly they may benefit in the short run, as they will face lower prices. But what is likely to happen as time goes by?

One possibility is that the original firm will be prepared to take losses in the short run by engaging in a pricing strategy that will eventually force the new entrant out of the market, so that prices will drift up again in due course. Or it may be that firms in the market will try to maintain profitability by cutting costs and quality, so consumers may end up having to consume an inferior product. So the benefits may be short-lived.

Market failure

Synoptic link

Market failure was discussed in Book 1, Chapter 7, although the focus there was on other forms of market failure. In this case the failure arises because firms may have market power to influence the market outcome, and thus cause a loss of allocative efficiency.

How is the market affected if the extent of competition in it is limited? By restricting output and raising price, firms are able to increase their profits, effectively increasing the market price to a level above the marginal cost of production. This implies that there is a loss of allocative efficiency in this situation. From society's point of view, too little of the product is being produced.

To the extent that the monopolist is a member of society, the increase in producer surplus might be regarded as a redistribution from consumers to producers. However, more crucial is the fact that there is a loss of consumer surplus that is not recoverable.

Regulation of monopoly and mergers

The effectiveness of the market system in allocating resources requires prices to act as signals to producers about consumer demand. Firms will be attracted into activities where consumer demand is buoyant and profitability is high, and will tend to exit from activities in which demand is falling and profitability is low.

This process relies on the existence of healthy competition between firms, and on freedom of entry to and exit from markets. In the absence of these conditions, resources may not be best allocated according to the pattern of consumer demand. For example, if there are barriers to entering a market, the existing firms in the market may have the power to restrict output and raise the price, producing less of the product than is desirable for society. As explained above, such barriers to entry may arise from features such as economies of scale or the patent system. In some situations, existing firms may take strategic action to deter entry.

This is one area of the economy in which governments often choose to intervene to protect consumers. In the UK, the Competition and Markets Authority (CMA) is responsible for this part of government policy (having taken over this responsibility from the Office of Fair Trading (OFT) and the Competition Commission (CC) in 2014). The CMA has the power to investigate markets that appear to be overly concentrated or in which competition appears weak. They can also take action to encourage competition in markets. This is known as **competition policy**, and will be discussed in more depth in Chapter 10.

One of the knotty problems that arises here is that if firms benefit from economies of scale, it may be more productively efficient to allow large firms to develop than to fragment the industry into lots of small firms in the name of encouraging competition. Thus, the authorities have to find a way of balancing the potential costs of losing allocative efficiency against the potential benefits of productive efficiency.

In seeking to evaluate the situation in a market, the competition authorities face a series of challenges. Apart from anything else, market conditions are always changing, so it becomes difficult to observe how firms are behaving. For example, the prices of foreign holidays could rise for many reasons other than the abuse of market power by tour operators or other firms in the market. Such price rises could be because of increases in the price of oil, affecting transport costs. They could equally be the effect of changes in the foreign exchange rate, or many other factors affecting the market. The authorities thus need to be careful in coming to a decision. They may need to investigate a variety of market conditions before judging a firm's behaviour. A key issue may be the extent to which the market is contestable. In other words, a judgement needs to be made as to the extent to which a firm faces potential competition, which may restrict the amount of market power that it can wield.

Merger and acquisition activity has led to the creation of some giant firms in recent years, and one responsibility of the competition authorities is to monitor such activity, which may be seen to have an effect on concentration in markets. Examples of past cases can be viewed on the archived websites of the OFT and the CC. In one enquiry, the CC investigated takeover bids for the Safeway supermarket chain from Morrisons, Tesco, Sainsbury's and ASDA. The Morrisons bid was accepted, as it was least likely to lead to a less competitive market. In an earlier investigation, the CC blocked a proposed takeover of Manchester United Football Club by BSkyB on the grounds that this would not be beneficial for consumers.

> **Key term**
>
> **competition policy** an area of economic policy designed to promote competition within markets to encourage efficiency and protect consumer interests

Summary

- Cost conditions in a market may affect the number of firms that can operate profitably.
- Firms that attain market dominance may be able to harness market power at the expense of consumers, reducing output and raising price.
- This is especially the case where the existing firm or firms are protected by barriers to entry.
- When firms do use such market power, there is a deadweight loss to society that reflects allocative inefficiency.
- However, this may in part be balanced by a gain in productive efficiency.
- Competition policy is a set of measures designed to encourage competition in markets.

Case study 5.1

A failed merger

This case study examines an episode in which a merger did not turn out the way that the firms involved anticipated.

In 2001 negotiations began between two firms in the telecoms-equipment business — the French firm Alcatel and Lucent Technologies of America — and 5 years later, in April 2006, an agreement was reached that the two firms would merge.

There seemed to be good commercial reasons for coming together. Alcatel, the bigger of the two firms, would gain entry into the lucrative American market, and the merger would make the combined firm one of the world's largest in the market. The combined revenue of the two firms from sales of network equipment would be slightly larger than that of Cisco Systems, the market leader at the time.

It was expected that the merger would not only give the firm a higher profile in the two key markets of America and Europe, but also enable the exploitation of economies of scale. By combining the companies, it was expected that about 10% of the existing workforce could be cut, saving $1.7 billion. This would be achieved by eliminating overlapping administrative, procurement and marketing costs, as well as reducing the workforce.

However, things did not work out as expected, and the merged company ran into problems. The firm found cost savings difficult to realise, in spite of 16,500 job losses from a workforce of 88,000 — and found that prices in the market were falling, squeezing profitability. The firm faced competition from new entrants, particularly from Chinese firms, and found difficulty in keeping up with the pace of technological change. It was also reported that the firm was suffering from a clash of cultures between the French and American parts of the business.

The result of all this was that in July 2008 it was announced that the French chairman (who was formerly the boss of Alcatel) and the American chief executive (formerly the boss of Lucent) were leaving the company and being replaced by a new executive team charged with the task of taking the company forward. The new chairman was neither French nor American.

Even the most carefully planned mergers can end up as failures

Follow-up question

From the passage, identify some of the causes for the failure of the merger. Discuss the extent to which these arose from the external environment rather than internal issues within the merged firm.

Case study 5.2

British supermarkets

In January 2003, the supermarket group Morrisons made an offer for the Safeway group. In the following 3 weeks, five other groups expressed an interest in buying Safeway, including the rival supermarkets Sainsbury's, ASDA and Tesco. Under the regulations in force, any merger or acquisition that would take the merged firm's market share above 25% could be referred to the Competition Commission for investigation, and the bids from Sainsbury's, ASDA and Tesco were duly investigated.

The commission concluded that a takeover of Safeway by any of these three would be 'expected to operate against the public interest, and should be prohibited'. However, the takeover of Safeway by Morrisons was allowed to go forward (subject to some conditions).

Figure 5.5 shows the estimated market shares of the largest grocery retailers in 2002 and in 2014.

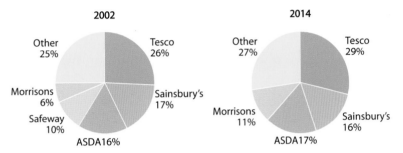

Sources: *Financial Times*; Kantar Worldpanel

Figure 5.5 Market shares of supermarkets in Great Britain

Follow-up questions

a With reference to the pattern of market shares in 2002, discuss why the Competition Commission reached its decision.

b Comparing 2002 with 2014, do you think that the acquisition of Safeway by Morrisons has been successful for the firm and for consumers?

c Calculate the four-firm concentration ratio for each of the years, and see whether the market concentration has increased.

d Given the pattern of market shares, do you think that the market was more or less competitive in 2014 than in 2002?

MICROECONOMICS

Part 3
The labour market

Chapter 6

Labour demand, labour supply and wage determination

The economic analysis of labour markets sheds light on a range of topical issues. How are wages determined? Differences in wages between people in different occupations and with different skills can be contentious. For example, why should premiership footballers or pop stars earn such high wages compared with nurses or firefighters? This chapter begins by looking at the labour market as an application of demand and supply analysis.

Learning objectives

After studying this chapter, you should:
- understand that the demand for labour is a derived demand
- be aware of the relationship between labour input and total and marginal physical product
- understand the concept of marginal revenue product
- be familiar with how a profit-maximising firm chooses the quantity of labour input to use in production
- be aware of the factors that influence the elasticity of demand for labour
- understand the decision of an individual worker as regards labour supply
- be aware of the choice made by the individual worker between work and leisure
- understand the reasons for earnings differentials between people working in different occupations and with different skills

Prior knowledge needed

This chapter builds upon material that was contained in Book 1, especially the early chapters that developed the demand and supply model. The present chapter applies this analysis to the labour market. The concepts of elasticity, producer surplus and externalities will also be drawn into the discussion.

Demand for labour

Key term

derived demand demand for a good not for its own sake, but for what it produces, e.g. labour is demanded for the output that it produces

Firms are involved in production. They organise the factors of production in order to produce output. Labour is one of the key factors of production used by firms in this process, but notice that labour is valued not for its own sake, but for the output that it produces. In other words, the fundamental reason for firms to demand labour is for the revenue that can be obtained from selling the output that is produced by using labour. The demand for labour is thus a **derived demand**, and understanding this is crucial for an analysis of the labour market.

To illustrate this, consider a firm that manufactures cricket bats. The firm hires labourers to operate the machinery that is used in production. However, the firm does not hire a labourer because he or she is a nice person. The firm aims to make profit by selling the cricket bats

Be clear in your mind about this notion of a derived demand, as it underpins much of the discussion of labour markets.

Key terms

marginal physical product of labour (MPP_L) the additional quantity of output produced by an additional unit of labour input

marginal revenue product of labour (MRP_L) the additional revenue received by a firm as it increases output by using an additional unit of labour input, i.e. the marginal physical product of labour multiplied by the marginal revenue received by the firm

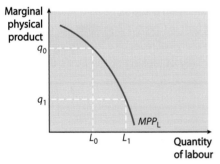

Figure 6.1 The marginal physical product of labour

produced, and the labourer is needed because of the labour services that he or she provides. This notion of derived demand underpins the analysis of labour markets.

It is important to be aware that although there is a tendency to talk about 'the' labour market, or about 'unemployment' in the aggregate, in reality there is not a single market in the economy, but a multitude of sub-markets. This partly reflects the fact that individual workers differ from each other in terms of their characteristics and skills. There are different markets for different types of labour, such as lawyers, accountants, cleaners and bricklayers. There may also be geographic sub-markets, given that labour may be relatively immobile. An employer may perceive that it operates in a particular industry, so there may be a labour market for an industry, or for particular skills within an industry. Indeed, a firm may find itself operating in several different sub-markets.

This interlocking pattern of labour markets is likely to evolve over time, as technology changes, bringing with it the need for different skills, and a different balance of skills.

The demand curve for labour

Consider the demand for a particular type of labour — in other words, a particular labour market. Given that the demand for labour is a derived demand, the first factor that will determine the demand for labour is the output that labour produces. Given the law of diminishing returns, which was introduced in Chapter 2, the additional output produced by labour as more labour is deployed is expected to diminish, other things remaining equal. This is because capital becomes relatively scarcer as the amount of labour increases without a corresponding increase in capital.

Important for the firm, then, is the **marginal physical product of labour (MPP_L)**, which is the amount of additional output produced if the firm increases its labour input by 1 unit (e.g. adding 1 more person-hour), holding capital constant. An example is shown in Figure 6.1. When labour input is relatively low, such as at L_0, the additional output produced by an extra unit of labour is relatively high, at q_0, since the extra unit of labour has plenty of capital with which to work. However, as more labour is added, the marginal physical product falls, so at L_1 labour the marginal physical product is only q_1.

Although the marginal physical product is important, what really matters to the firm is the *revenue* that it will receive from selling the additional output produced. In considering the profit-maximising amount of labour to employ, therefore, the firm needs to consider the marginal physical product multiplied by the marginal revenue received from selling the extra output, which is known as the **marginal revenue product of labour (MRP_L)**.

If the firm is operating under perfect competition, then marginal revenue and price are the same and MRP_L is MPP_L multiplied by the price. However, if the firm faces a downward-sloping demand curve for its product, it has to reduce the selling price in order to sell the additional output. Marginal revenue is then lower than price, as the firm must lower the price on *all* of the output that it sells, not just on the last unit sold.

Consider a firm operating under perfect competition, and setting out to maximise profits. Figure 6.2 shows the marginal revenue product curve.

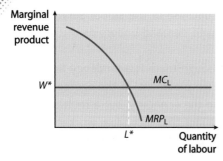

Figure 6.2 The labour input decision of a profit-maximising firm under perfect competition

The question to consider is how the firm chooses how much labour input to use. This decision is based partly on knowledge of the MRP_L, but it also depends on the cost of labour.

The main cost of using labour is the wages paid to the workers. There may be other costs — hiring costs and so on — but these can be set aside for the moment. Assuming that the labour market is perfectly competitive, so that the firm cannot influence the market wage and can obtain as much labour as it wants at the going wage rate, the wage can be regarded as the *marginal cost of labour* (MC_L).

Study tip

Notice here that we are treating the wage as the price of labour within the demand and supply model.

If the marginal revenue received by the firm from selling the extra output produced by extra labour (i.e. the MRP_L) is higher than the wage, then hiring more labour will add to profits. On the other hand, if the MRP_L is lower than the wage, then the firm is already hiring too much labour. Thus, it pays the firm to hire labour up to the point where the MRP_L is just equal to the wage. On Figure 6.2, if the wage is W^*, the firm is maximising profits at L^*. The MRP_L curve thus represents the firm's demand for labour curve. This approach is known as **marginal productivity theory**.

Key term

marginal productivity theory a theory which argues that the demand for labour depends upon balancing the revenue that a firm gains from employing an additional unit of labour against the marginal cost of that unit of labour

Extension material

Marginal productivity theory and profit maximisation

This profit-maximising condition can be written as:

wage = marginal revenue × marginal physical product of labour

which is the same as:

marginal revenue = wage/MPP_L

Remember that capital input is fixed for the firm in the short run, so the wage divided by the MPP_L is the firm's cost per unit of output at the margin. This shows that the profit-maximising condition is the same as that derived for a profit-maximising firm in Chapter 2: in other words, profit is maximised where marginal revenue equals marginal cost. This is just another way of looking at the firm's decision.

Quantitative skills 6.1

Calculating MPP_L and MRP_L

Table 6.1 shows how the total output produced by labour varies with labour input for a firm operating under perfect competition in the product market. The price of the product is £5.

Chapter 2 showed how marginal cost could be calculated from total cost. The same principle applies in calculating the MPP_L from the total output produced by different amounts of labour input. For example, suppose labour input is increased from 2 units to 3. The output produced by labour increases from 15 to 22, so the MPP_L is 22 − 15 = 7.

Table 6.1 Output and labour input

Labour input per period	Output (goods per period)
0	0
1	7
2	15
3	22
4	27
5	29

Exercise 6.1

This exercise builds on Quantitative skills 6.1.
a Calculate the marginal physical product of labour (MPP_L) at each level of labour input.
b Calculate the marginal revenue product of labour (MRP_L) at each level of labour input.

Suppose that the firm is also operating in perfect competition in the labour market, where the wage is £30.
c Plot the MRP_L on a graph and identify the profit-maximising level of labour input.
d Suppose that the firm faces fixed costs of £10. Calculate total revenue and total costs at each level of labour input, and check the profit-maximising level.

Factors affecting the position of the demand for labour curve

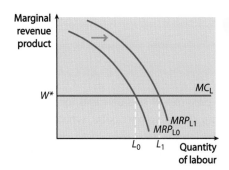

Figure 6.3 The effect of improved technology

There are a number of factors that determine the *position* of a firm's labour demand curve. First, anything that affects the marginal physical product of labour will also affect the MRP_L. For example, if a new technological advance raises the productivity of labour, it will also affect the position of the MRP_L. In Figure 6.3 you can see how the demand for labour would change if there were an increase in the marginal productivity of labour as a result of new technology. Initially demand is at MRP_{L0}, but the increased technology pushes the curve to MRP_{L1}. If the wage remains at W^*, the quantity of labour hired by the firm increases from L_0 to L_1. Similarly, in the long run, if a firm expands the size of its capital stock, this will also affect the demand for labour.

As MRP_L is given by MPP_L multiplied by marginal revenue, any change in marginal revenue will also affect labour demand. In a perfectly competitive product market, this means that any change in the price of the product will also affect labour demand. For example, suppose there is a fall in demand for a firm's product, so that the equilibrium price falls. This will have a knock-on effect on the firm's demand for labour, as illustrated in Figure 6.4. Initially, the firm was demanding L_0 labour at the wage rate W^*, but the fall in demand for the product leads to a fall in marginal revenue product (even though the physical productivity of labour has not changed), from MRP_{L0} to MRP_{L1}. Only L_1 labour is now demanded at the wage rate W^*. This serves as a reminder that the demand for labour is a derived demand that is intimately bound up with the demand for the firm's product.

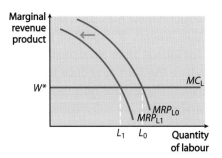

Figure 6.4 The effect of a fall in the demand for a firm's product on the demand for labour

A number of possible reasons could underlie a change in the price of a firm's product — it could reflect changes in the prices of other goods, changes in consumer incomes or changes in consumer preferences. All of these indirectly affect the demand for labour.

Summary

- The demand for labour is a derived demand, as the firm wants labour not for its own sake, but for the output that it produces.
- In the short run, a firm faces diminishing returns to increases in labour input if capital is held constant.
- The marginal physical product of labour is the amount of output produced if the firm employs an additional unit of labour, keeping capital input fixed.
- The marginal revenue product of labour is the marginal physical product multiplied by marginal revenue.
- With perfect competition in the product market, marginal revenue and price are the same, but if the firm needs to reduce its price in order to sell additional units of output, then marginal revenue is smaller than price.
- A profit-maximising firm chooses labour input such that the marginal cost of labour is equal to the marginal revenue product of labour. This is equivalent to setting marginal revenue equal to marginal cost.
- The firm has a downward-sloping demand curve for labour, given by the marginal revenue product curve.
- The position of the firm's labour demand curve depends on those factors that influence the marginal physical product, such as technology and efficiency, but also on the price of the firm's product.

Wage elasticity of the demand for labour

In addition to the factors affecting the *position* of the demand for labour curve, it is also important to examine its *shape*. In particular, what factors affect the firm's elasticity of demand for labour with respect to changes in the wage rate? In other words, how sensitive is a firm's demand for labour to a change in the wage rate (the cost of labour)?

In Chapter 5 of Book 1 you were introduced to the influences on the price elasticity of demand, and the most important were identified as being the availability of substitutes, the relative size of expenditure on a good in the overall budget and the time period over which the elasticity is measured. In looking at the elasticity of demand for labour, similar influences can be seen to be at work.

One significant influence on the elasticity of demand for labour is the extent to which other factors of production, such as capital, can be substituted for labour in the production process. If capital or some other factor can be readily substituted for labour, then an increase in the wage rate (ceteris paribus) will induce the firm to reduce its demand for labour by relatively more than if there were no substitute for labour. The extent to which labour and capital are substitutable varies between economic activities, depending on the technology of production, as there may be some sectors in which it is relatively easy for labour and capital to be substituted, and others in which it is quite difficult.

Whether capital can be substituted for labour varies, depending on the technology of production

Second, the share of labour costs in the firm's total costs is important in determining the elasticity of demand for labour. In many service activities, labour is a highly significant share of total costs, so firms tend to be sensitive to changes in the cost of labour. However, in some capital-intensive manufacturing activity, labour may comprise a much smaller share of total production costs.

Third, as was argued above, capital will tend to be inflexible in the short run. Therefore, if a firm faces an increase in wages, it may have little flexibility in substituting towards capital in the short run, so the demand for labour may be relatively inelastic. However, in the longer term, the firm will be able to adjust the factors of production towards a different overall balance. Therefore, the elasticity of demand for labour is likely to be higher in the long run than in the short run.

These three influences closely parallel the analysis of what affects the price elasticity of demand. However, as the demand for labour is a derived demand, there is an additional influence that must be taken into account: the price elasticity of demand for the product. The more price elastic is demand for the product, the more sensitive will the firm be to a change in the wage rate, as high elasticity of demand for the product limits the extent to which an increase in wage costs can be passed on to consumers in the form of higher prices.

In order to derive an industry demand curve for labour, it is necessary to add up the quantities of labour that firms in that industry would want to demand at any wage rate, given the price of the product. As individual firms' demand curves are downward sloping, the industry demand curve will also slope downwards. In other words, more labour will be demanded at a lower wage rate, as shown in Figure 6.5.

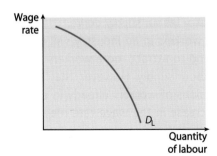

Figure 6.5 An industry demand for labour curve

Summary

- The elasticity of demand for labour depends upon the degree to which capital may be substituted for labour in the production process.
- The share of labour in a firm's total costs will also affect the elasticity of demand for labour.
- Labour demand will tend to be more elastic in the long run than in the short run, as the firm needs time to adjust its production process following a change in market conditions.
- As the demand for labour is a derived demand, the elasticity of labour demand will also depend on the price elasticity of demand for the firm's product.

Exercise 6.2

Using diagrams, explain how each of the following will affect a firm's demand for labour:

a a fall in the selling price of the firm's product
b adoption of improved working practices that improve labour productivity
c an increase in the wage (in a situation where the firm must accept the wage as market determined)
d an increase in the demand for the firm's product

Labour supply

So far, labour supply has been considered only as it is perceived by a firm, and the assumption has been that the firm is in a perfectly competitive market for labour, and therefore cannot influence the 'price' of labour. Hence the firm sees the labour supply curve as being perfectly elastic, as drawn in Figure 6.2, where labour supply was described as MC_L.

However, for the industry as a whole, labour supply is unlikely to be flat. Intuitively, you might expect to see an upward-sloping labour supply curve. The reason for this is that more people will tend to offer themselves for work when the wage is relatively high. However, this is only part of the background to the industry labour supply curve.

An increase in the wage rate paid to workers in an industry will have two effects. On the one hand, it will tend to attract more workers into that industry, thereby increasing labour supply. However, the change may also affect the supply decisions of workers already in that industry, and for existing workers an increase in the wage rate may have ambiguous effects.

Individual labour supply

Consider an individual worker who is deciding how many hours of labour to supply. Every choice comes with an *opportunity cost*, so if a worker chooses to take more leisure time, he or she is choosing to forgo income-earning opportunities. In other words, the wage rate can be seen as the opportunity cost of leisure. It is the income that the worker has to sacrifice in order to enjoy leisure time.

Now think about the likely effects of an increase in the wage rate. Such an increase raises the opportunity cost of leisure. This in turn has two effects. First, as leisure time is now more costly, there will be a substitution effect against leisure. In other words, workers will be motivated to work longer hours.

However, as the higher wage brings the worker a higher level of real income, a second effect comes into play, encouraging the consumption of more goods and services — including leisure, if it is assumed that leisure is a *normal good*.

Notice that these two effects work against each other. The substitution effect encourages workers to offer more labour at a higher wage because of the effect of the change in the opportunity cost of leisure. However, the real income effect encourages the worker to demand more leisure as a result of the increase in income. The net effect could go either way.

It might be argued that at relatively low wages the substitution effect will tend to be the stronger. However, as the wage continues to rise, the income effect may gradually become stronger, so that at some wage level the worker will choose to supply less labour and will demand more leisure. The individual labour supply curve will then be backward bending, as shown in Figure 6.6, where an increase in the wage rate above W^* induces the individual to supply fewer hours of work in order to enjoy more leisure time.

It is important to realise that decisions about labour supply may also be influenced by job satisfaction. A worker who finds his or her work to be satisfying may be prepared to accept a lower wage than a worker who really hates every minute spent at work. Indeed, firms may provide other **non-pecuniary benefits** — in other words, firms may provide benefits that are not fully reflected in wages. These are sometimes known as *fringe benefits*. Such benefits might include a subsidised canteen or other social facilities. They could also include in-work training, pension schemes or job security. If this is the case, then in choosing one job over another, workers may not only consider the wage rate, but the overall package offered by employers. In other words, by providing non-pecuniary benefits, firms may effectively shift the position of their labour supply curves, as workers will be prepared to supply more labour at any given wage rate. It may also be seen as a way in which firms can encourage loyalty, and thus hold on to workers when the job market is tight.

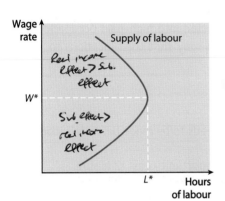

Figure 6.6 A backward-bending individual labour supply curve

Key term

non-pecuniary benefits benefits offered to workers by firms that are not financial in nature

Industry labour supply

At industry level, the labour supply curve can be expected to be upward sloping. Although individual workers may display backward-bending supply curves, when workers in a market are aggregated, higher wages will induce people to join the market, either from outside the workforce altogether or from other industries where wages have not risen.

The wage elasticity of supply

There are several factors that may influence the elasticity of labour supply: in other words, the extent to which an increase in the wage rate in a labour market will encourage an increase in the supply of labour. First, this may depend upon whether there is unemployment, so that there are workers ready to take up jobs. However, there are also likely to be obstacles to flexibility in labour supply. For example, the unemployed workers available for work may not have the skills needed for the vacancies available, so that training may be needed. It could be that the workers who are available are located in areas remote from where the vacancies are appearing. If the available workers are living in Newcastle, but the vacancies are in London, then they may not respond to the higher wages on offer, given the costs of transport, moving house, finding new schools for their children — or even being able to find out that the jobs are available. Labour supply may thus be relatively inelastic in the short run.

In the long run, if wage differentials persist, labour supply may be more elastic. More people may be attracted into high-paid occupations, industries or regions. Alternatively, firms may shift their locations to where labour is more plentiful.

Summary

- For an individual worker, a choice needs to be made between income earned from working and leisure.
- The wage rate can be seen as the opportunity cost of leisure.
- An increase in the wage rate will encourage workers to substitute work for leisure through the substitution effect.
- However, there is also an income effect, which may mean that workers will demand more leisure at higher income levels.
- If the income effect dominates the substitution effect, then the individual labour supply curve may become backward bending.
- However, when aggregated to the industry level, higher wages will encourage more people into the industry, such that the industry supply curve is not expected to be backward bending.
- Labour supply is likely to be more elastic in the long run than in the short run.

Labour market equilibrium

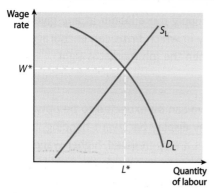

Figure 6.7 Labour market equilibrium

Bringing demand and supply curves together for an industry shows how the equilibrium wage is determined. Figure 6.7 shows a downward-sloping labour demand curve (D_L) based on marginal productivity theory, and an upward-sloping labour supply curve (S_L). Equilibrium is found at the intersection of demand and supply. If the wage is lower than W^* employers will not be able to fill all their vacancies, and will have to offer a higher wage to attract more workers. If the wage is higher than W^* there will be an excess supply of labour, and the wage will drift down until W^* is reached and equilibrium obtained.

Comparative static analysis can be used to examine the effects of changes in market conditions. For instance, a change in the factors that determine the position of the labour demand curve will induce a movement of labour demand and an adjustment in the equilibrium wage. Suppose there is an increase in the demand for the firm's product. This will lead to a rightward shift in the demand for labour, say from D_{L0} to D_{L1} in Figure 6.8. This in turn will lead to a new market equilibrium, with the wage rising from W_0 to W_1.

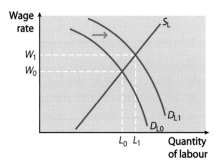

Figure 6.8 An increase in the demand for labour

This may not be the final equilibrium position, however. If the higher wages in this market now encourage workers to switch from other industries in which wages have not risen, this will lead to a longer-term shift to the right of the labour supply curve. In a free market, the shift will continue until wage differentials are no longer sufficient to encourage workers to transfer.

Summary

- Labour market equilibrium is found at the intersection of labour demand and labour supply.
- This determines the equilibrium wage rate for an industry.
- Comparative static analysis can be used to analyse the effects of changes in market conditions.
- Changes in relative wages between sectors may induce movement of workers between industries.

Labour markets

So far, the focus has been on the demand and supply of labour, seen sometimes through the eyes of a firm, sometimes through the eyes of a worker and sometimes looking at an industry labour market. As mentioned at the beginning of the chapter, it is important to remember that these are separate levels of analysis. In particular, there is no single labour market in an economy like the UK, any more than there is a single market for goods. In reality, there is a complex network of labour markets for people with different skills and for people in different occupations, and there are overlapping markets for labour corresponding to different product markets.

Transfer earnings

Many factors of production have some flexibility about them, in the sense that they can be employed in a variety of alternative uses. A worker may be able to work in different occupations and industries; computers can be put to use in a wide range of activities. The decision to use a factor of production for one particular job rather than another carries an opportunity cost, which can be seen in terms of the next best alternative activity in which that factor could have been employed.

For example, consider a woman who chooses to work as a waitress because the pay is better than she could obtain as a shop assistant. By making this choice, she forgoes the opportunity to work at, say, John Lewis. The opportunity cost is seen in terms of this forgone alternative. If John Lewis were to raise its rates of pay in order to attract more staff, there would come a point where the waitress might reconsider her decision and decide to be a shop assistant after all, as the opportunity cost of being a waitress has risen.

The threshold at which this decision is taken leads to the definition of **transfer earnings**. Transfer earnings are defined in terms of the minimum payment that is required in order to keep a factor of production in its present use.

Key term

transfer earnings the minimum payment required to keep a factor of production in its present use

Economic rent

In a labour market, transfer earnings can be thought of as the minimum payment that will keep the marginal worker in his or her present occupation or sector. This payment will vary from worker to worker; moreover, where there is a market in which all workers receive the same pay for the same job, there will be some workers who receive a wage in excess of their transfer earnings. This excess of payment to a factor over and above what is required to keep it in its present use is known as **economic rent**.

The total payments to a factor can thus be divided between these two — part of the payment is transfer earnings, and the remainder is economic rent.

Probably the best way of explaining how a worker's earnings can be divided between transfer earnings and economic rent is through an appropriate diagram. Figure 6.9 illustrates the two concepts. In the labour market as drawn, firms' demand for labour is a downward-sloping function of the wage rate. Workers' supply of labour also depends on the wage rate, with workers being prepared to supply more labour to the labour market at higher wages. Equilibrium is the point at which demand equals supply, with wage rate W^* and quantity of labour L^*.

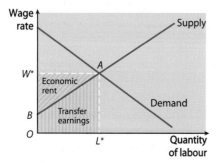

Figure 6.9 Transfer earnings and economic rent

Think about the nature of the labour supply curve. It reveals how much labour the workers are prepared to supply at any given wage rate. At the equilibrium wage rate W^*, there is a worker who is supplying labour at the margin. If the wage rate were to fall even slightly below W^*, the worker would withdraw from this labour market, perhaps to take alternative employment in another sector or occupation. In other words, the wage rate can be regarded as the transfer earnings of the marginal worker. A similar argument can be made about any point along the labour supply curve.

This means that the area under the supply curve up to the equilibrium point can be interpreted as the transfer earnings of workers in this labour market. In Figure 6.9 this is given by the area $OBAL^*$.

Total earnings are given by the wage rate multiplied by the quantity of labour supplied (here, area OW^*AL^*). Economic rent is thus that part of total earnings that is *not* transfer earnings. In Figure 6.9 this is the triangle BW^*A. The rationale is that this area represents the total excess that workers receive by being paid a wage (W^*) that is above the minimum required to keep them employed in this market.

If you think about it, you will see that this is similar to the notion of producer surplus, which is the difference between the price received by firms for a good or service and the price at which the firms would have been prepared to supply that good or service.

The balance between transfer earnings and economic rent

What determines the balance between the two aspects of total earnings? In this connection, the elasticity of supply of labour is of critical importance.

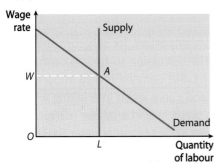

Figure 6.10 Perfectly elastic labour supply

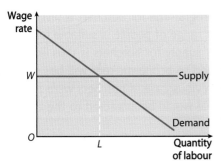

Figure 6.11 Perfectly inelastic labour supply

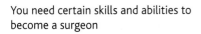
You need certain skills and abilities to become a surgeon

This can be seen by studying diagrams showing varying degrees of elasticity of supply. First, consider two extreme situations. Figure 6.10 shows a labour market in which supply is perfectly elastic. This implies that there is limitless supply of labour at the wage rate *W*. In this situation there is no economic rent to be gained from labour supply, and all earnings are transfer earnings. Any reduction of the wage below *W* will mean that all workers leave the market.

Now consider Figure 6.11. Here labour supply is perfectly inelastic. There is a fixed amount of labour being supplied to the market and, whatever the wage rate, that amount of labour remains the same. Another way of looking at this is that there is no minimum payment needed to keep labour in its present use. Now the entire earnings of the factor are made up by economic rent (i.e. the area *OWAL*).

This illustrates how important the elasticity of labour supply is in determining the balance between transfer earnings and economic rent. The more inelastic supply is, the higher the proportion of total earnings that is made up of economic rent.

Surgeons and butchers: the importance of supply

Consider an example of differential earnings — say, surgeons and butchers. First think about the surgeons. Surgeons are in relatively inelastic supply, at least in the short run. The education required to become a surgeon is long and demanding, and is certainly essential for entry into the occupation. Furthermore, not everyone is cut out to become a surgeon, as this is a field that requires certain innate abilities and talents. This implies that the supply of surgeons is limited and does not vary a great deal with the wage rate. If this is the case, then the earnings of surgeons are largely made up of economic rent.

The situation may be reinforced by the fact that, once an individual has trained as a surgeon, there may be few alternative occupations to which, if disgruntled, he or she could transfer. There is a natural limit to how many surgeons there are, *and* to their willingness to exit from the market.

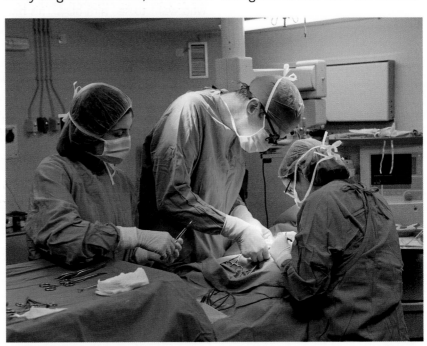

How about butchers? The training programme for butchers is less arduous than for surgeons, and a wider range of people is suitable for employment in this occupation. Labour supply for butchers is thus likely to be more elastic than for surgeons, and so economic rent will be relatively less important than in the previous case. If butchers were to receive high enough wages, more people would be attracted to the trade and wage rates would eventually fall.

In addition, there are other occupations into which butchers can transfer when they have had enough of cutting up all that meat: they might look to other sections of the catering sector, for example. This reinforces the relatively high elasticity of supply.

The importance of demand

Economic rent has been seen to be more important for surgeons than for butchers, but is this the whole story? The discussion so far has centred entirely on the supply side of the market. But demand is also important.

Indeed, it is the position of the demand curve when interacting with supply that determines the equilibrium wage rate in a labour market. It may well be that the supply of workers skilled in underwater basket weaving is strictly limited; but if there is no demand for underwater basket weavers then there is no scope for that skill to earn high economic rents. In the above example, it is the relatively strong demand for surgeons relative to their limited supply that leads to a relatively high equilibrium wage in the market.

Evaluation

This analysis can be applied to answer some questions that often appear about the labour market. In particular, why should the top footballers and pop stars be paid such high salaries, whereas valued professions such as nurses and firefighters are paid much less?

A footballer such as Wayne Rooney is valued because of the talent that he displays on the pitch, and because of his ability to bring in the crowds who want to see him play. This makes him a good revenue earner for his club, and reflects his high marginal productivity. In addition, his skills are rare — some would say unique. Wayne Rooney is thus in extremely limited supply. This combination of high marginal productivity and limited supply leads to a high equilibrium wage rate.

For nurses and firefighters, society may value them highly in one sense — that they carry out a vital, and sometimes dangerous, occupation. However, they are not valued in the sense of displaying high marginal productivity. Furthermore, the supply is by no means as limited as in the case of top-class professional footballers. These factors taken together help to explain why there are such large differences in salaries between occupations. This is one example of how marginal productivity theory helps to explain features of the real world that non-economists often find puzzling.

Summary

- In a modern economy, there is a complex network of labour markets for workers with different skills, working in different occupations and industries.
- The total payments to a factor of production can be separated into transfer earnings and economic rent.
- Transfer earnings represent the minimum payment needed to keep a factor of production in its present use.
- Economic rent is a payment received by a factor of production over and above what would be needed to keep it in its present use.
- The balance between transfer earnings and economic rent depends critically on the elasticity of supply of a particular kind of labour.
- The position of the demand curve is also important.

Education and the labour market

The above discussion has highlighted the importance of education and training in influencing wage differentials between occupational groups. Education and training might be regarded as a form of *barrier to entry* into a labour market, affecting the elasticity of supply of labour. Because of differences in innate talents and abilities — not to mention personal inclinations — wage differentials can persist even in the long run in certain occupations. However, economists expect there to be some long-run equilibrium level of differential that reflects the preference and natural talent aspects of various occupations.

How can education and training be viewed in this context? If an individual undertakes some form of education, some costs are incurred in the short run in the expectation of a future return in the form of higher earnings. This suggests that education can be viewed as *investment*. Indeed, it can be seen as investment in **human capital**: that is, the stock of skills and expertise that contribute to a worker's productivity.

Changes in the pattern of consumer demand for goods over time will lead to changes in those equilibrium differentials between occupations. For example, during the computer revolution, when firms were increasing their use of computers at work and households were increasing their use of home computers, there was a need for more computer programmers to create the software that people wanted, and a need for more computer engineers to fix the computers when they crashed. This meant that the wage differential for these workers increased. This in turn led to a proliferation of courses on offer to train or retrain people in these skills. Then, as the supply of such workers began to increase, so the wage differential narrowed.

This is what economists would expect to observe if the labour market is working effectively, with wages acting as signals to workers about what skills are in demand. It is part of the way in which a market system guides the allocation of resources.

Key term

human capital the stock of skills and expertise that contribute to a worker's productivity

Synoptic link

This notion of human capital will be encountered again in the macroeconomics part of the book, particularly in the context of the discussion of less developed countries, where investment in human capital is a crucial part of the process of economic and human development.

Individual educational choices

In specific cases, such as that of the computer programmers, you can see how individuals may respond to market signals. Word gets around that computer programmers are in high demand, and individual workers and job-seekers respond to that. However, not all education is geared so specifically towards such specific gaps in the market. How do individuals take decisions about education?

In trying to decide whether or not to undertake further education, an individual needs to balance the costs of such education against its benefits. One important consideration is that the costs tend to come in the short run, but the benefits only in the long run. Much of the discussion of student university tuition fees centres on this issue. Should students incur high debts now in the expectation of future higher earnings? Work through Exercise 6.3 to take this further.

In Exercise 6.3 you will have identified a range of benefits and costs. On the costs side are the direct costs in terms of tuition fees and living expenses, and there are also opportunity costs — the fact that you will have to delay the time when you start earning an income. But there are benefits to set against these costs, which may include the enjoyment you get from undertaking further study and the fact that university can be a great experience — that is, it can be a consumption good as well as an investment good. And, almost certainly, you have considered the fact that you can expect higher future earnings as a university graduate than as a non-graduate.

Figure 6.12 shows how average gross pay varies with the highest level of educational qualification achieved, using data from the UK Labour Force Survey. This shows that, on average, graduates with a degree receive higher gross pay than those who have taken some other form of higher education, who in turn receive more pay than those who have AS or A level as their highest qualification.

Exercise 6.3

Suppose you are considering undertaking a university education. Compile a list of the benefits and the costs that you expect to encounter if you choose to do so. Discuss how you would go about balancing the benefits and costs, remembering that the timing of these needs to be taken into account.

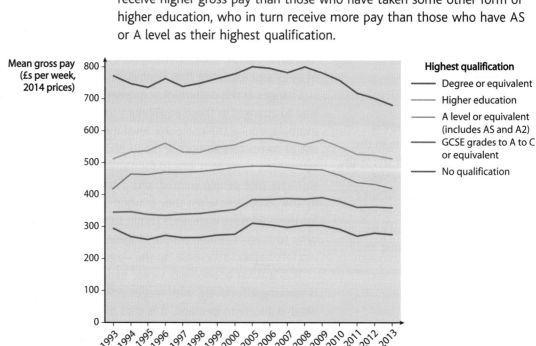

Source: John Simister, 'Is it worth studying economics at university?', *Economic Review*, April 2015

Figure 6.12 UK pay by educational level, 1993–2013

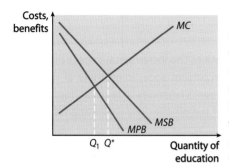

Figure 6.13 Education as a positive consumption externality

These data are a little difficult to interpret. They cannot be taken to mean that a university education necessarily increases the *productivity* of workers, because it may be that those who chose to undertake university education were naturally more able. This is the 'signalling' view of education — that the value of the degree is not so much what was learned during the programme of study as an indication that the person was capable of doing it. However, the fact that the returns to education are seen to vary across degree subjects suggests that employers do look for some value-added to emerge from university education. The evidence suggests that arts degrees have relatively little impact on average wages, whereas degrees in economics, management and law have larger effects.

In spite of such evidence that lifetime earnings can be boosted by education, people may still demand too little education for the best interest of society, as was discussed in Chapter 7 of Book 1. This may be because there are *externality effects* associated with education. Although education has been shown to improve productivity, it has also been found that *groups* of educated workers are able to cooperate and work together so that collectively they are even more productive than they are as individuals. From this point of view, an individual worker may not perceive the full social benefit of higher education.

Figure 6.13 is a reminder of this argument. If marginal social benefit (*MSB*) is higher than marginal private benefit (*MPB*), there is a tendency for individuals to demand too little education, choosing to acquire Q_1 education rather than the amount Q^*, which is the best for society. This argument may be used to suggest that government should encourage people to undertake more education.

Summary

- Wage differentials may act as signals to guide potential workers in their demand for training and retraining.
- People demand education partly for the effect it will have on their future earnings potential.
- Externality effects may mean that people choose to demand less education than is desirable for society as a whole.

Case study 6.1

Valuing professional footballers

The football transfer market was buoyant in the summer of 2014. Among the most prominent traders were the top English Premiership clubs such as Manchester United, Liverpool and Chelsea. The FA Premier League has the highest revenues of any domestic football league in the world, grossing more than £3 billion in revenues in the 2013/14 season according to Deloitte. The top Premiership clubs also compete in the highly lucrative UEFA Champions League. The battle between TV firms for broadcasting rights is a key factor in generating these revenues.

So not surprisingly, the top English Premiership clubs are able to outbid most of their rivals to attract the best players in the world. A survey published in November 2014 revealed that the average salary of a footballer playing in the English Premier League in the 2013/14 season had reached £2.3 million per year (£43,717 per week), comfortably more than footballers playing in the top leagues in Germany, Italy and Spain. These figures suggest that a high proportion of the TV revenues goes into players' salaries — rather than into lower ticket prices.

But is there any economic justification for Barcelona paying a transfer fee of £75 million to Liverpool for Luis Suárez or Manchester United paying £59.7 million to Real Madrid to obtain the services of Ángel di María?

From an economic and financial perspective, professional footballers are complex productive assets who are expected to provide a flow of services both on and off the field over the period of their employment contract. One way of valuing a professional footballer is to calculate the value of the expected flow of net benefits accruing to the holder of the asset — that is, the club. In other words, the value of a professional footballer should be related to the marginal revenue product (*MRP*) of the player.

Calculating the *MRP* of a professional footballer requires estimating the expected additional cash flows accruing to the club as a consequence of signing that player. Broadly speaking, there are two types of revenue stream that a player can generate. Firstly, there are the revenue streams associated with the player's on-the-field contribution to team performance. Team revenues tend to be 'win-elastic'. Winning teams tend to attract more spectators, generating higher match-day revenues. Media revenues can also be win-elastic with bigger viewing audiences for the more successful teams.

Sponsorship and merchandising revenues also tend to be higher for more successful teams. But a player's value will also depend on his expected image value off-the-field. Star players can generate greater revenues by virtue of being star players irrespective of their actual impact on team performance. Glamour as well as glory makes money in professional team sports, which when all is said and done are part of the entertainment industry. So from an economic perspective the fundamental value of a professional footballer can be stated as:

$$MRP = (MPC \times MWR) + PIV$$

where *MPC* is the (expected) marginal playing contribution, *MWR* is the marginal win revenue and *PIV* is the player image value. Calculating a player's value requires an estimate of the incremental impact of the player on the team performance, an estimate of the sensitivity of the team's revenues to team performance and an estimate of the off-the-field marketing value of the player.

Luis Suárez — is he worth the transfer fee?

Follow-up questions

a Explain what is meant by the 'marginal revenue product' of a footballer.

b What is meant by the statement that team revenues tend to be 'win-elastic'?

c Explain why 'glamour as well as glory makes money'?

d To what extent does the discussion of a footballer's *MRP* help to explain why professional footballers command such high wages?

Chapter 7

The UK labour market

Having explored some of the theory of how labour markets work, this chapter provides some context by looking at the UK labour market. The chapter introduces some important definitions that enable key dimensions of labour markets to be monitored and analysed. We will then explore some of the important changes that have affected labour markets in the UK in recent years.

> ## Learning objectives
>
> After studying this chapter, you should:
> - be familiar with key characteristics of the labour market
> - be aware of the structure of UK employment and earnings
> - be able to compare the UK labour market situation with that of other countries in the EU and countries elsewhere
> - be familiar with movements in labour productivity and hence unit labour costs in the UK and elsewhere
> - be able to evaluate the impact of changes that have affected the flexibility and operation of labour markets in the UK
> - be aware of the operation of a labour market in which there is a monopsony buyer of labour
> - understand how unemployment may arise in a market

Prior knowledge needed

Having discussed the economics of the labour market in Chapter 6, this chapter looks at the labour market in the UK.

The UK workforce

The way in which people earn a living is an important aspect of any economy. Indeed, it is a matter of concern to everyone at an individual level.

The default retirement age (which used to be 65) has been phased out, but it is still customary to think of the normal working age as between 16 and 64, and the people in that age range make up the **working population**. Notice that there is a sense in which the people in the working population age range must support those who are young (15 years of age and below), and those who are 65 or over. The **dependency ratio** shows the ratio of dependants to the working population.

Key terms

working population people between the ages of 16 and 64

dependency ratio the ratio of those aged 15 or below and 65 and above to the working population

> ## Quantitative skills 7.1
>
> ### Calculating ratios
>
> To calculate the dependency ratio, we need to know the age structure of the population. In mid-2012, the total population of England and Wales was 56.1 million. Of these, 10.7 million people were aged 15 or under, and 9.6 million were aged 65 or above. The size of the working population was 36.2 million. The dependency ratio is thus calculated as (10.7 million + 9.6 million) divided by 36.2 million, which equals 0.56.

If you need to use data on dependency ratios, and you turn to the internet, you need to be very careful to check the precise definitions that are used. For example, the World Bank expresses the dependency ratio as a percentage. The ONS often refers to the old age dependency ratio, which focuses on the number of people aged 65 and above relative to the working population, and also tends to express the ratio as a percentage or in per thousand terms. In at least one study, the ONS turns the ratio on its head, and discusses the dependency ratio as the ratio of the number of people of working age to the number of people of state pension age.

The dependency ratio is significant because people of working age need to support those who are too young or too old to work. In many advanced countries, there has been concern that as people now tend to live longer, the proportion of elderly people in the population is rising — in other words, the old age dependency ratio is tending to increase. This puts pressure on pension funds. For many developing countries, it is the percentage of young people in the population that results in a high dependency ratio. This puts pressure on the education system.

The dependency ratio does not tell the full story. At any point in time, not all of the working population are **economically active**, and the **workforce** comprises those who are in jobs, together with those who are unemployed, suggesting that there may be more dependants in the population than the ratio suggests. On the other hand, there may be people over 65 who are still working.

Looking at the overall situation for labour supply in the UK, in late 2014 just over 63% of people aged 16 and above were economically active. This means that they were in employment, self-employed or unemployed. Unemployment may arise for a number of reasons. It may reflect the fact that some people may not be prepared to accept jobs at the going wage rate. To the extent that this is so, such people may be regarded as being part of voluntary unemployment. However, there may also be involuntary unemployment — that is, people who would like to work but who are unable to find employment.

Key terms

economically active active in the labour force, including the employed, the self-employed and the unemployed

workforce people who are economically active, either employed or unemployed

In 2014, just over 63% of people in the UK were economically active

Key terms

ILO unemployment rate
measure of the percentage of the workforce who are without jobs but are available for work, willing to work and looking for work

participation rate the percentage of the population in a given age group who are economically active

The official measure of unemployment used in the UK is known as the **ILO unemployment rate**, as it is measured using the definition devised by the International Labour Organisation (ILO). This identifies the number of people available for work and seeking work, but who are without a job. The data are collected as part of the Labour Force Survey.

The **participation rate** captures the number of people within a given age group who are economically active. The overall participation rate for those aged 16 and above does not vary much from year to year. Since 1992 it has only varied between 62.2% and 63.8%. There tends to be a slight increase when the labour market is relatively healthy, which may encourage some people to believe that it is worth their while to join the workforce. Of the 18.9 million people who were economically inactive in late 2014, 9.9 million were above the official retirement age. There is a significant difference in the participation rate for men and women. In the UK in late 2014, the participation rate for men was about 70%, whereas for women it was 58%.

In late 2014, there were 9 million people aged between 16 and 64 who were economically inactive, of whom 6.8 million did not want a job. Some were inactive because they were students, others because they were looking after family members, or were sick or retired. There were also small numbers of 'discouraged workers' — that is, people who had withdrawn from the workforce believing that they had no chance of getting a job.

Figure 7.1 shows how the population aged 16 and over has been divided between the various categories in each year since 1992. This shows a gradual rise in the number of employees. The numbers unemployed fell in the middle of the period before rising again from 2009 as the recession began to bite. This is easier to see in Figure 7.2, which shows the percentage unemployment rate over this same period.

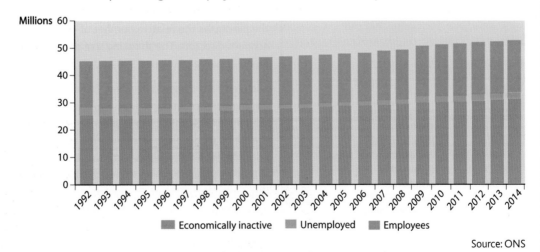

Source: ONS

Figure 7.1 Economic activity and inactivity in the UK, 1992–2014 (second quarter each year)

Figure 7.2 Unemployment in the UK, 1992–2014 (spring of each year)

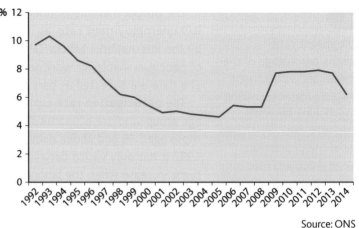

Source: ONS

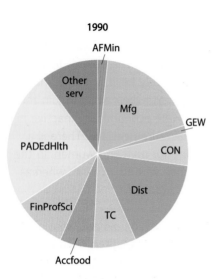

1990

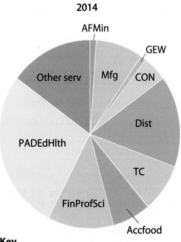

2014

Key

▨	AFMin	Agriculture, fishing and mining
▨	Mfg	Manufacturing
▨	GEW	Gas, electricity and water
▨	CON	Construction
▨	Dist	Distribution
▨	TC	Transport and communications
▨	Accfood	Accommodation and food
▨	FinProfSci	Financial, professional and scientific services
▨	PADEdHlth	Public administration, education and health
▨	Other serv	Other services

Figure 7.3 The structure of employee jobs in the UK, 1990 and 2014

The structure of economic activity

Over recent decades, the UK economy has gone through substantial structural change. You can see something of this in Figure 7.3, which compares the pattern of employment in the UK in 1990 and 2014. One of the key features is the change in the balance of employment between manufacturing activity and services. In 1990, 18% of jobs were in the manufacturing sector, and 73% in services, but in 2014, manufacturing only accounted for 8% of jobs, and 85% of employees were working in services. Service activity is clearly very important to the UK economy, particularly education, health and public administration, distribution, hotels and restaurants, and finance and business services.

Quantitative skills 7.2

Using graphs to show shares

A pie chart such as those in Figure 7.3 is a common way of showing the relative shares in a total. In this case, the size of each slice of the pie shows the relative number of employee jobs in the various economic sectors. The shrinking size of the pie slice representing manufacturing between 1990 and 2014 is readily apparent.

The pie chart is a good device if you are looking at one set of observations, or a couple (as here). However, if you want to be able to compare several different years, or several different countries, then the pie chart becomes less powerful, as it is difficult to assimilate the information. An alternative is to use a stacked bar chart where the shares are shown as proportions of a bar. You will meet an example of this very soon, in Figure 7.5, which is used in Exercise 7.1. This allows us to compare across five different countries/regions. Notice that if you want to show many component shares, this tool also becomes difficult to interpret.

Figure 7.4 shows the time-path of manufacturing jobs in the UK since 1978. This shows that there has been a steady decline over a long period, a process that has sometimes been described as *deindustrialisation*.

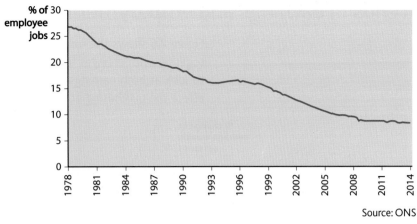

Source: ONS

Figure 7.4 Manufacturing jobs in the UK, 1978–2014

You should not be too surprised at such changes in the pattern of activity over time. In part they may reflect changes in the pattern of consumer demand as incomes have increased. As real incomes rise, the demand for some goods increases more rapidly than for others. For luxury goods, which have an income elasticity of demand greater than 1, the proportion of income spent on them increases as income itself increases. It is worth noting that the demand for many leisure items is likely to be income elastic. So, for example, as real incomes rise, it would be expected that the demand for capital goods associated with leisure activity, such as digital cameras and iPods, would rise more than proportionately with income. At the same time, the demand for some other goods and services may slacken. If the market economy is working effectively in encouraging the production of those goods and services that people wish to buy, then the structure of economic activity should also change, with some sectors expanding and others contracting.

Patterns of international trade have also changed over time, especially in the context of closer European integration, which may have affected the pattern of specialisation between countries. For example, as China has become a source of competitively priced manufactured goods, economies like the UK have been able to focus on the sorts of service sector activity at which they excel.

Exercise 7.1

Figure 7.5 shows the contribution of the major sectors to GDP in a range of locations. Compare and contrast the changes that have taken place in these locations between 1990 and 2011/12.

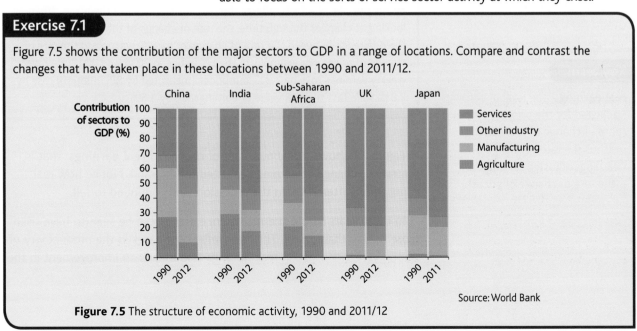

Source: World Bank

Figure 7.5 The structure of economic activity, 1990 and 2011/12

Trends in earnings and employment

Figure 7.6 shows the rate of change of earnings in the UK since 2001, together with changes in the retail price index. Notice that it is important to look at both earnings and prices because changes in prices (inflation) affect the purchasing power of earnings.

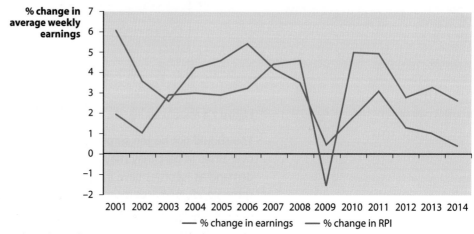

Figure 7.6 The rate of change of earnings and prices, 2001–14

Quantitative skills 7.3

Real and nominal earnings

When measuring variables that are expressed in money terms, it is important to adjust for the effects of inflation. When we think about wages and their effect on labour supply, what is important is the purchasing power of wages or earnings. If we ignore the fact that prices are changing over time, then this will provide a distorted view of the incentives facing workers in making choices about labour supply.

The *money wage* (often known as the *nominal wage*) is the wage as paid at a point in time to workers. The *real wage* is the money wage divided by the price level, which reflects the purchasing power of the wage. When looking at changes through time, the rate of change of the real wage is the difference between the rate of change of money wages and the rate of change of prices. For example, in the UK between 2011 and 2012, average weekly earnings rose by 1.3%, but prices (measured by RPI inflation) rose by 2.8%, so in fact the real value of earnings fell by 1.5%.

Figure 7.7 shows the annual rate of change of **real earnings**: that is, the rate of change of earnings adjusted for inflation. Notice how real earnings fell after 2009 in the recession, and continued to fall.

In most years before the recession, earnings can be seen to have risen more rapidly than prices. This may reflect increases in the productivity of labour. Whether a rise in real earnings also means an improvement in the

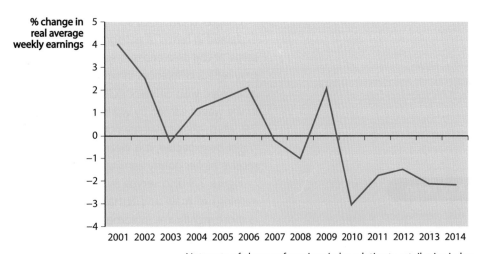

Note: rate of change of earnings index relative to retail price index.

Figure 7.7 The rate of change of real earnings, 2001–14

standard of living will depend on a number of things. For a start, the fact that average earnings have increased does not mean that all workers share in the benefits, so the distribution of the increases across different groups of workers may be important. Furthermore, it may be argued that the standard of living does not only depend upon income (earnings), but may also reflect other aspects of the quality of life, such as the environment in which people live, or the quality of leisure time that they can enjoy.

It is also important to be aware that the earnings that people receive differ for a wide variety of reasons. For one thing, it is the case that earnings differ between the various kinds of economic activity that take place within the economy. Figure 7.8 shows something of this. You can see that average weekly earnings in 2014 varied across sectors in the economy. Employees in accommodation and food services and in agriculture received relatively low pay, whereas those in the financial sector enjoyed substantially higher levels of remuneration — indeed, average pay for employees in finance and insurance was almost four times the average for workers in accommodation and food services.

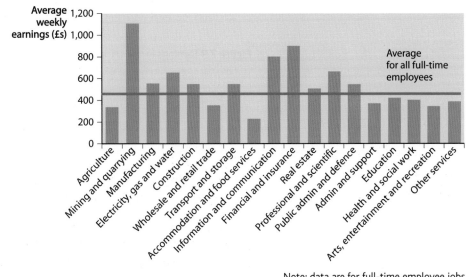

Note: data are for full-time employee jobs.
Source: ONS (Annual Survey of Hours and Earnings)

Figure 7.8 Average weekly earnings, 2014

Chapter 6 examined some of the ways in which this pattern can be explained in terms of economic analysis. One obvious point to notice is that some of the differences in earnings between economic sectors in the economy may reflect differences in occupational structure, which in turn may be associated with different skills requirements of different jobs. The differences in the wages earned by workers in different occupations can be seen in Figure 7.9, which shows average hourly earnings for various occupational groups. As might be expected, it is clear that managers, senior officials and professionals receive higher hourly earnings than less skilled occupations.

Figure 7.9 also serves as a reminder that there is a gender gap between earnings of male and female workers — and it would seem that the gap is more significant in some occupations than in others. It is also the case that earnings (and employment) show differences between age and ethnic groups, and one of the important issues to be examined is the extent to which such differences reflect **discrimination** in the labour force, or the extent to which they may be explained by other economic factors at work in the market. It has been noticeable that the gender gap has narrowed somewhat over the past decade — as you can see in Figure 7.10. However, it is still the case that men (on average) earn more than women.

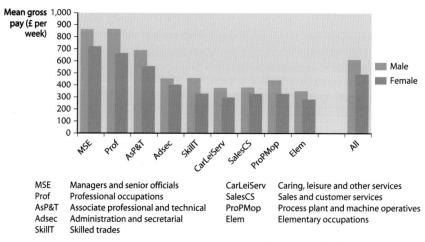

MSE   Managers and senior officials   CarLeiServ   Caring, leisure and other services
Prof   Professional occupations   SalesCS   Sales and customer services
AsP&T   Associate professional and technical   ProPMop   Process plant and machine operatives
Adsec   Administration and secretarial   Elem   Elementary occupations
SkillT   Skilled trades

Note: data are for full-time employee jobs.
Source: ONS

Figure 7.9 Earnings in the UK by occupation, 2014

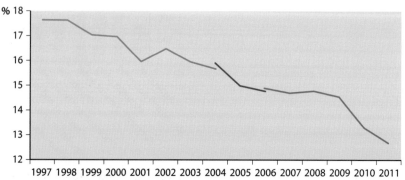

Note: data refer to full-time employees whose pay for the survey period was unaffected by absence; data show the percentage pay gap between women's and men's median earnings.
Source: *Social Trends*

Figure 7.10 The gender pay gap, 1997–2011

The mean and the median

You may have noticed that the footnote to Figure 7.10 refers to the pay gap between women's and men's median earnings. It is useful to be aware of what is meant by the median, which is sometimes used. You will be familiar with the notion of the *average* value of a variable. This is also known by statisticians as the *mean*. It is calculated as the sum of the values of a variable divided by the number of observations. The *median* is also a measure of central tendency, but the median is the middle observation. For example, suppose we had 5 observations on a variable, the values being 1, 3, 7, 14 and 65. The average would be (1 + 3 + 7 + 14 + 65)/5 =18. The median would be the middle observation, which is 7. We might think that in this instance, the median is more sensible for representing the series because the mean is affected by one very high value.

There are also some differences that emerge between ethnic groups within society. As with the gender differences, variations between ethnic groups reflect a number of factors, and are seen in a variety of ways. For example, people from some ethnic groupings are more likely to be self-employed, or may tend to work in certain occupations — some two-thirds of Chinese residents work in sales, distribution, hotels and restaurants; more than half of Indians and two-fifths of Pakistanis and Bangladeshis are self-employed. This then has knock-on effects on earnings, to the extent that these vary between occupations and sectors. It is also apparent that unemployment rates vary with ethnicity, as can be seen in Figure 7.11.

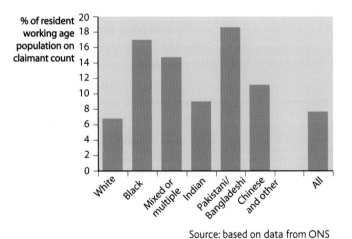

Source: based on data from ONS

Figure 7.11 Unemployment by ethnic group, 2013

International differences in productivity

Considering the UK economy in an international context, the relative cost of labour in different countries becomes important because this influences the relative competitiveness of UK goods in both overseas and domestic markets. In other words, the relative costs of production in different countries influence the prices that firms can charge. It thus becomes important to consider changes in **unit labour costs** over time, these being defined as the wages, salaries and other costs of using labour, divided by output per worker.

If unit labour costs in an economy rise more rapidly than in other countries, there will be a loss of competitiveness. Figure 7.12 compares annual changes in unit labour costs in the UK with changes in the member countries of the EU and with countries in the euro single currency area. This reveals that unit labour costs have grown more rapidly in the UK than elsewhere in the EU in recent years. If unit labour costs were to continue to grow more rapidly in the UK than in the EU then, ceteris paribus, this would imply a deterioration in the UK's competitive position.

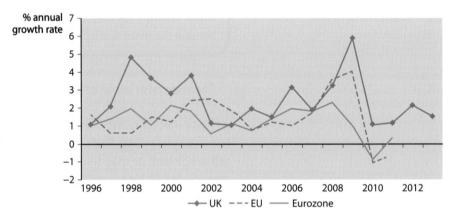

Source: HM Treasury

Figure 7.12 Unit labour cost growth in the UK and EU, 1996–2013

This in turn partly reflects different levels of productivity across countries. Productivity is a measure of productive efficiency: for example, **labour productivity** is output per unit of labour input. Different countries show appreciable differences in efficiency by this measure.

However, international comparisons of productivity are not straightforward, as measurements are subject to differences in data collection and differences in work practices. Figure 7.13 presents data for 2011 on GDP per head of population, expressed as index numbers, with the USA being the reference country and thus set to 100.

On this measure, the UK performs slightly better than Italy, Spain, France and Japan. As a measure of productivity levels, however, this is a misleading indicator. In particular, working hours are longer in the UK than in some other countries (especially within Europe), so in part, GDP per head reflects differences in the quantity of labour input. For this reason, GDP per hour worked is often seen as a more reliable indicator of relative productivity levels. This measure is graphed in Figure 7.14 and shows quite a different pattern. Indeed, on this basis Ireland shows higher productivity than the USA, and the UK's performance is much more modest.

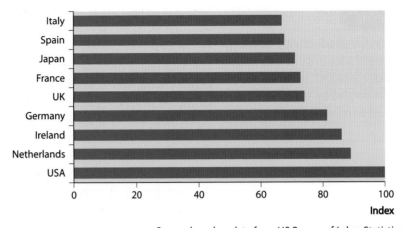

Source: based on data from US Bureau of Labor Statistics

Figure 7.13 GDP per head of population, selected countries, 2011 (USA = 100)

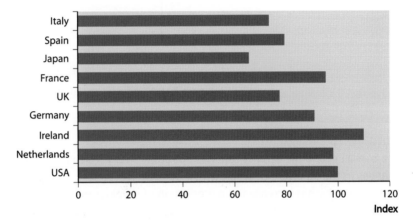

Source: based on data from US Bureau of Labor Statistics

Figure 7.14 GDP per hour worked, selected countries, 2011 (USA = 100)

Figure 7.15 shows the growth rate of labour productivity in selected countries from 2006 to 2014. The feature that stands out in this figure is the dramatic fall in labour productivity in France, Germany and the UK in 2009, when the recession affected many countries. The USA followed a different pattern, remaining more resilient, at least in terms of productivity.

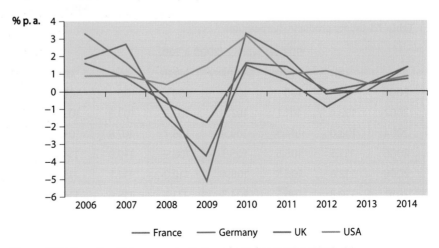

Figure 7.15 Growth of labour productivity, selected countries, 2006–14

total factor productivity the average productivity of all factors, measured as the total output divided by the total amount of inputs used

It is also important to realise that labour productivity is not the only relevant measure, as countries may also differ in their use of capital. An alternative measure is obtained by dividing the quantity of output by the total input of all factors of production. This is known as **total factor productivity**. This is naturally more difficult to measure, as the measurement of capital stock is especially prone to error and misinterpretation. However, some estimates of multifactor productivity growth are shown in Figure 7.16.

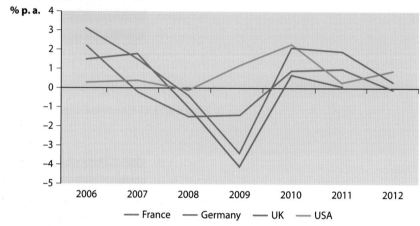

Figure 7.16 Multifactor productivity growth, selected countries, 2006–12

Summary
- The overall economic activity rate has not altered very much in the UK in recent years, but there have been changes in the structure of employment between sectors.
- Service activity has increased as a proportion of employment, and manufacturing has declined.
- This may reflect changes in the pattern of consumer demand, and of specialisation between countries.
- Earnings have risen by more than prices in most years.
- There have been significant differences in movements of unit labour costs and labour productivity over time between the UK and other countries in the EU.

Exercise 7.2

Table 7.1 provides data on two labour productivity measures, based on 2000 = 100. Discuss whether the UK's position improved or deteriorated between 2000 and 2014. How well has the UK performed relative to the other countries in the table? Explain your answer, and discuss why this might be important for the UK economy.

Table 7.1 Labour productivity measures

	GDP per worker (2000 = 100)					GDP per hour worked (2000 = 100)				
	UK	France	Germany	Japan	USA	UK	France	Germany	Japan	USA
2000	100	100	100	100	100	100	100	100	100	100
2002	103.4	101.1	102.1	103.3	103.3	103.5	103.3	104.4	103.4	104.5
2004	108.0	104.3	104.3	106.7	107.8	109.3	105.5	106.6	107.9	110.2
2006	111.5	106.5	105.3	108.9	110.0	114.0	109.9	108.8	110.1	112.5
2008	112.6	106.5	106.4	110.0	111.1	115.1	108.8	109.9	112.4	113.6
2010	110.3	106.5	104.3	111.1	115.6	114.0	108.8	108.8	115.7	119.3
2012	110.3	107.5	104.3	113.3	117.8	114.0	111.0	109.9	116.9	121.6

Source: calculated from ONS data

Flexibility and market failure in the labour market

So far, this chapter has focused on the measurement of various dimensions of the labour market, looking at different ways in which changes in the pattern of employment can be analysed. But why is this so important?

It is important because a flexible labour market allows the economy to be adaptable. It allows resources to be allocated efficiently and quickly, and allows the economy to maintain its international competitiveness, especially if its labour market is more flexible than that of its main competitors in global markets. A key aspect of this is for the labour market to be flexible in allowing changes in the structure of the economy to be achieved as the pattern of consumer demand changes and as the country's pattern of comparative advantage changes over time. In other words, a flexible labour market allows workers to switch between jobs or between occupations in response to changes in demand.

As with product markets, there are many ways in which labour markets may fail to achieve the most desirable results for society at large. Such market failure can occur on either the demand or the supply side of the market. On the demand side, it may be that employers — as the buyers of labour — have market power that can be exploited at the expense of the workers. Alternatively, it may be that some employers act against the interests of some groups of workers relative to others through some form of discrimination in their hiring practices or wage-setting behaviour. On the supply side, there may be restrictions on the supply of some types of labour, or it may be that trade unions find themselves able to bid wages up to a level that is above the free market equilibrium.

On another level, the very existence of unemployment might be interpreted as indicating disequilibrium in the labour market — although there may also be reasons to expect there always to be some unemployment in a modern economy. Finally, there are some forms of government intervention that may have unintended effects on labour markets.

Monopsony

One type of market failure in a product market occurs when there is a single *seller* of a good: that is, a monopoly market. As you may recall, a firm with this sort of market dominance is able to restrict output, and maximise profits by setting a higher price. A similar form of market power can occur on the other side of the market if there is a single *buyer* of a good, service or factor of production. Such a market is known as a **monopsony**.

In Chapter 6 it was assumed that firms in the labour market face perfect competition, and therefore must accept the market wage. However, suppose that one firm is the sole user of a particular type of labour, or is the dominant firm in a city or region, and thus is in a monopsony situation.

Such a monopsonist faces the market supply curve of labour directly, rather than simply accepting the equilibrium market wage. It views this supply curve as its average cost of labour because it shows the average wage rate that it would need to offer to obtain any given quantity of labour input.

Figure 7.17 shows a monopsonist's demand curve for labour, which is the marginal revenue product curve (MRP_L), and its supply curve of labour, seen by the firm as its average cost curve of labour (AC_L). If the market were perfectly competitive, equilibrium would be where supply equals demand, which would be with the firm using L^* labour at a wage rate W^*.

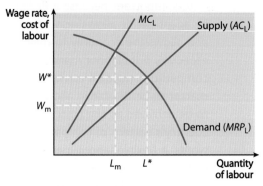

Figure 7.17 A monopsony buyer of labour

From the perspective of the monopsonist firm facing the supply curve directly, if at any point it wants to hire more labour, it has to offer a higher wage to encourage more workers to join the market — after all, that is what the AC_L curve tells it. However, the firm would then have to pay that higher wage to *all* its workers, so the *marginal cost* of hiring the extra worker is not just the wage paid to that worker, but the increased wage paid to all the other workers as well. So the marginal cost of labour curve (MC_L) can be added to the diagram.

If the monopsonist firm wants to maximise profit, it will hire labour up to the point where the marginal cost of labour is equal to the marginal revenue product of labour. Therefore it will use labour up to the level L_m, which is where $MC_L = MRP_L$. In order to entice workers to supply this amount of labour, the firm need pay only the wage W_m. (Remember that AC_L is the supply curve of labour.) You can see, therefore, that a profit-maximising monopsonist will use less labour, and pay a lower wage, than a firm operating under perfect competition. From society's perspective, this entails a cost, just as was seen in the comparison of monopoly and perfect competition in Chapter 3.

Exercise 7.3

Figure 7.18 shows a firm in a monopsonistic labour market.
a What would the wage rate be if this market were perfectly competitive, and how much labour would be employed?
b As a monopsony, what wage would the firm offer to its workers, and how much labour would it employ?
c Which area represents the employer's wage bill?
d What surplus does this generate for the firm?

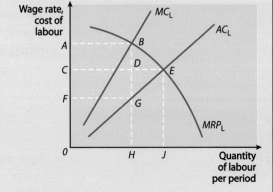

Figure 7.18 A monopsonistic labour market

Bilateral monopoly

It is important to notice that much of this analysis has treated the firm as being very passive in the negotiations. Suppose, however, that there is a bilateral monopoly, in which the monopoly trade union seller of labour faces a firm that is a monopsony buyer of labour. The resulting situation is illustrated in Figure 7.19. If unhindered by the trade union, the firm would offer a wage W_m and use L_m labour. However, if the union now negotiates a higher wage rate, what happens is that, as the wage moves upwards from W_m, the firm will take on more labour. The market will then move back towards the perfectly competitive level (at wage W^* and quantity L^*).

In this situation, the market power of the two protagonists works against both of them to produce an outcome that is closer to perfect competition. It is not possible to predict where the final resting

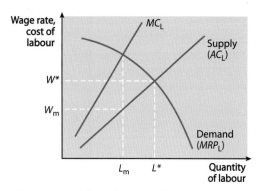

Figure 7.19 A bilateral monopoly

place for the market will be, but it will lie somewhere between L_m and L^*, depending upon the relative strengths and negotiating skills of the firm and the union.

Discrimination

In Chapter 6, it was explained that wage differentials across different labour markets within an economy such as the UK are to be expected because of differences in marginal productivity of different workers, and differences in economic rent and transfer earnings. However, the question often arises as to whether such economic analysis can explain all of the differentials in wages that can be observed.

Earlier in the chapter, it was noted that there is a gender gap in earnings that requires some investigation. For full-time workers the pay gap between male and female workers has narrowed since 1975, but for part-time workers it has not. It also appears that employment opportunities for ethnic minority groups have worsened since 1975 — in spite of legislation that has increasingly tried to ensure equal opportunities for all. It is important to explore the extent to which these differences can be explained by economic analysis, and the extent to which they reflect discrimination in pay or employment opportunities.

The mere fact that there is inequality does not prove that there is discrimination. You have seen the way in which education and training affects earnings, so differentials between different groups of people may reflect the different educational choices made by those different groups. The gender gap may also reflect the fact that childcare responsibilities interrupt the working lives of many women. This is important in terms of human capital and the build-up of experience and seniority. The increasing introduction of crèche facilities by many firms is reducing the extent of this contribution to the earnings gap, but it has not eliminated it. In addition, there have been changes in social attitudes towards female education beyond the age of 16. When girls were expected to become homemakers, education beyond 16 was not highly valued, so there were generations of women who missed out on education, and consequently

Childcare responsibilities interrupt the working lives of many women

found themselves disadvantaged in the labour market. Although attitudes have changed, however, such effects take a long time to work their way through the system.

Summary

- A market in which there is a single buyer of a good, service or factor of production is known as a monopsony market.
- A monopsony buyer of labour will employ less labour at a lower wage than if the market is perfectly competitive.
- Wage differentials and employment conditions are seen to vary between males and females and between ethnic groups, and only part of the variance can be explained by economic analysis, suggesting there may be discrimination.

Unemployment

In Book 1, unemployment was discussed at a *macroeconomic* level, as one of the key measures of an economy's overall performance. In that context a number of different causes of unemployment were identified.

Frictional unemployment was seen as arising when workers switch between jobs. This is a purely transitional phenomenon, and is necessary if the labour market is to be flexible in allowing people to transfer between firms or industries. When retraining is needed to ease the transition, the unemployment may be longer term: for example, when some sectors are declining and others are expanding, workers may need to be re-skilled in order to make the transfer. This is known as *structural unemployment*. It was also pointed out that in the macroeconomic context there may be a state of *demand-deficient unemployment*, in which aggregate demand in the economy is insufficient for the economy to reach full employment.

In a *microeconomic* context, unemployment might be seen from a different angle. While some frictional unemployment cannot be avoided, structural unemployment can be regarded as an indicator of some inflexibility in labour markets, slowing the process by which workers can move from one job to another.

One cause of structural unemployment may be that firms are not providing sufficient training to ensure a smooth transition. On-the-job training is an important way to enable workers to gain the skills that will make them more productive in the future. When firms are taking employment decisions, they are concerned not only with today's marginal revenue product of workers, but with the longer-term perspective.

Providing training

Providing training is costly to a firm, however, so it will need some assurance that it will be able to reap the benefits at a later date in the form of higher productivity. It may also be aware that firms choosing not to provide training may be able to poach its newly trained workers without having incurred the costs of the training. In other words, there is a potential *free-rider* problem here.

There may be some skills that are useful only within the firm. Such *firm-specific* skills do not pose quite the same problems. However, for generic transferable skills there is an incentive for firms to underprovide training. Some government intervention may therefore be needed to rectify this situation.

The replacement ratio

Unemployment could also arise where some people choose not to work simply because unemployment benefit is set at such a level that they are better off on benefits than accepting a low-paid job. This can be monitored through the **replacement ratio**, which is defined as the ratio of average weekly unemployment benefits to the wage that a claimant could receive from taking a job. This is quite difficult to measure precisely, as the wage that an individual could command depends upon his or her characteristics. However, the consensus of research is that the UK's replacement ratio is relatively low by European standards, especially compared with countries in northern Europe.

This is an area where the government has to maintain a careful balance in policy. On the one hand, it may be seen as important to provide protection for vulnerable people who are unable to obtain employment. On the other hand, if benefits are set at too generous a level, people may opt for unemployment rather than low-paid jobs. This is sometimes known as the **unemployment trap**. Unemployment that results from this is *voluntary unemployment*, in the sense that people are choosing to be unemployed because of the incentives that face them. To counter this, the government needs to ensure that 'work pays'.

Disequilibrium unemployment

One important potential cause of unemployment is disequilibrium in a labour market. Some examples of this have already been given. A wage set at a level that is above the equilibrium rate can cause unemployment in a labour market.

This is shown in Figure 7.20 where, given the demand curve D^*, the equilibrium wage is at W^*, with labour employed up to L^*. With the wage held above the equilibrium rate, at W_1, the supply of labour (S_1) exceeds the quantity of labour that firms are prepared to hire (D_1), and the difference $(S_1 - D_1)$ is unemployment — the number of workers who would like a job at the going wage rate, but are unable to find a job.

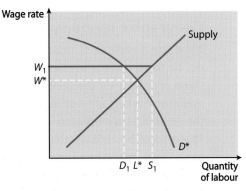

Figure 7.20 Disequilibrium unemployment

This could occur for a number of reasons. In some circumstances the introduction of a minimum wage could have this effect. Another possibility is that a trade union is able to negotiate a wage that is higher than the equilibrium rate. These situations will be analysed in Chapter 8.

Disequilibrium unemployment could also happen where there is inflexibility in the market. For example, suppose that a firm experiences a fall in the demand for its product. As the price of the product falls, so the marginal revenue product of labour falls, and the firm would want to move to a lower employment level and pay lower wages. This is shown in Figure 7.21. If previously the demand for labour was at D_0 then W_0 would have been the equilibrium wage rate, and employment would have been L_0, with no unemployment. When the demand for labour falls to D_1, there would be a new potential equilibrium with the wage at W^* and employment L^*. However, if the market is sluggish to adjust, perhaps because there is resistance to lowering wages from W_0 to W^*, then this will cause unemployment. In other words, with the wage remaining at W_0, workers continue to try to supply L_0 labour, but firms will only demand L_1, and the difference is unemployment. This situation of sticky wage adjustment is thus another cause of unemployment.

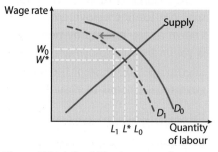

Figure 7.21 Inflexibility in wage adjustment

Labour mobility

A further reason for labour market inflexibility is that workers are not perfectly mobile. Mobility here can be seen in two important dimensions. First, there may be geographic immobility, where workers may be reluctant to move to a new region in search of appropriate employment. Second, there may be immobility between occupations. Both sorts of immobility can hinder the free operation of labour markets.

Geographic mobility

There are a number of reasons that help to explain why workers may not be freely mobile between different parts of the country. This will cause problems for the labour market if the available jobs and the available workers are not located in the same area. A key issue involves the costs that are entailed in moving to a new job in a new region. These could be considerable in social terms — people do not like to move away from their friends and relatives, or to leave the area that they know or where their favourite football team plays. Parents may not wish to disrupt their children's education. However, there are also strong economic considerations.

The relatively high rate of owner-occupied housing in the UK means that workers who are owner-occupiers may need a strong inducement to move to another part of the country in search of jobs. For council house tenants, too, it may be quite difficult to relocate to a different area for employment purposes because they will have to return to the bottom of the waiting list for housing. Differences in house prices in different parts of the country add further to the problem of matching workers to jobs.

There may also be information problems, in that it may be more difficult to find out about job availability in other areas. The internet may have reduced the costs of job search to some extent, but it is still easier to find jobs in the local area, where the reputation of firms is better known to locals. Where both partners in a relationship are working, this may also make it more difficult to find jobs further afield, and there is some evidence that females tend to be less mobile geographically than males.

International mobility of labour has increased in recent years, especially since the expansion of the EU in 2004, with the addition of ten new member countries. One of the features of the Single Market measures of 1992 was to allow free movement of people, goods, services and capital within the EU. Not all of the existing EU members allowed free movement of labour from the new members, but the UK did. As a result, it experienced large waves of migration from eastern Europe, especially from Poland. This was partly a response to the wage differential between the countries. As the marginal product of labour was higher in the UK than in Poland and other countries, wages in the UK were relatively high. This wage differential acted as an incentive for workers to move to the UK.

Exercise 7.4

Draw two labour market diagrams to represent the demand and supply of labour in the UK and Poland before the EU expansion. Show on the diagrams how the two markets would adjust to a flow of workers from Poland to the UK.

A Polish shop in London — higher wages attract Polish workers to the UK

Are migrant workers substitutes or complements?

In analysing the effect of in-migration on the domestic market, an important issue is whether the immigrant workers are substitutes for domestic labour, or whether they are complements. If the migrant workers compete with native workers for jobs, then the effect could be to push down the wage rate and leave some native workers without jobs. However, suppose the migrants are complementary to native workers? In other words, suppose the migrant workers come with different skills and characteristics to domestic workers, so they find jobs that native workers are unable or unwilling to take. In this case, the result could be an increase in national income and a consequent increase in the demand for native workers.

Occupational mobility

The difficulty that people face in moving between occupations is an important source of labour market inflexibility, and may result in structural unemployment. Over time, it is to be expected that the pattern of consumer demand will change, and if the pattern of economic activity is to change in response, it is important that some sectors of the economy decline to enable others to expand. As the UK economy has moved away from manufacturing towards service sector activities, people have needed to be occupationally mobile to find work.

There are costs involved for workers switching between occupations. A displaced farm worker may not be able to find work as a ballet dancer without some degree of retraining! As explained earlier, firms may be expected to underprovide training for their workers because of the free-rider problem. There may therefore be a need for some government intervention to ensure that training is provided in order to combat the problem of structural unemployment and to facilitate occupational mobility.

As with geographic mobility, another factor that may impede occupational mobility is the question of information. Workers may not have enough information to enable them to judge the benefits of occupational mobility. For example, they may not be aware of their aptitude for different occupations, or the extent to which they may gain job satisfaction from a job that they have not tried. These arguments do not apply only to workers displaced by structural change in the economy. They are equally valid for workers who are in jobs that may not necessarily be the best ones for them.

Summary

- Unemployment arises for a number of reasons at the microeconomic level.
- Structural unemployment, arising from changes in the structure of economic activity within an economy, may reflect inflexibility in a labour market, which slows the process by which workers move from declining into expanding sectors.
- Firms may underprovide training in transferable skills because of a possible free-rider effect.
- Unemployment in a market may arise if wages are held above the equilibrium level — because of trade union action, a minimum wage or sluggish adjustment to a fall in demand.
- Geographic immobility may impede the operations of the labour market, if workers are not readily able to move between different parts of the country.
- Occupational immobility may also contribute to the inflexibility of the labour market.

Chapter 8

Market failure and the government and the unions in the labour market

Product markets do not always work perfectly. For example, a firm (or small group of firms) may come to dominate a market and use its market power to increase its supernormal profits to the detriment of the consumer. It has also been shown that some government interventions in product markets do not always have their intended effects. This chapter explores some of the ways in which imperfections can be manifest in labour markets. It also examines the extent to which legislation has been able to outlaw discrimination on the basis of ethnic origin or gender. The role of trade unions in a modern economy is also discussed.

Prior knowledge needed

This chapter builds upon earlier analysis of market failure in Book 1, especially Chapters 7 and 8. These chapters introduced the notion of market failure, which is picked up again here in the context of labour markets.

Learning objectives

After studying this chapter, you should:
- understand ways in which labour markets may be imperfect
- be aware of ways in which governments may cause imperfections in labour markets through their interventions
- understand the role of trade unions in the economy
- understand the effects of trade union activity on the labour market
- understand the nature and causes of inequality in income and wealth

Market failure in labour markets

The previous chapter described features of the UK labour market. However, as with product markets, there are many ways in which labour markets may fail to achieve the most desirable results for society at large. Such market failure can occur on either the demand or the supply side of the market. On the demand side, it may be that employers — as the buyers of labour — have market power that can be exploited at the expense of the workers. Alternatively, it may be that some employers act against the interests of some groups of workers relative to others through some form of discrimination in their hiring practices or wage-setting behaviour. On the supply side, there may be restrictions on the supply of some types of labour, or it may be that trade unions find themselves able to bid wages up to a level that is above the free market equilibrium. In certain situations, government intervention may have unintended effects on labour markets.

Effects of government intervention

Labour markets can be a source of politically sensitive issues. Unemployment has been a prominent indicator of the performance of the economy, and there has been an increasing concern in recent years with issues of health and safety and with ensuring that workers are not exploited by their employers. This has induced governments to introduce a number of measures to provide the institutional setting for the operation of labour markets. However, such measures do not always have their intended effects.

Minimum wage

In its manifesto published before the 1997 election, the Labour Party committed itself to the establishment of the National Minimum Wage (NMW). This would be the first time that such a measure had been used in the UK on a nationwide basis, although **minimum wages** had sometimes been set in particular industries. The level of the NMW depends upon age: in 2014 it was set at £6.50 per hour for those aged 21 or over. The rate was £5.13 for those aged between 18 and 20 and £3.79 for those under 18. Apprentices were guaranteed £2.73 per hour.

The objectives of the minimum wage policy are threefold. First, it is intended to protect workers against exploitation by the small minority of bad employers. Second, it aims to improve incentives to work by ensuring that 'work pays', thereby tackling the problem of voluntary unemployment. Third, it aims to alleviate poverty by raising the living standards of the poorest groups in society.

The policy has been a contentious one, with critics claiming that it meets none of these objectives. It has been argued that the minority of bad employers can still find ways of exploiting their workers: for example, by paying them on a piecework rate so that there is no set wage per hour. Another criticism is that the policy is too indiscriminate to tackle poverty, and that a more sharply focused policy is needed for this purpose. For example, many of the workers receiving the NMW may not in fact belong to poor households, but may be women working part time whose partners are also in employment. But perhaps most contentious of all is the argument that, far from providing a supply-side solution to some unemployment, a National Minimum Wage is causing an increase in unemployment because of its effects on the demand for labour.

First, consider a firm operating in a perfectly competitive market, so that it has to accept the wage that is set in the overall market of which it is a part. In Figure 8.1 the firm's demand curve is represented by its marginal revenue product curve (MRP_L), and in a free market it must accept the equilibrium wage W^*. It thus uses labour up to l^*.

If the government now steps in and imposes a minimum wage, so that the firm cannot set a wage below W_{min}, it will reduce its labour usage to d_{min}, since it will not be profitable to employ labour beyond this point.

This effect will be similar for all the other firms in the market, and the results of this can be seen in Figure 8.2. Now the

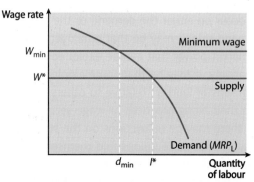

Figure 8.1 The effect of a minimum wage on a firm in a perfectly competitive labour market

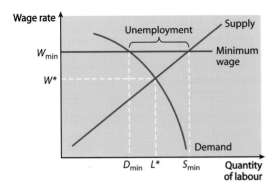

Figure 8.2 The effect of a minimum wage in a perfectly competitive labour market

demand curve is the combined demand of all the firms in the market, and the supply curve of labour is shown as upward sloping, as it is the market supply curve. In free market equilibrium the combined demand of firms in the market is L^*, and W^* emerges as the equilibrium wage rate.

When the government sets the minimum wage at W_{min}, all firms react by reducing their demand for labour at the higher wage. Their combined demand is now D_{min}, but the supply of labour is S_{min}. The difference between these $(S_{min} - D_{min})$ is unemployment. Furthermore, it is involuntary unemployment — these workers would like to work at the going wage rate, but cannot find a job.

Notice that there are two effects at work. Some workers who were formerly employed have lost their jobs — there are $L^* - D_{min}$ of these. In addition, however, the incentive to work is now improved (this was part of the policy objective, remember?), so there are now an additional $S_{min} - L^*$ workers wanting to take employment at the going wage rate. Thus, unemployment has increased for two reasons.

It is not always the case that the introduction of a minimum wage leads to an increase in unemployment. For example, in the market depicted in Figure 8.3 the minimum wage has been set below the equilibrium level, so will have no effect on firms in the market, which will continue to pay W^* and employ L^* workers. At the time of the introduction of the NMW, McDonald's argued that it was in fact already paying a wage above the minimum rate set.

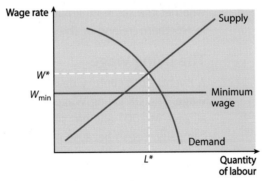

Figure 8.3 A non-binding minimum wage in a perfectly competitive labour market

This is not the only situation in which a minimum wage would *not* lead to unemployment. Suppose that the labour market in question has a monopsony buyer of labour. The firm's situation is shown in Figure 8.4. In the absence of a minimum wage, the firm sets its marginal cost of labour equal to its marginal revenue product, hiring L_0 labour at a wage W_0. A minimum wage introduced at the level W_{min} means that the firm now hires labour up to the point where the wage is equal to the marginal revenue product and, as drawn in Figure 8.4, this takes the market back to the perfectly competitive outcome.

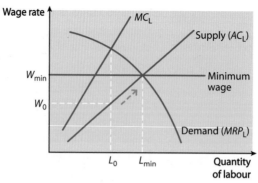

Figure 8.4 A minimum wage with a monopsony buyer of labour

Study tip

It is important to remain aware of the distinction between microeconomics and macroeconomics when discussing labour markets. Much of the discussion in this part of the book is of single labour markets. However, in designing macroeconomic policy it is more natural to think in terms of the labour market as a whole, if only because the headline indicator is the overall level of unemployment. As with the minimum wage, a policy designed at the macro level may not have equal effects across the economy.

Key term

living wage an estimate of how much income households need to afford an acceptable standard of living

Exercise 8.1

Discuss whether making the living wage enforceable would help to alleviate poverty. What other steps could be taken to achieve this objective?

Notice that the authorities would have to be very knowledgeable to set the minimum wage at exactly the right level to produce this outcome. However, any wage between W_0 and W_{min} will encourage the firm to increase its employment to some extent as the policy reduces its market power. Of course, setting the minimum wage above the competitive equilibrium level will again lead to some unemployment. Thus, it is critical to set the wage at the right level if the policy is to succeed in its objectives.

It is also important to remember that there is not just a single labour market in the UK. In fact, it could be questioned whether a single minimum wage set across the whole country could be effective, as it would 'bite' in different ways in different markets. For example, wage levels vary across the regions of the UK, and it must be questioned whether the same minimum wage could be as effective in, say, London as in Northern Ireland or the north of England.

The living wage

A twenty-first century development has been the concept of the **living wage**. The UK Living Wage Campaign was launched by a community alliance in 2001 and has since grown into a national movement. The campaign began because it was seen that the NMW was not providing people with enough funds to live on. The living wage is thus based on a calculation of the basic cost of living in the UK. It is an estimate of how much income households need to afford an acceptable standard of living, calculated by the Centre for Research in Social Policy at Loughborough University.

In 2014, the living wage was set at £9.15 in London and £7.85 in other parts of the country, compared with the NMW at £6.50. The difference between the living wage and the NMW has been growing over time (especially in London).

Unlike the NMW, the living wage has no legal status. However, the campaign for the living wage has been influential in affecting pay levels, particularly by appealing to firms' commitment to corporate social responsibility.

A maximum wage?

The controversy over the bonuses paid to bankers and other top executives has led some commentators to recommend that in addition to setting a minimum wage, the authorities should set a maximum wage, or a wage ceiling. It is argued that this would stem the excesses that characterise executive pay. An argument often put forward in this context is that high salaries and bonuses are needed to provide incentives for effort, but supporters of the maximum wage counter this by saying that the incentive effects are not strong at those levels of pay. This could reflect the diminishing marginal utility of income — the idea that additional increments of income provide less additional utility as incomes rise. It is also likely that attempts to introduce such a measure would be fraught with difficulties. For example, how would the level of the maximum wage be set? And, of course, the political pressures against such a policy would be enormous.

Anger at bankers' bonuses — should the authorities set a maximum wage?

Health and safety regulation

The government intervenes in the labour market through a range of measures designed to improve safety standards in the workplace.

Such regulation can impinge quite heavily on labour markets. One example is the EU Working Time Directive. This aims to protect the health and safety of workers in the European Union by imposing regulations in relation to working hours, rest periods, annual leave and working arrangements for night workers. The legislation came into effect in the UK in October 1998. Exceptions were made for junior doctors in training, for whom the directive was to be phased in gradually. There are some other workers who have signed contracts opting out of the directive. The UK implemented the 48-hour week later than countries elsewhere in Europe because of a special dispensation. Countries elsewhere complained about this, arguing that it gave UK firms an unfair competitive advantage. This seems to suggest that the directive does indeed have an effect on the labour market.

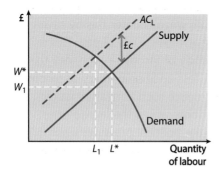

Figure 8.5 The effect of a health and safety regulation in a perfectly competitive market

The effect of these health and safety measures has been to raise the costs to firms of hiring labour. In the case of the Working Time Directive, firms may have to spread the same amount of work over a greater number of workers, and as there are some fixed hiring costs, this raises the cost of labour. Similarly, if firms have to spend more on ensuring safety, it adds to the firms' costs.

Figure 8.5 illustrates one way of viewing the situation. It shows a perfectly competitive labour market for an industry as a whole rather than an individual firm. Without regulation, the market reaches equilibrium with labour employed up to L^* at a wage of W^*. Suppose a health and safety regulation is introduced that adds a constant amount (of £c) to firms' cost per unit of labour employed. Firms then find that the average cost of labour is higher by £c — shown as AC_L in the diagram. They will thus employ labour up to the point where the average cost of labour is equal to the marginal revenue product. (Remember that this is a perfectly competitive labour market, so it is the average cost of labour that is significant in the market: each individual firm perceives this as its marginal cost.) This is at the quantity of labour L_1, and wage is given by W_1, which is the wage that attracts L_1 workers into the market.

The monopsony market could be analysed in a similar fashion, but the effects are comparable — there is a reduction in the amount of labour employed and a fall in the wage rate.

This sort of intervention can be justified by appealing to a merit good argument (which was discussed in Book 1, Chapter 8), which claims that the government knows better than workers what is good for them. Thus, individual workers' decisions about labour supply do not take health and safety sufficiently into account, and the regulation that adds to firms' costs is a way of protecting the workers, given that firms have an incentive to skimp on health and safety in order to keep costs down.

As with other policies, the judgement of the degree of regulation that is required is a difficult one to get right. If governments misjudge the amount of protection that workers need and set c too high, this could lead to lower employment than is optimal.

Some health and safety issues arise from externality effects. For example, firms transporting toxic or other dangerous substances may not face the full costs of their activities because they do not have the incentive to control the risk of affecting individuals. Regulation to enforce the appropriate transportation of such substances is a way of internalising such an externality.

Exercise 8.2

Use Figure 8.6 to explain how the externality effect in the paragraph above comes about.

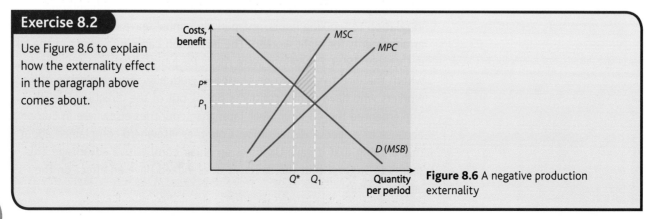

Figure 8.6 A negative production externality

Summary

- Governments have intervened in labour markets to protect low-paid workers, but policies need to be implemented with care because of possible unintended side-effects.
- The Labour government under Tony Blair introduced the National Minimum Wage in 1999.
- In a perfectly competitive labour market, a minimum wage that raises the wage rate above its equilibrium value may lead to an increase in unemployment.
- This is partly because firms reduce their demand for labour, but it also reflects an increased labour supply, as the higher wage is an incentive for more workers to join the market.
- A minimum wage that is set below the equilibrium wage will not be binding.
- A minimum wage established in a monopsony market may have the effect of raising employment.
- Health and safety legislation may help to protect workers, and may be interpreted as an example of a merit good.
- However, it adds to firms' costs, so may reduce employment.
- It is thus important to keep health and safety in perspective, and not overprotect at the expense of lower employment levels.

Trade unions

Key term

trade union an organisation of workers that negotiates with employers on behalf of its members

Trade unions are associations of workers that negotiate with employers on pay and working conditions. Guilds of craftsmen existed in Europe in the Middle Ages, but the formation of workers' trade unions did not become legal in the UK until 1824. In the period following the Second World War, about 40% of the labour force in the UK were members of a trade union. This percentage increased during the 1970s, peaking at about 50%, but since 1980 there has been a steady decline to below 30%.

Trade unions have three major objectives: wage bargaining, the improvement of working conditions, and security of employment for their members. In exploring the effect of the unions on a labour market, it is important to establish whether the unions are in a position to exploit market power and interfere with the proper functioning of the labour market, and also whether they are a necessary balance to the power of employers and thus necessary to protect workers from being exploited.

There have been some changes in the way in which trade unions have engaged in bargaining with employers, with a stronger focus on local agreements and on performance-related pay. In terms of marginal productivity theory, this emphasis on performance makes intuitive sense, as it strengthens the links between workers' productivity and their pay.

There are two ways in which a trade union may seek to affect labour market equilibrium. On the one hand, it may limit the supply of workers into an occupation or industry. On the other hand, it may negotiate successfully for higher wages for its members. It turns out that these two possible strategies have similar effects on market equilibrium.

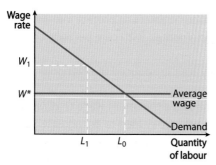

Figure 8.7 A trade union restricts the supply of labour

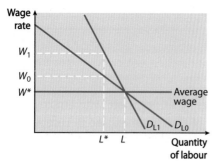

Figure 8.8 The importance of the elasticity of demand for labour

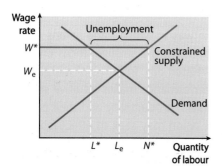

Figure 8.9 A trade union fixes the wage

Restricting labour supply

Figure 8.7 shows the situation facing a firm, with a demand curve for labour based on marginal productivity theory. The average going wage in the economy is given by W^*, so if the firm can obtain workers at that wage, it is prepared to employ up to L_0 labour.

However, if the firm faces a trade union that is limiting the amount of labour available to just L_1, then the union will be able to push the wage up to W_1. This might happen where there is a *closed shop*: in other words, where a firm can employ only those workers who are members of the union. A closed shop allows the union to control how many workers are registered members, and therefore eligible to work in the occupation.

In this situation the union is effectively trading off higher wages for its members against a lower level of employment. The union members who are in work are better off — but those who would have been prepared to work at the lower wage of W^* either are unemployed or have to look elsewhere for jobs. If they are unemployed, this imposes a cost on society. If they are working in a second-choice occupation or industry, this may also impose a social cost, in the sense that they may not be working to their full potential.

The extent of the trade-off depends crucially on the elasticity of demand for labour, as you can see in Figure 8.8. When the demand for labour is relatively more elastic, as shown by D_{L0}, the wage paid by the firm increases to W_0, whereas with the relatively more inelastic demand for labour D_{L1} the wage increases by much more, to W_1.

This makes good intuitive sense. The elasticity of demand is likely to be low in situations where a firm cannot readily substitute capital for labour, where labour forms a small share of total costs, and where the price elasticity of demand for the firm's product is relatively low. If the firm cannot readily substitute capital for labour, the union has a relatively strong bargaining position. If labour costs are a small part of total costs, the firm may be ready to concede a wage increase, as it will have limited overall impact. If the demand for the product is price inelastic, the firm may be able to pass the wage increase on in the form of a higher price for the product without losing large volumes of sales. Thus, these factors improve the union's ability to negotiate a good deal with the employer.

Negotiating wages

A trade union's foremost function can be regarded as negotiating higher wages for its members. Figure 8.9 depicts this situation. In the absence of union negotiation, the equilibrium for the firm is where demand and supply intersect, so the firm hires L_e labour at a wage of W_e.

If the trade union negotiates a wage of W^*, such that the firm cannot hire any labour below that level, this alters the labour supply curve, as shown by the kinked red line. The firm now employs only L^* labour at this wage. So, again, the effect is that the union negotiations result in a trade-off between the amount of labour hired and the wage rate. When the wage is at W^*, unemployment is shown on Figure 8.9 as $N^* - L^*$.

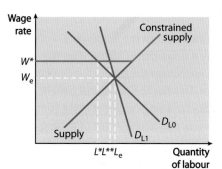

Figure 8.10 The effect of elasticity of demand for labour when the union fixes the wage

The elasticity of demand for labour again affects the outcome, as shown in Figure 8.10. This time, with the relatively more inelastic demand curve D_{L1}, the effect on the quantity of labour employed (falls from L_e to L^{**}) is much less than when demand is relatively more elastic (falls from L_e to L^*).

From the point of view of allocative efficiency, the problem is that trade union intervention in the market may prevent wages from acting as reliable signals to workers and firms, and therefore may lead to a sub-optimal allocation of resources.

Job security

One possible effect of trade union involvement in a firm is that workers will have more job security: in other words, they may become less likely to lose their jobs with the union there to protect their interests.

From the firm's point of view, there may be a positive side to this. If workers feel secure in their jobs, they may be more productive, or more prepared to accept changes in working practices that enable an improvement in productivity.

For this reason, it can be argued that in some situations the presence of a trade union may be beneficial in terms of a firm's efficiency. Indeed, the union may sometimes take over functions that would otherwise be part of the responsibility of the firm's human resource department.

Labour market flexibility

One of the most telling criticisms of trade unions has been that they have affected the degree of flexibility of the labour market. The most obvious manifestation of this is that their actions limit the entry of workers into a market.

This may happen in any firm, where existing workers have better access to information about how the firm is operating, or about forthcoming job vacancies, and so can make sure that their own positions can be safeguarded against newcomers. This is sometimes known as the *insider–outsider* phenomenon. Its effect is strengthened and institutionalised by the presence of a trade union, or by professional bodies such as the Royal College of Surgeons.

This and other barriers to entry erected by a trade union can limit the effectiveness and flexibility of labour markets by making it more difficult for firms to adapt to changing market conditions.

Asymmetric information and the labour market

Book 1, Chapter 8 introduced the problem of asymmetric information, where market failure can arise because some traders in a market have better information than others. This can happen in labour markets too.

The issue arises from the employer's perspective. When an employer is hiring new workers, a key concern is the quality of the workers applying for jobs. This is partly a question about their innate talents and abilities. It can be overcome to some extent by checking applicants' qualifications; indeed, this is why employers may insist on qualifications, even if they are not directly related to the requirements of the job.

However, there are other differences between workers that are important. Two workers with the same qualifications may show very different productivity. Some workers are naturally hardworking and conscientious, whereas others are always taking rest breaks and getting away with as little effort as possible. At the hiring stage, the employer may not be able to distinguish between the 'workers' and the 'shirkers'.

Suppose a firm pays a wage that is the average warranted by workers and shirkers combined. As time goes by, some workers are likely to quit and go to higher-paid jobs with other firms. The employees who are most likely to leave are the more productive ones, who realise that, if they are paid the average of what is right for the workers and shirkers taken together, they are being paid less than their own value. In the long run, the employer could be left with just the shirkers.

A rational response to this from the employer's perspective is to pay a wage that is higher than the average, in order to encourage the productive workers to stay with the firm. This has the additional benefit of increasing the penalty for being caught shirking (since a worker faces a greater opportunity cost of getting the sack if wages are higher). Thus, paying a higher-than-average wage has an additional incentive effect in that it discourages shirking.

This higher-than-average wage is known as the *efficiency wage*, and can be seen as a response by firms to the asymmetric information problem. One of the results in the labour market is to raise the level of involuntary unemployment, in the sense that at the higher wage there will be an increase in the number of workers who would be prepared to accept a job, but are unable to find employment.

Summary

- Trade unions exist to negotiate for their members on pay, working conditions and job security.
- If trade unions restrict labour supply, or negotiate wages that are above the market equilibrium, the net effect is a trade-off between wages and employment.
- Those who remain in work receive higher pay, but at the expense of other workers who either have become unemployed or work in second-choice occupations or industries.
- However, by improving job security, unions may make workers more prepared to accept changes in working practices that lead to productivity gains.
- Barriers to the entry and exit of workers may reduce firms' flexibility to adapt to changing market conditions.

Flexibility and unemployment

What makes for a flexible labour market? At the microeconomic level, where a prime concern is with achieving a good allocation of resources for society, the issue is whether workers can transfer readily between activities to allow resource allocation to change through time. This requires a number of conditions to be met. Workers need to have information about what jobs are available (and, perhaps, where those jobs are available), and what skills are needed for those jobs. Employers need to be able to identify workers with the skills and talents that they need. If workers cannot find the jobs that are available, or do not have the appropriate skills to undertake those jobs, the market will not function smoothly. Similarly, if employers cannot identify the workers with the skills that they need, that too will impede the working of the market.

Arguably, the problem has become acute in recent years, with a change in the balance of jobs between skilled and unskilled workers. As the economy gears up to more hi-tech activities, and low-skill jobs are outsourced or relocated to other countries, the need for workers to acquire the right skills becomes ever more pressing.

It could be argued that the rate of unemployment is indicative of the extent of flexibility in the labour market. Periods of prolonged unemployment may be suggestive of a slow adjustment to equilibrium because the labour market is insufficiently flexible. The overall unemployment rate in the UK since 1971 is presented in Figure 8.11, using the ILO measure.

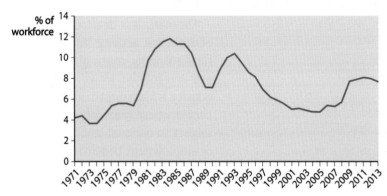

Figure 8.11 Unemployment in the UK since 1971

Synoptic link

Unemployment in the UK was discussed in Book 1, Chapter 11, and Figure 8.11 is included here as a reminder. The question of whether the economy will return rapidly to equilibrium will be discussed in the macroeconomic section of this book, in Chapter 15.

The large swings in unemployment that are visible on the graph are due to a number of causes. The large increase in the early 1980s reflected in part a change in the emphasis of economic policy. There was a new determination to bring inflation under control using monetary policy, whereas in earlier periods the government had been more concerned about achieving full employment. However, other things were happening as well. North Sea oil came on stream just before the second oil price crisis of 1979–80, a net effect of which was a loss in competitiveness of UK goods, which led to a decline in the manufacturing sector in the 1980s. There were also changes in the demographic structure of the population, which will be taken up at the end of the chapter.

The reduction in unemployment in the late 1980s was associated with what has come to be known as the 'Lawson boom', a period of relatively loose monetary policy that was followed by a severe recession in which unemployment rose again. But perhaps the most striking aspect of Figure 8.11 is the period after 1993, which showed a steady decline in the unemployment rate and a much steadier pattern until the end of 2008 when recession began to bite and unemployment started to increase again.

Informal labour markets

Key term

informal labour market
economic activity that is not
registered or recorded, and
so is not part of the formal
labour market

One way in which people cope with unemployment or low pay is by finding ways of generating income without actually taking a job or becoming formally self-employed: for example, by moonlighting or doing odd jobs without declaring the income. In other words, they join the **informal labour market**. The activities undertaken in this sector may involve the evasion of taxes or regulation, and are more likely to be in the service sector than in manufacturing. This is because the authorities may find it more difficult to identify where individuals are undertaking child care or motor vehicle repairs than if they are manufacturing furniture or computers. However, there are also likely to be activities being undertaken which are simply illegal, such as drug dealing and prostitution.

By its very nature, the extent of such activity is difficult to measure. However, European Social Survey data suggest that in the late 2000s, about one out of six employed persons in Europe was holding an informal main job. Estimates for the UK range between 10 and 13% of GDP, lower than the average for advanced countries, but still significant.

For many less developed countries, the informal sector is a vital part of economic activity. Where subsistence agriculture is a key part of the rural economy, much of the production that takes place is informal and unregulated. However, even in the non-agricultural sector, informal activity is widespread. In this context, the informal sector includes people whose main job is informal, which means that they are not subject to national labour legislation, income taxation, social protection or employment benefits such as notice of dismissal, annual leave or severance pay. Figure 8.12 shows some estimates of the size of the informal economy in non-agricultural activities in selected countries.

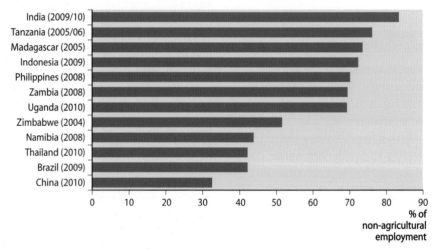

Source: ILO Department of Statistics, June 2012

Figure 8.12 Employment in the informal economy in non-agricultural activities, selected countries (latest year available)

The sheer size of the informal sector underlines its importance for these economies. The existence of the sector creates a dilemma for the authorities. On the one hand, it may be tempting to formalise the enterprises by bringing them into the regulatory framework. This would have advantages in providing some protection for vulnerable people and bringing them into taxation. On the other hand, informal sector employment is encouraging enterprise. By seeking to regulate such activity, it could be suppressed.

Policies to improve the flexibility of the labour market

If it is so important for labour markets to be flexible, what steps could be taken to promote flexibility? A number of obstacles to flexibility have been identified in this chapter and the previous one. To what extent are these amenable to policy intervention?

Training, skills and information

The process of structural change in an economy may be impeded if the people looking for work, perhaps because they have been released from a declining sector, do not have the requisite skills for the sectors that are expanding. It is also important for unemployed workers to have good information about the jobs available.

The 1997 Labour government launched a package of policy measures known as the New Deal, which was aimed at reducing long-term unemployment. These measures were aimed at three age groups, responding to the fact that youth unemployment was perceived as a particular problem. Young people aged 18–24 years old who had been unemployed for a period of more than 6 months were to be assigned a personal adviser to provide them with information about available jobs and contacts with potential employers. If they were still without a job after a further 4 months, they would either enter a year of full-time education or training; or take up a job with the voluntary sector or the environmental task force for 6 months; or go into subsidised employment which would include on-the-job training. Similar targeted programmes were provided for the older age groups.

Such measures are designed to improve the flexibility of the labour market, by providing unemployed workers with information and skills training. Furthermore, employers receive a subsidy to take on workers, who can then be observed in the workplace, which provides a better insight into their potential than any interview or other screening process.

The New Deal provided training, subsidised employment and voluntary work to the unemployed

Trade union reform

As we have seen, by negotiating for a wage that is above the equilibrium level, trade unions may trade off higher wages for lower levels of employment. The potential disruption caused by strike action can also impede the workings of a labour market.

Some indication of this disruption can be seen in Figure 8.13. Clearly, compared with the 1970s and 1980s, the amount of disruption through strikes in recent years has been very low, although even the 1979 figure pales into insignificance beside the 162 million working days lost in the General Strike of 1926. In fact, however, the 1970s and 1980s were a tempestuous period, in which trade union action severely disrupted UK industry. So why has life become so much quieter?

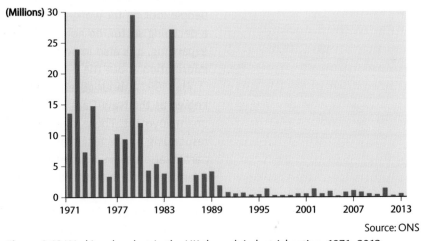

Source: ONS

Figure 8.13 Working days lost in the UK through industrial action, 1971–2013

It is perhaps no surprise that unions should have worked hard to protect their members during the 1980s, when unemployment was soaring and the Thatcher government was determined to control inflation — including inflation of wages. Legislation was introduced in the early 1980s to begin to reform the trade unions, and after the highly disruptive miners' strike ended in 1985, the government introduced a number of further reforms designed to curb the power of the trade unions, making it more difficult for them to call rapid strike action. For example, secret ballots were to be required before strike action could be taken. This may help to explain why trade union membership has been in decline since the 1980s. By weakening the power of trade unions in this way, some labour market inflexibility has been removed.

Another factor may have been changes in the structure of economic activity during this period. Manufacturing employment was falling, whereas the service sectors were expanding. Traditionally, union membership has been higher among workers in the manufacturing sector than in services.

Regional policy

There have always been differences in average incomes and in unemployment rates between the various regions of the UK. In broad terms, there are two possible responses to this — either persuade workers to move to regions where there are more jobs, or persuade the firms to move to areas where labour is plentiful. Each of these solutions poses problems. Housing markets limit the mobility of workers, and it is costly for firms to relocate their activities.

The regions most affected in the past were those that specialised in industries that subsequently went into decline: for example, coal mining areas or towns and regions dominated by cotton mills. In a broad context, it is desirable for the economy to undergo structural change as the pattern of international comparative advantage changes, but this is painful during the transition period. Thus, successive governments have implemented regional policies to try to cope with the problems experienced in areas of high unemployment.

At the same time, the booming regions can be affected by the opposite problem — a shortage of labour. Thus, measures have been taken to encourage firms to consider relocating to regions where labour is available. These have included leading by example, with some civil service functions being moved out of London.

EU funding has helped in this regard, with Scotland, Wales and Northern Ireland all qualifying for grants. Between 1999 and 2012, Regional Development Agencies (RDAs) set up by the Labour government had responsibility for promoting economic development in their regions. There were nine of these agencies covering the country. Although differentials have narrowed, it is difficult to know how much of this narrowing can be attributed to the success of regional policy. It has also been pointed out that there are some areas that have been receiving regional aid for more than 70 years, but are still disadvantaged, so it is difficult to argue that regional policy has had outstanding success. The RDAs were abolished as part of government efforts to reduce the budget deficit, and ceased operating in March 2012.

Technology and unemployment

One of the greatest fallacies perpetuated by non-economists is that technology destroys jobs. Bands of labourers known as Luddites rioted between 1811 and 1816, destroying textile machines, which they blamed for high unemployment and low wages. In the twenty-first century there is a strong lobbying group in the USA arguing that outsourcing and cheap labour in China are destroying US jobs.

In fact, new technology and an expansion in the capital stock should have beneficial effects — so long as labour markets are sufficiently flexible. Consider a market in which new technology is introduced. If firms in an industry invest in technology and expand the capital stock, this affects the marginal revenue product of labour and hence the demand for labour, as shown in Figure 8.14, where demand shifts from D_1 to D_2. In this market, the effect is to raise the wage rate from W_1 to W_2 and the employment level from L_1 to L_2.

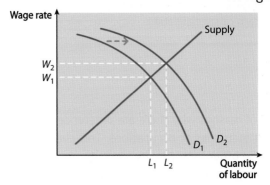

Figure 8.14 An increase in capital

However, it is important to look beyond what happens in a single market, as the argument is that it is all very well expanding employment in the technology sector — but what about the old industries that are in decline? Suppose the new industries absorb less labour than is discarded by the old declining industries? After all, if the effect of technology is to allow call centres to create jobs in India at the expense of the USA or the UK, does this not harm employment in those countries?

The counter-argument to this lies in the notion of the gains from specialisation introduced in Book 1, Chapter 1. This argues that countries can gain from international trade through specialising in certain activities. Setting up call centres in India frees UK workers to work in sectors in which the UK has a comparative advantage, with the result that the UK can import (and thus consume) more labour-intensive goods than before.

There is one proviso, of course. It is important that the workers released from the declining sectors have (or can obtain) the skills that are needed for them to be absorbed into the expanding sectors. This recalls the question of whether the labour market is sufficiently flexible to allow the structure of economic activity to adapt to changes in the pattern of comparative advantage. However, it also serves as a reminder that policy should be aimed at enabling that flexibility, and not at introducing protectionist measures to reduce trade, which would be damaging overall for the economy.

Summary

- An important factor influencing the rate of unemployment is the degree of flexibility in labour markets.
- The New Deal was a package of measures introduced with the objective of reducing long-term unemployment, through providing information to jobseekers and training.
- Trade union reforms were introduced during the 1980s and have contributed to flexibility in labour markets.
- Regional policy has attempted to reduce the differentials in unemployment rates between the regions of the UK.
- Adjustment in labour markets is needed in order to cope with the changing international pattern of specialisation.

Inequality of income and wealth

Chapter 7 identified a number of reasons why there are differences in pay between individuals in different industries or occupations. This chapter has also noted that there may be other reasons why some groups in society, such as trade union members, are paid at different rates. To what extent might this be considered a form of market failure?

Marginal productivity theory suggests that an important underlying cause of differences in pay is the differing marginal productivity of individual workers, who have different skills and abilities. To this extent, inequalities in income may be justified in terms of economic analysis. However, if differences in income arise from discrimination or the operation of trade unions in the labour market, this could be seen as a form of market failure, being unjustified by economic analysis. If females are paid less for undertaking the same work simply because of their gender, this may be seen as a form of market distortion. In addition, there may be those in society whose medical condition prevents them from earning.

Different households or groups in society may have different degrees of access to resources, which may then affect their income-earning potential. This is especially apparent in some less developed countries, where some people may not have access to education, healthcare or clean water. Furthermore, it may be that some jobs are only open to those people lucky enough to have good connections.

It is important to be aware of the distinction between income and wealth. Income is the *flow* of wages and other income in a period, whereas wealth is the *stock* of accumulated assets. If an individual saves part of his or her income, this accumulates as wealth. However, wealth may also come from other sources — in particular, from legacies. Differences in the distribution of wealth can also lead to differences in income, insofar as wealth generates a flow of income in the form of interest and dividend payments.

Inequality in the distribution of income and wealth may be significant in society if it becomes excessive, or if there are households and individuals who become vulnerable because of low income and wealth. A sense of social justice suggests that the vulnerable groups in society should be protected, and that the effects of discrimination should be addressed.

In the UK, the government uses its fiscal policy to affect the distribution of income, through the use of taxation and transfer payments that help to provide some social security for vulnerable groups. This will be discussed further in Chapter 12.

Exercise 8.4

Discuss the extent to which differences in earnings in the UK economy reflect differences in marginal productivity as opposed to the effects of discrimination or access to resources.

Synoptic link

Inequality may also have macroeconomic effects. Chapter 12 will consider the topic in a macroeconomic perspective, explaining how inequality can be identified, and its relationship with poverty.

Summary

- Differences in income between individuals may arise because of differences in marginal productivity, reflecting differences in skills and abilities.
- Discrimination or the restrictive practices of trade unions may also lead to inequalities in income.
- Further differences may arise from differences in access to resources.
- Differences in the distribution of wealth may feed back to exacerbate differences in income.
- Where differences arise from a form of market failure, it may be necessary for governments to intervene to protect certain groups in society.
- In the UK, taxation and benefit payments are used to influence the distribution of income and of wealth.

Working informally

In many developing countries, the majority of people are active in the informal sector, working without a written contract for unregistered private enterprises in jobs that generally lack basic social or legal protections or employment benefits. Informal employment includes both self-employed people — for instance, own-account workers or micro-entrepreneurs — and employees. Besides regular informal employees, there are casual day labourers: that is, wage workers without a fixed employer, particularly present in agriculture and construction. Somewhere in between the employee/self-employed distinction, there are the so-called industrial outworkers or home-workers, people usually working on a piece-rate basis (for instance, sewing garments) for an employer or an intermediary, without direct supervision and owning the means of production.

To make ends meet, many informal workers hold multiple occupations and engage in multiple activities on a daily basis or across the year. For instance, women may be selling pancakes in front of their houses during the morning hours and then, once the demand for breakfast dries up, switch to stitching and selling garments for the rest of the day. This diversification may be beneficial in that it reduces the risks associated with fluctuating demand or input prices. However, it also results in a lack of specialisation and of economies of scale, thereby reducing productivity.

Why do workers and firms operate in the informal economy? One view is that they are excluded from the formal economy and stay in the informal one to make a living; another view is that they actually choose to operate informally, even if they would have the opportunity to be formal.

The informal economy may be seen as a form of exclusion, acting as a sort of 'workplace of last resort' for workers who cannot afford to stay unemployed. However, even if they are active in the informal economy, people may still be underemployed, working just occasionally, when the opportunity arises. Firms may also be excluded from the formal economy if they

In many developing countries, the majority of people are active in the informal sector

are not able to afford the costs associated with the formal sector — for instance, costs related to taxation and compliance with regulations.

Informality may be seen as a choice in some situations. Informal firms are not necessarily on the verge of closure due to low productivity or throat-cutting competition. They may well be dynamic micro-enterprises that choose informality to avoid paying the costs associated with formal registration — both the monetary costs and the costs in terms of time or effort needed to deal with the bureaucracy. Thus, with a reduction in these costs, firms would regularise and, at least potentially, thrive in the formal sector by taking advantage of the benefits associated with official status, such as secure property rights and access to credit.

The policy response towards firms in the informal sector depends on whether they are there because of exclusion or because of choice. In the former case, increasing the productivity of firms should be the main focus. When firms are informal because of choice, the strategy usually proposed is a mix of 'carrot and stick', in which the carrot relates to lower costs of formalisation — for instance, through a simplification of the administrative procedures required to register a firm — while the stick is stronger enforcement of regulation.

Source: based on an article by Mirco Tonin that appeared in *Economic Review*, September 2012

Follow-up questions

a Discuss the distinction drawn in the passage between exclusion and choice as explaining the persistence of the informal sector in developing countries.

b Suggest some policies that the authorities could introduce to deal with the informal sector. Should these be designed to encourage or to suppress the sector?

MICROECONOMICS

Part 4
Market failure and government intervention

Chapter 9

The environment

This part of the book explores aspects of market failure and government intervention, building upon the coverage of market failure in Book 1, Chapters 7 to 9. The first chapter of this part of the book analyses how market failure may affect the environment in which we live. This is an important issue for societies around the world, and a good example of how economic analysis can be applied to help us to understand real-world issues. Chapter 10 looks at some key ways in which governments intervene in markets.

Learning objectives

After studying this chapter, you should:
- be familiar with the three functions of the environment — to supply resources and amenities, and to act as an absorber of waste
- be able to apply the concept of externalities in the context of production and consumption effects on the environment
- be aware of why there may be a relationship between the level of development in an economy and the quality of the environment
- be familiar with the relationship between economic growth and the environment
- be able to analyse environmental policies

Prior knowledge needed

In tackling this chapter, you may wish to remind yourself of key concepts that will be used. Externalities are at the heart of much discussion of the environment — these were discussed in Book 1, Chapter 7. Reference is also made to the circular flow of income, expenditure and output, which was introduced in Book 1, Chapter 13.

Functions of the environment

Book 1, Chapter 1 discussed the factors of production, identifying the various inputs into the production process. These included natural resources, both renewable and non-renewable. The examples mentioned were forests, oil and coal, which, of course, are all closely related to the environment. However, the environment is more complex than being simply a provider of inputs for the production process. Figure 9.1 identifies three crucial functions of the environment in today's world.

Figure 9.1 Three functions of the environment

Resources

One important function of the environment is to supply resources that are required in the production process. Firms need energy as an input to production, in the form of oil, natural gas, electricity, etc. Notice that electricity can be generated by a range of processes, using either renewable methods from wind farms or non-renewable methods based on coal or oil. This important distinction will be explored soon.

Amenities

The environment also supplies amenities to households. People get utility from visiting a pleasant clean beach, walking in the woods or playing the park. Enjoying clean air and living in a pleasant location contributes to people's quality of life. The provision of amenities is therefore an important function that the environment fulfils.

Absorber of waste

Perhaps less often noticed is the third function that the environment provides, as an absorber of waste. Firms and households generate waste, which somehow has to be absorbed. The environment is crucial in the process of waste disposal.

Sustainability?

Figure 9.1 illustrates the situation. The environment provides inputs for firms in the form of natural resources and amenities to households. Both firms and households generate waste. Firms and households interact with each other, as was captured in the circular flow of income, expenditure and output, which was set out in Book 1, Chapter 13. As part of the circular flow, households supply their factors services such as labour to firms in return for income, which households can then use to purchase goods and services from firms.

A key issue to be explored is whether this process is sustainable in the long run. In other words, does the environment have the capacity to support the three functions indefinitely? To what extent can the environment continue to supply the natural resources that firms need to produce? To what extent can the amenities provided by the environment be conserved for the future? Does the absorption of waste cause damage to the environment that will affect its capacity to continue to provide resources and amenities in the future? These questions are some of the most important facing the global economy, and will be explored in this chapter using economic analysis.

Sustainable development was defined in Book 1, Chapter 12 as 'development that meets the needs of the present without compromising the ability of future generations to meet their own needs'. This argues that society should not use up all its resources for current consumption without taking into account the needs of future generations.

Another way of expressing the definition of sustainable development is to say that the stock of capital should not decline over time. In other words, generations in the future should inherit a stock of resources that enables them to enjoy at least as high a quality of life as that enjoyed by today's generation.

The environment acts as an absorber of waste, but how sustainable is this process?

Synoptic link

Notice that the notion of sustainable development is important when considering economic growth in macroeconomics. This was discussed briefly in Book 1, Chapter 12 and will reappear (again briefly) in Chapter 11 of this book, especially in Case study 11.1.

Extension material

Weak and strong sustainability

If we want to be more explicit about what is meant by saying that the stock of capital should not decline over time, we need to be more explicit about what is meant by 'capital' in this context. In economic analysis, the focus is normally on three types of capital — financial capital, manufactured capital and human capital. However, it could be argued that consideration should also be given to two other forms of capital: namely, social capital and natural capital. *Social capital* refers to the way in which society works, through the strength of institutions, the way in which people collaborate and provide mutual support, and the networks connecting people. *Natural capital* refers to the stock of natural assets, including the earth's geology, soil, air, water and all living things.

A weak view of sustainability is that the total stock of capital should not decline over time, which implies that a decrease in natural capital can be compensated by an increase in manufactured or human capital. A stronger view of sustainability would argue that there should be no decline in natural capital. This approach would suggest, for example, that the benefits from exploiting non-renewable resources should be partly devoted to investment that ensures that a renewable substitute is available at the point when the non-renewable resource reaches depletion.

Study tip

Issues around the environment can arouse strong views, and may draw you into making normative judgements, rather than remaining objective and focusing on positive analysis. In responding to questions, make sure your discussion is based on economic analysis, and not on your own personal value judgements.

Summary

- The environment fulfils three key functions in today's world.
- The environment provides resources needed in the production process and amenities for households.
- It also has a role in absorbing the waste produced by firms and households.
- Sustainability is a key issue in this context — can the environment continue to fulfil these three functions in the long term?

Externalities and the environment

Key term

externality a cost or a benefit that is external to a market transaction, borne (or enjoyed) by a third party, and not reflected in market prices

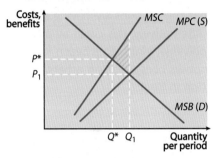

Figure 9.2 A negative production externality

Externalities arise in situations where there are items of cost or benefit associated with transactions, and these are not reflected in market prices, and thus affect third parties to the transaction. In these circumstances a free market will not lead to an optimum allocation of resources.

A production externality

Figure 9.2 shows the effect of a production externality in a market. Here, *MSB (D)* represents the market demand curve for a good, and *MPC (S)* represents the marginal private costs faced by firms in the industry, and the market supply curve in a competitive market. The market equilibrium is at Q_1, where demand equals supply. However, suppose there is a negative production externality present — perhaps the firms in the market cause pollution of some kind. This implies that the marginal social cost (*MSC*) is higher than *MPC*, so the best position for society would be at Q^*. In the presence of the externality, too much of this good is supplied, and there is a welfare cost imposed on society, given by the shaded area in the figure. This is an example of market failure.

> ### Quantitative skills 9.1
>
> **Interpreting areas on diagrams (a reminder)**
> Why does the shaded area represent the welfare cost imposed on society by the externality? Note that Q^* represents the best position for society, where *MSB = MSC*, but the free market outcome is at Q_1. Between these two levels of output, marginal social cost exceeds marginal private cost because of the externality. For every unit of output in this range, a cost is imposed on society given by the vertical distance by which *MSC* exceeds *MPC*. The sum of all those differences is the total welfare cost resulting from the externality, which is the shaded triangle.

Note that the optimum position is not characterised by *zero* pollution. In other words, from society's point of view it pays to abate pollution only *up to* the level where the marginal benefit of reducing pollution is matched by the marginal cost of doing so. Reducing pollution to zero would be too costly.

A consumption externality

Figure 9.3 shows the effect of a consumption externality in a market. In the figure, you can see that marginal social benefit (*MSB*) is higher than marginal social benefit (*MSC*), so in a free market, equilibrium will occur at Q_2, although the optimum position for society would be at Q^*. In other words, there is a positive consumption externality.

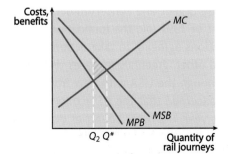

Figure 9.3 A positive consumption externality

An example might be journeys undertaken by rail. When people choose to travel by rail instead of using their cars, or when firms choose rail transport over road, they gain benefits. For example, an individual going to a meeting can sit on a train and read a book or do some work — and avoid the stress of driving. These are the private benefits from taking the train. However, there are benefits to society as well, because using the train eases congestion on the roads and reduces the pollution caused by traffic fumes. Hence there is a positive consumption externality, with marginal social benefits being higher than marginal private benefits. In this case, the market failure results in the consumption of too little of the good (i.e. too few rail journeys).

Remember that one of the functions of the environment is to provide amenities to consumers. A possible market failure that could arise here is where so many people flock to a beach or historical site that it becomes congested, perhaps to the extent that the site itself becomes subject to damage. For example, it could be that popular paths across the hills become worn out. One way of interpreting this sort of situation is that people do not appreciate the impact that their actions are having on what may seem to be a free resource. Alternatively, this could be another example of an externality, where the individual visitor to a beach faces the average cost of congestion, but also imposes congestion on others. This parallels the discussion of road congestion in Book 1.

The NIMBY syndrome

Exercise 9.1

You discover that your local authority has chosen to locate a wind farm close to your home. What costs and benefits for society would result? Would these differ from your private costs and benefits? Would you object?

One problem that arises in trying to deal with externalities is that you cannot please all of the people all of the time. For example, it may well be that it is in society's overall interests to relocate unsightly facilities — it may even be that everyone would agree about this; but such facilities have to be located somewhere, and someone is almost bound to object because they are the ones to suffer. This is the **NIMBY (not in my back yard)** syndrome.

For example, many people would agree that it is desirable for the long-run sustainability of the economy that cleaner forms of energy are developed. One possibility is to build wind farms. People may well be happy for these to be constructed — *as long as* they do not happen to be living near them. This may not be the best example, however, as the effectiveness of wind farms is by no means proven, and there is a strong movement against their use on these grounds.

International considerations

Externalities that cross international boundaries cause particularly difficult problems. Economic activity carried out in one country can have externality effects on people and firms located in neighbouring countries — and further afield in some cases.

Global warming and climate change

Global warming is widely seen to require urgent and concerted action at a worldwide level. The Kyoto summit of 1997 laid the foundations for action, with many of the developed nations agreeing to take action to reduce emissions of carbon dioxide and other 'greenhouse' gases that are seen to be causing climate change. Although the USA withdrew from the agreement in early 2001, apparently concerned that the US economy might be harmed, in November of that year 178 other countries did reach agreement on how to enforce the Kyoto Accord. The absence of US cooperation was potentially significant, however, as the USA was the world's largest emitter of carbon dioxide, responsible for about a quarter of the world's greenhouse gas emissions.

At the heart of the Kyoto Accord was the decision of countries to reduce their greenhouse gas emissions by an agreed percentage by 2010. The method chosen to achieve these targets was based on a tradable pollution permit system. This was seen to be especially demanding for countries such as Japan, whose industry is already relatively energy-efficient. Japan was thus concerned that there should be sufficient permits available for purchase. More explicitly, it was concerned that sloppy compliance by Russia would limit the amount of permits on offer. The issues of monitoring and compliance were thus seen as critical.

Further summit meetings were held to try to maintain the Kyoto protocol, which appeared to have been salvaged in Doha in 2012. Some progress was made, but countries such as the USA, Canada and Japan remained sceptical, and China is reluctant to negotiate beyond Kyoto. This is significant, as China has been experiencing such rapid economic growth. The effect of this is shown in Figure 9.4, which shows carbon dioxide emissions of China, the USA, India and the EU since 1960. The dramatic rise in emissions in China after 2002 is very clear.

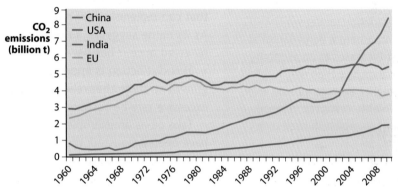

Figure 9.4 Carbon dioxide emissions, selected countries, 1960–2010

Source: World Bank

Exercise 9.2

Use the internet to find out whether further progress has been made to tackle climate change.

Summary

- The presence of externalities in production and consumption results in market failure.
- This can affect the ability of the environment to fulfil its three functions in the short and long run.
- Externalities can cross international boundaries, causing particular problems.

The environment and economic growth

Synoptic link

Economic growth will be discussed in the macroeconomics section of this book in Chapter 11.

An important consideration is whether economic growth can be sustainable — in the sense that was introduced early in the chapter. How will the process of economic growth affect the environment?

One argument that has been advanced is that, as a society begins to take off in terms of economic growth, there is likely to be some degradation of the environment. Industry begins to expand, but may be relying on inefficient technology for the production process. As household incomes rise, there is an increase in demand for car ownership,

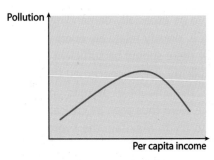

Figure 9.5 The environmental Kuznets curve

Key terms

environmental Kuznets curve
a relationship between economic growth and environmental degradation, under which environmental degradation at first increases as an economy expands, but then may improve at higher average income levels

renewable resource a resource that can replenish itself over time

non-renewable resource
a resource that cannot be renewed once its supply is exhausted

or for other goods that make demands on the environment. There is also likely to be an increased need for waste disposal, which also puts pressure on the environment. This approach suggests that pollution and environmental degradation will increase as growth takes off.

However, as the economy continues to expand, businesses may be able to adopt cleaner and more efficient production technology, and the pace of growth in demand for car ownership may slow. It is also possible for the government to devote resources to protecting the environment, once the pressure to alleviate poverty diminishes. This suggests that there will come a point at which the rate of pollution will begin to drop.

These arguments suggest that the relationship between pollution and per capita incomes may follow an inverted U-shape, sometimes known as the **environmental Kuznets curve**, as depicted in Figure 9.5.

Renewable and non-renewable resources

An important consideration in evaluating the impact of economic growth on the environment is bound up with the distinction between renewable and non-renewable resources. A **renewable resource** is one that can replenish itself naturally over time, such as forests, water or air. As its name suggests, a **non-renewable resource** is one that cannot be renewed once it has been used, such as coal, gas or minerals.

This distinction is important when discussing sustainability. Can a growth strategy that relies on using up non-renewable resources at an excessive rate be sustainable in the long run?

Take oil as an example. Reserves of oil are finite, and once all reserves have been exhausted, they cannot be renewed. From an economic analysis point of view, it might be argued that the market mechanism will help to cope with this problem. As reserves become depleted, the cost of extracting the oil rises, and market prices will rise. As market prices rise, it becomes profitable to exploit less accessible reserves, or to extract oil from shale. It also becomes more profitable to develop alternative sources of energy. In this way the market mechanism may guide the economy towards alternative energy sources. The key issue then becomes the pace at which remaining reserves are being exhausted, and whether the alternative sources can be developed sufficiently quickly to meet market demand, or whether some form of intervention is needed to encourage the research and development of new renewable sources of energy.

However, this is not the complete picture because there are externality effects of relying on oil as an energy source. These come through the impact of energy use on climate change. In addition, the rapid economic growth that has been experienced by countries like China and India in recent years has vastly increased the demand for energy, so that the rate at which resources are being depleted has increased.

Renewable resources are not without their own problems. In principle, forests are renewable, given careful planting and restocking. Here again, however, the rate of usage can intervene. If deforestation proceeds at too rapid a rate, the forests may cease to be renewable. Fish stocks are potentially renewable, but over-fishing of some species may mean extinction.

The tragedy of the commons

Can economic analysis help us to understand why such behaviour should occur? In other words, can we explain why over-fishing should take place? One approach looks at the impact of property rights. This has become known as the *tragedy of the commons*.

To illustrate this phenomenon, consider a village in which the land (or certain plots of land) are owned communally by the inhabitants of the village. There are many English place names that betray the existence of this in the past — such as Wimbledon Common, for example.

Suppose there is a plot of land on which any resident of the village can graze cattle. When the number of cattle is small, this probably works very well, but as more and more people graze their cattle — and own more cattle to graze — the quality of grazing begins to decline, raising costs for everyone, in the sense that it takes longer for cattle to find enough grazing to sustain them. The marginal entrant adding an extra cow to the grazing faces the average cost, but also imposes higher costs on all existing herdspeople. There is an externality present, and the land may be grazed until it is no longer productive.

The problem arises not only because of the externality, but because of the characteristics of the good. The grazing land in the example is rivalrous, but not excludable, because the property rights in the land are shared amongst the villagers, and each has an incentive to consume the good regardless of the impact on others in the long run.

Extension material

Four types of good

The winner of the Nobel Prize for Economic Sciences in 2009 was Elinor Ostrom. She noted that we can identify four types of good based on two key characteristics of a good: namely, its non-rivalry and non-excludability. The four goods are summarised in Table 9.1, which shows a matrix of possibilities.

Table 9.1 Four types of good

		Non-rivalrous	
		High	Low
Non-excludable	High	Public goods	Commons
	Low	Club goods	Private goods

In the top left-hand corner are goods that are both non-rivalrous and non-excludable. From Book 1, Chapter 8 you should recognise such goods as being *public goods*. In the bottom right are goods that are low on both dimensions: these are *private goods*. A private good (such as a burger) is low in non-excludability because once you own the good you can prevent others from consuming it, and rivalrous because once you have consumed it, nobody else can do so.

Club goods (in the bottom left) are non-rivalrous but excludable. An example would be a jazz club. Here, the music is non-rivalrous, in the sense that one person's listening to the music does not leave any less for anybody else. However, it is excludable in the sense that only members of the club can gain entry to the performance.

The tragedy of the commons arises for goods that are rivalrous but not excludable.

Property rights

The existence of a system of secure property rights is an essential underpinning for the economy. The legal system exists in part to enforce property rights, and to provide the set of rules under which markets operate. When property rights fail, there is a failure of markets.

One of the reasons underlying the existence of some externalities is that there is a failing in the system of property rights. For example, think about the situation in which a factory is emitting toxic fumes into a residential district. One way of viewing this is that the firm is interfering with local residents' clean air. If those residents could be given property rights over clean air, they could require the firm to compensate them for the costs it was inflicting. However, the problem is that, with such a wide range of people being affected to varying degrees (according to prevailing winds and how close they live to the factory), it is impossible in practical terms to use the assignment of property rights to internalise the pollution externality. This is because the problem of coordination requires high transaction costs in order for property rights to be individually enforced. Therefore, the government effectively takes over the property rights on behalf of the residents, and acts as a collective enforcer.

Nobel prize winner Ronald Coase argued in 1991 that externality effects could be internalised in conditions where property rights could be enforced, and where the transaction costs of doing so were not too large.

Summary

- Economic growth can have a significant impact on the environment.
- The environmental Kuznets curve suggests that there may be a relationship over time between the level of per capita incomes in a country and the state of the environment.
- The distinction between renewable and non-renewable resources is important in shaping how economic growth affects the environment.
- The tragedy of the commons can lead to the depletion of a scarce resource which is rivalrous but non-excludable, which is affected by the pattern of property rights.

Environmental policy options

Key term

internalising an externality
an attempt to deal with an externality by bringing an external cost or benefit into the price system

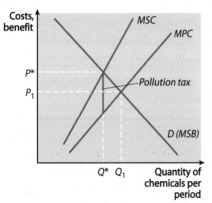

Figure 9.6 Reducing the emission of toxic fumes

One approach to dealing with such market situations is to bring those externalities into the market mechanism — a process known as **internalising an externality**. An example is the London congestion charge, which may be seen as an attempt to internalise the externality effects of traffic congestion. In the case of pollution, this principle would entail forcing the polluting firms to face the full social cost of their production activities. This is sometimes known as the *polluter pays* principle.

Taxes or regulation?

Figure 9.6 shows a situation in which there is a negative production externality, caused by chemicals firms that pollute the atmosphere in their production process. One approach to reaching the optimal output of chemicals at Q^* in line with the principle that the polluter should pay would be to impose a tax on firms such that polluters face the full cost of their actions. In Figure 9.6, if firms were required to pay a tax equivalent to the vertical distance between marginal private cost (*MPC*) and marginal social cost (*MSC*), they would choose to produce at Q^*, paying a tax equal to the green line on the figure.

This is not the only way of reaching the objective, however. Another possibility would be to impose environmental standards, and prohibit emissions beyond a certain level. This amounts to controlling quantity rather than price; and, if the government has full information about marginal costs and marginal benefits, the two policies will produce the equivalent result, as was discussed in Book 1, Chapter 7.

Evaluation of taxes and regulation

For any intervention by the government, care is needed to ensure that taxes or regulations have their intended effects. In other words, it is important to guard against the possibility of government failure. If taxes are set at too high (or too low) a level, or if regulations are too stringent (or too loose), the best result for society in terms of resource allocation will not be achieved. Furthermore, it is important to remember that markets are interconnected, so intervention in one market may have knock-on effects on resource allocation elsewhere.

A key problem comes in determining the appropriate level at which a tax should be set in order to counter the effects of an externality. This is because the tax needs to reflect the additional social cost that is being inflicted on society — and this is very difficult to calculate in many cases. You might argue that the extent to which people are prepared to pay to install double glazing in order to counter noise pollution could be a measure of the impact of noise — but this cannot be the whole answer. In some other instances, it could be even more difficult to find an agreed measurement. For example, how could we put a value on the increased probability of being involved in a traffic accident? Some of these issues will be considered in Chapter 10 when we discuss the use of cost–benefit analysis.

Hypothecation

Within the transport sector, a contentious issue has been the level of duties levied on petrol and diesel, and road taxes. Motorists have claimed that they are being unfairly treated by heavy duties and high road taxes — not to mention the fines imposed when drivers are caught on speed cameras. Such arguments lead towards the notion of **hypothecation**.

Literally speaking, 'hypothecation' comes from the phrase 'hypothetical dedication'. In the transport arena, what this means is that revenues raised from the taxation of transport should be dedicated to expenditures that are concerned with transportation. For example, the revenues from gasoline tax in the USA are dedicated to the funding of transportation infrastructure.

Another example of hypothecation is the London Congestion Charge, where it was agreed that any net revenues raised by the scheme would be ploughed back into improving London's transport network. This is seen as one way of enabling improvements in public transport systems and traffic management, with private road users footing the bill. As a way of making charges politically acceptable to those who pay them, hypothecation may be an effective device. However, does it make sense in terms of economic analysis? If there are significant externalities associated with private motoring that affect other aspects of the economy, then there is a case for taxing motorists more heavily, and for using some of the revenues to correct for other distortions of resource allocation: for example, in remedying environmental damage.

Exercise 9.3

Discuss approaches that could be adopted to limit noise pollution.

Key term

hypothecation in the context of the transport sector, the principle that revenues raised from taxing transport should be used to improve the transport system

Exercise 9.4

Singapore has, for many years, imposed a range of financial instruments on motorists. These have included heavy customs duties and other charges for people wanting to put a new car on to Singapore's roads; there are also charges for taking a car into the Central Business District. The revenues raised from these measures have enabled the Singapore government to make substantial improvements to the road infrastructure in the city. Explain how this illustrates the principle of hypothecation.

Subsidising public transport

In formulating a vision of the future pattern of transport in the UK, the environment is seen to be a central concern. For example, there is a major concern about the emission of greenhouse gases from private motoring, which suggests that car usage needs to be managed, rather than being allowed to continue to expand in line with demand. This requires greater encouragement to use public transport, or a shift towards more fuel-efficient cars. However, individual consumers will not switch towards public transport unless its quality can be improved — which then requires investment to bring about those improvements and make public transport a more attractive alternative.

One way of encouraging more use of public transport might be through a subsidy. Figure 9.7 shows how this might work. Here, S_0 represents the supply curve in the absence of a subsidy, so that with demand at D, the market equilibrium is with price P_0 and quantity of bus journeys Q_0. If the authorities introduce a subsidy of an amount BC, this encourages the bus companies to supply more bus journeys at any given price, so the effective supply curve is now S_1, and the equilibrium moves to a lower price P_1 and higher quantity Q_1.

How effective is such a policy likely to be? Figure 9.7 was drawn with the demand curve relatively steep. This is probably realistic to some degree, as the demand for bus journeys is probably not too sensitive to price, so a subsidy has relatively little impact on the number of bus journeys undertaken. In addition, the cost to the authorities is relatively high. It is shown by the shaded area ($ABCP_1$) in Figure 9.7. This seems to suggest that the use of subsidies will be expensive and ineffective. This will be reinforced if increases in the real income of consumers cause the demand curve to shift to the left over time — in other words, if bus journeys can be regarded as an inferior good — which again seems a reasonable assumption.

In evaluating such a policy measure, it is important to realise that the benefits from encouraging more bus travel may go beyond the individual market. If the demand for bus journeys is inelastic, this makes subsidies relatively expensive. Nonetheless, in combination with measures to discourage private motor vehicles (reducing the number of city-centre parking spaces, introducing bus lanes and so on), subsidies can be an effective way of changing people's attitudes towards transport modes.

There may also be a case for subsidising rural bus travel, where there are communities that would otherwise be isolated. In other words, subsidies for bus travel may contribute to social inclusion of rural communities where bus routes might prove unprofitable for the private sector in the absence of some form of subsidy. The Rural Bus Subsidy Grant and Rural Bus Challenge policies were introduced in 1998. An evaluation undertaken for the Department for Transport after 5 years of operation suggested that these measures had been successful in meeting their objectives.

The rural subsidies apart, subsidies have not been widely used as a way of encouraging more usage of buses and coaches. Such subsidies as have been provided tend to be aimed at rather different targets — for example, bus passes for the elderly, which are intended to provide protection for vulnerable individuals, rather than being part of a transport policy.

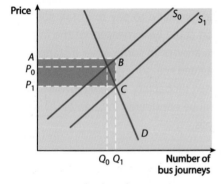

Figure 9.7 A subsidy to bus companies

Rural bus travel has been subsidised in recent years

Tradable pollution permits

Another approach to tackling externalities caused by pollution is to use a tradable *pollution permit system*, under which the government issues or sells permits to firms, allowing them to pollute up to a certain limit. These permits are then tradable, so that firms that are relatively 'clean' in their production methods and do not need to use their full allocation of permits can sell their polluting rights to other firms, whose production methods produce greater levels of pollution.

One important advantage of such a scheme lies in the incentives for firms. Firms that pollute because of their relatively inefficient production methods will find they are at a disadvantage because they face higher costs. Rather than continuing to purchase permits, they will find that they have an incentive to produce less pollution — which, of course, is what the policy is intended to achieve. In this way, the permit system uses the market to address the externality problem — in contrast to direct regulation of environmental standards, which tries to solve pollution by overriding the market.

A second advantage is that the overall level of pollution can be controlled by this system, as the authorities control the total amount of permits that are issued. After all, the objective of the policy is to control the overall level of pollution, and a mixture of 'clean' and 'dirty' firms may produce the same amount of total emissions as uniformly 'slightly unclean' firms.

However, the permit system may not be without its problems. In particular, there is the question of enforcement. For the system to be effective, sanctions must be in place for firms that pollute beyond the permitted level, and there must be an operational and cost-effective method for the authorities to check the level of emissions.

Furthermore, it may not be a straightforward exercise for the authorities to decide upon the appropriate number of permits to issue in order to produce the desired reduction in emission levels. Some alternative regulatory systems share this problem, as it is not easy to measure the extent to which marginal private and social costs diverge.

One possible criticism that is unique to a permit form of regulation is that the very different levels of pollution produced by different firms may seem inequitable — those firms that can afford to buy permits can pollute as much as they like. On the other hand, it might be argued that those most likely to suffer from this are the polluting firms, whose public image is likely to be tarnished if they acquire a reputation as heavy polluters. This possibility might strengthen the incentives of such firms to clean up their production. Taking the strengths and weaknesses of this approach together, it seems that on balance such a system could be effective in regulating pollution.

Information

In some cases, it may be that the market failure that is affecting the environment arises from an information failure. It might be that people do not fully understand the implications of their actions for the environment. For example, there may be those who do not appreciate the importance of recycling waste, or tourists who remain unaware of the damage they may be causing in visiting popular beauty spots.

In order to tackle this problem, a first step is to deal with the information problem. Campaigns to promote recycling schemes or responsible tourism are examples of attempts to improve information provision in order to influence behaviour. Behavioural economists may also point to attempts to influence behaviour by encouraging recycling or appealing to people to take their litter home on the basis that this is good social behaviour.

Government expenditure

The government can help to tackle environmental problems caused by market failure by undertaking appropriate expenditure. The National Infrastructure Plan sets out the various ways in which the UK government has attempted to improve the country's infrastructure, with many of the projects having significant impacts on the environment. Between 2010 and the end of 2014, it was noted that over 2,500 different infrastructure schemes had been completed, including improvements to the rail network and a number of flood and coastal defence improvement projects and waste management systems. In December 2014, the Treasury announced £2.3 billion of further investment in flood defences and £15 billion of road improvements.

Public–private partnerships

The discussion of public goods in Book 1, Chapter 8 pointed out that, although public goods would be underprovided in a free market, this did not necessarily mean that the government needed to take on the role of provider. Instead, intervention in the market may take the form of encouraging private sector involvement. One way in which this has been tackled is through public–private partnerships.

The Private Finance Initiative (PFI)

PFI was launched in 1992 as a way of trying to increase the involvement of the private sector in the provision of public services. This established a partnership between the public and private sectors. The public sector specifies, perhaps in broad terms, the services that it requires, and then invites tenders from the private sector to design, build, finance and operate the scheme. In some cases, the project might be entirely freestanding: for example, the government may initiate a project such as a new bridge that is then taken up by a private firm, which will recover its costs entirely through user charges such as tolls. In other cases, the project may be a joint venture between the public and private sectors. The public sector could get involved with such a venture in order to secure wider social benefits, perhaps through reductions in traffic congestion that would not be reflected in market prices, and thus would not be fully taken into account by the private sector. In other cases, it may be that the private sector undertakes a project and then sells the services to the public sector.

The aim of PFI was to improve the financing of public sector projects. This was partly achieved by introducing a competitive element into the tendering process, but in addition it enabled the risk of a project to be shared between the public and private sectors. This should enable efficiency gains to be made. By 2012, the Treasury was able to announce that more than 700 projects had reached financial completion, having secured around £55 billion of private sector investment.

However, PFI has been much debated — and much criticised. One effect of PFI is to reduce the pressures on public finances by enabling greater private sector involvement in funding. But it might be argued that this may in fact raise the cost of borrowing, if the public sector would have been able to borrow on more favourable terms than commercial firms. The introduction of a competitive element in the tendering process may be beneficial, but on the other hand, it could be argued that the private sector may have less incentive than the public sector to give due attention to health and safety issues. In other words, there may be a concern that private firms will be tempted to sacrifice safety or service standards in the quest for profit. Achieving the appropriate balance between efficiency and quality of service is an inevitable problem, whatever way transport is financed and provided, but it becomes a more critical issue to the extent that the use of PFI switches the focus more towards efficiency and lower costs.

PF2

Having undertaken a major review of the PFI, the Treasury announced a new approach to public–private partnerships in 2012, to be known as PF2, aiming to strengthen the partnership between the public and private sectors through public sector minority equity holdings in PF2 projects. This was expected to accelerate delivery, and ensure greater transparency and flexibility in provision.

A key issue is how to set priorities amongst competing projects, all of which may have beneficial environmental effects. This is discussed in the following chapter.

Exercise 9.5

Discuss the extent to which improvements in road infrastructure will help to address environmental issues.

Summary

- In seeking to counter the harmful effects of externalities, governments look for ways of internalising the externality, by bringing external costs and benefits within the market mechanism.
- For example, the 'polluter pays' principle argues that the best way of dealing with a pollution externality is to force the polluter to face the full costs of its actions.
- Attempts have been made to tackle pollution through taxation, the regulation of environmental standards, subsidies, and the use of pollution permits.
- In some cases, the allocation of property rights can be effective in curbing the effects of externalities — so long as the transaction costs of implementing it are not too high.

Case study 9.1

The Mekong River

The Mekong River is the world's twelfth longest river, rising in China and flowing through Myanmar, Laos, Thailand, Cambodia and Vietnam. Some 60 million people live in the lower Mekong Basin. The river provides drinking water, food, irrigation, hydropower, transportation and commerce to these people. Nearly half of the population of Cambodia benefit directly or indirectly from the resources provided by the Tonie Sap Lake, which is one of the world's largest freshwater fisheries, and is fed by water from the Mekong River. The Mekong Delta provides more than half of rice production in Vietnam, and an estimated third of its GDP.

In 1995, an agreement between Cambodia, Laos, Thailand and Vietnam led to the formation of the Mekong River Commission, to oversee a process of consultation between the countries on projects that would have significant impact on the river.

Laos is a low-income country with aspirations to develop and initiate economic growth. The Laotian government's strategy for achieving this includes improving infrastructure — in particular, improving

electricity supply. In pursuit of this objective, the Xayaburi Dam project was launched on a remote stretch of the Mekong River in the north of the country. The Mekong River Commission had been notified of the project in 2010, but no consensus was reached. Preliminary construction began in 2012 in violation of the agreement.

The Xayaburi is just one of 11 planned dam projects, which could have major consequences for countries downstream.

A demonstration led by Thai villagers affected by the proposed construction of the Xayaburi dam

Follow-up questions

a Identify the nature of the externality involved in the Xayaburi Dam project.
b Discuss the difficulties of devising a policy that would address the market failure resulting from the project.

Case study 9.2

Recycling and market failure

With rising affluence in the world, growing consumption has led to one of the most worrying issues in the field of environmental economics — waste management. With reference to municipal waste management, the main problem is to correct an imbalance in the quantity of waste produced and the means of its disposal. This occurs as the pricing mechanisms of the free market do not take account of externalities such as disposal costs and damage costs arising from the usage of raw materials, or the social benefits that arise from recycling schemes.

Due to the growing problem of finding landfill sites, governments have introduced initiatives to reduce waste. Recycling has been seen as a way of minimising the overall waste output and becoming more sustainable.

Individuals benefit from recycling, but do not necessarily perceive the full social benefits of the process.

Follow-up questions

a Identify the type of externality involved in the use of landfill sites to dispose of household waste.

b Identify the externality that may arise from the way in which households perceive recycling.

c Use diagrams to analyse the effects of these externality effects, and identify the welfare cost on society if there is no regulation.

d Discuss the policy options that could be invoked to address these effects.

Chapter 10

Other forms of government intervention in markets

The previous chapter discussed ways in which environmental policy may be designed. Attention now switches to other ways in which the government may intervene in order to correct market failure. A first question concerns how priorities can be set amongst competing projects, and the discussion here centres on the application of cost–benefit analysis. Market failure can occur when there is imperfect competition in a market, such that there is a need to protect the interests of consumers and prevent them from being exploited. Finally, the problems of providing a sustainable pension scheme are discussed.

Learning objectives

After studying this chapter, you should:
- be aware of the importance of social cost–benefit analysis as a method of appraising capital projects where there is a potential market failure involved
- be familiar with the process of undertaking cost–benefit analysis
- be able to discuss the uses and limitations of the cost–benefit approach to decision making in a range of contexts
- understand the economic underpinnings of competition policy
- appreciate that there may be situations in which unremitting competition may not be in the best interests of society
- be familiar with the roles of the Competition and Markets Authority
- be aware of the issues that may affect its judgements of a market under investigation
- be familiar with the general institutional background of competition policy in the UK
- understand the issues surrounding the operation of pension policy

Prior knowledge needed

Market failure was introduced in Part 3 of Book 1, and this chapter looks at ways in which governments may choose to intervene in markets.

Social cost–benefit analysis

The importance of externalities in regard to environmental and other issues means that it is especially important to be aware of externalities when taking decisions that are likely to affect the environment. This is especially important for large-scale projects that can have far-reaching effects on the economy, such as the construction of a new dam or a major road-building project. If good decisions are to be taken, it is crucial to be able to measure the external costs and benefits that are associated with those decisions.

This suggests that in taking such decisions, it is important to be able to weigh up the costs and benefits of a scheme. If it turns out that the benefits exceed the costs, it might be thought appropriate to go ahead. However, in valuing the costs and the benefits, it is clearly important to include some estimate for the externalities involved in order that the decision can be based on all relevant factors. In other words, it is important to take a 'long and wide view' and not to focus too narrowly on purely financial costs and benefits.

A further complication is that, with many such schemes, the costs and benefits will be spread out over a long period of time, and it is important to come to a reasonable balance between the interests of present and future generations.

Social cost–benefit analysis (CBA) is a procedure for bringing together the information needed to make appropriate decisions on such large-scale schemes. This entails a sequence of key steps.

1 Identify relevant costs and benefits

The first step is to identify all relevant costs and benefits. This needs to cover all of the direct costs of the project. These can probably be identified relatively easily, and include the production costs, labour costs and so on.

The indirect costs also need to be identified, and this is where externality effects need to be considered. For example, in constructing a dam across a river, there are the visible direct costs that are inevitably entailed in such a large engineering project. But there are also the indirect costs — that is, the *opportunity costs*. How many people and businesses will be uprooted by the project, and how much land that could have been used for agriculture will be flooded as a result of the new dam? Similarly, in a road-building scheme, it is important to think in terms not only of the costs of construction, but also of the opportunity cost — how else could the land being used for the road have been used? How will the increase in traffic affect the quality of life enjoyed by local residents? For example, they may suffer from noise from the traffic using the road, or from the traffic fumes. Similarly, direct and indirect benefits need to be identified. The dam may bring benefits in terms of hydroelectric power, or irrigation for crops. A new road may increase the efficiency of transportation, and reduce costs for firms.

2 Valuation

If the costs and benefits are to be compared, they all need to be given a monetary valuation. It is likely that some of them will be items that have a market price attached to them. For these, valuation is not a problem. However, for externalities, or for other indirect costs and benefits without a market valuation, it is necessary to establish a **shadow price** — an estimate of the monetary value of each item. Notice that this can be quite difficult, as some of the external costs may be elusive, especially if the impact is on the quality of life, rather than on measureable production loss.

Key terms

social cost–benefit analysis (CBA) a process of evaluating the worth of a project by comparing its costs and benefits, including both direct and social costs and benefits — including externality effects

shadow price an estimate of the monetary value of an item that does not carry a market price

161

3 Discounting the future

It is also important to recognise that costs and benefits that will flow from the project at some point in the future need to be expressed in terms of their value in the present. From today's perspective, a benefit that is immediate is more valuable than one that will only become relevant in 20 years' time. In order to incorporate this notion into the calculations, we need to **discount** the future at an appropriate rate, and calculate the **net present value** of the future stream of costs and benefits associated with the project under consideration. Notice that a government taking decisions on behalf of future generations may choose a higher discount rate than consumers who prefer to enjoy benefits in the present. Equally, a government that is feeling vulnerable may prefer to provide benefits in the present to persuade the electorate, rather than taking decisions that will not bear fruit until the distant future. In other words, there may be a political backdrop to take into account.

Key terms

discount a process whereby the future valuation of a cost or benefit is reduced (discounted) in order to provide an estimate of its present value

net present value the estimated value in the current time period of the discounted future net benefit of a project

Quantitative skills 10.1

Discounting the future

Discounting the future is a bit like reversing the process of compound interest.

Suppose you have an asset worth £100 which is accumulating interest at 5% per year. In 5 years' time, it will be worth the original £100 plus the interest that is added each year. Over 5 years, the amount would be 100 multiplied by 1.05 each year, where 1.05 is 1 plus the interest rate expressed as a decimal. This is equal to $100 \times (1.05)^5 = £127.63$.

Discounting puts this into reverse, asking what £100 would be worth today, given a 5% discount rate. This present value is calculated as $100 \div (1.05)^5 = £78.35$.

The further into the future the project is discounted, the smaller is the present value of the future return in each year. The present value sums all of these future values to give the discounted value now of the net returns from the future across the life over which the return is expected.

The decision-making process

If it is possible to identify all the private and external costs of a project, to place a monetary valuation on each of them and to choose an appropriate discount rate, then there is a framework for taking decisions about a project. The bottom line is whether the total social benefits expected to arise from a project outweigh the social costs.

This may sounds straightforward, but it is important to remember all the assumptions on which such decisions would be based. In particular, the valuations made of the various elements of benefits and costs may be considered to be at least partially subjective, and different members of society may take different views of what is an appropriate discount rate. However, this does not mean that CBA is unhelpful. For example, a government may be choosing between a range of different development projects. By using consistent assumptions in valuation and discount rates across the projects, it may be possible to produce a coherent *ranking* of alternative projects, and thus identify the project that would produce the highest benefit : cost ratio.

Summary

- A number of approaches have been proposed to measure externalities. Measurement may enable a social cost–benefit analysis to be made of projects involving a substantial externality element.
- The first step is to identify all direct and indirect (private and external) benefits and costs of a project.
- Each component must then be valued.
- An appropriate discount rate needs to be applied to those benefits and costs that will arise in the future.
- The project with the highest ratio of benefits to costs is likely to be the one that is most beneficial for society.

Exercise 10.1

Suppose there is a proposal to construct a new industrial estate close to where you live. Identify the costs and benefits of the scheme, including direct costs and benefits and not forgetting externalities. Discuss how you could bring these components together to analyse the overall net benefit of the project.

Applications of cost–benefit analysis

CBA can be used in any situation in which a large-scale investment project is being contemplated. It is even more important where a choice has to be made between competing alternative projects. Given that resources are limited, a decision to go ahead with one project has an opportunity cost in terms of the next best alternative project that will not go ahead.

Such large-scale projects arise in a variety of settings where some form of market failure is present. The presence of externalities is one such situation, but intervention to provide infrastructure may also be needed in other circumstances, such as where there are public goods, merit goods or environmental considerations. For example, there may be projects in transport, education and health, or in relation to environmental issues.

Transport

Transport is a crucial sector in the economy for many reasons, not least because an efficient transport system facilitates the operation of markets, whether they are in manufacturing or in commerce. The

163

workforce needs transport for travel to work, and consumers need transport to take advantage of amenities for shopping and leisure. Furthermore, the transport sector has major effects on the environment and has externality effects in terms of traffic congestion. There are also aspects of public goods in the provision of infrastructure for transport. The need to coordinate the provision of transport infrastructure across different modes of travel (road, rail, etc.) adds further to the need for some sort of government involvement in the provision of transport infrastructure.

Roads

The Department for Transport (DfT) routinely applies cost–benefit analysis to major road schemes using a standard approach. This is based on computer software that has been in use since the 1970s: the COBA (Cost–Benefit Analysis) program. In evaluating transport projects, the DfT appraises on the basis of five key objectives: environment, safety, economy, accessibility and integration.

Suppose that a new section of trunk road is proposed. What are the steps that COBA goes through in order to reach an evaluation of the project? There are three key procedures to invoke. First, the expected construction cost needs to be measured. Second, the benefits to users must be evaluated. These costs and benefits should ideally incorporate all of the costs and benefits that will be associated with the scheme, including some that would not normally be given a monetary value. Third, it is important to be aware that the scheme is likely to provide a stream of costs and benefits over a period of time. In taking decisions in the present period, analysts need to be careful not to give too much weight to benefits (or costs) that will only accrue in the very long term. It would not be sensible to regard benefits that will appear in 30 years' time as highly as benefits that will flow after only 5 years. Future costs and benefits thus need to be converted into their 'present values' through a process of discounting future values.

Figure 10.1 shows the process adopted within the COBA system, reproduced from the Department for Transport's *COBA Manual*. Notice that the first step is to identify user costs on the existing road network (A1 in the diagram), so that the benefits from the scheme can be evaluated as the reduction in user costs. In other words, first check the existing scenario, and then see how this will improve as a result of the new project. The costs of the project are then deducted to give an estimate of the net present value of the project. If this is positive, the scheme may be viewed favourably, although, of course, there may be other schemes under consideration and these might come out with a higher net present value. In this case, the process enables the DfT to set priorities among a range of projects, remembering that the opportunity cost of a project can be seen in terms of the net present value of the next best alternative. If funds are committed to a particular project, this may have to be at the expense of another scheme, given the limits of the overall budget.

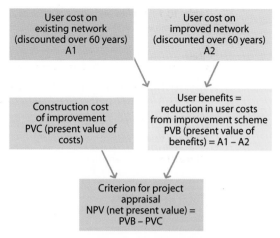

Source: Department for Transport, *COBA Manual*, 2006

Figure 10.1 The COBA appraisal process

In many ways, the difficult part of applying such a system comes in the way in which the user costs are evaluated. In order for the process to be carried out, it is vital that a monetary value is placed on the various user costs involved, both with the existing road network and under the new proposal. Under the COBA process, the user costs include changes in time, operating costs and the cost of accidents. In other words, the question is whether the new scheme will allow speedier travel, cheaper travel and safer travel. The costs of the scheme are appraised in terms of the capital costs (including the preparation and supervision costs), and any changes in the capital cost of maintaining the proposed new network as compared to the existing one.

The need to assign monetary values is both the strength and the weakness of COBA. It is a strength because it enables external benefits and costs to be brought into consideration. It is a weakness because such valuations may be contentious, although the process is now so well established that at least some of the issues are familiar to analysts. It might also be argued that, as long as similar methods are applied consistently across a range of projects, then at least the ranking procedure should be reliable.

Rail: the HS2 project

The High Speed 2 project is a high-profile project designed to link eight of Britain's largest cities, and is expected to require investment of more than £16 billion in Phase 1. Construction is due to start in 2017 and to be completed by 2025. It is expected that this will increase capacity on the rail network, and 'allow more passengers to use trains and more freight operators to use rail rather than road' (Department for Transport, 2012).

An appraisal based on cost–benefit analysis was carried out to evaluate the economic case for the project. The first step was to itemise the quantifiable benefits and costs of the project, calculating the estimated present value of benefits and costs over a 60-year time horizon. Table 10.1 summarises the main components.

Table 10.1 Benefits and costs of HS2 over 60 years as at October 2013 (£ million, present value at 2011 prices)

Item	Phase 1	Full network
Transport benefits (business)	16,921	40,529
Transport benefits (other)	7,673	19,323
Other quantifiable benefits	407	788
Indirect taxes (loss to government)	−1,208	−2,912
Net transport benefits	**23,793**	**57,727**
Wider economic impacts	4,341	13,293
Total net benefits	**28,134**	**71,020**
Total costs	29,919	62,606
Revenues	13,243	31,111
Net cost to government	**16,676**	**31,495**

The table shows the estimated benefits and costs for the project, measured in present value (PV) terms, based on projections for the growth of future demand. The estimates show the breakdown between the first phase of the project (Phase 1) and the situation when the full network is in operation.

Quantitative skills 10.2

Calculating a benefit:cost ratio

In comparing the benefits and costs of a project, it is customary to calculate the ratio of benefits to costs. This shows the relative strength of the benefits relative to the costs. For Phase 1, this calculation would entail dividing the total net benefits (£28,134 million) by the net cost (to the government: £16,676 million), which equals 1.7. For the full network, the calculation gives a benefit:cost ratio of 2.3. Make sure that you can replicate this answer from the table. The interpretation of this is that the benefits of the full network are 2.3 times higher than the cost, and thus potentially beneficial for society.

This is not the final story, however. It is also important to take into account the impact that the project will have on the environment. The issues taken into account covered noise in running HS2 services, greenhouse gases, air quality, landscape, heritage and townscape, biodiversity and the water environment — and option values (that is, the value attached to having the option of using a transport service, whether or not it is actually used). Of course, some of these items are more difficult to quantify in monetary terms than others, and after a thorough review, it was estimated that these impacts considered jointly would have a small negative effect on the value for money of the scheme, reducing the benefit:cost ratio by 0.1, leaving the conclusion as before, that the project would bring substantial net benefits.

Further assessment tested the robustness of this conclusion, by exploring how the ratio would differ under alternative assumptions underpinning the analysis, including assumptions about the sensitivity of demand to economic growth, variations in costs of construction, fares and the valuation of time.

Other applications of cost–benefit analysis

Cost–benefit analysis can be important in many other contexts where a government is considering investment in large-scale projects. In the provision of education and healthcare, there may be a need for investment in new schools or hospitals, or in the equipment needed to achieve a high standard of provision. The same methodology for calculating the benefit:cost ratio can be applied, although the benefit and cost components may be different according to the project.

In education, there may be externalities involved, as was set out in Book 1, Chapter 7. Educated people tend to earn more and to be more productive. However, there may be external benefits if educated people are even more productive when they work together, or if the educated are more socially responsible. It may be possible to quantify the returns to education by comparing the average earnings of people with differing levels of education, but it is much more difficult to quantify the external benefits. In less developed countries, there may be an information failure associated with education, if parents do not perceive the full potential of education of their children. This may also be difficult to estimate, but in principle cost–benefit analysis could be undertaken to justify enforcing a school attendance policy, or finding some other way of encouraging parents to send their children to school.

In the area of healthcare provision, there may also be a role for cost–benefit analysis. One important aspect of this is caught up with the idea that prevention is often better than cure. If a disease can be prevented from taking hold, there may be cost savings in the future, but these may be difficult to quantify. For example, a less developed country could undertake a cost–benefit analysis to decide on a vaccination programme, or (in the case of HIV/AIDS, for example) an information campaign to avoid having to spend on curative medicine in the future. There may also be benefits if less production is lost by people becoming ill.

Evaluation

How effective is the use of social cost–benefit analysis in helping governments to take good decisions about investment projects? On the one hand, it could be argued that the assumptions needed for the calculations are highly speculative. It may be almost impossible to predict how the economy will look in 60 years' time, so trying to estimate future demand, economic growth and the state of the environment over that sort of time period is likely to be subject to a substantial range of uncertainty. On the other hand, it might be argued that the process at least forces consideration of the unquantifiable impact of projects, rather than basing decisions purely on monetary considerations. Furthermore, it may enable the *relative* net benefits of alternative projects to be compared under similar assumptions about the future path of the economy, even if those assumptions are speculative. The separation of decision making into independent government departments may make this less likely to happen.

Exercise 10.2

Suppose there is a proposal to construct a new stretch of motorway close to where you live. Discuss how you would seek to evaluate the proposal.

Summary

- Cost–benefit analysis (CBA) can be used for appraising large-scale investment projects where there is a potential market failure present.
- CBA has been used by the Department for Transport for many years to evaluate the likely impact of road projects.
- CBA was also used when considering whether to go ahead with the HS2 project.
- The methodology can also be used in assessing projects that affect the environment, and the provision of education and healthcare.
- The assumptions underpinning the analysis need to be considered carefully when evaluating the impact of a project over a long timescale.

Competition and the government

<blockquote>
Key term

competition policy an area of economic policy designed to promote competition within markets to encourage efficiency and protect consumer interests
</blockquote>

Part 1 of this book explored market structure, and discussed the possibility that firms may have market power that enables them to make abnormal profits in some market situations. This can give rise to a form of market failure and has led governments to introduce measures designed to promote competition, in order to address issues of resource misallocation and to protect consumers. Such measures are known as **competition policy**.

A key focus of such legislation in the past has been monopoly, as economic analysis highlighted the allocative inefficiency that can arise in a monopoly market if the firm sets out to maximise profit. More recently, however, the scope of legislation has widened, and since 1997 competition policy has been toughened significantly.

Underlying this aspect of government policy has been the growing belief that competition induces firms to eliminate X-inefficiency as well as encouraging better resource allocation. However, this must always be balanced against the possible sacrifice of economies of scale if competition can only be enabled by fragmentation of the production process. The question of contestability is also important, as it is possible that the very threat of competition may be sufficient to affect firms' behaviour.

X-inefficiency does not occur only in the private sector, and a further set of measures has tried to address the question of efficiency in the provision of public sector services by encouraging the private sector to be involved in partnerships with the public sector in its economic activities.

Economic analysis and competition policy

The final section of Chapter 3 undertook a comparison of perfect competition and monopoly, and it is this analysis that lies at the heart of competition policy. Figure 10.2 should remind you of the discussion.

Here it is assumed there is an industry that can operate either under perfect competition, with a large number of small firms, or as a multi-plant monopolist. For simplicity, it is also assumed that there is no cost difference between the two forms of market structure, so that the long-run supply schedule (*LRS*) under perfect competition is perceived by the

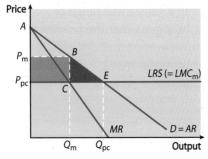

Figure 10.2 Perfect competition and monopoly compared

monopolist as its long-run marginal cost curve. In other words, in long-run equilibrium the monopoly varies output by varying the number of plants it is operating.

Under perfect competition, output would be set at Q_{pc} and market price would be P_{pc}. However, a monopolist will choose to restrict output to Q_m and raise price to P_m. Consumer surplus will be reduced by this process, partly by a transfer of the blue rectangle to the monopoly as profits, and partly by the red triangle of deadweight loss. Competition policy is intended to alleviate this deadweight loss, which imposes a cost on society.

Indeed, this analysis led to a belief in what became known in the economics literature as the *structure–conduct–performance paradigm*. This was discussed in Chapter 5.

Thus, under perfect competition firms cannot influence price, and all firms act competitively to maximise profits, thereby producing good overall performance of the market in allocating resources. On the other hand, under monopoly the single firm finds that it can extract consumer surplus by using its market power, and as a result the market performs less well.

This point of view leads to a distrust of monopoly — or, indeed, of any market structure in which firms might be seen to be conducting themselves in an anti-competitive manner. Moreover, it is the structure of the market itself that leads to this anti-competitive behaviour.

If this line of reasoning is accepted, then monopoly is always bad, and mergers that lead to higher concentration in a market will always lead to allocative inefficiency in the market's performance. Thus, legislation in the USA tends to presume that a monopoly will work against the interests of society. However, there are some important issues to consider before pinning too much faith on this assumption.

Cost conditions

The first issue concerns the assumption that cost conditions will be the same under perfect competition as under monopoly. This simplifies the analysis, but there are many reasons to expect economies of scale in a number of economic activities. If this assumption is correct, then a monopoly firm will face lower cost conditions than would apply under perfect competition.

In Figure 10.3, *LRS* represents the long-run supply schedule if an industry is operating under perfect competition. The perfectly competitive equilibrium would be at output level Q_{pc} with the price at P_{pc}. However, suppose that a monopolist had a strong cost advantage, and was able to produce at constant long-run marginal cost LMC_m. It would then maximise profit by choosing the output Q_m, where MR_m is equal to LMC_m, and would sell at a price P_m. In this situation the monopolist could actually produce more output at a lower price than a firm operating under perfect competition.

Notice that in the monopoly situation the market does not achieve allocative efficiency because, with these cost conditions, setting price equal to marginal cost would require the firm to produce Q^* output. However, this loss of allocative efficiency is offset by the improvements in productive efficiency that are

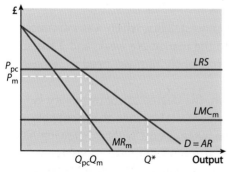

Figure 10.3 Suppose that monopoly offers much better cost conditions

achieved by the monopoly firm. This is sometimes known as dynamic efficiency, whereas allocative efficiency is a more static concept that considers the best use of existing resources with existing technologies.

It could be argued that the monopolist should be regulated, and forced to produce at Q^*. However, what incentives would this establish for the firm? If a monopolist knows that whenever it makes supernormal profits the regulator will step in and take them away, it will have no incentive to operate efficiently. Indeed, Joseph Schumpeter argued that monopoly profits were an incentive for innovation, and would benefit society, because only with monopoly profits would firms be able to engage in research and development (R&D). In other words, it is only when firms are relatively large, and when they are able to make supernormal profits, that they are able to devote resources to R&D. Small firms operating in a perfectly competitive market do not have the resources or the incentive to be innovative.

Figure 10.4 illustrates a less extreme case. As before, equilibrium under perfect competition produces output at Q_{pc} with price at P_{pc}. The monopoly alternative faces lower long-run marginal cost, although with a less marked difference than before: here the firm produces Q_m output in order to maximise profits, and sets price at P_m.

Analysis of this situation reveals that there is a deadweight loss given by the red triangle; this reflects the allocative inefficiency of monopoly. However, there is also a gain in productive efficiency represented by the green rectangle. This is part of monopoly profits, but under perfect competition it was part of production costs. In other words, production under the monopoly is less wasteful in its use of resources in the production process.

Is society better off under monopoly or under perfect competition? In order to evaluate the effect on total welfare, it is necessary to balance the loss of allocative efficiency (the red triangle) against the gain in productive efficiency (the green rectangle). In Figure 10.4 it would seem that the rectangle is larger than the triangle, so society overall is better off with the monopoly. Of course, there is also the distribution of income to take into account — the area $P_m ABP_{pc}$ would be part of consumer surplus under perfect competition, but under monopoly it becomes part of the firm's profits.

Contestability

A second important issue concerns contestability, which was introduced in Chapter 4. If barriers to entry into the market are weak, and if the sunk costs of entry and exit are low, the monopoly firm will need to temper its actions to avoid potential entry.

Thus, in judging a market situation, the degree of contestability is important. If the market is perfectly contestable, then the monopoly firm cannot set a price that is above average cost without allowing hit-and-run entry. In this case, the regulator does not need to intervene. Even without perfect contestability, the firm may need to set a price that is not so high as to induce entry. In other words, it may choose not to produce at the profit-maximising level of output, and to set a price below that level.

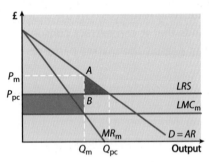

Figure 10.4 Cost conditions again — a less extreme example

Concentration and collusion

The structure–conduct–performance argument suggests that it is not only monopolies that should be the subject of competition policy, but any market in which firms have some influence over price. In other words, oligopolies also need careful attention because of the danger that they will collude, and act *as if* they were a joint monopoly. After all, it was argued that where a market has just a small number of sellers there may be a temptation to collude, either in a cartel or tacitly. For this reason, government authorities may be wary of markets in which concentration ratios are simply high, even if not 100%.

For this reason, it is important to examine whether a concentrated market is *always* and *necessarily* an anti-competitive market. This is tantamount to asking whether structure necessarily determines conduct. A high concentration ratio may mean that there are a small number of firms of more or less equal size, or it could mean that there is one large firm and a number of smaller competitors. In the latter case you might expect the dominant firm to have sufficient market power to control price.

With a small number of equally sized firms, it is by no means certain that they will agree to collude. They may be very conscious of their respective market shares, and so act in an aggressively competitive way in order to defend them. This may be especially true where the market is not expanding, so that a firm can grow only at the expense of the other firms. Such a market could well display intense competition, causing it to drift towards the competitive end of the scale. This would suggest that the authorities should not presume guilt in a merger investigation, since the pattern of market shares may prove significant in determining the firms' conduct, and hence the performance of the market. An example of this was discussed in Case study 5.2 in the context of the battle for Safeway.

Globalisation

Another significant issue is that a firm that comes to dominate a domestic market may still face competition in the broader global market. This may be especially significant within the European single market.

In this regard, there has been a longstanding debate about how a domestic government should behave towards its large firms. Some economists believe that the government should allow such firms to dominate the domestic market in order that they can become 'national champions' in the global market. This has been especially apparent in the airline industry, where some national airlines are heavily subsidised by their national governments in order to allow them to compete internationally. Others have argued that, if a large firm faces competition within the domestic market, this should help to encourage its productive efficiency, enabling it to become more capable of coping with international competition.

> ### Exercise 10.3
>
> Discuss whether a concentrated market is necessarily anti-competitive.

Summary

- Competition policy refers to a range of measures designed to promote competition in markets and to protect consumers in order to enhance the efficiency of markets in resource allocation.
- One view is that market structure determines the conduct of firms within a market, and this conduct then determines the performance of the market in terms of allocative efficiency.
- A profit-maximising monopolist will produce less output at a higher price than a perfectly competitive market, causing allocative inefficiency.
- However, there may be situations in which the monopolist can enjoy economies of scale, and thereby gain in productive efficiency.
- In the presence of contestability, a monopolist may not be able to charge a price above average cost without encouraging hit-and-run entry.
- In a concentrated market, the pattern of market shares may influence the intensity of competition between firms.
- A firm that is a monopoly in its own country may be exposed to competition in the international markets in which it operates.

Competition policy in the UK

In the UK, competition policy has tended to be less rigid than in the USA, with its natural distrust of monopoly. Policy has therefore been conducted in such a way as to take account of the issues discussed above. This has meant that cases of monopoly or concentrated markets have been judged on their individual merits on a case-by-case basis.

This pragmatic approach was embedded in UK legislation from the start — which was the 1948 Monopolies and Restrictive Practices (Inquiry and Control) Act. This Act set up the Monopolies and Restrictive Practices Commission to investigate markets in which a single firm (or a group of firms in collusion) supplied more than one-third of a market. The commission was asked to decide whether such a market was operating in the public interest, although at that stage the legislation was not very precisely defined.

Since then the legislation has been steadily tightened through a sequence of Acts, the most recent of which are the Competition Act of 1998 and the Enterprise Act of 2002. The Competition Act is in two sections ('chapters'), one dealing with anti-competitive agreements between parties (e.g. firms) and the other dealing with anti-competitive practices by one or more parties — that is, the abuse of a dominant position in a market.

Cartels are covered by Chapter 1 of the 1998 Act, but less formal agreements between firms are also within the scope of the Act: for example, price fixing, agreements to restrict output and agreements to share a market. The Enterprise Act elevated the operation of a cartel to a criminal offence (as opposed to a civil offence).

Since April 2014, the conduct of the policy has been entrusted to the Competition and Markets Authority (CMA) (previously it was implemented by two agencies: the Office of Fair Trading (OFT) and the Competition Commission). The CMA investigates mergers and anti-competitive practices in markets.

A merger is subject to investigation if the firms involved in the proposed merger or acquisition have a combined market share in the UK of more than 25% and if the combined assets of the firms exceed £70 million worldwide.

Probably the best way of understanding how competition policy operates is by exploring an example of how it has worked in practice. First, however, there is a very important issue to be examined.

The relevant market

The first step in any investigation is to identify the **relevant market**. Until the scope of the market has been defined, it is not possible to calculate market shares or concentration ratios.

How should the market be defined in this context? In other words, which products should be included? Or over which region should the market be defined? Take the market for sugar — is this defined as the market for all sugar, or just for granulated sugar? Is organic sugar a separate product? Or, regarding the market for rail travel in Scotland, do bus services need to be considered as part of the Scottish market for travel?

One way of addressing this question is to apply the *hypothetical monopoly test*. Under this approach, the product market is defined as the smallest set of products and producers in which a hypothetical monopolist controlling all such products could raise profits by a small increase in price above the competitive level.

> **Key term**
>
> **relevant market** a market to be investigated under competition law, defined in such a way that no major substitutes are omitted but no non-substitutes are included

Extension material

Identifying the relevant market

The hypothetical monopoly test is effectively a question about substitution. If in a hypothetical market an increase in price will induce consumers to switch to a substitute product, then the market has not been defined sufficiently widely for it to be regarded as a monopoly. This is demand-side substitutability. One way of evaluating it would be to consult the cross-price elasticity of demand — if it could be measured. This would determine which products were perceived as substitutes for each other by consumers.

For example, in 2003 a number of supermarkets put in bids to take over the Safeway chain. The first step in the investigation was to define the relevant market. One issue that was raised was whether discount stores such as Lidl and Aldi, which sell a limited range of groceries, should be considered part of the same market as supermarkets selling a wide range of grocery products. In the south of the country, the cross-price elasticity of Sainsbury's demand was 0.05 with respect to Lidl's price, but 1.48 with respect to Tesco's price. This suggested that Sainsbury and Tesco were in the same market, but Lidl was not.

It is also important to consider the question of substitutes on the supply side: in other words, whether an increase in price may induce suppliers to join the market. Supply-side substitutability is related to the notion of contestability, in the sense that one way a market can be seen to be contestable is if other firms can switch readily into it — that is, if there are potential substitutes.

An example of an investigation: airports

BAA plc

In 1987 the British Airports Authority was privatised, and BAA plc was established. The new company was responsible for the airports that had previously been under the aegis of the British Airports Authority — namely, the three London airports (Heathrow, Gatwick and Stansted), plus airports in Scotland (Aberdeen, Edinburgh, Glasgow and Prestwick). Prestwick was sold in 1991, and Southampton was acquired in 1990. BAA plc had an effective monopoly on flights in and out of London and a stranglehold on flights in and out of Scotland.

One of the objectives in setting up BAA plc was to have a single enterprise that would be able to plan ahead and take strategic decisions, and to provide the airport capacity needed to meet the expected growth in demand. In addition, it was hoped that the provision of the infrastructure needed for air travel would help to encourage competition amongst the airlines providing the transport services.

In the event, things did not work out well, and after 20 years of operation, BAA plc was seen to have failed to provide sufficient capacity to meet demand in the South East region. There was also mounting criticism of the way in which BAA was managing its airports — especially Heathrow. In March 2007, the OFT referred the case to the Competition Commission for investigation under the Enterprise Act 2002. The brief for the investigation was 'to investigate whether any feature, or combination of features, of the market or markets for airport services in the UK as exist in connection with the supply of airport services by BAA Limited prevents, restricts or distorts competition in connection with the supply or acquisition of any goods or services in the UK or a part of the UK. If so there is an "adverse effect on competition"' (Competition Commission, 2008).

In terms of market share, it was clear that BAA was in a very strong position. The Competition Commission noted that its seven airports accounted for more than 60% of all passengers using UK airports. In the South East, Heathrow, Gatwick, Stansted and Southampton between them accounted for 90% of air passengers; in Scotland, 84% of air passengers were accounted for by Edinburgh, Glasgow and Aberdeen. The key issue is whether this market position was damaging competition, and hence working against consumer interests.

BAA's dominant market position was found to be having an adverse effect on competition

Competition between airports

An important aspect of this is whether there is scope for competition between airports, and what effect such competition would have on the nature and quality of service that would be offered. In order to approach this question, the Competition Commission looked at evidence relating to non-BAA airports that could be regarded as being in potential competition with each other — for example, Birmingham International Airport and East Midlands Airport, Cardiff International Airport and Bristol International Airport, and other combinations. Some evidence was found which suggested that there could be competition between airports, particularly in relation to the low-cost airlines. However, competition is most likely where there is spare capacity — which is not the case for Heathrow and Gatwick.

Competition also requires there to be the potential for substitution in demand. In other words, there needs to be some overlap in the potential catchment area for competing airports. In relation to BAA's airports in Scotland, it was found that there was some overlap in catchment between Glasgow and Edinburgh — but not with Aberdeen. In the South East, there was little evidence of competition between BAA's London airports and non-BAA airports (apart from some competition between Southampton and Bournemouth). However, there was significant overlap in the catchment areas of these airports, suggesting the possibility of some competition (subject to capacity constraints).

The Competition Commission came to the view that the shortage of capacity in the South East had partly arisen from the common ownership of the three BAA London airports, and that had these airports been under separate ownership, the incentives to expand capacity and improve the quality of service being offered would have been higher.

Having concluded that there was evidence that the market structure was having an adverse effect on competition, the Competition Commission in its provisional findings recommended that BAA should sell two of its three airports in the South East, and should not be allowed to continue to own airports in both Glasgow and Edinburgh.

Since that time, BAA has become Heathrow Airport Holdings Ltd, owning four airports: Heathrow, Southampton, Glasgow and Aberdeen. It sold Gatwick in 2009, Edinburgh and Prestwick in 2012, and Stansted in 2013. Southampton Airport was acquired by AGS Airports in 2014.

Summary

- Competition policy in the UK is implemented through the Competition and Markets Authority, which replaced the Office of Fair Trading and the Competition Commission in April 2014.
- The main pillars of policy are legislation dealing with agreements between firms and the abuse of a dominant position.
- A key step in any investigation is to define the relevant market.
- The CMA carries out a preliminary investigation of mergers that meet the criteria in terms of market share and size of assets.
- It then decides whether to initiate a thorough investigation.
- Some mergers are allowed to proceed without referral.
- The CMA may permit the merger to go ahead, may impose conditions on the firm, or may prohibit it.

A final area in which governments intervene that has not been discussed so far is pensions policy. It is clear that in the UK and many other advanced economies, pensions are coming under pressure in terms of funding. This results from changes in the demographic structure of the population, with people living longer and population growth rates slowing.

The result of this demographic shift is that governments are finding they have to pay a greater share of national income on pension schemes, whilst at the same time facing a shrinking tax base. The recent credit crisis and subsequent deterioration in government finances has created added pressure.

In the UK, the basic state pension in 2014/15 was £113.10 per week for a single person. This is funded through compulsory National Insurance (NI) contributions which people pay during their working life.

With an ageing population, pensions are increasingly expensive. In addition, people over 65 are more likely to require indirect spending, such as healthcare treatment on the NHS, and as older people are not likely to be working, they will not be paying income tax and National Insurance contributions.

Pensioners are one of the groups most at risk of relative poverty. This age-related poverty has been made worse by other factors such as rising fuel costs and inflation, which affects pensioners the most because many are on fixed incomes. There are fears that because of inadequate income, some pensioners may have to cut back on basic necessities such as heating and power. This is why government has introduced schemes such as the winter fuel allowance, which is an additional benefit to help pay energy bills. However, there is a continuing trade-off between reducing relative poverty (through means-tested benefits) and creating sufficient incentives for people to save for their retirement.

Solutions to the pension problem

The difficulty is that any long-term solution to the pension crisis tends to be politically unpopular. Solutions tend to involve higher taxes, a longer working life and increased commitments to provide private pensions. It is often much easier for a government to delay making politically unpopular decisions and leave it 'for a later date'.

One possible solution from a funding perspective is to raise the retirement age. In 1909, the first state pension was given to people over 70. At that time, the life expectancy for people over 70 was quite short. But in the twenty-first century, life expectancy is much higher. Therefore, given that people live longer, there is a case for increasing the retirement age, maintaining the same portion of the life span in retirement. Indeed, the government has already announced plans to increase the pension age. The age at which people qualify for the state pension will increase to 67 for both men and women by 2028. By 2046, it will be 68. However, the government may be tempted to bring this date forward.

Raising the retirement age has key benefits. It reduces government spending, it increases the size of the labour force, enabling a bigger productive capacity, and it can help finance a more worthwhile state pension. It is one of the few budget cuts that can reduce the long-term deficit without causing lower aggregate demand and lower economic growth. Given recent levels of debt and the prolonged recession, this makes raising the retirement age quite an attractive proposition. However, there are some drawbacks. It means that people who planned to retire at a certain date now have to delay it. In addition, raising the retirement age may increase inequality. High earners can still afford to retire early due to their private pensions, but low-paid manual workers will have to keep working.

To reduce the burden on government spending and taxation, the government has tried to increase the role of the private sector in pension provision. The idea is that by placing greater emphasis on the private sector, the government can avoid increasing tax rates, which may reduce incentives to work.

However, private pensions have also come under pressure with the low rates of interest that have prevailed since the financial crisis. Pension funds rely on investing the funds that are lodged with them and funding the pension payments from the returns that they receive. In periods when returns are low, this can create problems.

Exercise 10.4

Explain possible solutions to the pension problem and discuss which you think would be most effective.

Summary

- The UK and other advanced economies are experiencing the effects of an ageing population.
- This puts pressure on government resources because the government has to pay pensions for a longer period and because the elderly tend to need more healthcare treatment.
- Pensioners are at particular risk of relative poverty.
- Possible solutions to the pension problem include raising the retirement age and encouraging more people to contribute to private pensions.

Case study 10.1

The economic impacts of transport infrastructure

Cost–benefit analysis

Traditionally, major transport investment projects have been appraised by the use of cost–benefit analysis (CBA), which enables decision-makers to take into account the direct impacts of a project on a common basis, whether or not they are actually priced in a market. For most road projects where tolls are not paid, virtually all of the benefits will fall into this category. What is not usually included is any wider economic impact which the project may have on enhancing productivity, stimulating growth or affecting the distribution of income.

Traditional CBA lies behind the COBA model, which has been used for appraising road projects in the UK for many years. It does not include the non-user costs and benefits, principally the impacts on the environment through pollution, global warming effects, noise, visual intrusion, etc. But there is no reason why such effects cannot be included; all that is needed is a valid monetary valuation of the impact. Often, however, proponents of a scheme which fails to achieve a sufficient benefit:cost ratio score to be adopted claim that there are unmeasured benefits to the economy, such that if the project were to be completed, it would enhance the competitiveness of an area, reduce unemployment and so on. Can we simply add on a set of benefits to allow for this?

One key issue arises from the nature of demand for transport. The demand derives from the benefit that arises from making a journey. Assuming that no-one simply travels for the sake of travelling, but only for a specific purpose — for instance, work, shopping or leisure — then the willingness to pay for travel depends on the benefit derived from the activity in question. Put another way, travel is an input into the final activity. Thus the marginal value of the travel depends on the marginal value of the activity it enables.

If these activities are supplied under conditions of perfect competition then the willingness to pay for travel will reflect exactly the marginal value of the activity. In such circumstances, the transport benefits will exactly reflect the total economic benefit and hence there is no 'wider economic benefit' to be added.

Imperfect competition

Now let us consider what happens when there is imperfect competition in the markets which use transport: output markets and labour markets. In the case of output markets, the prices charged will no longer be equal to marginal costs and thus any change in the cost of transport will not be reflected directly in the price of the activity. Now there are several possible outcomes, depending on the extent of the mark-up of price over marginal cost. The mark-up will itself depend on such factors as the market size, scale economies, the degree of competition or potential competition and the elasticity of demand for the activity.

What does this mean for the overall value of a project? There are several different forces at work here. Lower transport costs increase competition and this pushes price closer to marginal cost, such that for a given reduction in cost there is a bigger reduction in price and hence a larger gain in consumer surplus. In addition, firms can increase their markets as their transport costs fall, and hence can exploit scale economies more. This may be anti-competitive, but as long as the fall in costs is greater than the increase in mark-up, the gains will again be greater than in the case of perfect competition. However, the improvements to transport also aid the process of agglomeration, which boosts the productivity of all the firms in the area affected by the transport improvement. Agglomeration economies arise through the increasing concentration of particular activities in one area (localisation economies), through the clustering of different types of activity which enhance the forward and backward linkages between different activities, and through the more efficient provision of a range of services to all industries (urbanisation economies). This has the effect of reducing costs even further and

What is the wider economic impact of major transport projects?

boosting the potential benefits. The net effect will depend on the interaction of all these effects in the particular case.

Perhaps some of the most interesting impacts are to be found in labour markets. A simple perfect market explanation would predict that wages will be equalised if barriers to mobility are reduced. This is likely to be too simplistic. Three types of response could occur. First, there may be an effect on labour market participation: lower costs of access to jobs could induce more workers into the labour market. Second, those with jobs could be induced to work longer hours as the time spent commuting has been reduced. Third, workers could be induced to move from less productive jobs in more peripheral areas to more productive jobs in core areas. Now each of these could simply be seen as a reallocation, but if the move towards jobs in the core also leads to agglomeration effects of the type discussed above, then productivity would rise further and the wage differential between core and periphery could increase. This increasing differential might induce even more workers to move jobs towards the core as the real wage after allowing for commuting continues to increase.

The key to understanding the impact of transport projects is thus to recognise that there are no guaranteed wider benefits; much will depend on the details of the particular project.

Source: 'The economic aspects of transport infrastructure investments', by Roger Vickerman, *Economic Review*, April 2007

Follow-up questions

a Identify the sorts of impact that would normally be included in a cost–benefit analysis.

b Explain why 'under conditions of perfect competition...the willingness to pay for travel will reflect exactly the marginal value of the activity'.

c Explain why the extent of the mark-up over marginal cost depends on the factors listed in the passage.

d If there are 'no guaranteed wider benefits' from transport projects, should an attempt be made to consider them?

Case study 10.2

Cinemas in Basingstoke and Edinburgh

In September 2005, the OFT referred to the Competition Commission (CC) a completed takeover of Ster Century by Vue Entertainment Holdings. Before the merger, Vue was the third largest operator of cinemas in the UK, with 42 cinemas and 409 screens; Ster owned and operated 6 cinemas in the UK with 73 screens; these were located in Basingstoke, Cardiff, Edinburgh, Leeds, Norwich and Romford.

In investigating the merger, the CC had first to define what was the relevant market. It decided to restrict the market definition to cinema exhibition, and that the appropriate scale for market investigation was a local geographic area. The main focus was on cinemas within a 20-minute drive-time of the acquired cinemas. Evidence suggested that cinema-goers tend to decide which film they wish to see first of all, and then where to see it as a secondary decision, normally going to the closest cinema, although there may be some variation in the quality of cinema, which may be reflected in ticket prices. It was not thought that the merger would significantly increase Vue's negotiating position with screen advertising contracts, distributors or other suppliers, so there would not be an impact at the national level.

In Basingstoke, the merger meant that Vue owned the only two cinemas within a 20-minute drive of the city.

Vue argued that it was in competition with cinemas in Winchester, Alton, Bracknell, Reading and Woking, but the CC did not find this to be a strong argument. As a result, a substantial lessening of competition (SLC) was expected to occur, which was likely to lead to higher prices for cinema tickets and a reduced incentive to maintain quality.

The situation in Edinburgh was quite different. After the merger there were still a 'significant number of competing cinemas and screens' in the city. The CC therefore took the view that there would be no SLC resulting from the merger in this case.

Vue mounted a defence of its position in Basingstoke. One argument put forward related to the market for DVDs, claiming that the DVD market was constraining cinemas in their pricing policy. In addition, Vue offered to agree a price cap, restricting any increase in ticket price in Basingstoke to the average percentage ticket price rise across the whole Vue cinema circuit for each type of ticket. Vue also promised to maintain quality by spending at least as much as the average across its circuit on site maintenance. Vue also promised to keep both cinemas open, and to offer a broad range of films to ensure consumer choice.

Follow-up questions

a Explain what is meant by 'relevant market' and why it is important for an investigation of this sort.

b Why might it be important to check whether the merger would significantly affect Vue's bargaining power with its suppliers?

c How convincing do you find Vue's defence?

d What decision would you have taken if you had been the CC?

Microeconomics key terms

abnormal, supernormal or economic profits profits above normal profits

allocative efficiency achieved when society is producing the appropriate bundle of goods and services relative to consumer preferences

arbitrage a process by which prices in two market segments will be equalised as a result of purchase and resale by market participants

average cost total cost divided by the quantity produced; sometimes known as unit cost

average revenue the average revenue received by the firm per unit of output; it is total revenue divided by the quantity sold

barrier to entry a characteristic of a market that prevents new firms from readily joining the market

behavioural economics a branch of economics that builds on the psychology of human behaviour in decision making

budget line shows the boundary of an individual's consumption set, given the amount available to spend and the prices of the goods

cartel an agreement between firms on price and output with the intention of maximising their joint profits

competition policy an area of economic policy designed to promote competition within markets to encourage efficiency and protect consumer interests

conglomerate merger a merger between two firms operating in different markets

constant returns to scale found when long-run average cost remains constant with an increase in output — in other words, when output and costs rise at the same rate

contestable market a market in which the existing firm makes only normal profit, as it cannot set a price higher than average cost without attracting entry, owing to the absence of barriers to entry and sunk costs

corporate social responsibility actions that a firm takes in order to demonstrate its commitment to behaving in the public interest

dependency ratio the ratio of those aged 15 or below and 65 and above to the working population

derived demand demand for a good not for its own sake, but for what it produces, e.g. labour is demanded for the output that it produces

discount a process whereby the future valuation of a cost or benefit is reduced (discounted) in order to provide an estimate of its present value

discrimination a situation in a labour market where some people receive lower wages that cannot be explained by economic factors

diseconomies of scale occur for a firm when an increase in the scale of production leads to higher long-run average costs

dominant strategy a situation in game theory where a player's best strategy is independent of those chosen by others

dynamic efficiency a view of efficiency that takes into account the effect of innovation and technical progress on productive and allocative efficiency in the long run

economic rent a payment received by a factor of production over and above what would be needed to keep it in its present use

economically active active in the labour force, including the employed, the self-employed and the unemployed

economies of scale occur for a firm when an increase in the scale of production leads to production at lower long-run average cost

economies of scope economies arising when average cost falls as a firm increases output across a range of different products

environmental Kuznets curve a relationship between economic growth and environmental degradation, under which environmental degradation at first increases as an economy expands, but then may improve at higher average income levels

equi-marginal principle that a consumer does best in utility terms by consuming at the point where the ratio of marginal utilities from two goods is equal to the ratio of their prices

external economies of scale economies of scale that arise from the expansion of the industry in which a firm is operating

externality a cost or a benefit that is external to a market transaction, borne (or enjoyed) by a third party, and not reflected in market prices

firm an organisation that brings together factors of production in order to produce output

fixed costs costs that do not vary with the level of output

game theory a method of modelling the strategic interaction between firms in an oligopoly

horizontal merger a merger between two firms at the same stage of production in the same industry

human capital the stock of skills and expertise that contribute to a worker's productivity

hypothecation in the context of the transport sector, the principle that revenues raised from taxing transport should be used to improve the transport system

ILO unemployment rate measure of the percentage of the workforce who are without jobs but are available for work, willing to work and looking for work

income effect of a price change reflects the way that a change in the price of a good affects purchasing power

industry long-run supply curve (LRS) under perfect competition, the curve that, for the typical firm in the industry, is horizontal at the minimum point of the long-run average cost curve

informal labour market economic activity that is not registered or recorded, and so is not part of the formal labour market

internal economies of scale economies of scale that arise from the expansion of a firm

internalising an externality an attempt to deal with an externality by bringing an external cost or benefit into the price system

labour productivity a measure of output per worker, or output per hour worked

law of diminishing marginal utility states that the more units of a good that are consumed, the lower the utility from consuming those additional units

law of diminishing returns a law stating that if a firm increases its inputs of one factor of production while holding inputs of the other factor fixed, eventually the firm will get diminishing marginal returns from the variable factor

living wage an estimate of how much income households need to afford an acceptable standard of living

long run the period over which the firm is able to vary the inputs of all its factors of production

marginal cost the cost of producing an additional unit of output

marginal physical product of labour (MPP_L) the additional quantity of output produced by an additional unit of labour input

marginal principle the idea that economic agents may take decisions by considering the effect of small changes from the existing situation

marginal productivity theory a theory which argues that the demand for labour depends upon balancing the revenue that a firm gains from employing an additional unit of labour against the marginal cost of that unit of labour

marginal revenue the additional revenue received by the firm if it sells an additional unit of output

marginal revenue product of labour (MRP_L) the additional revenue received by a firm as it increases output by using an additional unit of labour input, i.e. the marginal physical product of labour multiplied by the marginal revenue received by the firm

marginal utility the additional utility gained from consuming an extra unit of a good or service

market structure the market environment within which firms operate

minimum efficient scale the level of output at which long-run average cost stops falling as output increases

minimum wage legislation under which firms are not allowed to pay a wage below some threshold level set by the government

monopolistic competition a market that shares some characteristics of monopoly and some of perfect competition

monopoly a form of market structure in which there is only one seller of a good or service

monopsony a market in which there is a single buyer of a good, service or factor of production

multinational corporation a firm that conducts its operations in a number of countries

Nash equilibrium a situation occurring within a game when each player's chosen strategy maximises payoffs given the other player's choice, so no player has an incentive to alter behaviour

natural monopoly monopoly that arises in an industry in which there are such substantial economies of scale that only one firm is viable

net present value the estimated value in the current time period of the discounted future net benefit of a project

***n*-firm concentration ratio** a measure of the market share of the largest *n* firms in an industry

NIMBY (not in my back yard) a syndrome under which people are happy to support the construction of an unsightly or unsocial facility, so long as it is not in their back yard

non-pecuniary benefits benefits offered to workers by firms that are not financial in nature

non-renewable resource a resource that cannot be renewed once its supply is exhausted

normal profit the return needed for a firm to stay in a market in the long run

oligopoly a market with a few sellers, in which each firm must take account of the behaviour and likely behaviour of rival firms in the industry

participation rate the percentage of the population in a given age group who are economically active

perfect competition a form of market structure that produces allocative and productive efficiency in long-run equilibrium

perfect/first-degree price discrimination a situation arising in a market whereby a monopoly firm is able to charge each consumer a different price

predatory pricing an anti-competitive strategy in which a firm sets price below average variable cost in an attempt to force a rival or rivals out of the market and achieve market dominance

price taker a firm that must accept whatever price is set in the market as a whole

principal–agent problem arises from conflict between the objectives of the principals and their agents, who take decisions on their behalf

prisoners' dilemma an example of game theory with a range of applications in oligopoly theory

product differentiation a strategy adopted by firms that marks their product as being different from their competitors'

productive efficiency when a firm operates at minimum average cost, choosing an appropriate combination of inputs and producing the maximum output possible from those inputs

rational decision making a decision that allows an economic agent to maximise their objective, by setting the marginal benefit of an action equal to its marginal cost

real earnings the level of earnings adjusted for the price level; the rate of change of real earnings is thus the rate of change of earnings adjusted for inflation (the rate of change of prices)

relevant market a market to be investigated under competition law, defined in such a way that no major substitutes are omitted but no non-substitutes are included

renewable resource a resource that can replenish itself over time

replacement ratio the ratio of unemployment benefits to the wage that a claimant could receive in employment

satisficing behaviour under which the managers of firms aim to produce satisfactory results for the firm (e.g. in terms of profits) rather than trying to maximise them

shadow price an estimate of the monetary value of an item that does not carry a market price

short run the period over which a firm is free to vary its input of one factor of production (labour), but faces fixed inputs of the other factors of production

short-run supply curve for a firm operating under perfect competition, the curve given by its short-run marginal cost curve above the price at which $MC = SAVC$; for the industry, the horizontal sum of the supply curves of the individual firms

social cost–benefit analysis (CBA) a process of evaluating the worth of a project by comparing its costs and benefits, including both direct and social costs and benefits — including externality effects

static efficiency efficiency at a particular point in time

substitution effect of a price change reflects the way that a change in the price of a good affects relative prices

sunk costs costs incurred by a firm that cannot be recovered if the firm ceases trading

sustainable development 'development that meets the needs of the present without compromising the ability of future generations to meet their own needs' (Brundtland Commission, 1987)

tacit collusion a situation occurring when firms refrain from competing on price, but without communication or formal agreement between them

total cost the sum of all costs that are incurred in producing a given level of output

total factor productivity the average productivity of all factors, measured as the total output divided by the total amount of inputs used

total revenue the revenue received by a firm from its sales of a good or service; it is the quantity sold, multiplied by the price

trade union an organisation of workers that negotiates with employers on behalf of its members

transfer earnings the minimum payment required to keep a factor of production in its present use

unemployment trap a situation in which people choose to be unemployed because the level of unemployment benefit is high relative to the wage available in low-paid occupations

unit labour cost wages, salaries and other costs of using labour, divided by output per worker

utility the satisfaction received from consuming a good or service

variable costs costs that vary with the level of output

vertical merger a merger between two firms in the same industry, but at different stages of the production process

workforce people who are economically active, either employed or unemployed

working population people between the ages of 16 and 64

X-inefficiency occurs when a firm is not operating at minimum cost, perhaps because of organisational slack

Questions

Microeconomics practice questions

Part 1: How competitive markets work

1 Chloe gains 50 utils from consuming one bar of chocolate, and 95 utils from consuming two bars. What is her marginal utility from consuming the second bar?

- **A** 5 utils
- **B** 45 utils
- **C** 50 utils
- **D** −5 utils

2 Which of the following summarises the equi-marginal principle?

- **A** $MU_x/MU_y = P_y/P_x$
- **B** $MU_x/MU_y = P_x/P_y$
- **C** $MU_y/MU_x = P_x/P_y$
- **D** $MU_x \times P_x = MU_y \times P_y$

3 Figure 1 shows Jack's budget line between music CDs and DVDs given his available budget.

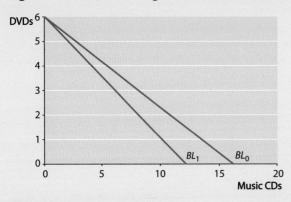

Figure 1 A shift in the budget line

Following a change in the price of apples, the budget line has moved from BL_0 to BL_1. Which of the following could have led to this change?

- **A** A fall in the price of music CDs
- **B** An increase in the price of music CDs
- **C** A fall in the price of DVDs
- **D** An increase in Jack's budget

4 Which of the following statements is **not** true?

   A The more you consume of a good, the less additional pleasure you get from extra units of the good.

   B The income effect of a price change reflects the way that a change in the price of a good affects spending power.

   C An increase in the budget that a consumer has to allocate to spending on goods causes the budget line to move inwards.

   D The substitution effect of a price change reflects the way that a change in the price of a good affects relative prices.

Part 2: Competition and market power

1 A rise in long-run average costs necessarily indicates that the firm is experiencing:

   A Diminishing returns

   B Increasing returns to scale

   C Diseconomies of scale

   D Increasing revenues

2 The diagram below shows the short-run cost curves of a firm.

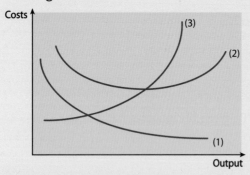

Figure 2 Short-run cost curves

Which of the following is correct?

   A Curve (1) is the average total cost curve

   B Curve (1) is the total cost curve

   C Curve (2) is the average fixed cost curve

   D Curve (3) is the marginal cost curve

3 X-inefficiency occurs when a firm:

   A Is producing at the lowest marginal cost

   B Is operating above its long-run average cost curve

   C Sets price equal to marginal cost

   D Is producing more goods than are demanded

4 A firm that aims to maximise profits will produce the output at which:

   A The marginal revenue is zero

   B Total cost is equal to total revenue

   C The difference between total revenue and total cost is greatest

   D Average revenue is less than average cost

5 In the short run, a firm will continue in business so long as:

   A Average revenue is greater than marginal cost

   B Average revenue is greater than average variable cost

   C Marginal cost is greater than marginal revenue

   D Average revenue is greater than average fixed cost

6 Which of the following may be found under conditions of perfect competition?

A Product differentiation

B Barriers to the entry of new firms

C Price discrimination

D An individual firm faces a perfectly elastic demand curve

7 A firm operating in a perfectly competitive market is currently making supernormal profits. In the long run:

A There will be an increase in the price of the product

B The firm's output and price will fall

C Firms will leave the industry

D The firm's output will rise and its price will fall

8 A perfectly competitive firm's total costs for various levels of output are shown in the table below.

Units of output	1	2	3	4	5	6	7	8	9	10
Total cost (pence)	7	13	18	22	25	29	34	40	47	55

If the market price is 6p, which of the following ranges of output would a profit-maximising firm choose to produce?

A 1–2

B 3–4

C 5–6

D 7–8

9 A profit-maximising monopolist will produce the output at which:

A Marginal revenue is zero

B Average revenue is equal to average cost

C Marginal cost is equal to marginal revenue

D The difference between marginal revenue and marginal cost is greatest

10 The monopoly power of a business will tend to rise if:

A Barriers to the entry of new firms increase

B It diversifies into new product lines

C There is a rise in monopoly profits

D There is a reduction in tariffs on similar goods

11 A monopolistically competitive firm is in long-run equilibrium. Which of the following combinations applies to such a firm?

	Allocative efficiency	Productive efficiency	Supernormal profit
A	Yes	No	No
B	No	No	Yes
C	No	Yes	Yes
D	No	No	No

12 Which market structure is characterised by barriers to entrys and interdependence between the few firms operating in the market?

A Monopoly

B Perfect competition

C Oligopoly

D Monopolistic competition

13 Mobile phone companies operating in an oligopolistic market usually employ price competition or advertising as means of increasing market share. Use game theory to explain how firms might behave in such a market.

14 Evaluate pricing and non-pricing strategies that car retailers might employ as means of competing with rival firms.

15 Which of the following conditions is most likely to explain the small number of firms controlling over 90% of the market for detergents?

A High sunk costs
B Absence of legal barriers
C Low start-up costs
D High contestability

16 If a firm switches from a policy of profit maximisation to a policy of revenue maximisation, then which of the following will be true?

	Price	Output	Profit
A	Higher	Higher	Higher
B	Lower	Higher	Higher
C	Lower	Higher	Lower
D	Lower	Lower	Lower

17 In order to produce at the allocatively efficient level of output, a monopolist would produce the output at which:

A Average total cost is at its minimum level
B Price is equal to marginal cost
C Marginal revenue is equal to marginal cost
D Price is equal to average total cost

18 A firm may adopt a limit price with the primary aim of:

A Deterring the entry of new firms
B Increasing its supernormal profits
C Increasing producer surplus
D Deterring investigation by the competition authorities

19 Increased expenditure on advertising by firms in an industry is likely to:

A Decrease the concentration ratio in the industry
B Decrease sunk costs
C Decrease contestability
D Reduce the revenues of marketing firms

20 A necessary condition for a monopolist to practise price discrimination is that:

A The price elasticity of demand must be the same in both markets
B The two markets must be geographically separate
C The cost of separating the two markets must be greater than the revenue obtained from charging different prices in the two markets
D The markets must be completely separated

Part 3: The labour market

1 The demand for workers in the UK vegetable farming industry will decrease if:

A The price that supermarkets are prepared to pay for vegetables increases

B The increase in world population causes increased demand for vegetables

C It becomes cheaper to use machinery to harvest the vegetables

D More people become vegetarians

2 The demand for labour in a particular industry will be inelastic if:

A The prices of the products produced by the workers form a large proportion of consumers' incomes

B It is possible to substitute capital for labour

C The proportion of total costs accounted for by wage costs is very small

D The demand for the product is price elastic

3 **The National Minimum Wage**

The UK government introduced a National Minimum Wage (NMW) in 1999 at a rate of £3.60 and by October 2012 this had been increased to £6.19 for workers over the age 21, with lower rates for younger workers. One aim of this was to prevent the exploitation of workers by firms that paid very low wages.

Some business owners and economists argued that an NMW would cause widespread unemployment, especially in labour-intensive industries such as hotels and catering. However, there is only limited evidence of this because it is difficult to replace workers with machines in this industry. There is a ready supply of workers because only limited qualifications are required and also because of the availability of immigrant workers from eastern Europe.

a Explain **one** reason why the government intervenes in labour markets by imposing a National Minimum Wage.

b Outline **two** factors that influence the demand for labour in the hotel industry.

c To what extent might an increase in the National Minimum Wage lead to job losses in the hotel industry? Illustrate your answer with an appropriate labour market diagram.

d Apart from the National Minimum Wage, discuss the factors that might influence the supply of labour to the hotel industry or to another occupation of your choice.

Part 4 Market failure and government intervention

1 The government is considering investing in an infrastructure project that is expected to bring direct benefits with a present value of £2 billion over a 10-year period. The present value of the net costs is estimated to be £2.5 billion. The benefit:cost ratio is:

A £0.5 billion

B 0.8

C 1.25

D −£0.5 billion

2 In addition to the direct costs outlined in the previous question, external benefits are estimated to be £1.6 billion and external costs are expected to be £0.5 billion. The benefit:cost ratio is:

A £3.6 billion

B 0.8

C 1.2

D 1.25

3 In the project outlined in questions 1 and 2, should the government proceed with the investment? What additional information would be needed? Explain your answer.

4 In 2002, Aberdeen Journals was fined £1.3 million by the Office of Fair Trading following allegations about predatory pricing. Which characteristic is likely to have been observed?

A Price set above average total cost in the short run

B Price set at the output at which average total cost is equal to average revenue

C Output determined by the level at which marginal revenue is zero

D Price set below average variable cost in the short run

5 The UK government has agreed many contracts under the Private Finance Initiative (PFI) for the building of new hospitals over the last 10 years. A significant reason for the government's use of PFI contracts is that:

A It had a budget surplus

B There was a surplus of building workers

C The number of people requiring treatment in hospitals was declining

D PFI enabled hospitals to be built without an immediate increase in the budget deficit

MACROECONOMICS

Part 5
Macroeconomic policy and performance

Chapter 11

Growth and development

This chapter explores the relationship between economic growth and human development and looks at ways in which economic and human development can be recognised. Countries in different parts of the world have followed different paths to development — with varying degrees of success. Differences partly reflect the different characteristics of each country. Less developed countries (LDCs) do seem to share some characteristics, but each country also faces its own configuration of problems and opportunities. This chapter explores some of the common characteristics that LDCs display, but also examines some of the key differences between them. It will also examine how overseas aid and international trade can promote growth and development and discuss the role of multilateral organisations such as the IMF, World Bank and WTO in this process.

Learning objectives

After studying this chapter, you should:
- understand what is meant by economic and human development
- be familiar with the most important economic and social indicators that can help to evaluate the standard of living in different societies
- recognise the strengths and limitations of such indicators in providing a profile of a country's stage of development
- be aware of the importance of political and cultural factors in influencing a country's path of development
- be aware of the diversity of experience of less developed countries
- be aware of significant differences between regions of the world in terms of their level and pace of development
- understand the importance of the structure of economic activity in an economy
- be able to evaluate the impact of aid and trade on economic and human development
- be aware of the respective roles of multilateral organisations in promoting trade and development

Prior knowledge needed

Economic growth was discussed in Book 1, Chapter 12, using the growth of GDP per capita as an indicator.

Key term

development a process by which real per capita incomes are increased and the inhabitants of a country are able to benefit from improved living conditions, i.e. lower poverty and enhanced standards of education, health, nutrition and other essentials of life

Defining development

The first step is to define what is meant by 'development'. You might think that it is about economic growth — if a society can expand its productive capacity, surely that is development? But development means much more than this. Economic growth may well be a necessary ingredient, since development cannot take place without an expansion of the resources available in a society; however, it is not a sufficient ingredient, because those additional resources must be used wisely, and the growth that results must be the 'right' sort of growth.

Wrapped up with development are issues concerning the alleviation of poverty — no country can be considered 'developed' if a substantial portion of its population is living in absolute poverty. Development also requires structural change, and possibly changes in institutions and, in some cases, cultural and political attitudes.

In recognition of the multifaceted nature of development, the United Nations Millennium Summit in 2000 agreed a set of **Millennium Development Goals (MDGs)** that encapsulated their views of the main priorities for development. These were:

- eradicate extreme poverty and hunger
- achieve universal primary education
- promote gender equality and empower women
- reduce child mortality
- improve maternal health
- combat HIV/AIDS, malaria and other diseases
- ensure environmental sustainability
- develop a global partnership for development

These eight goals represent key facets of development that need to be addressed. The original aim was to achieve specific targets for each of the goals by 2015. Substantial progress was made in relation to some of the goals, although not all of the specific targets were met, especially in some regions of the world. The United Nations has worked with governments, civil society and other partners to create an ambitious post-2015 agenda to build upon the progress that was made up to 2015.

In thinking about these goals, you can begin to understand the various dimensions of development, and realise that it is about much more than economic growth — although growth may be seen as a prerequisite for the achievement of the goals. At the same time, failure to achieve these goals will retard economic growth.

To summarise, development is about more than just economic growth. Achieving higher real income per capita is a necessary part of development, but it is not all there is to it. A country will not be recognised as achieving development unless it is also able to alleviate poverty, improve education levels and health standards, and provide an enhanced physical and cultural environment. Furthermore, such improvements must reach all inhabitants of the country, and not be confined to certain groups within society. In other words, economic growth may be *necessary* for development to take place, but it is not *sufficient*. Expanding the resources available within a society is the first step, but those resources also need to be used well.

Key term

Millennium Development Goals (MDGs) targets set for each less developed country, reflecting a range of development objectives to be monitored each year to evaluate progress

One of the Millennium Development Goals was to achieve universal primary education

Summary

- Economic growth is one aspect of economic development, in that it provides an increase in the resources available to members of society in less developed countries.
- However, in addition, development requires that the resources made available through economic growth are used appropriately to meet development objectives.
- The Millennium Development Goals were set by the Millennium Summit of the United Nations in September 2000.
- These eight goals comprise a set of targets for each less developed country, which were to be achieved by 2015.
- An ambitious programme for the post-2015 period is to be agreed to build on the progress made.

Exercise 11.1

Visit the Millennium Development Goals website at **www.un.org/ millenniumgoals/**. Discuss which of the goals you see as being of most importance for development and explore the extent to which progress has being made towards the goals in two or three countries of your choice.

Which are the less developed countries?

There is no single definitive list of countries that are regarded as being the *less developed countries* (LDCs), and it is important to be aware that this term is used to refer to a wide range of countries with differing characteristics. The discussion in this chapter will be illustrated using indicators for a selection of countries from different regions of the world, but try to remember the wide diversity among the countries that are classified as LDCs. Although it is tempting to generalise, you need to be a little wary of doing so. Different countries have different characteristics, and face different configurations of problems and opportunities. Therefore, a policy that works for one country might fail totally in a different part of the world.

In broad terms, the countries regarded as LDCs are concentrated in four major regions: sub-Saharan Africa, Latin America, South Asia and South East Asia. This excludes some countries in the 'less developed' range, but relatively few. For some purposes it may be necessary to treat China separately, rather than including it as part of South East Asia, partly because of its sheer size, and partly because it has followed a rather different development path.

Indicators of development

GNI per capita

The first step is to be able to measure 'development'. We might begin by comparing average income levels across countries. This was done in Book 1 with reference to data for GDP per capita. However, when we want to focus on the standard of living that is experienced by people in different countries, it is important to recognise that although GDP is an indicator of the total level of activity in an economy during a period, this does not take into account flows of income from abroad. This is significant for some countries, where nationals of the country work abroad and send some of their income back to their families. Gross national income (GNI) takes these flows into account, and is the standard measure used by the World Bank to compare income levels across countries. **GNI per capita** will therefore be used as the indicator of average incomes within a country.

GNI does have some advantages as a measure. First, it is relatively straightforward and thus is widely understood. Second, it is a well-established indicator and one that is available for almost every country in the world, so it can be used to compare income levels across countries.

Figure 11.1 provides data on GNI per capita for a selection of countries from each of the four major groupings. These countries will be used as examples throughout this discussion: they are colour-coded by region, with high-income countries grouped together. Because of the diversity of countries in each of the regions, such a selection must be treated with a little caution. Singapore, South Korea and China have been chosen to represent East Asia and the Pacific, in order to highlight three of the countries that have achieved rapid economic growth over a sustained period.

Key term

GNI per capita GDP plus net income from abroad, expressed as an average per person

Study tip

Do not be tempted to learn by heart lots of statistics about individual countries, as this will not be expected of you. Being aware of the general differences in the stage of development reached by countries in different regions may be helpful, but the detail is not necessary.

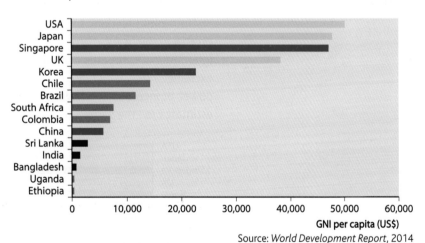

Source: *World Development Report*, 2014

Figure 11.1 GNI per capita, selected countries, 2012 (US$)

The extreme differences that exist around the globe are immediately apparent from the data. GNI per capita in Ethiopia is just $410, whereas in the USA the figure is $50,120. In trying to interpret these data, a number of issues need to be borne in mind, as the comparison is not as straightforward as it looks.

Exchange rate problems

The data presented in Figure 11.1 are expressed in terms of US dollars. This allows economists to compare average incomes using a common unit of measurement. At the same time, however, it may create some problems.

It is important to compare average income levels in order to evaluate the standard of living, and compare standards across countries. In other words, the aim is to assess people's command over resources in different societies, and to be able to compare the purchasing power of income in different countries.

GNI is calculated initially in terms of local currencies, and subsequently converted into US dollars using official exchange rates. Will this provide information about the relative local purchasing power of incomes? Not necessarily.

One reason for this is that official exchange rates are sometimes affected by government intervention. Indeed, in many of the less developed countries, exchange rates are pegged to an international currency — usually the US dollar. In these circumstances, exchange rates are more likely to reflect the government's policy and actions than the relative purchasing power of incomes in the country under scrutiny. For example, a government may choose to maintain an overvalued currency in order to try to maximise the earnings from its exports. In the case of China, the government has been tempted into the opposite situation, maintaining an undervalued currency in order to maximise export volume.

Where exchange rates are free to find their own equilibrium level, they are likely to be influenced strongly by the price of internationally traded goods, which is likely to be a very different combination of goods than that typically consumed by residents in these countries. Again, it can be argued that official exchange rates may not be a good reflection of the relative purchasing power of incomes across countries.

The United Nations International Comparison Project has been working on this problem for many years. It now produces an alternative set of international estimates of GNI based on *purchasing power parity* (PPP) exchange rates, which are designed to reflect the relative purchasing power of incomes in different societies more accurately. Figure 11.2 shows estimates for the same set of countries that were given in Figure 11.1.

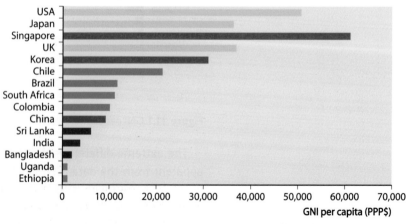

Source: *World Development Report*, 2014

Figure 11.2 GNI per capita, 2012 (PPP$)

Comparing the two graphs, you will notice that the gap between the low-income and high-income countries seems a bit less marked when PPP dollars (PPP$) are used as the unit of measurement. In other words, the US dollar estimates exaggerate the gap in living standards between rich and poor countries. This is a general feature of these measurements — that measurements in US dollars tend to understate real incomes for low-income countries and overstate them for high-income countries compared with PPP$ data. Put another way, people in the lower-income countries have a stronger command over goods and services than is suggested by US-dollar comparisons of GNI per capita. You will also see that in some cases, using PPP$ alters the rankings of the countries — for example, compare Singapore with Japan or the USA in the two figures.

Figure 11.3 shows the relative size of GNI per capita in PPP$ for the regional groupings of countries around the world in 2013. The gap in income levels between the LDCs and the 'very high human development' countries shows very clearly in the graph; equally, the gap between the countries of sub-Saharan Africa and South Asia, on the one hand, and those in East Asia and Latin America, on the other, is apparent. The graph also puts into context the position of the transition economies of Central and Eastern Europe and the CIS, and the Arab states. The Arab states are rather different in character because their oil resources have enabled them to increase their average income levels.

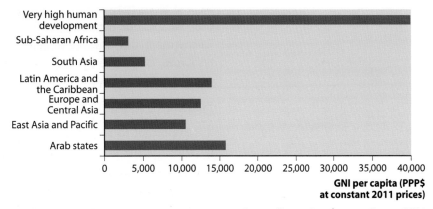

Source: *Human Development Report*, 2014

Figure 11.3 GNI per capita, regional groupings, 2013 (PPP$)

The informal sector and the accuracy of data

Synoptic link

The informal sector was discussed in the microeconomics part of the book, in Chapter 8.

Even when measured in PPP$, GNI has limitations as a measure of living standards. One limitation that is especially important when considering low-income countries is that in many LDCs there is considerable *informal economic activity*, which may not be captured by a measure like GNI, based on monetary transactions. Such activity includes subsistence agriculture, which remains important in many countries, especially in sub-Saharan Africa. In other words, GNI may not capture production that is directly used for consumption. Remember that GNI is measured by adding up the total transactions that take place in an economy. In the case of barter or production for consumption, there are no transactions to be measured, so they will not be captured in GNI.

Income distribution

Another important limitation of GNI per capita as a measure of living standards is that it is an *average* measure, and so does not reveal information about how income is distributed among groups in society.

In Brazil, the poorest 10% of households received less than 1% of total income in 2009, whereas the richest 10% received 43%. In Belarus, on the other hand, the poorest 10% received 4% of income and the richest 10% received 21%. These are extreme examples of the degree of inequality in the distribution of income within countries. This will be discussed further in Chapter 12.

Social indicators

A further question that arises is whether GNI can be regarded as a reasonable indicator of a country's *standard of living*. GNI provides an indicator of the total resources available within an economy in a given period, calculated from data about total output, total incomes or total expenditure. This focus on summing the transactions that take place in an economy over a period can be seen as a rather narrow view of what constitutes a country's standard of living. After all, it may be argued that the quality of people's lives depends on more things than simply the material resources that are available.

For one thing, people need to have knowledge if they are to make good use of the resources that are available. Two societies with similar income levels may nonetheless provide a very different quality of life for their inhabitants, depending on the education levels of the population. Furthermore, if people are to benefit from consuming or using the available resources, they need a reasonable lifespan coupled with good health. So, good standards of health are also crucial to a good quality of life.

Differing priorities

It is important to remember that different societies tend to set different priorities for the pursuit of growth and the promotion of education and health. Some countries have higher levels of health and education than other countries with similar levels of GNI per capita. This needs to be taken into account when judging relative living standards by comparing GNI per capita. For a given level of real GNI per capita, there may be substantial differences in living standards between a country that places a high priority on providing education and healthcare, and one that devotes resources to military expenditure. In the longer term, there may also be significant differences between a society that spends its resources on present consumption, and one that engages in investment in order to increase consumption in the future.

A reasonable environment in which to live may be seen as another important factor in one's quality of life. There are some environmental issues that can distort the GNI measure of resources. Suppose there is an environmental disaster — perhaps an oil tanker breaks up close to a beautiful beach. This reduces the overall quality of life by degrading the landscape and preventing enjoyment of the beach. However, it does not have a negative effect on GNI; on the contrary, the money spent on clearing up the damage actually adds to GNI, so that the net effect of an environmental disaster may be to *increase* the measured level of GNI!

The Human Development Index

To deal with the criticism that GNI per capita fails to take account of other dimensions of the quality of life, in 1990 the United Nations Development Programme (UNDP) devised an alternative indicator, known as the **Human Development Index (HDI)**. This was designed to provide a broader measure of the stage of development that a country had reached. It has since become a widely used indicator.

The basis for the HDI is that there are three key aspects of human development: resources, knowledge of how to make good use of those resources, and a reasonable life span in which to make use of those resources (see Figure 11.4). The three components are measured by, respectively, GNI per capita in PPP$, indicators of education (mean years of schooling and expected years of schooling) and life expectancy. The measurements are then combined to produce a composite index ranging between 0 and 1, with higher values reflecting higher human development.

GNI per capita (in PPP$) represents resources in this set-up, and is intended to reflect the extent to which people have command over resources. The education indicators pick up two rather different aspects of this important component of human development. *Mean* years of education can be seen as a way of reflecting educational attainment, as it measures the average number of years of schooling that were received by people aged 25 and above in their lifetime. It thus tells us something about the extent to which there has been past investment in education. *Expected* years of schooling, on the other hand, reveals something about the current state of education in an economy. That is, it identifies the number of years of schooling that a child of school entrance age can expect to receive, given current patterns of enrolment and access to education. Life expectancy is the natural indicator of expected lifespan, and is also closely related to the general level of health of people in the country.

Values of the HDI for 2013 are charted in Figure 11.5 for the selected countries. You can see that the broad ranking of the countries in Figure 11.1 is preserved, but the gap between low and high human development is less marked. Exceptions are South Africa and Brazil, which are ranked lower on the basis of the HDI than on GNI per capita: what this suggests

Figure 11.4 Components of the Human Development Index

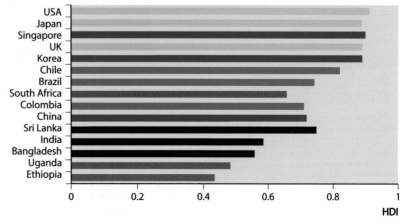

Source: *Human Development Report*, 2014

Figure 11.5 The Human Development Index, 2013

197

is that these countries have achieved relatively high income levels, but other aspects of human development have not kept pace. There are other countries in the world that share this feature. You will see that there are also countries that seem to perform better on HDI grounds than on GNI per capita — for example, China and Sri Lanka.

Figures 11.6 and 11.7 show the levels of two of the measures that enter into the HDI: life expectancy and mean years of schooling. It would seem that life expectancy is primarily responsible for the low ranking of South Africa in the HDI, as its level of life expectancy is out of kilter with its average income level and mean years of schooling. In contrast, Bangladesh and India perform quite well in terms of lifespan, but relatively poorly in terms of education. By comparing these data, you can get some idea of the diversity between countries that was mentioned earlier.

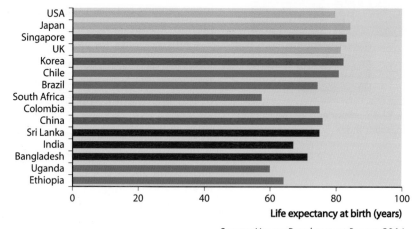

Source: *Human Development Report*, 2014

Figure 11.6 Life expectancy at birth

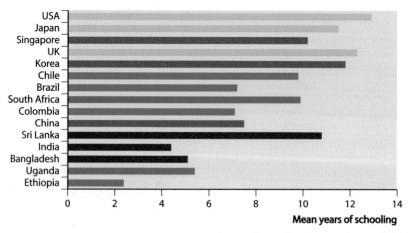

Source: *Human Development Report*, 2014

Figure 11.7 Mean years of schooling

In part, this diversity reflects differing priorities that governments have given to different aspects of development. Countries such as Brazil have aimed primarily at achieving economic growth, while those such as Sri Lanka have given greater priority to promoting education and healthcare.

A development diamond

Another way of putting a country into perspective is to construct a *development diamond*. An example is shown in Figure 11.8. This compares Ethiopia's performance with the average for countries in its region: sub-Saharan Africa. On each axis, the value of the variable achieved by Ethiopia is expressed as a proportion of the value for sub-Saharan Africa. In this instance, Ethiopia is seen to have low life expectancy, relatively much lower GNI per capita but shows stronger achievement on mean years of schooling. These combined with other indicators contribute to the HDI value, which is lower than the average for sub-Saharan Africa.

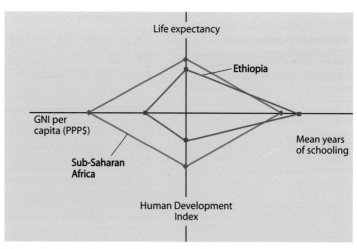

Figure 11.8 Development diamond for Ethiopia compared with all countries in sub-Saharan Africa

There is a view that growth should be the prime objective for development, since by expanding the resources available the benefits can begin to trickle down through the population. An opposing view claims that by providing first for basic needs, more rapid economic growth can be facilitated. The problem in some cases is that growth has not resulted in the trickle-down effect, and inequality remains. It may be significant that countries such as Brazil and South Africa, where the GNI per capita ranking is high relative to the HDI ranking, are countries in which there remain high levels of inequality in the distribution of income.

The HDI may be preferred to GNI per capita as a measure of development on the grounds that it reflects the key dimensions of development as opposed to growth. However, it will always be difficult to reduce a complex concept such as development to a single statistic. The diverse characteristics of LDCs demand the use of a range of alternative measures in order to identify the configuration of circumstances and problems facing a particular country.

Beyond the HDI

The UNDP has recognised that the HDI does not encompass all the dimensions of human development that should be taken into account when evaluating the state of development in an LDC. It now produces some additional indicators intended to capture other key facets of the quality of life. These include indicators that adjust the HDI to take into account inequality in societies. It also produces indicators to highlight gender inequality, which is an important feature of many LDCs, where females receive less education than men, and are more exposed to health risks.

The UNDP also produces an index that tries to capture poverty. This is based on the idea that what we mean by poverty is best reflected in deprivations. In other words, people may be considered poor if they lack access to key components of what makes for a good life. In constructing this index, the UNDP considers indicators that include poor nutrition, high child mortality, low years of schooling and lack of access to clean water, sanitation, electricity and so on.

Synoptic link

Some of the issues surrounding sustainability were raised in Chapter 9 in the context of the analysis of the environment.

Evaluation

An important question is whether any of these measures can capture the progress that has been made by LDCs towards escaping poverty and starting on the road to development. Furthermore, can rapid economic growth be compatible with sustainability?

Over the years, many commentators have suggested alternative indicators that will capture more dimensions of the stage of development reached by LDCs. These include a range of indexes developed by the United Nations, building on the methodology used to produce the HDI. None is perfect, but each adds something to the understanding of the development process. However, no single indicator will ever be sufficient to capture the diversity of experience of countries, and the various measures are best used alongside each other. A number of approaches to understanding levels of well-being in developed countries will be explored at the end of the chapter.

Exercise 11.2

Table 11.1 presents some indicators for two countries, A and B.

Table 11.1 Selected standard of living indicators for two countries, 2012

	Country A	Country B
GNI per capita (PPP$)	11,788	11,477
Life expectancy (in years at birth)	56.9	75.3
Adult literacy rate (%)	93.0	95.1
People living with HIV/AIDS (% of adults aged 15–49)	17.9	<0.1
Infant mortality rate (per 1,000 live births)	44.6	14.0

Source: *Human Development Report*, 2014

a Discuss the extent to which GNI (here measured in PPP$) provides a good indication of relative living standards in the two countries.

b Discuss what other indicators besides those listed in the table might be useful in this evaluation.

Summary

- Less developed countries (LDCs) are largely located in four major regions: sub-Saharan Africa, Latin America, South Asia and South East Asia.
- These regions have shown contrasting patterns of growth and development.
- GNI (or GDP) is a widely used measure of the total amount of economic activity in an economy over a period of time.
- The trend rate of change of GNI may thus be an indicator of economic growth.
- However, converting from a local currency into US dollars may distort the use of GNI as a measure of the purchasing power of local incomes.
- There may be variation in the effectiveness of data collection agencies in different countries, and variation in the size of the informal sector.
- Average GNI per person also neglects the important issue of income distribution.
- GNI may neglect some important aspects of the quality of life.
- The Human Development Index (HDI) recognises that human development depends upon resources, knowledge and health, and therefore combines indicators of these key aspects.
- Different countries have different characteristics, and face different configurations of problems and opportunities.

The structure of economic activity

Key terms

primary production production using natural resources, including the extraction of raw materials and the growing of crops

secondary production the production of manufactured goods

tertiary production the production of the service sector; may include the quaternary sector, which includes production based on information technology and information products

stages of economic growth a process described by economic historian Walt Rostow, which set out five stages through which he claimed that all developing countries would pass

An important characteristic of an economy is the way in which economic activity is made up of different sectors. This can be envisaged in terms of a division into **primary**, **secondary** and **tertiary** production activities. The primary sector involves the extraction of raw materials and the growing of crops. It includes agriculture, the extraction of minerals (and oil), forestry, fishing and so on. The secondary sector is where these raw materials or crops are processed or transformed into goods. It includes various forms of manufacturing activity, ranging from the processing of food to the manufacture of motor vehicles or computer equipment. The tertiary sector is concerned with the provision of services. It includes transport and communication, hairdressing, financial services and so on. A subset of tertiary activity involves intellectual services. This is sometimes known as the quaternary sector and includes hi-tech industry, information technology, some forms of scientific research and other 'information products'.

Stages of economic growth

The economic historian Walt Rostow examined the pattern of development that had been followed in history. He argued in 1960 that all of the more developed countries could be seen to have passed through five **stages of economic growth**. Figure 11.9 gives a general impression of how income per capita changes through these stages.

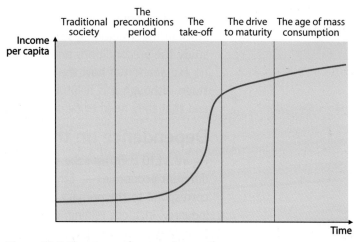

Figure 11.9 The stages of economic growth

In the first stage — the *traditional society* — land is the basis of wealth, most of the production that takes place is in the primary sector (especially agriculture), and investment is low. Some societies can remain in this stage or get trapped in it. Income per capita is static in this phase.

In order to escape from this situation, Rostow argued that a country must establish the *preconditions* for economic growth. In this period, agricultural productivity begins to increase. This enables resources to be released from the agricultural sector so that some diversification into secondary production can take place. Such changes are typically accompanied by a range of social and political changes. It is also important in this stage that some resources are devoted to the provision of the infrastructure that is needed for industrialisation to take place, especially in terms of transport and communications and market facilities.

In the *take-off* stage the economy passes through a 20–30-year period of accelerated growth, with investment rising relative to GDP. Barriers that held back economic growth are overcome. The process of growth in this period tends to be driven by a few leading sectors. A key element of this period is the emergence of entrepreneurs — people who are able to recognise opportunities for productive investment, and who are willing to accept the risk of carrying out that investment. A flow of funds for investment is also needed. Such funds may come from domestic savings, but it may also be necessary to draw in funds from external sources.

The *drive to maturity* stage is a period of self-sustaining growth. New sectors begin to emerge to complement the leading sectors that emerged during the take-off, so that the economy becomes more diversified and balanced, including a focus on tertiary activity. In this period, investment continues to take a relatively high proportion of GDP.

The final period is the *age of mass consumption*, in which the economy is now fully diversified, output per head continues to rise, but consumption now takes a higher proportion of GDP. Countries in this stage have effectively become developed.

Rostow's analysis has been much criticised. For example, it has been suggested that, as an economic historian, Rostow was more concerned with describing the way in which economies had developed in the past than with providing an explanation of *why* they had developed in this way. Nor does his approach provide much helpful guidance for designing policy that would stimulate development in those countries that are still stuck in the 'traditional society' stage, except insofar as countries could study the preconditions and try to replicate them. For example, he offers no explanation of how the barriers to growth disappear in the take-off stage, although it is helpful to be aware that there may be such barriers, and that they need to be overcome.

Dependence on the primary sector

Figure 11.10 contrasts the structure of economic activity in two very different economies — Ethiopia and the UK. These data do not exactly correspond to the primary, secondary and tertiary divisions, as 'Other industry' includes mining, construction, electricity, water and gas. Nonetheless, the contrast is striking. In the UK, the agricultural sector has dwindled almost to nothing, and services have become the dominant form of activity, although industry accounts for 20% of GDP. In Ethiopia, manufacturing activity takes up less than 4% of GDP. Agriculture, on the other hand, is the largest single sector.

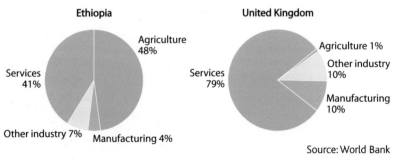

Source: World Bank

Figure 11.10 The structure of economic activity, 2012 (% of GDP)

Many LDCs have an economic structure that is strongly biased towards agriculture. Figure 11.11 shows the percentage of GDP coming from the agricultural sector (measured in terms of value added). In interpreting these data, it is important to be aware that labour productivity tends to be lower in agriculture than in other sectors. The data therefore understate the importance of agriculture in the structure of the economy, as the percentage of the labour force engaged in agriculture is higher than the agricultural share of output. This is further reinforced by the importance of unrecorded agricultural production in the subsistence sector. In other words, if farmers produce food for their own consumption, this will not be included in GDP.

Summary
- Economic activity can be classified into primary, secondary and tertiary production activities.
- Primary activity centres on agriculture and mineral extraction; secondary activity focuses mainly on manufacturing activity; tertiary activity is concerned with the provision of services.
- Many LDCs have an economic structure that is biased towards the primary sector.
- Agriculture is often characterised by low productivity.

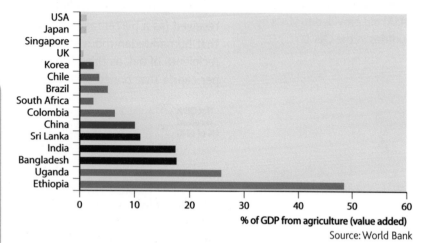

Figure 11.11 The importance of agriculture, 2012

The high importance of agriculture can affect less developed countries in a number of ways. Agriculture tends to display lower productivity than other sectors, and there is less scope for exploiting increasing returns to scale than in manufacturing activity. High dependence on agriculture thus tends to be correlated with low income per head. In addition, primary producers tend to face difficulties in international markets, with volatility in commodity prices and a long-run tendency for agricultural prices to fall relative to prices of manufactured goods.

Overseas assistance and international trade

The problems faced by many LDCs in seeking to stimulate development have given rise to much discussion over a long period. International trade is an essential ingredient of growth and development, as LDCs need to be able to gain access to physical capital goods that they are not able to produce for themselves, so they need a way of earning foreign exchange. This has been challenging, because the dependence on primary goods for export leaves LDCs vulnerable to price fluctuations, and they find it difficult to break into global markets because of barriers to entry.

If LDCs could enter a phase of economic growth and rising incomes, one result would be an increase in world trade. This would benefit nations around the world, and the more developed industrial countries would be likely to see an increase in the markets for their products. This might be a reason for the governments of more developed countries to help LDCs with the growth and development of their economies. Of course, there may also be a humanitarian motive for providing assistance — to reduce global inequality.

There may also be market failure arguments for providing aid. For example, it may be that governments have better information about the riskiness of projects in LDCs than private firms have. In relation to the provision of education and healthcare, it was argued earlier that there may be externality effects involved. However, LDC governments may not have the resources needed to provide sufficient education for their citizens. Similarly, it was argued that some infrastructure may have public good characteristics that require intervention.

Official aid is known as **official development assistance (ODA)**, and is provided through the Development Assistance Committee of the OECD. Figure 11.12 shows the relationship between the amount of ODA received (as a percentage of GNI) and GNI per capita in 2010. It suggests that humanitarian motives are not always paramount in determining the recipients of aid, as there are countries with relatively high levels of GNI per capita that nonetheless receive overseas assistance.

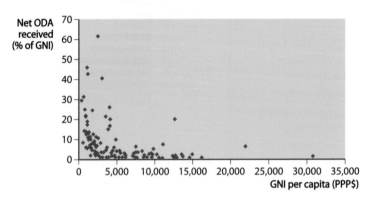

Figure 11.12 ODA and GNI per capita, 2010

The relationship shown in Figure 11.12 is inconclusive in this respect, but there is some suggestion that humanitarian motives are not the only driver of overseas aid. From a donor's perspective, it might be that the government of a country wishes to demonstrate to its electorate that the aid it is giving is being well used, so it may direct its funds towards countries that are in a position to make good use of the funds. In many cases, this may not be the countries with very low GNI per capita or those facing the greatest development challenges. There may also be political motives for donors to give to certain countries: for instance, if their foreign policy objectives make it desirable to support countries in some regions.

At a meeting of the United Nations in 1974, the industrial countries agreed that they would each devote 0.7% of their GNP to ODA. This goal was reiterated at the Millennium Summit as part of the commitment to achieving the Millennium Development Goals. Progress towards this target has not been impressive. Figure 11.13 shows the performance of donor countries relative to this target, and you can see that only five countries had achieved the 0.7% UN target by 2012. The amount of ODA provided by the UK as a percentage of GNI increased after 1997, but the USA's share has fallen. However, it should be borne in mind that in terms of US dollars, the USA is by far the largest contributor.

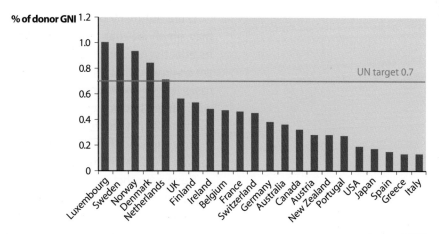

Source: OECD

Figure 11.13 Official development assistance in 2012

An encouraging sign is that total ODA flows increased in the late 1990s and the early years of the new millennium, as can be seen in Figure 11.14. This seemed to represent an enhanced awareness of the importance of such flows for many LDCs. Indeed, at the summit meeting of G8 at Gleneagles in July 2005 the commitment to the UN target for ODA was reiterated. In the UK, the government has expressed its continuing commitment to providing overseas assistance. In the 2013 Budget, official development assistance was one of the areas of spending that was protected by the chancellor, in spite of much criticism from parts of the media. You should be aware that the increase in ODA included funds devoted to debt forgiveness, as brokered by the World Bank under the Heavily Indebted Poor Countries Initiative.

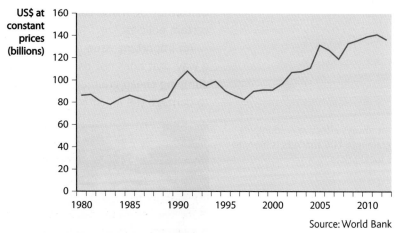

Source: World Bank

Figure 11.14 Total ODA received, 1980–2012

A World Bank study of the effectiveness of aid, published in 1997, reported that 'foreign aid to developing countries since 1970 has had no net impact on either the recipients' growth rate or the quality of their economic policies'. Some evidence was found to suggest that aid was more effective in countries where 'sound economic management' was being practised. In other words, it was argued that aid might prove effective in stimulating growth only if the country were also implementing 'good' economic policies — particularly in terms of openness to trade, low inflation and disciplined fiscal policy.

There are many possible reasons for the ineffectiveness of aid. It may simply be that providing aid to the poorest countries reduces its effectiveness, in the sense that the resources of such countries are so limited that the funding cannot be efficiently utilised. In some cases it may be related to the fact that aid flows are received by LDC governments, which can be inefficient or corrupt, so there are no guarantees that the funds are used wisely by these governments. Or it might simply be that the flows of aid have not been substantial enough to have made a difference.

There are other explanations, however. For example, some donor countries in the past have regarded aid as part of their own trade policy. By tying aid to trade deals, the net value of the aid to the recipient country is much reduced: for instance, offering aid in this way may commit the recipient country to buying goods from the donor country at inflated prices.

In other cases, aid has been tied to use in specific projects. This may help to assure the donor that the funds are being used for the purpose for which they were intended. However, it is helpful only if appropriate projects were selected in the first place. There may be a temptation for donors to select prestige projects that will be favourably regarded by others, rather than going for the LDC's top-priority development projects. In 1994, 66.1% of total aid was untied (45.8% in the case of aid from the UK), but by 2010 this proportion had increased to 79.4% (99.9% from the UK).

Another distinction is between overseas assistance that is given by one country to another (bilateral aid), and funds that are channelled through organisations such as the World Bank or the UN (multilateral aid). Multilateral aid is less likely to be tied to trade agreements, but in some cases may be made conditional on the recipient country implementing certain policies.

An important issue for all sorts of aid is that it should be provided in a way that does not damage incentives for local producers. For example, dumping cheap grain into LDC markets on a regular basis would be likely to damage the incentives for local farmers by depressing prices.

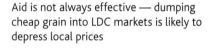
Aid is not always effective — dumping cheap grain into LDC markets is likely to depress local prices

Study tip

The giving (and receiving) of overseas aid can become quite an emotive topic with some people. If it is a topic on which you feel strongly, try to remember in the exam that you are supposed to be analysing the issue based on economic arguments, so don't let your personal views overcome your economic analysis.

Exercise 11.3

Examine the arguments for and against providing assistance to those countries in most need of it, as opposed to those best equipped to make good use of it.

A final issue to notice is that in some cases, the acceptance of foreign aid by a country may result in a phenomenon known as *Dutch disease*. The discovery of a large natural gas field in the Netherlands in the late 1950s resulted in a revaluation of the currency, causing a loss of competitiveness in the manufacturing sector and an acceleration of the deindustrialisation process. It has been argued that a flow of foreign aid into a country can have a similar effect, if the receipt of aid causes the exchange rate to rise, thus reducing the competitiveness of the country's exports.

Summary

- Official development assistance (ODA) comprises grants and concessional funding provided from the OECD countries to LDCs.
- The countries most in need of ODA may not be in a position to use it effectively.
- In some cases the direction of ODA flows is influenced by the political interests of the donor countries.
- The more developed countries have pledged to devote 0.7% of their GNPs to ODA, but few have reached this target.
- Some evidence suggests that aid has been ineffective except in countries that have pursued 'good' economic policies.
- The tying of aid to trade deals or to specific projects can limit the aid's benefits to recipient LDCs.

The Bretton Woods institutions

At the end of the Second World War in 1945, a conference was held at Bretton Woods, New Hampshire, USA, to establish a system of fixed exchange rates. This became known as the Dollar Standard, as countries agreed to fix their currencies relative to the US dollar. John Maynard Keynes was an influential delegate at the conference. In addition to establishing the exchange rate system that operated until the early 1970s, the conference set up three key institutions with prescribed roles, in support of the international financial system.

International Monetary Fund

The **International Monetary Fund (IMF)** was set up with a specific brief to offer short-term assistance to countries experiencing balance of payments problems. Thus, if a country were running a deficit on the current account, it could borrow from the IMF in order to finance the deficit. However, the IMF would insist that, as a condition of granting the loan, the country put in place policies to deal with the deficit — typically, restrictive monetary and fiscal policies.

World Bank

The International Bank for Reconstruction and Development was the second institution established under the Bretton Woods agreement. It soon became known as the **World Bank**. The role of the World Bank is to provide longer-term funding for projects that will promote development.

Key terms

International Monetary Fund (IMF) a multilateral institution that acts as a bank for central banks and sets standards for regulation of banks that are accepted globally

World Bank a multilateral organisation that provides financing for long-term development projects

Much of this funding is provided at commercial interest rates, as the role of the bank was seen to be the channelling of finance to projects that normal commercial banks would perceive as being too risky. However, some concessional lending is also made through the International Development Association (IDA), which is part of the World Bank.

World Trade Organization

Initially, Bretton Woods set up the **General Agreement on Tariffs and Trade (GATT)**, with a brief to oversee international trade. This entailed encouraging countries to reduce tariffs, but the GATT also provided a forum for trade negotiations and for settling disputes between countries. The GATT was replaced by the **World Trade Organization (WTO)** in 1995. Between them, these organisations have presided over a significant reduction in the barriers to trade between countries — not only tariffs, but other forms of protection too.

Heavily Indebted Poor Countries (HIPC) Initiative

In the run-up to the millennium it was clear that many countries' international debt burdens had become unsustainable. Pressure was put on the World Bank and the UN to offer debt forgiveness to LDCs to herald the millennium. This will be discussed in Chapter 19.

The Washington Consensus

It has been noted that institutions such as the World Bank and the IMF have tended to impose conditions on countries in return for lending or debt forgiveness. These conditions were based on the prevailing views about how economies would respond to policy changes.

At a conference in 1989, John Williamson drew up a set of ideas about economic policy that he believed represented accepted views. These ideas became known as the *Washington Consensus*. The ten core policies were:

- fiscal discipline
- reordering public expenditure priorities
- tax reform
- liberalising interest rates
- a competitive exchange rate
- trade liberalisation
- liberalising inward foreign direct investment
- privatisation
- deregulation
- secure property rights

Exercise 11.4

Consider each of the core policies of the Washington Consensus. Explain how each of them might be expected to promote economic growth and human development. Which do you consider to be of most importance?

It was argued that countries that adopted these measures would be able to initiate a process of economic development, and the list formed the basis of the conditions imposed on countries. The measures reflect a market-oriented view of how economies operate. Although many countries did adopt some or all of these policies, it became clear that the consensus was not a complete solution. For example, China offered an alternative model, blending the introduction of market reforms with continuing state control.

It has also been argued that the set of measures neglects a number of key issues surrounding governance and the need to establish reliable and robust institutions to underpin the economy. In addition to the consensus measures, successful development also needs attention to be given to improving the way that markets work, especially in terms of the need for flexible labour markets, and there needs to be targeted poverty reduction and social safety nets to bring together macro and micro aspects of the economy. This has led to initiatives centred on the notion of *inclusive growth*. Under this approach, it becomes important to ensure that growth provides genuine benefits for the populace.

Summary

- The Bretton Woods conference in 1945 set up three major multilateral organisations: the IMF, the World Bank and the GATT (which later became the WTO).
- The IMF has the role of providing short-term finance for countries experiencing balance of payments problems.
- The World Bank provides longer-term financing for development projects.
- The WTO oversees the conduct of international trade.
- The HIPC Initiative was designed to address the problems of debt in the poorest countries.
- Under the HIPC Initiative, debt relief is provided to countries that have shown a commitment to World Bank-approved policies and that have implemented a Poverty Reduction Strategy Paper (PRSP).
- The World Bank and IMF encouraged the adoption of policies known as the Washington Consensus, although this proved to be oversimplified in practice.

Happiness and well-being

The justification given for wanting economic growth is that it expands choice for people and provides the resources needed to enable them to enjoy an enhanced quality of life. Increasing attention is being given to whether economic growth can actually deliver this. To put it another way, does higher income bring more happiness?

In the mid-1970s, Richard Easterlin drew attention to a paradox. He argued that, although happiness and income appear to be correlated at a point in time, happiness does not appear to increase as income increases through time. In other words, rapid economic growth does not seem to bring with it an increase in happiness.

Figure 11.15 shows an overall life satisfaction index produced by the United Nations. This is based on surveys carried out by Gallup in countries around the world. The index is based on a 10-point scale, with 10 indicating the most satisfied. It is intended to capture people's perceptions of how satisfied they are with their life.

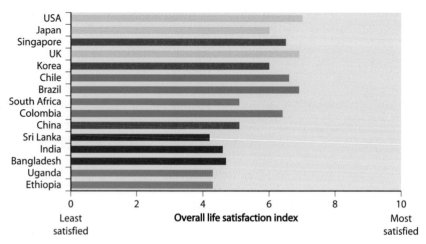

Source: *Human Development Report*, 2014

Figure 11.15 Overall life satisfaction index, 2007–12

Summary

- Economic growth, measured by the rate of change of GDP or GNI, offers only a partial picture of the progress of an economy.
- The Easterlin paradox argues that, although there may be a correlation between the level of income and the level of happiness, this does not mean that happiness necessarily increases in step with the growth of GNI.
- Recent research is beginning to shed light on ways in which it is possible to identify indicators of happiness.
- These are based partly on quantifiable indicators, and partly on surveys of people's perceptions of their own happiness or anxiety.

Exercise 11.5

Discuss the alternative that can be used to evaluate relative living standards across countries. Which do you regard as being most informative?

Perhaps the first attempt to shift the focus towards happiness rather than material prosperity was when Bhutan's ruler announced in 1972 that he was committed to improving 'gross national happiness', based on Buddhist spiritual values rather than measuring output. The ideas have gradually begun to catch on, and there have been attempts to refine the analysis and measurement of happiness.

In the UK, the Office for National Statistics publishes national well-being measures in spring and autumn each year, in an attempt to monitor how the nation as a whole is doing. The measures focus on a wide range of aspects of the quality of life, including personal well-being, relationships, health, education, the economy, personal finance and the environment, amongst other things. Similar work is being undertaken in other European countries, with the aim of being able to compare well-being.

The aim is to identify a range of quantifiable indicators that can be monitored over time, as well as conducting surveys to discover how people's perceptions of their own happiness and anxiety change over time.

There have been other attempts to produce indicators that capture different aspects of the quality of life. For example, an alternative indicator was proposed by William Nordhaus and James Tobin in 1972, known as the *Measure of Economic Welfare*. This began with GNP and then made various adjustments so that it only included the consumption and investment items that contribute positively to economic well-being. For example, they argued that the value of informal production should be added, but that there should be deductions for negative externalities such as environmental damage. This indicator was later relaunched as the *Index of Sustainable Economic Welfare*. The most recent refinement of this approach is the *Genuine Progress Indicator* proposed by the Center for Sustainable Economy and the Institute for Policy Studies based in Washington DC. The hope is that this sort of indicator would be able to capture key issues relating to the sustainability of economic growth.

It is unlikely that any single indicator will be able to provide all the characteristics needed to encapsulate the various dimensions of economic and human development, and a range of indicators will need to be considered side-by-side to gauge the quality of life in different countries, or in the same country through time.

Case study 11.1

Development and the service sector

Tourism has undergone significant change during recent decades as globalisation has proceeded. Individuals in developed countries are now looking for far more from their holidays. Europeans, for example, are no longer content just to bake on the beach in the Mediterranean. Holidaymakers are looking further afield, to places such as Thailand and Kenya, seeking new experiences.

Developing countries have tended to be reliant on agriculture as a source of employment and growth, and this has proved problematic. Due to the variable nature of this sector (as a result of changing weather conditions), and a number of other factors, countries have struggled to grow and to raise standards of living.

While the development of the industrial sector offers opportunities to relocate surplus agricultural workers, resulting in increased output levels, in practice this transition has not run so smoothly. Many agricultural workers do not have the relevant skills for the industrial sector and all too often have moved to the urban areas, typically to shanty towns, to find that there are no jobs available for them. Many of these individuals have consequently experienced a fall in their living standards. The industrial sectors of less developed countries have also found it difficult to gain entry to developed countries' markets. Development of the service sector therefore provides a key method to diversify a developing country's economy, with tourism having the advantage that the tourists go to the 'product'.

Tourism has been recognised as an effective way of helping developing countries to meet a number of the Millennium Development Goals (MDGs). These MDGs include poverty alleviation, gender equality and the promotion of environmental sustainability. The sector lends itself to alleviating poverty due to its labour-intensive nature, which creates many job opportunities for the poor. Tourism is often the only viable strategy for development of poor rural communities.

The type of employment created is also suited to female employees. This raises opportunities available to women and improves gender equality — there is substantial inequality between men and women in many less developed countries. Tourism also encourages the protection of the environment as countries' natural resources can attract tourists, creating the incentive to look after it.

At times, support for this sector has been low due to concerns regarding the dependency of developing countries on developed countries, possible exploitation of the environment and various negative aspects associated with the industry. However, with changes brought about in part by the demands of tourists — for example, a more ethical and sustainable approach — there has been a shift in the way in which tourism is viewed. The World Tourism Organisation (UNWTO) is the UN agency dedicated to the promotion of tourism. It points out that the business volume of tourism equals or exceeds that of exports of oil, food products or cars. The agency focuses on tourism as a way of alleviating poverty in less developed countries and doing so in a responsible and sustainable way.

Source: an earlier version of this appeared in 'Tourism and development' by Jill Whittock, *Economic Review*, September 2007

On safari in Kenya — tourism is a way of alleviating poverty in less developed countries

Follow-up question

Evaluate the potential for tourism to be used as a driving force in the development of an LDC.

Chapter 12

Income distribution and welfare

This chapter explores an important aspect of macroeconomic performance: namely, the way that income and wealth are distributed in an economy. Part of macroeconomic policy is concerned with the redistribution of resources so as to reduce inequality between groups in society. In order to evaluate the effectiveness of such policies, it is important to be able to measure and monitor changes in inequality through time and to compare the degree of inequality across countries. The chapter will also explore the related issue of poverty and how to measure it.

Learning objectives

After studying this chapter, you should:
- be familiar with ways of identifying and monitoring inequality, including Lorenz curves and the Gini index
- be familiar with ways of measuring relative and absolute poverty
- be aware of the changing pattern of inequality in the UK
- understand the main causes of inequality and poverty
- be familiar with policies designed to affect the distribution of income and wealth

Prior knowledge needed

No prior knowledge is needed for this chapter.

The distribution of income and wealth

Synoptic link

Chapter 8 discussed the inequality of income and wealth from a microeconomic perspective, including a discussion of some of the causes of inequality. Be aware of the links here between microeconomic and macroeconomic approaches to this topic.

The distinction between income and wealth was discussed in Chapter 8, noting that income relates to the flow of wages and other income in a period, whereas wealth refers to the accumulated stock of assets.

There are reasons based in microeconomic analysis for expecting there to be differences in income between individuals and groups in society. This becomes an issue at the macroeconomic level partly because there may be a link between the degree of inequality in society and the rate of economic growth. It is also potentially significant because a high level of inequality in a society may need to be tackled by fiscal policy either through the tax system or through government expenditure. This cannot be treated in isolation from other policies being implemented at the macroeconomic level.

This issue may become especially significant for some less developed countries, where the need to address concerns about extreme poverty and provide for the basic needs of the society may have a high priority. One of the problems with this is that there may be a Catch-22 situation, in which economic growth may be impeded by the existence of extreme

Poverty needs to be tackled to enable economic growth

poverty, but extreme poverty cannot be tackled until economic growth has taken place. The government then faces a difficult dilemma: should the focus of policy be on alleviating poverty in order to enable economic growth, or should it be to promote economic growth in order to have the resources to tackle poverty?

Inequality is not only of concern to less developed countries. In the advanced countries, there is still unrest that arises from the existence of inequality between groups, or between regions within a country. Dealing with this by redistributing resources may have an opportunity cost in diverting resources from other priorities. Furthermore, taxing the rich heavily in order to divert resources to the poor may affect the incentives for high-paid workers.

These are some of the issues to be addressed in relation to this topic. However, the first step is to explore ways in which the distribution of income (and wealth) can be described and monitored.

Measuring inequality in society

An important limitation of GNI per capita as a measure of living standards is that it is an average measure, and so does not reveal information about how income is distributed among groups in society. Inequality is present in all societies, and always will be. However, the degree of inequality varies from one country to another; and before exploring the causes of inequality, and the policies that might be used to influence how income and wealth are distributed within society, it is necessary to be able to characterise and measure inequality. This is important in order to be able to judge relative standards of living in different countries or different periods.

One way of presenting data on this topic is to rank households in order of their incomes, and then calculate the share of total household income that goes to the poorest 10%, the poorest 20% and so on.

Quantitative skills 12.1

Deciles and quantiles

When the groups are divided into tenths in this way, they are referred to as deciles; thus, the poorest 10% is the first decile, the next 10% is the second decile and so on. Similarly, the poorest 20% is the first quintile. This is useful in trying to explore the pattern of the distribution of income because it quantifies the difference between income going to low-income and high-income households.

According to the World Bank, the top decile (richest 10%) of households in Brazil receives 55.8 times higher income than the lowest decile (poorest 10%). In Belarus, on the other hand, the ratio is only 5.5. These are extreme examples of the degree of inequality in the distribution of income within countries.

Table 12.1 presents some data for three developed countries. Notice that the unit of measurement is normally the household rather than the individual, on the presumption that members of a household tend to share their resources — a millionaire's life-partner may not earn any income, but he or she is not usually poor.

Table 12.1 Distribution of income in the USA, the UK and Japan, by quintiles (%)

	UK, 2010	USA, 2010	Japan, 2008
First decile	2	1	3
First quintile	6	5	7
Second quintile	11	10	13
Third quintile	16	16	17
Fourth quintile	23	23	23
Top quintile	44	46	40
Top decile	29	30	25
Ratio top quintile : first quintile	7.3	9.2	5.7

Source: *World Development Indicators*

It can be seen that in the UK households in the top quintile receive 7.3 times more income than those in the poorest quintile. On the basis of these data, inequality in the UK is lower than that in the USA, but higher than that in Japan.

The Lorenz curve

Key term

Lorenz curve a graphical way of depicting the distribution of income within a country

The structure of this information is quite different from the sorts of data that economists normally encounter, and it would be helpful to find an appropriate type of diagram to allow the data to be presented visually. The usual types of graph are not well suited to presenting such data visually, but there is a method of presenting the data visually via the **Lorenz curve**. Some Lorenz curves are shown in Figure 12.1.

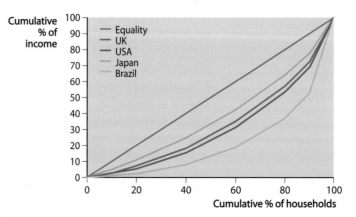

Source: *World Development Indicators*

Figure 12.1 Lorenz curves

Lorenz curves are constructed as follows. The curves for the UK, USA and Japan are based on the data in Table 12.1. The first step is to convert the numbers in the table into *cumulative* percentages. In other words (using the UK as an example), the data show that the poorest 20% receive 6.6% of total household income, the poorest 40% receive 6.6% + 11.5% = 18.1%, the poorest 60% receive 18.1% + 16.3% = 34.4%, and so on. It is these cumulative percentages that are plotted to produce the Lorenz curve, as in Figure 12.1. (The figure also plots the lowest and highest deciles.)

Suppose that income were perfectly equally distributed between households. In other words, suppose the poorest 10% of households received exactly 10% of income, the poorest 20% received 20% and so on. The Lorenz curve would then be a straight line going diagonally across the figure.

To interpret the country curves, the closer a country's Lorenz curve is to the diagonal equality line, the more equal is the distribution. You can see from the figure that Japan comes closest to the equality line, bearing out the earlier conclusion that income is more equally distributed in that country. The UK and the US curves are closer together, but there seems to be slightly more inequality in the USA, as its Lorenz curve is further from the equality line. Brazil has also been included on the figure, as an example of a society in which there is substantial inequality.

Exercise 12.1

Use the data provided in Table 12.2 to calculate the ratios of top decile income to bottom decile income, and of top quintile income to bottom quintile income. Then draw Lorenz curves for the two countries, and compare the inequalities shown for Belarus and South Africa with each other and with the countries already discussed.

Table 12.2 Income distribution in Belarus and South Africa

	Percentage share of income or consumption	
	South Africa	Belarus
Lowest decile	1	4
Lowest quintile	2	9
Second quintile	4	14
Third quintile	8	18
Fourth quintile	16	23
Highest quintile	70	36
Highest decile	54	21

The Gini index

The Lorenz curve is fine for comparing income distribution in just a few countries. However, it would also be helpful to have an index that could summarise the relationship in a numerical way. The **Gini index** does just this. It is a way of trying to quantify the equality of income distribution in a country, and is obtained by calculating the ratio of the area between the equality line and the country's Lorenz curve (area *A* in Figure 12.2) to the whole area under the equality line (area *A* + *B* in Figure 12.2).

Notice that the Gini index
is sometimes presented as a
proportion rather than an index,
and may be called the *Gini
coefficient*. This should be treated
in the same way as the Gini index:
for example, in Table 12.3, the UK
would have a Gini coefficient
of 0.38.

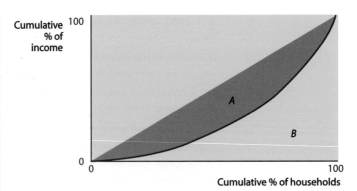

Figure 12.2 The Gini index and the Lorenz curve

Table 12.3 The Gini index

Country	Gini index
USA	41
UK	38
Japan	32
Brazil	53

Source: *World Development Indicators*

This is often expressed as a percentage (but sometimes as a proportion). The closer the Gini index is to 100, the further the Lorenz curve is from equality, and thus the more unequal is the income distribution. The Gini index values for the countries in Figure 12.1 are shown in Table 12.3.

Some measurement issues

When measuring income inequality, some important measurement issues need to be borne in mind. For example, in talking about the 'poorest' and 'richest' households, you need to be aware that absolute income levels per household may be a misleading indicator, given that households are of different sizes and compositions. Thus, when looking at the income distribution in the UK, it is important to make adjustments for this.

The way this is done is by the use of *equivalence scales*. These allow a household to be judged relative to a 'reference household' made up of a childless couple. It can then be decided that a household with a husband, wife and two young children rates as 1.18 relative to the childless couple with a rating of 1. So if the couple with two children had an income of, say, £40,000 per year, this would be the equivalent of $\frac{40,000}{1.18}$ = £33,898. In order to examine the inequality of income, it is these equivalised incomes that need to be considered.

A further question is whether income is the most appropriate indicator. People tend to smooth their consumption over their lifetimes, and it has been argued that it is more important to look at consumption (expenditure) than income when considering inequality.

Then there is the question of housing costs. In the short run, households have no control over their spending on housing. Some measures of inequality therefore choose to exclude housing costs from the calculations in order to focus on the income that households have at their disposal for other expenditures. As housing tends to constitute a higher proportion of the budgets of poor households, measures of inequality that exclude housing costs tend to show greater levels of inequality.

It is also important to bear in mind that the standard of living that households can achieve depends partly on government-provided services, such as health and education. Remember that rich as well as poor households may benefit from these.

Finally, in considering inequality in a society, it may be important to examine inequalities in the distribution of wealth as well as income. Wealth can be regarded as the accumulated stock of assets that households own, and in the UK wealth is more unequally distributed than income.

It is interesting to note that many people remain unaware of where they fit into the income distribution of their country. A survey in the USA in 2000 found that 19% of Americans believed that they were in the top 1% of earners.

Figure 12.3 shows how a Lorenz curve can be used to demonstrate the effect that taxes and benefits have on the distribution of income.

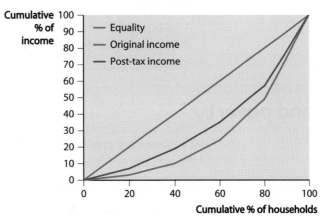

Figure 12.3 The effect of taxes and transfers on income distribution in the UK, 2012/13

Original income is income before any benefits or taxes, including income from earnings, pensions and investments. Post-tax income includes cash benefits provided by the state but deducts direct taxes and an estimate of indirect tax payments. In Figure 12.3, the Lorenz curve for post-tax income moves towards the equality line, indicating that some redistribution of income has taken place.

The Gini index can be used to see how the overall income distribution has changed over time. This is shown in Figure 12.4.

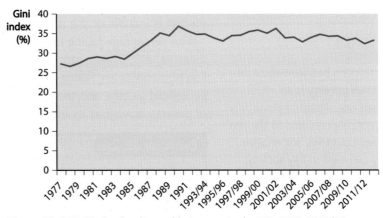

Figure 12.4 Gini index for disposable income in the UK, 1977–2012/13

The figure shows that income inequality worsened slightly during the 1980s, but has remained fairly steady since then.

Summary

- Microeconomic analysis identifies a number of reasons why different individuals and groups in society may receive differential pay.
- At the macroeconomic level, income distribution is important partly because fiscal policy is a key tool in redistributing income and wealth.
- The degree of inequality may also affect economic growth and social stability.
- One indicator of inequality is the ratio of the top to the lowest decile of households in the income distribution.
- The Lorenz curve offers a graphical way of portraying the distribution of income.
- These data can be quantified in the form of the Gini index.

Inequality and poverty

All societies are characterised by some inequality — and some poverty. Although the two are related, they are not the same. Indeed, poverty might be regarded as one aspect of inequality.

If there is a wide gap between the richest and poorest households, it is important to evaluate just how poor those poorest households are, and whether they should be regarded as being 'in poverty'. This requires a definition of poverty.

One approach is to define a basket of goods and services that is regarded as being the minimum required to support human life. Households that are seen to have income that falls short of allowing them to purchase that basic bundle of goods would be regarded as being in **absolute poverty**.

Poverty can also be defined in *relative* terms. If a household has insufficient income for the members of the household to participate in the normal social life of the country, then they are said to be in **relative poverty**. This is also defined in terms of a poverty line. The line is often defined as 50% of the median adjusted household disposable income (the median is income of the middle-ranked household).

The percentage falling below the poverty line is not a totally reliable measure, as it is also important to know *how far* below the poverty line households are falling. Thus the income gap (the distance between household income and the poverty line) is useful to measure the intensity of poverty as well as its incidence.

Key terms

absolute poverty the situation of a household whose income is insufficient to purchase the minimum bundle of goods and services needed for survival

relative poverty a situation in which household income falls below 50% of median adjusted household income

Study tip

This distinction between absolute and relative poverty is an important one. Absolute poverty is almost entirely confined to the less developed countries, but relative poverty can exist in any society, even the advanced nations, because some individuals may be excluded from normal society.

Exercise 12.2

Imagine that you are the Minister for Poverty Alleviation in a country in which the (absolute) poverty line is set at $500. Of the people living below the poverty line, you know that there are two distinct groups, each made up of 50 individuals. The people in group 1 have an income of $450, whereas those in group 2 have only $250. Suppose that your budget for poverty alleviation is $2,500.

a Your prime concern is with the most needy: how would you use your budget?

b Suppose instead that your prime minister instructs you to reduce the percentage of people living below the poverty line: do you adopt the same strategy for using the funds?

c How helpful is the poverty line as a strategic target of policy action?

Causes of inequality and poverty

Inequality arises through a variety of factors, some relating to the operation of the labour market, some reflecting patterns in the ownership of assets, and some arising from the actions of governments.

Labour market explanations

As explained in the microeconomics part of the book, there are several ways in which the labour market is expected to give rise to inequalities in earnings. Inequality could arise from demand and supply conditions in labour markets, which respond to changes in the pattern of consumer demand for goods and services, and changes in international comparative advantage between countries. Furthermore, differences in the balance between economic rent and transfer earnings in different occupations and economic sectors reinforce income inequalities.

However, a by-product of changes in the structure of the economy may be rising inequality between certain groups in society. For example, if there is a change in the structure of employment away from unskilled jobs towards occupations that require a higher level of skills and qualifications, then this could lead to an increase in inequality, with those workers who lack the skills to adapt to changing labour market conditions being disadvantaged by the changes taking place. In other words, if the premium that employers are prepared to pay in order to hire skilled or well-qualified workers rises as a result of changing technology in the workplace, then those without those skills are likely to suffer.

The decline in the power of the trade unions may have contributed to the situation, as low-paid workers may find that their unions are less likely to be able to offer employment protection. It has been argued that this is a *good* thing if it increases the flexibility of the labour market. However, again a balance is needed between worker protection and having free and flexible markets.

Ownership of assets

Perhaps the most obvious way in which the ownership of assets influences inequality and its changes through time is through inheritance. When wealth accumulates in a family over time, and is then passed down to succeeding generations, this generates a source of inequality that does not arise from the current state of the economy or the operations of markets.

Wealth is considerably less evenly distributed than income. During 2008–10 people in the highest decile were estimated to own 44% of identified wealth in the UK. The Gini index for wealth in 2003 was 67, which is much higher than that for income, indicating that wealth is much less evenly distributed than income.

Notice, however, that although wealth and income are not the same thing, inequality in wealth can also lead to inequality in income, as wealth (the ownership of assets) leads to an income flow, from rents and profits, which then feeds back into an income stream.

A significant change in the pattern of ownership of assets in recent decades has been the rise in home ownership and the rise in house prices. For those who continue to rent their homes, and in particular for those who rent council housing, this is a significant source of rising inequality.

Many developed countries have seen
a change in the age structure of the
population

Demographic change

A feature of many developed countries in recent years has been a
change in the age structure of the population. Improved medical drugs
and treatments have meant that people are living longer, and this has
combined with low fertility rates to bring about an increase in the
proportion of the population who are in the older age groups. This has
put pressure on the provision of pensions, and increased the vulnerability
of this group in society. State pensions have been funded primarily by the
contributions of those in work, but if the number of people of working
age falls as a proportion of the whole population, then this funding
stream comes under pressure.

Government intervention

There are a number of ways in which government intervention influences
the distribution of income in a society, although not all of these
interventions are expressly intended to do so. Most prominent is the
range of transfer payments and taxation that has been implemented.
Another example is the minimum wage legislation discussed earlier, which
was also intended to protect the poor. Overall, these measures have a
large effect on income distribution, as was shown earlier in the chapter.

Benefits

There are two forms of benefit that households can receive that help to
equalise the income distribution. First, there are various types of *cash
benefits*, such as income support, child benefit, incapacity benefit and
working families tax credit. These benefits are designed to protect families
in certain circumstances whose income would otherwise be very low.
Second, there are *benefits in kind*, such as health and education. These
benefits accrue to individual households depending on the number of
members of the household and their age and gender.

Of these benefits, the cash benefits are far more important in
influencing the distribution of income. For the lowest quintile in 2009/10,
such benefits made up nearly 60% of gross income, and they were also
significant for the second quintile.

Key terms

direct tax a tax levied directly on income

marginal tax rate tax on additional income, defined as the change in tax payments divided by the change in taxable income

progressive tax a tax in which the marginal rate rises with income

indirect tax a tax on expenditure, e.g. VAT

regressive tax a tax bearing more heavily on the relatively poorer members of society

Exercise 12.3

Table 12.5 shows the amount of tax paid by an individual as income increases. Calculate the average and marginal tax rates at each of the income levels. (*Remember the definition of the marginal tax rate provided above.*)

Table 12.5

Income	Tax paid
£1,000	£100
£2,000	£300
£3,000	£600
£4,000	£1,000

Taxation

Direct taxes (taxes on incomes) tend to be **progressive**. In other words, higher-income groups pay tax at a higher rate. In 2010/11, people earning more than £1 million in the year on average paid 44.4% of the income as tax, whereas those in the £15,000–19,999 income range paid 11.3% in tax.

In the UK, the main direct taxes are income tax, corporation tax (paid by firms on profits), capital gains tax (paid by individuals who sell assets at a profit) and inheritance tax. There is also the council tax, collected by local authorities.

With a tax such as income tax, its progressive nature is reflected in the way that the percentage rates payable increase as an individual moves into higher income ranges. In other words, the **marginal tax rate** increases as income increases. The progressive nature of the tax ensures that it does indeed contribute to reducing inequality in the income distribution — although its effects are less than those of the cash benefits discussed earlier.

Table 12.4 shows average tax rates for taxpayers in different income bands in 2010/11. Notice that the table shows *average* rather than *marginal* tax rates. When average rates are rising, marginal tax rates are higher than the average. Exercise 12.3 illustrates this.

Table 12.4 Income tax payable in the UK by annual income, 2010/11

Income band	Number of taxpayers (m)	Average rate of tax payable (%)	Average amount of tax payable (£)
£6,475–£7,499	0.9	1.3	91
£7,500–£9,999	2.6	4.3	382
£10,000–£14,999	6.4	7.7	956
£15,000–£19,999	5.2	11.3	1,960
£20,000–£29,999	6.9	13.7	3,350
£30,000–£49,999	5.7	15.4	5,800
£50,000–£99,999	2.1	22.3	14,600
£100,000–£199,999	0.3	29.8	35,700
£200,000–£499,999	0.1	37.8	109,000
All incomes	30.5	18.3	5,220

Source: *Social Trends*, no. 41

The effect of **indirect taxes** can sometimes be **regressive**: in other words, indirect taxes may impinge more heavily on lower-income households. Indirect taxes are taxes that are paid on items of expenditure, rather than on income.

An example of an indirect tax is value added tax (VAT), which is charged on most goods and services sold in the UK. However, there are also tobacco taxes, excise duties on alcohol and oil duties. These specific taxes are levied per unit sold.

An indirect tax could be regressive where a product is consumed by a higher proportion of low-income households — for example, evidence suggests that a higher proportion of unskilled workers smoke cigarettes than professional groups. If expenditure on the product is a higher proportion of income of low-paid workers than it is for the rich, then a tax on the product will fall more heavily on the poor than on the rich.

Long-term policy

An economic analysis of the causes of inequality suggests that there are some long-term measures that can be taken to reduce future inequality, although they may take quite a while to become effective. Policies that encourage greater take-up of education, and provide skills retraining, may be important in the long run if the unskilled are not to be excluded from the benefits of economic growth.

It could be argued that some inequality is inevitable within a free market, capitalist society. Indeed, it could be argued that without some inequality, capitalism could not operate, as it is the pursuit of gain that provides firms with the incentive to maximise profits, workers with the incentive to provide labour effort, and consumers with the incentive to maximise their utility. It is the combination of these efforts by economic agents that leads to good resource allocation, through the working of Adam Smith's 'invisible hand', a term he coined in 1776. In a world in which every individual was guaranteed the same income as everyone else, there would be no incentive for anyone to strive to do better. However, few would argue for this. More important is that there should be equality of opportunity.

Weak institutions and poor governance in developing countries mean that measures such as taxation and transfers to influence the distribution of income are largely untried or ineffective. The economist Simon Kuznets argued that there is expected to be a relationship between the degree of inequality in the income distribution and the level of development that a country has achieved. He claimed that in the early stages of economic development, income is fairly equally distributed, with everyone living at a relatively low income level. However, as development begins to take off, there will be some individuals at the forefront of enterprise and development, and their incomes will rise more rapidly. So in this middle phase the income distribution will tend to worsen. At a later stage of development, society will eventually be able to afford to redistribute income to protect the poor, and all will begin to share in the benefits of development.

This can be portrayed as the relationship between the Gini index and the level of development. The thrust of the Kuznets hypothesis is that this should reveal an inverted U-shaped relationship, as shown in Figure 12.5. The empirical evidence in support of the relationship is not strong, although there is some support for the idea that it does hold in some regions of the world.

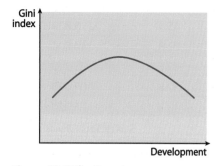

Figure 12.5 The Kuznets curve

Exercise 12.4

Using appropriate economic analysis, discuss the various policy measures available to a government wishing to ensure an equitable distribution of income without damaging incentives to work.

Summary

- Some degree of inequality in income and wealth is present in every society.
- Absolute poverty measures whether individuals or households have sufficient resources to maintain a reasonable life.
- Relative poverty measures whether individuals or households are able to participate in the life of the country in which they live: this is calculated as 50% of median adjusted household disposable income.
- Inequality arises from a range of factors.
- The distribution of wealth is strongly influenced by the pattern of inheritance, but in recent years changing patterns of home ownership, coupled with rises in house prices, have also been significant.
- The natural operation of labour markets gives rise to some inequality in income.
- Government action influences the pattern of income distribution, with the net effect being a reduction in inequality.
- Most effective in this is the provision of cash benefits to low-income households.

Case study 12.1

Inequality and economic growth

If you visit Rio de Janeiro, you may be surprised to see high metal fences in front of many of the luxurious multi-storey buildings along the lovely beaches of Copacabana. However, it is not really surprising, given that Rio has one of the highest crime rates in Brazil, exacerbated by the high level of income inequality. It is not uncommon to find a substantial gap between the rich and the poor in many societies. Inequality exists in both developing and developed countries. For example, the economist Paul Krugman has noted that the 13,000 richest families in the USA have almost as much income as the 20 million poorest households; those 13,000 families have incomes 300 times that of average families. Thus, it is important to examine the effects of such income inequality not only on crime rate and social behaviour, but also on the economy.

Level of income inequality

The level of income inequality depends primarily on the distribution of assets and wages as well as on government policy. First, an important factor is the distribution of productive assets such as land. If land ownership is concentrated among a few owners, which is typical of many agriculture-dominated developing economies, then income inequality tends to be high in such countries. In addition, if the ownership of minerals

and natural resources is concentrated among the elite, then countries well endowed with natural resources — especially mineral resources such as oil, diamonds, copper and so on — tend also to have higher asset and income inequality than other types of economy. Another factor that explains variations across countries is the rural–urban inequality within developing countries, which is the result of urban bias.

Overall, income inequality depends to a large extent on earnings inequality, as in many countries earnings account for 60–70% of total income. In some countries, rising wage inequality has often been ascribed to technological change. New technologies generate a demand for skills. This favours higher-skilled workers over lower-skilled ones and leads to increasing wage differentials between skilled and unskilled workers. In addition, education tends to play an important role in reducing income inequality.

Thus, if some groups in a society do not have access to education, this leads to higher earnings inequality and therefore higher income inequality. Thus, earnings inequality is clearly an important contributor to the increases in overall income inequality witnessed in many countries recently.

Economic performance and output

But how does inequality influence economic performance and output? More unequal societies tend to develop larger groups of people who are excluded from opportunities that others enjoy. Poor people may not have the same chances in life as richer people, and may thus never quite realise their full productive potential. This may be because they do not get as good an education as those afforded by richer families, or because they can't get loans to start up a business as easily, or because they can't afford the insurance they would require to undertake some risky — but productive — venture. An income distribution with lots of poor people, or unequally distributed opportunities, would under-utilise its aggregate productive potential to a greater degree than a distribution with relatively fewer poor people, or one where opportunities were more equitably distributed. Both theory and empirical evidence suggest that these incomplete realisations of economic potential are not of concern only to those who care about equity *per se*. They also affect aggregate economic potential, and therefore aggregate output and its rate of growth.

The impact on growth may also be negative when the gap between the rich and the poor widens excessively. For instance, rural economies with very high land concentration in a few hands and landlessness for the majority face very high shirking and supervision costs. For these reasons, these economies tend to be less efficient (e.g. to have lower yields per hectare) than more equitable agrarian systems, even when accounting for the economies of scale in marketing, processing and shipping which benefit larger farms.

Political instability and social problems

Finally, high levels of income inequality can also create political instability and social problems and very negatively affect growth over both the short and long term. There is increasing evidence of a strong relation between inequality and the crime rate. Income differences between households create *psychological stress* for the relatively poor that may explain higher morbidity, mortality and violence rates. Social tensions, in turn, erode the security of property rights, augment the threat of expropriation, drive away domestic and foreign investment and increase the cost of business security and contract enforcement.

In Rio de Janerio, the slum areas or 'favelas' sit alongside middle-class districts, reflecting the high level of income inequality in Brazil

Follow-up questions

a Identify the key causes of inequality in a society.

b In your own words, outline the main ways in which inequality may have an impact on economic growth.

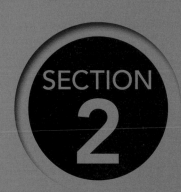

SECTION
2

MACROECONOMICS

Part 6
Aggregate demand and aggregate supply

Chapter 13

Views of the macroeconomy and the economic cycle

Macroeconomic thinking has gone through many changes in the period since the Second World War. The approaches to macroeconomic policy adopted by governments during this time have reflected developments in economic analysis, with different schools of thought holding quite different positions based on different assumptions about how the macroeconomy works. This chapter reminds you of the *AD/AS* model that was introduced in Book 1 and uses the model to explain how both theory and policy have evolved. It will also explain issues surrounding the economic cycle.

Learning objectives

After studying this chapter you should:
- understand the *AD/AS* model
- be able to distinguish between alternative approaches to aggregate supply and to evaluate them
- be familiar with the notion of the Phillips curve, and why it might be seen to be vertical in the long run
- understand what is meant by the natural rate of unemployment
- be able to evaluate the applicability of the Phillips curve in explaining the relationship between inflation and unemployment and its relevance for policy-makers
- be familiar with the economic cycle
- be able to analyse the economic cycle and use the multiplier and accelerator to explain why it may occur
- be aware of the concept of the output gap, and its causes and consequences

Prior knowledge needed

This chapter builds upon the *AD/AS* model that was introduced in Part 5 of Book 1. You may wish to look back at some of the detail of the analysis.

Aggregate demand and aggregate supply revisited

In order to understand and monitor the performance of the macroeconomy, and to design policies that will influence the path it takes, it is necessary to have a model that shows how (and if) equilibrium will be attained. The aggregate demand and aggregate supply (*AD/AS*) model provides a starting point for this analysis.

It is important to distinguish carefully between the short run and the long run, especially in relation to the aggregate supply curve. It is also important to appreciate that there has been debate amongst

Key terms

aggregate demand curve (AD)
a curve showing the relationship between the level of aggregate demand in an economy and the overall price level; it shows planned expenditure at any given overall price level

short-run aggregate supply curve (SAS) a curve showing how much output firms are prepared to supply in the short run at any given overall price level

macroeconomists about the nature of equilibrium at the macroeconomic level, about the shape of the long-run *AS* curve and about the speed with which equilibrium will be reached. These differing views have been important in the approach to macroeconomic policy that has been adopted.

Figure 13.1 illustrates short-run macroeconomic equilibrium. Suppose that the economy begins in equilibrium with the **aggregate demand curve** AD_0 and the **short-run aggregate supply curve** SAS_0. Recall from Book 1 that the main components of aggregate demand are consumption, investment, government spending and net exports.

The short-run aggregate supply curve shows how much output firms would be prepared to supply in the short run at any given overall price level. Macroeconomic equilibrium is achieved with real output given by Y_0 and with the overall price level at P_0.

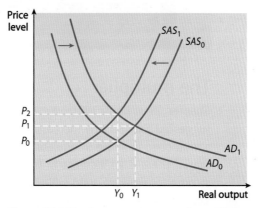

Figure 13.1 Short-run macroeconomic equilibrium

If for some reason there is an increase in aggregate demand from AD_0 to AD_1, then the immediate response is a movement along the *SAS* curve, with real output increasing to Y_1 and the price level rising to P_1. What is happening here is that firms are responding to the increase in demand, expanding their production as prices rise.

The macroeconomy may not settle at this new position. As prices rise, there will be further adjustments. For example, workers may bid for higher wages to compensate for the higher prices, and firms may charge higher prices for the components that they supply to other firms. Or it may be that firms have to pay workers at overtime rates in order to induce them to work longer hours — especially if the economy is close to its full employment position. These effects will feed back on to the costs faced by firms. As this happens, firms will be prepared to supply less output at any given overall price level, and the short-run aggregate supply curve will shift to the left. In Figure 13.1, this is represented by the shift from SAS_0 to SAS_1. The overall price rises again, but real output now falls back. Indeed, in Figure 13.1, the level of real output returns to its original level at Y_0, but with a higher overall price level at P_2.

This suggests that an increase in aggregate demand may lead to higher real output in the short run, but that this may not be a permanent increase.

The multiplier

Chapter 13 of Book 1 introduced the concept of the **multiplier**, which suggested that for any increase in autonomous spending, there would be a multiplied increase in equilibrium output. The idea of the multiplier is that, if there is an increase in (say) government expenditure, this provides income for workers, who will then spend that income and create further expenditure streams.

Notice that it is the act of spending that allows these effects to be perpetuated. If the workers who receive additional income do not spend some of that income, the effects are diluted. The amounts that are not spent are referred to as 'withdrawals'. There are three ways in which these withdrawals take place. First, it may be that households decide to save some of the extra income that they receive instead of spending it. The amount of additional income that is saved is known as the *marginal propensity to save* (s). Second, some of the extra income will be spent on imports, and the marginal propensity to import (m) represents the fraction of extra income spent on imported goods or services. Third, a proportion of the extra income (t) is taken back by the government as taxes on income. The overall size of these induced effects will depend upon the marginal propensity to withdraw. The **marginal propensity to withdraw** (MPW) is thus the sum of these three effects ($s + m + t$).

Key terms

multiplier the ratio of a change in equilibrium real income to the autonomous change that brought it about; it is calculated as 1 divided by the marginal propensity to withdraw

marginal propensity to withdraw the sum of the marginal propensities to save, tax and import; it is the proportion of additional income that is withdrawn from the circular flow

Quantitative skills 13.1

Calculating the multiplier

The size of the multiplier can then be calculated. For example, suppose that households save 5% of extra income ($s = 0.05$) and spend 10% of the extra income on imports ($m = 0.1$), and that 25% goes in tax ($t = 0.25$). The MPW is then $0.05 + 0.1 + 0.25 = 0.4$, and the multiplier is $1 \div 0.4 = 2.5$. An increase in the savings rate to 15% would increase the MPW to 0.5 and reduce the multiplier to 2.

In terms of the *AD/AS* diagram, the existence of the multiplier means that if there is an increase in an item of autonomous expenditure (e.g. investment or government spending), the *AD* curve moves further to the right than it otherwise would have done, because of the multiplier effects.

Long-run equilibrium

It was argued above that economic growth in the short run may be short-lived because the adjustments to an increase in aggregate demand may offset the initial increase in real output. Indeed, it could be argued that there is a full capacity level of real output beyond which no increase in real output can be sustained. This full capacity level of output corresponds to the notion of full employment. In the short run, output may rise beyond this, but only if firms are able to employ workers on overtime, which is not likely to be sustainable in the long term as it adds to the firms' labour costs. This suggests that the **long-run aggregate supply curve** is different in character from the short-run version.

Figure 13.2 illustrates the situation. As before, *AD* is the aggregate demand curve, with the chief components of aggregate demand again being consumption, investment, government spending and net exports. *LRAS* is the aggregate supply curve, which becomes vertical at the full capacity level of output. In other words, Y^* represents the maximum amount of output that the economy can produce in a period if all its resources are being fully utilised. This can be described as the full employment level of output. The intersection of *AD* and *LRAS* provides the equilibrium position for the economy, with P^* in Figure 13.2 being the equilibrium price level. Remember that the *AD* curve is very different in nature from the individual demand curve for a commodity. Here the relationship is between the *total* demand for goods and services and the *overall* price level.

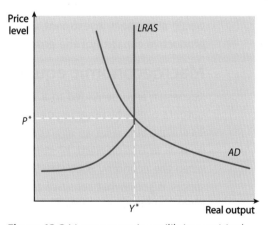

Figure 13.2 Macroeconomic equilibrium revisited

Approaches to macroeconomic equilibrium

Arguably, macroeconomic analysis began with the publication of J.M. Keynes's book *The General Theory of Employment, Interest and Money* in 1936. Before Keynes, the neoclassical view of the economy had focused primarily on microeconomics and the way that markets operated. The Great Depression of the 1930s, with its unprecedented high unemployment, had cast doubt on the neoclassical approach, and Keynes drew attention to how the economy could be analysed in the aggregate.

new classical (monetarist) school a group of economists who believed that the macroeconomy always adjusts rapidly to the full employment level of output; they also argued that monetary policy should be the prime instrument for stabilising the economy

natural rate of unemployment the equilibrium full employment level of unemployment

Keynesian school a group of economists who believed that the macroeconomy could settle in an equilibrium that was below the full employment level

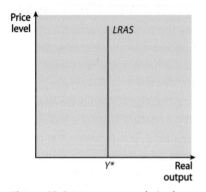

Figure 13.3 Aggregate supply in the long run: the 'monetarist' view

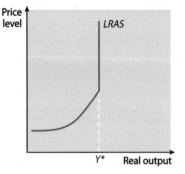

Figure 13.4 Aggregate supply in the long run: the 'Keynesian' view

Keynes's ideas were dominant in the period after the Second World War, and the focus of Keynesian macroeconomic thinking was on aggregate demand, with the notion that governments could influence the level of aggregate demand, and thus affect macroeconomic equilibrium.

During the 1970s, an influential school of macroeconomists, which became known as the **monetarist or new classical school**, argued that the economy would always converge on an equilibrium level of output that they referred to as the *natural rate of output*. They also argued that the adjustment to this natural rate would be rapid, perhaps almost instantaneous, because of the way in which economic agents formed expectations about the future course of the economy.

Associated with this long-run equilibrium was a **natural rate of unemployment**. In this case, the long-run relationship between aggregate supply and the price level would be vertical, as shown in Figure 13.3. Here $Y*$ is the full employment level of aggregate output — the natural rate of output. In this view of the world, a change in the overall price level does not affect aggregate output because the economy always readjusts rapidly back to full employment. Indeed, no change in aggregate demand can affect aggregate output, as it is only the price level that will adjust to restore equilibrium.

In contrast, the new **Keynesian school** held that the macroeconomy was not sufficiently flexible to enable continuous full employment. They argued that the economy could settle at an equilibrium position below full employment, at least in the medium term. In particular, inflexibilities in labour markets would prevent adjustment. For example, if firms had pessimistic expectations about aggregate demand, and thus reduced their supply of output, this would lead to lower incomes because of workers being laid off. This would then mean that aggregate demand was indeed deficient, so firms' pessimism was self-fulfilling. Pessimistic expectations would also affect investment, and thus have an impact on the long-run productive capacity of the economy.

Macroeconomic equilibrium and unemployment

Keynesian arguments led to a belief that there would be a range of outputs over which aggregate supply would be upward sloping. Figure 13.4 illustrates such an aggregate supply curve, and will be familiar from Book 1. In this diagram, $Y*$ still represents full employment; however, when the economy is operating below this level of output, aggregate supply is somewhat sensitive to the price level, becoming steeper as full employment is approached.

The policy implications of the monetarist *LRAS* curve are strong. If the economy always converges rapidly on the full employment level of output, no manipulation of aggregate demand can have any effect except on the price level. This is readily seen in Figure 13.5, where, regardless of the position of the aggregate demand curve, the level of real output remains at $Y*$. If aggregate demand is low at AD_0, then the price level is also relatively low, at P_0. An increase in aggregate demand to AD_1 raises the price level to P_1 but leaves real output at $Y*$. In such a world, only supply-side policy (which affects the position of the aggregate supply curve) has any effect on real output.

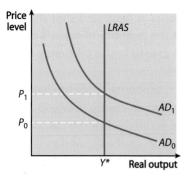

Figure 13.5 An increase in *AD* with a vertical *LRAS* curve

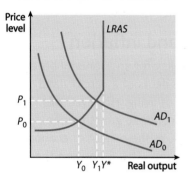

Figure 13.6 An increase in *AD* with a Keynesian *LRAS*

Macroeconomic equilibrium and economic growth

Economic growth was defined in Book 1, Chapter 12. **Short-run economic growth** was seen as an increase in actual GDP, whereas **long-run economic growth** was defined in terms of an expansion of the productive capacity of the economy. How can economic growth be analysed in terms of the *AD/AS* model?

First, consider short-run economic growth with a Keynesian *LRAS* curve, as shown in Figure 13.6.

Under Keynesian assumptions, if aggregate demand is at such a position as AD_0, the equilibrium price level could be at P_0 with real output at Y_0, which is below the full employment level of Y^*. Notice that this full employment level is equivalent to the full potential productive capacity of the economy. If there were to be an increase in aggregate demand from AD_0 to AD_1, the new equilibrium would be at a price level P_1 with real output rising to Y_1, closer to the full capacity output level.

Notice that this is short-run economic growth. Actual real GDP has increased, but productive capacity is still unreachable at Y^*.

Under the pure new classical approach, the adjustment of the economy is so rapid that such a situation is not possible, as the economy always moves rapidly to the natural (full employment) rate of output. You can see that these different approaches have very different implications for the design of policy, which will be explored in Chapter 15.

Economic growth in the long run would be reflected in a rightward shift of the long-run aggregate supply curve. It is the process by which the total resources available to inhabitants of a country expand as time goes by. The measurement of economic growth is normally based on changes in real GDP over time, but it is important to recall that GDP is subject to the fluctuations of the economic cycle, which will be explored later in this chapter.

In some ways, economic growth may be seen as the most fundamental policy objective for an economy. It is economic growth that enables a country to improve the standard of living of its inhabitants, which is ultimately what most societies wish to achieve. However, care needs to be taken in this respect, as the standard of living of people in a country does not only depend upon the *quantity* of resources that are available. The standard of living also depends upon the *quality* of those resources, and on the way in which they are divided up among members of a society. For this purpose, the members of a society may need to include future generations as well as the present one, in the sense that economic growth that is achieved at the expense of the environment may leave future generations worse off. In other words, the unremitting pursuit of economic growth without regard to the costs may not be the best policy.

Nonetheless, economic growth is a central target of economic policy, as without it the well-being of a country's inhabitants is likely to stagnate. Indeed, a policy objective such as low inflation may be regarded as a target because achieving it is expected to encourage investment in order to enable a higher rate of economic growth. Thus other targets may be seen as subservient to economic growth.

So what determines the position of the *LRAS*? A rightward shift in the *LRAS* may be the result of an increase in the quantity of factors of production available in the economy, or an increase in the efficiency with which those factors of production are utilised.

The quantity of factors of production in an economy tends to change very slowly through time. The labour force grows relatively slowly in normal circumstances, especially in a mature economy like the UK, where the rate of natural population increase is slow. Since the expansion of the EU in 2004, there has been in-migration of workers from the new EU member states — especially from eastern European countries such as Poland. This would be expected to have an effect on the productive capacity of the economy, by shifting the long-run aggregate supply curve to the right. Similarly, the quantity of capital services available changes relatively slowly through time, depending on the degree to which firms are willing to undertake investment. Remember that investment in future productive capacity can only be undertaken at the expense of current consumption.

The other way in which productive capacity can be increased is through improvements in the efficiency with which factors of production can be utilised. Another way of viewing this is to look for improvements in productivity.

Macroeconomic equilibrium and inflation

Economic growth is a prime objective of policy for an economy because it expands the resources available to the residents of a country and thus enables improvements in the standard of living. However, this does not mean that a country can pursue economic growth without having regard for the possible consequences, as the pursuit of economic growth may have other effects on the economy. This is because the macroeconomy is interconnected, so changes in one area can have knock-on effects elsewhere.

One possible consequence of a single-minded pursuit of economic growth is that it could endanger macroeconomic stability. This is especially the case when the economy is close to its capacity level. Trying to boost economic growth by persistently stimulating aggregate demand in such a position will push up the overall price level, but may have no discernible effect on real output. An extreme example of this was shown in Figure 13.5, where the long-run aggregate supply curve was assumed to be vertical under new classical assumptions.

It is important to be aware that the increase in *AD* shown in Figure 13.5 does not of itself result in inflation. It shows that an increase in aggregate demand results in a higher price *level*, but this does not mean that there will be persistent inflation. It is only if *AD* persists in shifting to the right that there will be persistent increases in price — that is, inflation.

If economic growth stems from an expansion in the economy's productive capacity, the picture is different. A rightward shift of the long-run aggregate supply curve does not have consequences for an increase in the price level or inflation — indeed, with aggregate demand unchanged, a shift to the right of the *LRAS* curve results in a *lower* equilibrium overall price level, thus reducing inflationary pressure.

This clearly has implications for policy design. In the pursuit of economic growth, it is important to distinguish between demand-led and supply-led growth, and there needs to be an awareness of the position of the economy relative to the full employment or capacity level, and the current stage of the economic cycle. This will be explored in the next chapter.

Economic policy objectives — a reminder

You will realise from the discussion above that there are several targets for macroeconomic policy. However, we can put these into perspective by recognising that policy is aimed at a relatively small number of ultimate objectives, which we can summarise as

- economic stability
- economic growth
- international competitiveness

We could argue that the most important of these overarching objectives is economic growth. It is through economic growth that it becomes possible to improve the quality of life of a nation's citizens, as it is only through economic growth that the quantity of resources available to citizens can be expanded. This is not to say that the other two objectives are unimportant. Economic stability is important — but partly because it creates an environment within which economic growth can take place. For example, if we have price stability, then firms will have more confidence to invest in the future, thus stimulating economic growth. Similarly, maintaining or improving the international competitiveness of domestically produced goods also contributes to economic stability and provides a solid demand base to encourage firms to expand by selling in global markets — again helping to increase economic growth. In the chapters following, we will examine a range of different policy approaches, and you will find that some of these are likely to be more useful in achieving some of the objectives.

China has experienced an unprecedented period of growth since 1978

Summary

- In using the *AD/AS* model, it is useful to distinguish between monetarist (new classical) and Keynesian views about the shape of aggregate supply.
- Monetarist economists have argued that the economy always converges rapidly on equilibrium at the natural rate of output, implying that changes in aggregate demand have an impact only on prices, leaving real output unaffected. The aggregate supply curve in this world is vertical.
- The Keynesian view is that the economy may settle in an equilibrium that is below full employment, and that there is a range over which the aggregate supply curve slopes upwards.
- Long-run economic growth is an increase in the productive capacity of an economy.
- The *AD/AS* model can be used to analyse the effect of changes in aggregate demand on economic growth, unemployment and inflation.
- Economic growth may be seen as the ultimate target of macroeconomic policy, as it allows an improvement in the well-being of a country's inhabitants.

Unemployment and inflation

The *AD/AS* model is helpful in analysing equilibrium in the macroeconomy. It identifies the equilibrium price level and the level of real output given the position of the aggregate demand and supply curves. However, in reality the macroeconomy is in a continual state of change. Economic growth takes place as the economy progresses through time, and the normal situation is one of inflation, rather than a static price level.

A first step towards looking at the macroeconomy in a more dynamic setting is to examine the **Phillips curve**, which postulates a relationship between unemployment and the rate of inflation. This is named after an economist from New Zealand, Bill Phillips, who in 1958 identified a long-run empirical relationship between the rate of unemployment and the rate of change of money wages. He claimed that this relationship had remained stable for a period of almost a hundred years. This was rapidly generalised into a relationship between unemployment and inflation (by arguing that firms pass on increased wages in the form of higher prices).

Figure 13.7 shows what became known as the Phillips curve. Although Phillips began with data, he also came up with an explanation of why such a relationship should exist. At the heart of his argument was the idea that when the demand for labour is high, firms will be prepared to bid up wages in order to attract labour. To the extent that higher wages are then passed on in the form of higher prices, this would imply a relationship between unemployment and inflation: when unemployment is low, inflation will tend to be higher, and vice versa.

From a policy perspective, this suggests a trade-off between unemployment and inflation objectives. If the Phillips curve relationship holds, attempts to reduce the rate of unemployment are likely to raise inflation. On the other hand, a reduction in inflation is likely to result in higher unemployment. This suggests that it might be difficult to maintain

Key term

Phillips curve an empirical relationship suggesting that there is a trade-off between unemployment and inflation

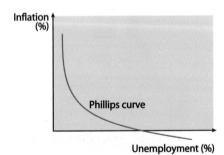

Figure 13.7 The Phillips curve

full employment and low inflation at the same time. For example, Figure 13.8 shows a Phillips curve that is drawn such that to achieve an unemployment rate of 5%, inflation would need to rise to almost 15% per annum; this would not be acceptable these days, when people have become accustomed to much lower inflation rates. Furthermore, to bring inflation down to zero would require an unemployment rate of 15%. Having said that, as recently as 1990 the UK economy was experiencing inflation of nearly 10% and unemployment of 7%, which is not far from this example.

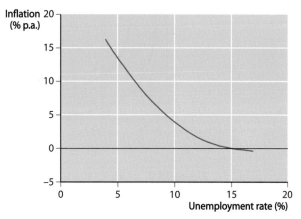

Figure 13.8 The Phillips curve unemployment/inflation trade-off

Nonetheless, the Phillips curve trade-off offers a tempting prospect to policy-makers. For example, if an election is imminent, it should be possible to reduce unemployment by allowing a bit more inflation, thereby creating a feel-good factor. After the election, the process can be reversed. This suggests that there could be a political business cycle induced by governments seeking re-election. In other words, the conflict between policy objectives could be exploited by politicians who see that in the short run an electorate is concerned more about unemployment than inflation.

The 1970s provided something of a setback to this theory, when suddenly the UK economy started to experience both high unemployment and high inflation simultaneously, suggesting that the Phillips curve had disappeared. This combination of stagnation and inflation became known as **stagflation**.

One possibility is that the Phillips curve had not in fact disappeared, but had moved. Suppose that wage bargaining takes place on the basis of *expectations* about future rises in retail prices. As inflation becomes embedded in an economy, and people come to expect it to continue, those expectations will be built into wage negotiations. Another way of viewing this is that expectations about price inflation will influence the *position* of the Phillips curve.

Figure 13.9 shows how this might work. PC_0 represents the initial Phillips curve. Suppose we start with the economy at the *natural rate of unemployment U_{nat}*. If the economy is at point A, with inflation at π_0 and unemployment at U_{nat}, the economy is in equilibrium. If the government then tries to exploit the Phillips curve by allowing inflation to rise to π_1, the economy moves in the short run to point B. However, as people realise that inflation is now higher, they adjust their expectations. This eventually begins to affect wage negotiations; the Phillips curve then moves to PC_1, and unemployment returns to the natural rate. The economy settles at C and is again in equilibrium, but now with higher inflation than before — and the same initial rate of unemployment. For this reason, the natural rate of unemployment is sometimes known as the **non-accelerating inflation rate of unemployment (NAIRU)**.

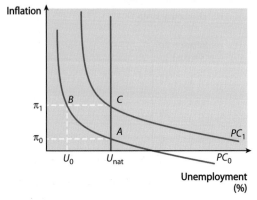

Figure 13.9 The expectations-augmented Phillips curve

The problem that arises with this is of how to get back to the original position with a lower inflation rate. This can happen only if people's expectations adjust so that lower inflation is expected. This means that the economy has to move down along PC_1, pushing up unemployment in order to reduce inflation. Then, once expectations adjust, the Phillips curve will move back again until the natural rate of unemployment is restored. If this takes a long time, then the cost in terms of unemployment will be high.

Figure 13.10 shows some empirical data for the UK since 1986. From 1986 until 1993 (or even until 1995), the pattern seems consistent with a Phillips curve relationship. However, after that time inflation seems to have stabilised, and unemployment is gradually falling — as if, with stable inflation, people's expectations have kept adjusting and allowed unemployment to fall. Unemployment rose again during the recession that began in the late 2000s and you can see that in 2010 the RPI actually fell.

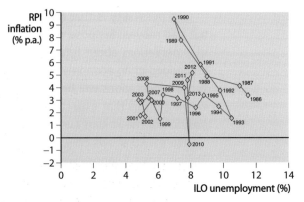

Figure 13.10 Unemployment and inflation in the UK, 1986–2013

Notice that an important assumption here is that economic agents base their behaviour on expectations about the future course of the economy. But how do they form these expectations?

One possibility is that expectations are formed based on the past performance of the economy. Economic agents observe the economy in one period, and then adapt to that when forming expectations about the future. This is known as *adaptive expectations*. Their expectations are shaped by the past.

The new classical economists rejected this view, arguing that economic agents would always take decisions on the basis of all the information available. In other words, they would not simply assume that the economy would behave consistently with past experience. Instead they would use all of the information available, understanding how the economy operates and avoiding systematic errors. For example, they would have as good an information set as the government and would thus be able to predict how the government would react to changes in the economy. This theory is known as *rational expectations*, and helps to explain how it is that the economy will reach its equilibrium so rapidly.

Policy and the Phillips curve

Summary

- The Phillips curve claims a trade-off relationship between unemployment and inflation, although the appearance of stagflation in the 1970s cast doubt on the hypothesis.
- The position of the Phillips curve may be seen to depend on people's expectations about future inflation, so that in the long run the Phillips curve may be vertical at the natural rate of unemployment (or the non-accelerating inflation rate of unemployment — the NAIRU).

How important is the Phillips curve for the design of macroeconomic policy? When policy-makers first came across the trade-off between unemployment and inflation, it became tempting to exploit the trade-off for electoral purposes. It seemed possible to expand the economy in the run-up to an election, getting unemployment to fall and creating a feel-good factor, whilst allowing inflation to creep up ready to be brought back down after the election. This is clearly not helpful for the economy in the long run.

The disappearance of the Phillips curve in the 1970s put a damper on this approach, and it became apparent that the cost of bringing inflation back under control was high.

Some commentators argued that the Phillips curve (even if it did exist) could not be used for short-term political expediency because, once economic agents realised what the government was doing, they would factor it into their expectations formation process, and would thus discount the government's attempts to manipulate the economy. If the new classical economists were correct, trying to affect the natural rate was doomed to failure.

The economic cycle

Key terms

economic cycle a phenomenon whereby GDP fluctuates around its underlying trend, following a regular pattern
output gap the difference between actual GDP and its trend value

Historically, the performance of economies has tended to fluctuate over time in a cyclical fashion. This is known as the **economic cycle**. It is illustrated in Figure 13.11. The economic cycle describes the way in which GDP fluctuates through time around an upward trend. At any point in time, GDP may be below or above its trend value, the difference being known as the **output gap**. This is defined as the actual level of output minus the potential level. If the economy is in recession, with actual GDP below potential GDP, then the gap is negative; if actual GDP is above the trend level, the gap is positive.

Consider an economy at point *A* on Figure 13.11. At this stage in the cycle, the economy is entering a period of recession, in which GDP is falling. This continues until point *B*, the trough of the cycle, at which point

GDP stops falling and begins to grow again. At point *C*, the economy is showing growth in actual GDP, but GDP is still below its trend value; only at point *D* does the economy hit the trend. In other words, between points *A* and *D*, the output gap is negative. Beyond point *D* the economy moves into a boom period (as at point *E*), where GDP grows more rapidly than its trend value, and the level of GDP is above its trend value; the output gap is positive. At point *F* the cycle reaches its peak and stops increasing; beyond this point actual GDP again begins to fall, and then the story repeats. Notice that in practice the economy is regarded as being in **recession** when GDP falls in two successive quarters.

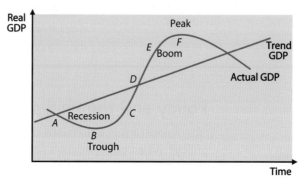

Figure 13.11 The economic cycle

This process highlights the important distinction between growth in the short run, and growth in the long run. The term *long-run economic growth* is used to refer to the process by which there is an increase in the trend, or potential, rate of growth of GDP. One way of looking at this is that long-run economic growth occurs when there is an increase in long-run aggregate supply — an increase in the productive capacity of the economy. Indeed, this is the process by which GDP is able to follow an upward trend over time as productive capacity increases. However, there are also short-run changes in the actual level of GDP: for example, between points *B* and *C* on Figure 13.11, there will be an observed increase in real GDP. This is *short-run economic growth*, and is not to be confused with the changing capacity of the economy through time. This short-run economic growth can occur (for example) because unemployed factors of production are being drawn into use when the economy is recovering or in boom.

From a policy perspective, it is important to know at what stage the economy is located. When the output gap is negative, and the level of output is below trend, then it may be tempting for policy-makers to try to 'fill the gap' by stimulating aggregate demand. However, this would be dangerous when the output gap is positive, as the main effect would be on the price level. This will be explained more carefully later.

Figure 13.12 shows the rate of change of (actual) real GDP each year since 1950. Also marked on the graph is the long-run average rate of growth, which was about 2.6% p.a. between 1950 and 2007 (just before the onset of the financial crisis and subsequent recession. This shows that the rate of growth of actual real GDP has been relatively volatile over this period — sometimes showing substantial variation from one year to the next, the most extreme example being when the annual growth rate fell from +7.1% in 1973 to −1.4% in 1974. This graph suggests that the economic cycle is not very regular, and certainly the growth rate appears to become more stable towards the end of the period shown. One classic example of a cycle occurred from 1984 to 1993, as shown in Figure 13.13; here the output gap was positive from 1985 to 1988, then became negative as the economy went into recession.

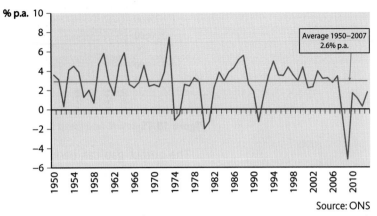

Source: ONS

Figure 13.12 Growth of real GDP, 1950–2013 (% change over previous year)

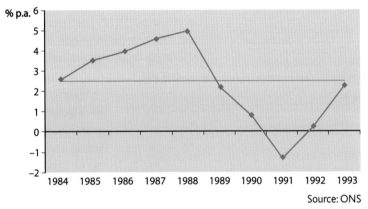

Source: ONS

Figure 13.13 A classic economic cycle

In mid-2008, the Chancellor of the Exchequer took the unprecedented step of stating publicly that the UK was heading for its biggest recession since the Second World War. Figure 13.14 shows quarterly data for the period 2003 to 2008, showing the information that was available to the chancellor when he made this claim. He proved to be correct. Figure 13.15 shows actual GDP since 1950, together with the trend that would have been followed on the basis of the average growth rate between 1950 and 2007. The periods when the output gap was positive and negative can be seen clearly — as can the recession that set in after 2007.

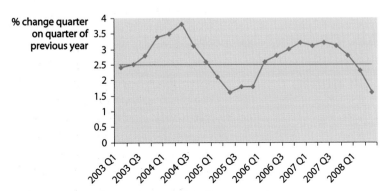

Figure 13.14 The UK economy heading for recession?

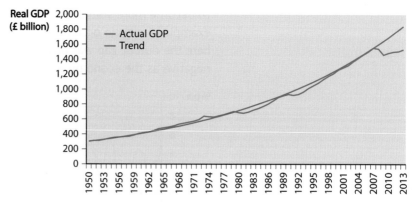

Figure 13.15 Actual and trend real GDP

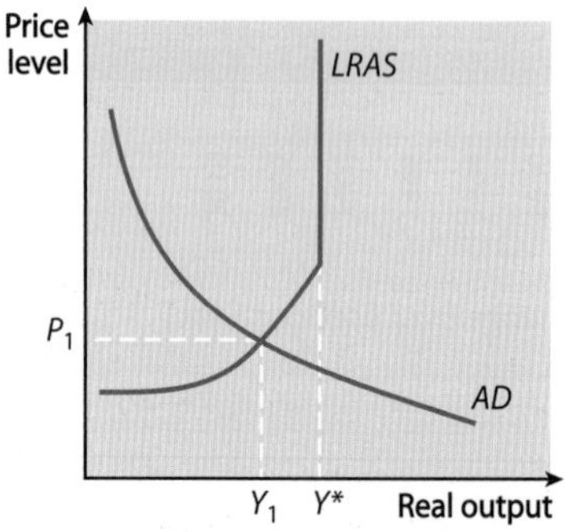

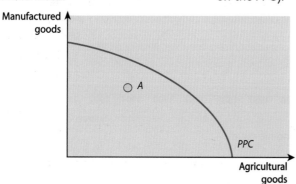

Figure 13.16 The output gap in the *AD/AS* model

Figure 13.17 The output gap and the *PPC*

The output gap can be identified through an *AD/AS* diagram, as in Figure 13.16. The figure shows a Keynesian *LRAS* curve, with the *AD* located in such a position that the equilibrium level of output is at Y_1, which is below the natural rate at Y^*. The output gap is the difference between the actual and potential levels of output (i.e. $Y^* - Y_1$). The gap could also be shown in relation to the production possibility curve (*PPC*), as in Figure 13.17. The figure shows a country's *PPC* between agricultural and manufactured goods. If it is producing at a point such as *A*, it is operating below its potential capacity output (which would be any point on the *PPC*).

Figure 13.18 shows the growth rates of GDP per capita in selected countries from 1971 to 2012. Although the graph looks a little congested, it is useful because it shows that there are some periods when fluctuations occur simultaneously across countries. For example, look at what happened in 1974/75, when all countries shown were negatively affected by the oil price shock of 1973/74. Notice that all countries enjoyed a more stable period of growth between about 1984 and 1990. So there may be periods in which there are common cycles across countries. On the other hand, there are also exceptions to this — for example, Japan's negative growth in 1998 and 1999, which was not shared by the other countries in the graph. The recession of the late 2000s clearly affected all of these economies, sending growth strongly negative in 2008 and 2009.

It is important to be aware that if countries do follow common patterns — at least in some periods — then this implies that domestic economic policy may not be the only influence on an economy's performance.

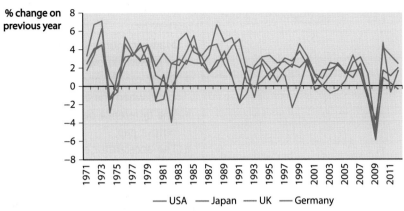

Source: World Bank

Figure 13.18 Growth of real GDP per capita in selected OECD countries, 1971–2012

The accelerator

The idea of the multiplier is based on the induced effects of expenditure that spread the initial effects of an increase in spending. A similar notion is that of the **accelerator**. The notion of the accelerator arises from one of the driving forces behind firms' investment. Although some investment is needed to replace old equipment (known as depreciation), most investment is needed when firms wish to expand capacity. If there is an increase in demand for a firm's product (or if a firm expects there to be an increase in demand), it may need to expand capacity in order to meet the increased demand. This suggests that one of the determinants of the level of investment is a *change* in expected demand. Notice that it is the change in demand that is important, rather than the level, and it is this that leads to the notion of the accelerator.

Suppose that the economy is in recession and begins to recover. As the recovery begins, demand begins to increase, and firms have to undertake investment in order to expand capacity. However, as the economy approaches full capacity, the growth rate slows down — and hence investment falls, as it reacts to the change in output.

The multiplier and accelerator interact with each other. If there is an increase in output following an increase in aggregate demand, the accelerator induces an increase in investment. The increase in investment then has a multiplier effect that induces an additional increase in demand. In this way, the multiplier and accelerator reinforce each other. The downside to this is that the same thing happens when output slows as this leads to a fall in investment, which has negative multiplier effects. This interaction between the multiplier and the accelerator can result in cyclical fluctuations in the level of output.

> **Key term**
>
> **accelerator** a theory by which the level of investment depends upon the change in real output

Exercise 13.3

Which of the following represent genuine economic growth, and which may just mean a move to the *PPC*?

a An increase in the rate of change of potential output.
b A fall in the unemployment rate.
c Improved work practices that increase labour productivity.
d An increase in the proportion of the population joining the workforce.
e An increase in the utilisation of capital.
f A rightward shift of the long-run aggregate supply curve.

Summary

- Many economies display fluctuations around an underlying trend rate of growth, known as the economic cycle.
- Short-run economic growth occurs at some points in the economic cycle when the economy is in recovery or boom.
- The difference between actual and trend real GDP is known as the output gap.
- The accelerator effect reinforces the multiplier when investment by firms responds to a change in output.
- The interaction between the multiplier and the accelerator can give rise to fluctuations in equilibrium output.

Case study 13.1

The UK economy and the financial crisis

In late 2008, the UK was hit by a combination of events that caused widespread consternation.

The British economy — and many others in the developed world — had enjoyed a long period of relative stability, with stable inflation rates and steady economic growth.

During 2007, a combination of circumstances interrupted this period of calm. The price of oil began to rise steeply, and other commodity prices rose in world markets, as food prices spiralled. This began to affect inflation in the UK, which moved beyond its target range during 2008.

The credit crunch then hit the economy, with parts of the banking sector needing to be bailed out by intervention from the government. The government's budget deficit rose as a result. Bank lending was slow to recover, and confidence in the economy was low.

Follow-up questions

a Use an *AD/AS* diagram to illustrate the effect of an increase in the price of oil. Comment on the effects on the overall price level and real output.

b Use the same diagram to show the effects of a fall in lending by the banking sector, and again analyse the effects on the overall price level and real output.

SECTION
2

MACROECONOMICS

Part 7
The application of
policy instruments

Chapter 14

The operation of fiscal and monetary policy

This chapter explores the main policy instruments that the authorities can use in seeking to control the performance of the UK economy, and evaluates the extent to which such methods of control are likely to be effective. Fiscal policy has always been an important part of the government's armoury of instruments, and the way that the government carries out its expenditure and taxation policies has important impacts on performance. Monetary policy has been the most prominent method of influencing the economy in recent years, and will be explored here. The role of the exchange rate is also significant, which was covered in Book 1, Chapter 17.

Learning objectives

After studying this chapter, you should:
- understand the alternative types of fiscal policy instrument, including the use of alternative tax instruments and government spending
- understand the consequences of a fiscal budget deficit or surplus
- appreciate the difference between direct and indirect taxation as means of raising revenue
- be familiar with the prime instruments of monetary policy
- be aware of the functions and measures of money, and the importance of interest rates in the economy
- appreciate the importance of the impact of the exchange rate on the conduct of monetary policy
- be able to understand the monetary transmission mechanism
- be familiar with the operation of monetary policy and its effectiveness in helping to manage the economy

Prior knowledge needed

This chapter builds upon the introductory discussion of fiscal and monetary policy that appeared in Chapter 15 of Book 1.

Policy targets and instruments

At the macroeconomic level, the government has a number of key objectives. The most fundamental of these objectives is economic growth, as this allows improvements in the standard of living. However, in order to achieve economic growth, it is crucial to maintain economic stability, thus providing the economic environment within which economic growth can take place. It is also important to be aware of international competitiveness — and to achieve an acceptable distribution of income and wealth (as was discussed in Chapter 12). Finally, there is a need to ensure that economic growth is sustainable. The government has three main types of policy instrument with which to attempt to meet these macroeconomic objectives: fiscal, monetary and supply-side policies.

The term *fiscal policy* covers a range of policy measures that affect government expenditures and revenues through the decisions made by the government on its expenditure, taxation and borrowing. Fiscal policy is used to influence the level and structure of aggregate demand in an economy. The effectiveness of fiscal policy also depends crucially on the whole policy environment in which it is utilised.

Monetary policy entails the use of monetary variables such as money supply and interest rates to influence aggregate demand. It will be shown that under a fixed exchange rate system, monetary policy becomes wholly impotent, as it has to be devoted to maintaining the exchange rate. So, the effectiveness of monetary policy depends upon the policy environment in which it is used. In recent years, the prime use of monetary policy has been in seeking to create a stable macroeconomic environment.

Supply-side policies comprise a range of measures intended to have a direct impact on aggregate supply — specifically, on the potential capacity output of the economy. These measures are often microeconomic in character and are designed to increase output and hence economic growth.

Study tip

Supply-side measures were discussed in Book 1, Chapter 15. They may be seen as ways in which policy can affect the position of the long-run aggregate supply curve. Do not forget to review these policies alongside those relating to fiscal and monetary policy.

Fiscal policy

Key term

fiscal policy decisions made by the government on its expenditure, taxation and borrowing

Fiscal policy covers a range of policy measures that affect government expenditures and revenues, as was explained in Book 1, Chapter 15. As the government has discretion over the amount of expenditure that it undertakes and the amount of revenue that it chooses to raise from taxation, these can be manipulated in order to influence the course of the economy.

What is the role of fiscal policy in a modern economy? Traditionally, fiscal policy was used to affect the level of aggregate demand in the economy, under the influence of Keynesian thinking. The overall balance between government receipts and outlays affects the position of the aggregate demand curve, which is reinforced by multiplier effects. When government outlays exceed government receipts, the result is a *fiscal deficit*. This occurs when the revenues raised through taxation are not sufficient to cover the government's various types of expenditure.

The overall size of the budget deficit may limit the government's actions in terms of fiscal policy. In addition, the overall pattern of revenue and expenditure has a strong effect on the overall balance of activity in the economy. A neutral government budget can be attained either with high expenditure and high revenues, or with relatively low expenditure and revenues. Such decisions affect the overall size of the public sector relative to the private sector. Over the years, different governments in the UK have taken different decisions on this issue — and different countries throughout the world have certainly adopted different approaches.

In part, such issues are determined through the ballot box. In the run-up to an election, each political party presents its overall plans for taxation and spending, and typically they adopt different positions as to the overall balance. It is then up to those voting to give a mandate to whichever party offers a package that most closely resembles their preferences.

Notice that there is a limit to how effective this process can be. The policies adopted by a government during its term of office cover a wide range of different issues, and individual voters may approve of some but not others — but they only get to vote once every 5 years or so, and then only on the whole package of measures. When the election comes round, the debates may be dominated by issues that happen to be contentious at the time, rather than the overall ideology of the parties. Furthermore, if the election turns out to be indecisive, so that the result is a coalition across parties with differing manifestos, the resulting policies may turn out to be a mixture. Another pertinent issue is whether voters will be fooled by being offered (or given) tax cuts just before an election, as they may know that the reality will be different in the long term.

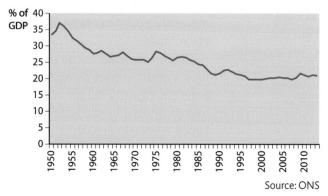

Source: ONS

Figure 14.1 Government final consumption, 1950–2013

Figure 14.1 shows the time path of government consumption as a share of GDP since 1950; it shows minor fluctuations around a downward trend, suggesting that the public sector has been gradually reducing its share of the economy, although it has been fairly constant since the mid-1990s. Notice that this does not give the full picture, as public sector investment is not taken into account in these data. There are one or two periods in the figure where the decline seems to have been especially rapid. In the early 1950s, this partly reflects the winding down of government activity after the rebuilding that followed the Second World War. The decline in the 1980s reflects the privatisation drive of that period, when the government was withdrawing from some parts of the economy.

Figure 14.2 provides an international perspective, showing the share of current and capital expenditure by governments in a range of countries. This reveals something of a contrast between, on the one hand, Korea and Switzerland, and on the other hand, many European countries, where governments have been more active in the economy. In part this reflects the greater role that government plays in some countries in providing services such as education and healthcare, whereas in other countries the private sector takes a greater role, often through the insurance market.

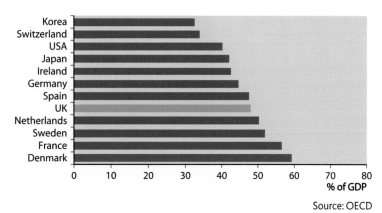

Source: OECD

Figure 14.2 Total government spending as a percentage of GDP, selected countries, 2012

Direct and indirect taxes

Fiscal policy, and taxation in particular, has not only been used to establish a balance between the public and private sectors of an economy. In addition, taxation remains an important weapon against some forms of market failure, and it also influences the distribution of income. In this context, the choice of using direct or indirect taxes is important.

Direct taxes are taxes levied on income of various kinds, such as personal income tax. Such taxes are designed to be progressive and so can be effective in redistributing income: for example, a higher income tax rate can be charged to those earning high incomes. In contrast, *indirect taxes* — taxes on expenditure, such as VAT and excise duties — tend to be regressive. As poorer households tend to spend a higher proportion of their income on items that are subject to excise duties, a greater share of their income is taken up by indirect taxes. Even VAT can be regressive if higher-income households save a greater proportion of their incomes.

When Margaret Thatcher came to power in 1979, one of her first actions was to introduce a switch away from direct taxation towards indirect taxes. VAT was increased and the rate of personal income tax was reduced. In support of this move, it was pointed out that if an income tax scheme becomes too progressive, it can provide a disincentive towards effort. If people feel that a high proportion of their income is being taken in tax, their incentives to provide work effort are weak. Indeed, a switch from direct to indirect taxation is regarded as a sort of supply-side policy intended to influence the position of aggregate supply.

Margaret Thatcher introduced a switch away from direct taxation towards indirect taxation

Sustainability of fiscal policy

Another important issue that came to the fore during the 1990s concerned the sustainability of fiscal policy. This is wrapped up with the notion that current taxpayers should have to fund only expenditure that benefits their own generation, and that the taxpayers of the future should make their own decisions, and not have to pay for past government expenditure that has been incurred for the benefit of earlier generations.

In this context, what is significant is the overall balance between receipts and outlays through time. If outlays were always larger than receipts, the spending programme could be sustained only through government borrowing, thereby shifting the burden of funding the deficit to future generations. This could also be a problem if it made it more difficult for the private sector to obtain funds for investment, or if it added to the national debt.

The Labour governments of 1997–2010 initiated a rules-based approach to fiscal policy, in the form of the so-called **'Golden Rule' of fiscal policy**, which stated that, on average over the economic cycle, the government should borrow only to invest and not to fund current expenditure. This was intended to help achieve equity between present and future generations. It should perhaps be noted that this was a self-imposed guideline, so there would be no penalty for breaking the rule other than a loss of political credibility. The Coalition government that followed was less committed to the concept of the Golden Rule, and the onset of the financial crisis — and the need to bail out commercial banks in order to safeguard the financial system — rendered the Golden Rule impossible to follow.

If receipts and outlays more or less balance over the economic cycle, the economy is not in a position whereby the current generation is forcing future generations to pay for its consumption. However, it is not practical to impose this rule at every part of the cycle, so the Golden Rule was intended to apply over the economic cycle as a whole.

Key term

Golden Rule of fiscal policy a rule stating that, over the economic cycle, net government borrowing will be for investment only, and not for current spending

There was also a commitment to keep public sector net debt below 40% of GDP — again, on average over the economic cycle. Figure 14.3 shows data for this since 1997. The Golden Rule seemed secure until the onset of the credit crunch. However, the financial support offered to Northern Rock and other banks in the bailout of 2008 had a noticeable effect on public sector net debt, as is all too clear in the figure. Even without the financial sector interventions, net debt rose over the 40% mark in the last quarter of 2008 and continued to rise thereafter. This reflected other measures taken by the government to try to mitigate the effects of the recession. One example was the reduction in the rate of VAT from 17.5 to 15%. This is tantamount to a fiscal expansion, but when it was introduced, it was made clear that it was intended as a temporary boost for a specified period. This statement enabled the government to maintain that it was not breaching its long-term fiscal commitment. The rate of VAT returned to 17.5% in January 2010, and was increased to 20% in January 2011.

The sudden fall in the public sector net debt (including financial sector interventions) in 2014 results from the reclassification of Lloyds Banking Group from the public to the private sector, following sales by the UK government of part of its share holdings in the group.

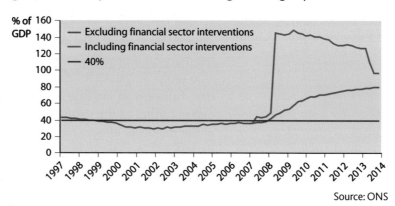

Source: ONS

Figure 14.3 Public sector net debt as a percentage of GDP, 1997–2014

Summary

- Fiscal policy concerns the use of government expenditure and taxation to influence aggregate demand in the economy.
- The overall balance between private and public sectors varies through time and across countries.
- Direct taxes help to redistribute income between groups in society, but if too progressive they may dampen incentives to provide effort.
- Indirect taxes tend to be regressive.
- The Golden Rule of fiscal policy was that the government should aim to borrow only for investment, and not for current expenditure (averaged over the economic cycle).
- There was also a commitment to keep the national debt below 40% of GDP; this commitment did not survive the financial crisis and recession of the late 2000s.

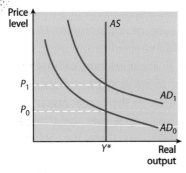

Figure 14.4 Demand-side policy with a vertical *AS* curve

Fiscal policy and the *AD/AS* model

It is important to understand how fiscal policy can be analysed using the *AD/AS* model. As already noted, the overall balance between government receipts and outlays affects the position of the aggregate demand curve, which is reinforced by multiplier effects. When government outlays exceed government receipts, the result is a *fiscal deficit*. This occurs when the revenues raised through taxation are not sufficient to cover the government's various types of expenditure. An increase in the fiscal deficit has the effect of shifting the aggregate demand curve to the right.

Figure 14.4 shows that shifting the aggregate demand curve in this way affects only the overall price level in the economy when the aggregate supply curve is vertical — and remember that the monetarist school of thought argued that it would always be vertical. Hence a key issue for a government considering the use of fiscal policy is knowing whether there is spare capacity in the economy, because otherwise an expansion in aggregate demand from increased government spending will push up prices, but leave real output unchanged.

Under the multiplier, any increase in autonomous spending leads to a multiplied increase in equilibrium output. The idea of the multiplier is that, if there is an increase in (say) government expenditure, this provides income for workers, who will then spend that income and create further expenditure streams. The size of these induced effects will depend upon the marginal propensity to withdraw.

In terms of the *AD/AS* diagram, the existence of the multiplier means that if there is an increase in government expenditure, the *AD* curve moves further to the right than it otherwise would have done, because of the multiplier effects. However, this does not mean that equilibrium income will increase by the full multiplier amount. Looking more closely at what is happening, you can see that there are some forces at work that are acting to weaken the multiplier effect of an increase in government expenditure.

One way in which this happens is through interest rates. If the government finances its deficit through borrowing, a side effect is to put upward pressure on interest rates, which then may cause private sector spending — by households on consumption and by firms on investment — to decline, as the cost of borrowing has been increased. This process is known as the **crowding out** of private sector activity by the public sector. It limits the extent to which a government budget deficit can shift the aggregate demand curve, especially if the public sector activity is less productive than the private sector activity that it replaces. In principle, there could also be a **crowding in** effect if the government runs a surplus and thus puts downward pressure on interest rates.

Automatic and discretionary fiscal policies

It is important to distinguish between automatic and discretionary changes in government expenditure. Some items of government expenditure and receipts vary automatically with the economic cycle. They are known as **automatic stabilisers**. For example, if the economy enters a period of recession, government expenditure will rise because of the increased payments of unemployment and other social security benefits, and revenues will fall because fewer people are paying income tax, and because receipts from VAT are falling. This helps to offset the recession without any active intervention from the government.

More important, however, is the question of whether the government can or should make use of discretionary fiscal policy in a deliberate attempt to influence the course of the economy. As already mentioned, the key issue is whether or not the economy has spare capacity, because attempts to stimulate an economy that is already at full employment will merely push up the price level.

There are many examples of how excessive government spending can create problems for the economy. Such problems arose in a number of Latin American economies during the 1980s. In Brazil, a range of policies was brought to bear in an attempt to reduce inflation, including direct controls on prices. However, with no serious attempt to control the fiscal deficit, inflation continually got out of control, reaching almost 3,000% in 1990. Only when the deficit was reduced did it become possible to bring inflation down to a more reasonable level. More recently, the collapse of the economy of Zimbabwe was accompanied by inflation at such a high level that the printing presses could not keep up with the need for banknotes.

The conduct of fiscal policy

Having discussed the policy environment, the next step is to see how the effectiveness of fiscal policy is determined by the economic models that have been introduced, and by the assumptions made.

Fiscal policy is the manipulation of the government's taxation and expenditure in order to influence the economy. For a period after the Second World War, the prime aim of economic policy was to maintain full employment, and the main way of trying to achieve this was through an active fiscal policy. It was thought that by manipulating aggregate demand through changes in the government's fiscal balance, the economy could be stabilised close to full employment.

Figure 14.5 shows how this is intended to work. The figure shows an economy with $LRAS$ being the aggregate supply curve, becoming vertical at the full employment level of output Y^*. Suppose that the economy is initially operating with the aggregate demand curve AD_0, such that short-run equilibrium is with real output at Y_0 and an overall price level at P_0. The intention of fiscal policy is to raise the real output level in order to take the economy closer to full employment. An increase in government spending would shift the AD curve to AD_1, and real output would increase to Y_1 in the new equilibrium. The overall price level would also rise, to P_1.

The active use of fiscal policy to influence the economy in this way went out of fashion under the influence of the monetarist school of macroeconomists. As has been explained, they argued that the aggregate supply curve is vertical, such that the economy will return of its own accord to full employment relatively quickly. If this is the case, then active fiscal policy is damaging to the economy. Figure 14.6 shows an expansionary fiscal policy under the assumption of a vertical aggregate supply curve. The increase in government spending again has the effect of shifting the aggregate demand curve to the right, from AD_0 to AD_1, but now the impact is *only* on the overall price level, which increases from P_0 to P_1.

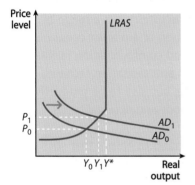

Figure 14.5 An expansionary fiscal policy

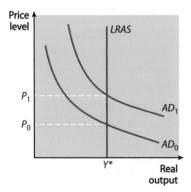

Figure 14.6 Fiscal policy with a vertical *AS* curve

Therefore, according to monetarist economists, if the government continues trying to simulate the economy by increasing spending, the result will be that the price level will keep rising, but that real output will remain unchanged. Some countries in Latin America acted in this way during the 1980s, and the result was hyperinflation. Eventually, the continuing inflation acts to discourage investment, and causes the economy to have a lower productive capacity than it otherwise could have reached.

Balance between the public and private sectors

Both economic analysis and the UK experience support the view that fiscal policy should not be used as an active stabilisation device. However, this does not mean that there is no role for fiscal policy in a modern economy. Earlier, it was pointed out that decisions about the size of government expenditure and revenue influence the overall balance between the public and private sectors. The balance that is achieved can have an important influence on the overall level of economic activity, and upon economic growth, so the importance of designing an appropriate fiscal policy should not be underestimated.

An important theme that runs through much economic analysis is that governments may be justified in intervening in the economy in order to correct market failure. Some of this intervention requires the use of fiscal policy: for example, taxes to correct for the effects of externalities, or expenditure to ensure the provision of public goods. In other words, fiscal policy can be an instrument that operates at the microeconomic level, as well as having macroeconomic implications.

Take infrastructure as an example. Infrastructure covers a range of goods that are crucial for the efficient operation of a market economy. Businesses need good transport links and good communication facilities. Households need good healthcare, education and sanitation facilities, not only in order to enjoy a good standard of life, but also to be productive members of the labour force. Both public goods and externality arguments come into play in the provision of infrastructure, so there needs to be appropriate government intervention to ensure that such goods are adequately provided. The consequence of failing to do this will be to lower the productive capacity of the economy below what would otherwise have been possible. In other words, the aggregate supply curve will be further to the left than it need be.

On the other hand, too much government intervention may also be damaging. One of the most compelling arguments in favour of privatisation was that when the managers of public enterprises are insufficiently accountable for their actions, X-inefficiency becomes a major issue, so public sector activity tends to be less efficient than private sector enterprise. On this argument, too large a public sector may have the effect of lowering aggregate productive capacity below its potential level.

These arguments suggest that an important role for fiscal policy is in affecting the supply side of the economy, ensuring that markets operate effectively to make the best possible use of the economy's resources.

Synoptic link

Public goods were discussed in Book 1, Chapter 8.

Income distribution

The other key role for fiscal policy is in affecting the distribution of income within society. Taxes and transfers can have a large effect on income distribution. This in turn may have effects on the economy by affecting the incentives that people face in choosing their labour supply. This was discussed in Chapter 12.

Achieving a balance of taxation between direct and indirect taxes is an important aspect of the government's redistributive policy. A switch in the balance from direct to indirect taxes will tend to increase inequality in a society. The incentive effects must also be kept in mind. High marginal tax rates on income can have a disincentive effect; if people know that a large proportion of any additional work they undertake will be taxed away, they may be discouraged from providing more work. In other words, cutting income tax can encourage work effort by reducing marginal tax rates. This is yet another reminder of the need for a balanced policy — one that recognises that, while some income redistribution is needed to protect the vulnerable, disincentive effects may arise if the better-off are over-taxed.

Raising revenue

An important rationale for fiscal policy is the need to raise revenue in order to finance the government's expenditure. But does an increase in the tax rate necessarily lead to a rise in tax revenue? Arthur Laffer argued that the answer to this was 'no'. He pointed out that changes in tax rates have two effects on tax revenue. The arithmetic says that an increase in the tax rate will increase the tax revenue. However, there is also an economic effect. As tax rates rise, incentive effects come into play, tending to work against the arithmetic effect, as people have less incentive to supply effort at the higher tax rates. The relationship can be captured in the so-called *Laffer curve*, an inverted U-shaped relationship between the tax rate and the amount of revenue raised, as shown in Figure 14.7.

At low rates of tax, revenue increases, but beyond t^*, the revenue begins to fall. If an economy has been operating with a tax rate above t^*, then a *reduction* in the tax rate would actually *increase* the revenue raised by the tax. It is worth noting that Laffer himself pointed out that he had not invented the concept, as it can be found in the writings of Keynes, not to mention Ibn Khaldun, a fourteenth-century Muslim philosopher.

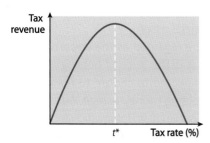

Figure 14.7 The Laffer curve

Summary

- Fiscal policy entails changes in taxation and in the government's expenditure to influence the level or pattern of aggregate demand.
- Fiscal policy has gone out of fashion as a short-run stabilisation device.
- Fiscal policy retains a key role in ensuring an appropriate balance between private and public sectors, and ensuring the provision of public goods and tackling externality effects.
- It also plays a key role in influencing the distribution of income between groups within society.
- In doing this, an appropriate balance needs to be found between achieving a desired level of equity between individuals, and providing incentives to work.
- The Laffer curve suggests that there may be situations in which a reduction in the tax rate may result in an increase in tax revenue.

Monetary policy

Monetary policy has become the prime instrument of government macroeconomic policy, with the interest rate acting as the key control variable. Monetary policy involves the manipulation of monetary variables in order to influence aggregate demand in the economy, with the intention of meeting the government's inflation target.

In order to understand how monetary policy can influence the level of aggregate demand, it is important to examine the characteristics of key monetary variables — the money supply, interest rates and the exchange rate.

Money supply

The **money stock** is the quantity of money that is in circulation in the economy. In a modern economy, money performs four important functions. First, it is a medium of exchange. In other words, money is what is used when people undertake transactions — for example, when you buy a sandwich or a burger for lunch. Second, money is a store of value: people (or firms) may choose to hold money in order to undertake transactions in the future. If this were not the case, there would be no reason for people to accept money in exchange for goods or services. Money is also a unit of account: it is a way of setting prices so that the value of different goods and services can be compared. Finally, money is a standard of deferred payment. Firms signing contracts for future transactions need to be able to set prices for those transactions.

Firms and households choose to hold some money. They may do this in order to undertake transactions, or as a precaution against the possible need to undertake transactions at short notice. In other words, there is a *demand for money*. However, in choosing to hold money they incur an opportunity cost, in the sense that they forgo the possibility of earning interest by purchasing some form of financial asset.

This means that the interest rate can be regarded as the opportunity cost of holding money; put another way, it is the price of holding money. At high rates of interest, people can be expected to choose to hold less money, as the opportunity cost of holding money is high. *MD* in Figure 14.8 represents a money demand curve. It is downward sloping.

Suppose the government wants to set the money supply (*MS*) at *M** in Figure 14.8. This can be achieved in two ways. If the government controls the supply of money at *M**, equilibrium will be achieved only if the interest rate is allowed to adjust to *r**. An alternative way of reaching the same point is to set the interest rate at *r** and then allow the money supply to adjust to *M**. The government can do one or the other — but it cannot set money supply at *M** and hold the interest rate at any value other than *r** without causing disequilibrium. In other words, it is not possible to control both money supply and interest rates simultaneously and independently.

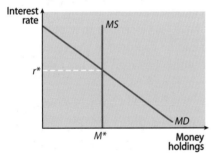

Figure 14.8 The demand for money

Measuring money stock

An important characteristic of money is **liquidity**. This refers to the ease with which an asset can be spent. Cash is the most liquid asset, as it can be used for transactions. However, if you are holding funds in a savings account whereby you must either give notice of withdrawal or forfeit some

The notes and coins in circulation are known as 'narrow money'

Key terms

narrow money (M0) notes and coins in circulation and as commercial banks' deposits at the Bank of England

broad money (M4) M0 plus sterling wholesale and retail deposits with monetary financial institutions such as banks and building societies

return to withdraw it instantly, then such funds are regarded as being less liquid, as they cannot costlessly or instantly be used for transactions.

One traditional way of measuring the money stock was from the *monetary base*, which comprised all notes and coins in circulation. Together with the commercial banks' deposits at the Bank of England, this was known as **M0** or **narrow money**. This was intended to measure the amount of money held for transactions purposes. However, with the increased use of electronic means of payment, M0 has become less meaningful as a measure, and the Bank of England stopped issuing data for M0 in 2005.

However, there are many assets that are 'near-money', such as interest-bearing current account deposits at banks. These are highly liquid and can readily be converted into cash for transactions. **M4** or **broad money** is a measure of the money stock that includes M0 together with sterling wholesale and retail deposits with monetary financial institutions such as banks. In other words, it includes all bank deposits that can be used for transactions, even though some of these deposits may require a period of notice for withdrawal. However, M4 is held not only for transactions purposes, but also partly as a store of wealth.

A problem with attempting to control the money supply directly is that the complexity of the modern financial system makes it quite difficult to pin down a precise definition or measurement of money. For this and other reasons, the chosen instrument of monetary policy is the interest rate. By setting the interest rate, monetary policy affects aggregate demand.

It is also important to realise that the lending behaviour of the commercial banks can influence money supply, as by increasing their lending, banks can create credit. This makes it more difficult for the central bank to exert control over money supply. This could be achieved by forcing the banks to hold a proportion of their assets as cash or liquid assets, but this method was abandoned in favour of controlling via the interest rate.

Interest rates

Although the previous section talked about 'the interest rate', this is a simplification. In the real-world economy, there are many different interest rates. For example, if you borrow from a bank, you will pay a higher interest rate than would be paid to you on your savings. Indeed, it is this difference between the rates for savers and borrowers that enables the banks to make a profit.

Similarly, interest rates on financial assets differ depending on the nature of the asset. In part, these differences reflect different degrees of risk associated with the assets. A risky asset pays a higher interest rate than a relatively safe asset. A long-term asset tends to pay a higher interest rate than a short-term asset, although the differences have been quite small in the early part of the twenty-first century. This will be discussed further in Chapter 18.

The exchange rate

In considering the tools of monetary policy, it is also important to consider the **exchange rate** — that is, the rate at which one currency exchanges against another. This is because the exchange rate, the interest rate and the money supply are all intimately related. If UK interest rates are high relative to elsewhere in the world, they will attract overseas investors, increasing the demand for pounds. This will tend to lead to an appreciation in the exchange rate — which in turn will reduce the competitiveness of UK goods and services, reducing the foreign demand for UK exports and encouraging UK residents to reduce their demand for domestic goods and buy imports instead.

Under a fixed exchange rate regime, the monetary authorities are committed to maintaining the exchange rate at a particular level, so could not allow an appreciation to take place. In this situation, monetary policy is powerless to influence the real economy, as it must be devoted to maintaining the exchange rate. Under a floating exchange rate system, monetary policy is freed from this role, but even so it must be used in such a way that the current account deficit of the balance of payments does not become unsustainable in the long run. In other words, the use of interest rates to target inflation has implications for the magnitude of the current and financial accounts of the balance of payments.

Key term

exchange rate the price of one currency in terms of another

Study tip

The importance of the balance of payments and the exchange rate for macroeconomic policy was analysed in Book 1, Chapter 17 — including in the 'extension material', which covered some important areas. It is important that you are familiar with this topic when discussing policy issues.

Summary

- Monetary policy entails the manipulation of monetary variables in order to influence aggregate demand in the economy.
- The prime instrument of monetary policy is the interest rate.
- People hold money in order to undertake transactions (among other reasons), and the interest rate can be regarded as the opportunity cost of holding money.
- There are several alternative definitions of money, depending upon how wide or narrow is the focus.
- There is not a single interest rate in the economy, but a variety of rates associated with the wide range of financial assets available.
- The monetary authorities can control either the money supply or interest rates, but not both independently.
- The exchange rate is also closely associated with money supply and the interest rate, and cannot be ignored in policy design.

How does monetary policy work?

In evaluating the tools of monetary policy, it is important to understand the route by which a change in a monetary variable can have an effect on the real economy. In other words, how can a change in money supply, or the interest rate, affect the level of equilibrium output in the economy?

The monetary transmission mechanism

In drawing this analysis together, an important issue concerns the relationship between the rate of interest and the level of aggregate demand. This is critical for the conduct of monetary policy. Indeed, the interest rate has been seen as the prime instrument of monetary policy in recent years — and monetary policy is seen as the prime instrument of macroeconomic policy. By setting the interest rate, monetary policy is intended to affect aggregate demand through the so-called **monetary transmission mechanism**.

At a higher interest rate, firms undertake less investment expenditure because fewer projects are worthwhile. In addition, a higher interest rate may encourage higher saving, which also means that households undertake less consumption expenditure. This may then reinforce the impact on investment because if firms perceive consumption to be falling, this will affect their expectations about future demand, and further dampen their desire to undertake investment. Furthermore, if UK interest rates are high relative to elsewhere in the world, they will attract overseas investors, increasing the demand for pounds. This will tend to lead to an appreciation in the exchange rate, which in turn will reduce the competitiveness of UK goods and services, reducing the foreign demand for UK exports and encouraging UK residents to reduce their demand for domestic goods and buy imports instead. All these factors lower the level of aggregate demand, shifting the AD curve to the left.

This can be seen by looking at Figure 14.9. The initial equilibrium is with real output at Y_0, the price level at P_0 and the rate of interest at r_0. An increase in the rate of interest to r_1 will need to be balanced by a decrease in money supply to maintain money market equilibrium. However, more significant is the effect on investment, which is shown in the middle panel of the figure. The increase in the rate of interest leads to a fall in investment from I_0 to I_1. This will cause the aggregate demand curve to move from AD_0 to AD_1, resulting in a lower overall price level P_1 and a lower real output level at Y_1. The lower level of real output arises because the LRAS curve was drawn under Keynesian assumptions with an upward-sloping segment.

> ### Key term
>
> **monetary transmission mechanism** the channel by which monetary policy affects aggregate demand

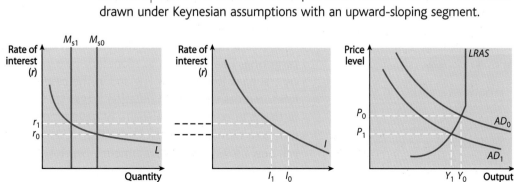

Figure 14.9 The interest rate and aggregate demand

Notice that this may not be the end of the story. If one of the effects of the higher interest rate is to discourage investment, this will also have long-term consequences. Investment allows the productive capacity of the economy to increase, leading to a rightward drift in the *LRAS* curve. With lower investment, this process will slow down, leaving the economy with lower productive capacity than it otherwise would have had.

The *AD/AS* graph is drawn in terms of the overall price level. However, in a dynamic context, high interest rates may be needed in order to maintain control of inflation. A reduction in interest rates would, of course, have the reverse effect. However, notice that the interaction of the money supply, interest rates and the exchange rate makes policy design a complicated business.

In creating a stable macroeconomic environment, the ultimate aim of monetary policy is not simply to keep inflation low, but to improve the confidence of decision-makers, and thereby encourage firms to invest in order to generate an increase in production capacity. This will stimulate economic growth and create an opportunity to improve living standards.

Monetary policy in practice

The monetary transmission mechanism explains the way in which a change in the interest rate affects aggregate demand in the economy. In summary, suppose there is a reduction in the interest rate. From firms' point of view, this lowers the cost of borrowing, and would be expected to encourage higher investment spending. Furthermore, consumers may also respond to a fall in the interest rate by increasing their expenditure, both because this lowers the cost of borrowing — so there may be an increase in the demand for consumer durable goods — and because households may perceive that saving now pays a lower return, so may decide to spend more. Thus a fall in the interest rate is expected to have an expansionary effect on aggregate demand. In terms of the *AD/AS* model, this has the effect of shifting the aggregate demand curve to the right. The effectiveness of this will depend upon the shape of the aggregate supply curve and the starting position of the aggregate demand curve.

An expansionary monetary policy intended to stimulate aggregate demand would be damaging if the economy were close to (or at) full employment, as the main impact would be on the overall price level rather than real output. This suggests that monetary policy should also not be used to stimulate aggregate demand. However, monetary policy can still play an important role in managing the economy. This arises through its influence on the price level and hence the rate of change of prices — that is, inflation.

Soon after the general election of 1997, the UK introduced **inflation targeting**. This approach to monetary policy gives independence to the central bank (the Bank of England in the case of the UK) to set interest rates in order to meet an inflation target set by the government. The idea of this is to boost the credibility of government policy, by establishing a firm commitment to controlling inflation, as the control of money supply will now be out of the government's control. It cannot expand money supply to boost aggregate demand in order to create a temporary boom that might bolster its popularity in the lead-up to an election.

Exercise 14.2

Outline the mechanism by which an increase in the rate of interest affects aggregate demand in an economy.

Key term

inflation targeting an approach to monetary policy in which the central bank is given independence to set interest rates in order to meet an inflation target

Monetary policy in the UK thus became the responsibility of the Bank of England. The Bank's Monetary Policy Committee (MPC) meets each month to decide whether or not the interest rate needs to be altered. If the rate of inflation threatens to accelerate beyond the target rate, the Bank of England can intervene by raising interest rates, thereby having a dampening effect on aggregate demand and reducing the inflationary pressure. In reaching its decisions, the MPC takes a long-term view, projecting inflation ahead over the next 2 years. In the case of the British approach to this policy, the target range is *symmetric*: in other words, the MPC is required to take action (or explain itself) if the inflation rate falls below the target range as well as if it rises above it. In contrast, the European Central Bank faces an *asymmetric target*, being only required to act when the inflation rate rises about the target range, but without a lower range.

However, decisions to change the rate of interest are not taken solely in the light of expected inflation. In its deliberations about the interest rate, the MPC takes a wide variety of factors into account, including developments in:

- financial markets
- the international economy
- money and credit
- demand and output
- the labour market
- costs and prices (e.g. changes in oil prices)

A good example was in 2008, when the UK and other countries were struggling to cope with the 'credit crunch'. At this time, inflation was accelerating, and had reached a rate that was more than one percentage point above the target. This being so, it might have been expected that the Bank of England would raise interest rates in order to stem aggregate demand and bring inflation back into line with the target. However, this would have been damaging in other ways, pushing the economy further into recession. With house prices falling, an increase in interest rates could also have damaged this sector. It was also thought that there were other pressures affecting the world economy that would in any case mean that the rate of inflation was likely to slow down of its own accord. In the event, inflation accelerated way beyond its target range, but the MPC refrained from raising the bank rate because of fears that the recession would become even deeper, or that the economy would recover more slowly. This is a good example of how different policy targets may come into conflict, and of how it may be prudent not to stick to a rule just for its own sake.

It is also important to remember that the transmission mechanism has a third channel in addition to the effects of the change in interest rate on consumption and investment. This third channel arises through the exchange rate, so that monetary policy cannot be considered in isolation from exchange rate policy. The channels of the transmission mechanism are summarised in Figure 14.10.

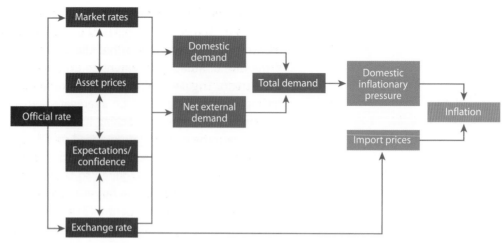

Figure 14.10 The transmission of monetary policy

Evaluation of monetary policy

For a decade after the responsibility for monetary policy was delegated to the Bank of England, monetary policy was seen to be highly effective in enabling the achievement of the inflation target. You can see this in Figure 14.11. Inflation stayed within the required one percentage point of its target, moving outside that range in only one month between May 1997 and April 2008. However, matters then took a turn for the worse with the onset of the financial crisis and the ensuing recession, and inflation accelerated beyond its limit before coming back into range.

In looking at the relationship between interest rates and inflation, it is useful to be aware that there are long time lags between initiating a change in the interest rate and the final impact on the inflation rate. The Bank of England has noted that it can take about 2 years before the full effect on inflation has worked through the system. Decisions about the interest rate therefore need to be based on the forecast of inflation between 2 and 3 years ahead.

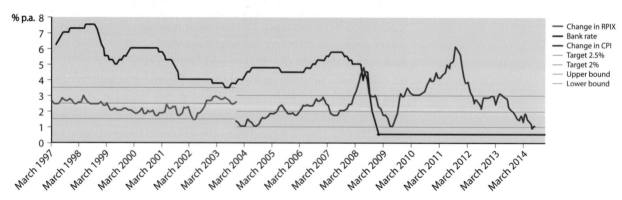

Sources: ONS, Bank of England

Figure 14.11 UK interest rates and the inflation target, 1997–2014

The need to combat recession led to the bank rate being reduced to 0.5% in March 2009. This situation creates problems for monetary policy, as having reached such a low level for bank rate, it is no longer possible to reduce the interest rate any further — it would not be possible for the bank rate to be negative. Keynes had pointed to the danger that such a

Key terms

liquidity trap a situation in an economy when interest rates can fall no further, and monetary policy cannot influence aggregate demand

quantitative easing a process by which liquidity in the economy is increased when the central bank purchases assets from the commercial banks

situation would arise, referring to this as the **liquidity trap**. He argued that in a deep recession, monetary policy would become ineffective in affecting aggregate demand. Interest rates could fall no further, and any increase in money supply would be absorbed by an increase in the cash holdings of firms and individuals, as they would not buy financial assets with such a low return.

The Bank of England announced that it would start to inject money directly into the economy, effectively switching the instrument of monetary policy away from the interest rate and towards the quantity of money. This would be achieved by a process known as **quantitative easing**, by which the Bank purchases assets such as government and corporate bonds, thus releasing additional money into the system through the banks and other financial institutions from which it buys the assets. The hope was that this would allow banks to increase their lending, and thus combat the threat of deflation — and perhaps help to speed recovery. This suggests that the Bank did not believe that the economy was in a liquidity trap, so that an increase in money supply could still affect aggregate demand. You will find further discussion of this in Chapter 20, which explores the role of the Bank of England in more detail.

It is important to be aware that the UK was certainly not alone in facing this combination of circumstances. A number of countries had also enjoyed relative stability for several years, followed by a more turbulent period. This in itself suggests that the conduct of monetary policy cannot claim full responsibility for the period of calm, nor perhaps be entirely blamed for the subsequent problems. The process of globalisation that has been taking place means that the UK economy cannot be viewed in total isolation from events occurring elsewhere in the world, and macroeconomic policy is interconnected — through movements in the exchange rate and through trading links. This is illustrated by Figure 14.12, which shows annual inflation (in % p.a.) since 1981 for the world as a whole and for two country groupings. You can see how inflation in the world as a whole accelerated in the 1990s before stabilising during the 2000s, then rising in 2007/08, only to plummet as the recession set in. Until the beginning of the twenty-first century, Latin America displayed more instability than the world as a whole, whereas the high-income OECD countries experienced inflation rates below the world average throughout the period.

Exercise 14.3

Discuss why rules-based fiscal or monetary policy may help to reinforce the effectiveness of policy measures.

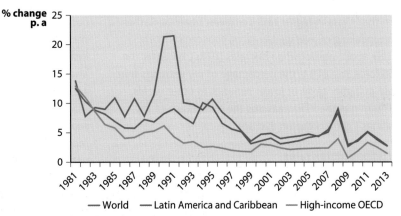

Figure 14.12 World inflation, 1981–2013

It is also important to realise that for monetary policy to be and remain effective, it must be viewed in combination with other policies being implemented at the same time — in particular, there needs to be coordination with fiscal policy.

Summary

- Monetary policy is the use of financial variables, such as money supply or the rate of interest, to influence the performance of the economy.
- Money supply does not provide a reliable control mechanism, so the prime instrument of monetary policy is the interest rate.
- The transmission mechanism from the interest rate to aggregate demand works through investment and consumption, and indirectly via the exchange rate.
- The Bank of England's Monetary Policy Committee has the responsibility for setting the interest rate at such a level as to achieve the government's inflation target, taking account of the general domestic and international economic environment.
- Monetary policy cannot focus solely on meeting the inflation target, but must also operate with an awareness of other developments in the macroeconomy.
- It is also important that monetary policy is coordinated with other policy measures being implemented that affect the macroeconomy.

Case study 14.1

Fiscal policy and the supply side

How do tax changes (for example, an increase in the personal allowance) affect incentives? What is the likely effect of these changes on people's working behaviour? This depends upon the 'marginal' and the 'average' tax rates that people face, and how these will have been affected by a change in this 'personal allowance'.

The 'marginal' and 'average' concepts are common throughout economics. These can be applied to the tax system and incentives to work. We want to estimate the effect of changes to the income tax system on whether and how much an individual works. In this case, the equivalent to marginal cost is the *marginal effective tax rate* (METR) — the proportion of the next pound I earn that I lose in higher taxes or lower benefits. Rather than speaking of average tax rates, economists prefer to talk about *participation tax rates* (PTRs). If I enter the workforce, my PTR is the percentage of my earnings that I lose in higher taxes or lower benefits. In other words, 100% minus the PTR measures the percentage of my earnings I get to keep on average.

Participation tax rates

How do the marginal and participation tax rates influence individuals' choices? When I am deciding whether to work

an extra hour, it is the marginal tax rate that matters. If I can earn £10 an hour, but face a marginal tax rate of 40%, I have to decide whether I would rather have £6 or do something else with the extra hour, like have a lie-in. If my marginal tax rate is 20%, the choice is between £8 and an extra hour in bed. The argument that lowering an individual's marginal tax rate is likely to encourage them to work more is as simple as saying that they are more likely to get out of bed in the first case than in the second.

The participation tax rate matters when an individual is deciding whether to work at all. Imagine a mother with school age children deciding whether to go back to work. Her decision is likely to be whether to take a full-time (or part-time) job, rather than whether to work 1 hour rather than none. In that case, it is not her marginal gain from her first hour of work that matters, but the total increase in her after-tax income if she takes the job. In fact, many people are unable to choose the precise number of hours they work in practice. As a result, economists modelling labour supply tend to use what are known as 'discrete choice' models — people choose to work full time, part time, or not at all. In such a setting, it is the participation tax rates which people face at each discrete amount of work that influence their decision, rather than any marginal tax rate.

Case study 14.1 (continued)

Increases in the personal allowance

During the period of the Coalition government, every budget saw an increase in the income tax personal allowance (the amount you can earn before you start paying income tax). What can we say about the effect of this increase in the personal allowance on the work incentives of the low-income individuals whom the policy is designed to benefit? Thinking first about marginal tax rates, researchers at the Institute for Fiscal Studies calculated that the government's policy on the income tax personal allowance will have taken 1.8 million individuals out of income tax altogether by 2014/15. Each of these people will keep 20p more of every additional pound they earn as a result. This might make individuals more inclined to work an extra hour, but it seems unlikely that many of the individuals facing lower marginal tax rates as a result of the policy will have had the flexibility to increase the hours they work in response, particularly given the state of the economy.

The much broader effect of the policy on people's incentive to work comes through its impact on average tax rates. Take an individual choosing whether to take a job with a salary of £15,000, or to remain unemployed. With a personal allowance of £10,000, they pay a total of £1,000 in income tax. With a personal allowance of £7,455 the same individual pays a total of £1,509 in income tax. Despite facing exactly the same marginal income tax rate of 20%, the raising of the personal allowance has had a substantial effect on their work incentives, by reducing the total tax they pay, and hence reducing their participation tax rate.

The substitution effect

Does this allow us to conclude with certainty that such individuals are more likely to work as a result of the increases in the personal allowance? Unfortunately not. So far, we have been discussing the impact of changes to the income tax system in terms of how people respond to changes in the returns for working. As taxes on income decrease, the returns for working increase. This means that taking leisure time (any time that is not spent working) becomes relatively more expensive. In other words, the opportunity cost of leisure has increased. As a consequence, we would expect people to substitute work for leisure. This effect is known as the *substitution effect*.

The participation tax rate will affect a mother's decision to return to work

The income effect

However, we also need to consider responses to the impact of changes to the income tax system on an individual's take-home pay. Suppose that an individual can buy everything she wants with a post-tax income of £50,000. If her participation tax rate falls as a result of the changes to the personal allowance, she can earn this amount with a lower pre-tax income. As a result, she can reduce the amount that she works and instead enjoy more leisure time, while maintaining a post-tax income of £50,000. This is known as the *income effect*.

The income effect moves in the opposite direction to the substitution effect; while higher returns for working provide an individual with an incentive to work more, the higher post-tax income that she can enjoy for any given amount of work might lead her to work less. The overall impact of tax changes on people's work patterns is therefore determined by the relative size of these two effects, and so we cannot say for certain that the increases in the personal allowance will lead to an increase in labour supply.

Economic theory alone cannot tell us for sure what the impact on work of changes to the personal allowance will be, as there are two potentially confounding effects: the substitution effect of changes in returns for working and the income effect of changes in post-tax income. As with so many economic questions, the answer lies in the data, not just the theory.

Source: adapted from Andrew Hood, 'To work or not to work', *Economic Review*, September 2013

Follow-up question

Discuss the extent to which this analysis suggests that fiscal policy can be viewed as contributing to supply-side policy. How would this be shown using the *AD/AS* model?

Chapter 15

Approaches to macroeconomic policy

Previous chapters have highlighted the evolution of macroeconomic thinking over time, and the way that different schools of thought emerged with contrasting views of how the macroeconomy works. This chapter focuses on the key differences between the assumptions of the competing schools, and explores the way in which these shaped (and were shaped by) the development of approaches towards macroeconomic policy. This discussion will be set in the context of the changing macroeconomic environment.

Prior knowledge needed

Chapter 14 of Book 1 introduced the different views of the Monetarists and Keynesians in relation to the shape of the aggregate supply curve. This chapter sets this discussion into a broader context.

Learning objectives

After studying this chapter, you should:
- be familiar with the key differences in assumptions about the macroeconomy that have been the focus of debate
- be able to explain why approaches to macroeconomic policy have changed in accordance with economic circumstances
- be aware of the main macroeconomic events that have shaped the development of macroeconomic thinking and policy design

Synoptic link

This chapter draws together analysis from a number of other parts of the book in order to uncover the debates that have been ongoing in macroeconomics over a long period. You may wish to dip into other chapters to remind yourself of some of the arguments.

Debates in macroeconomic thinking

The discussion so far has highlighted the way that macroeconomists have disagreed about how the macroeconomy works. How could this happen? Economists claim to use scientific method and to share a common way of thinking about the world. So why should there be different (and sometimes opposing) views about the macroeconomy? Perhaps the main reason is that although macroeconomists share the same methodology, they may rest their analysis on different assumptions. In particular, different assumptions have been made about three key issues: the elasticity of aggregate supply, the flexibility of prices and wages, and the role of expectations.

The elasticity of aggregate supply

The previous chapter highlighted the debate between the monetarist (new classical) school and the (new) Keynesians in terms of the shape of the aggregate supply curve. This emerges as a fundamental source of difference between these two differing views of the macroeconomy.

The new classical economists held the viewpoint that the macroeconomy would always return rapidly to its equilibrium (natural) rate of output and unemployment. This being the case, the long-run aggregate supply curve would be vertical at the natural rate, corresponding to full employment. In other words, the economy would always tend rapidly to the potential capacity level of real output.

Unemployment could be caused if the wage rate does not adjust downwards

The Keynesian view, on the other hand, was that there would be a range of output below full employment where the long-run aggregate supply curve would be upward sloping, so it would be possible for an economy to be caught in equilibrium at a level of real output that was below the full capacity output of the economy.

This has great significance for the design of macroeconomic policy. If the economy always makes a rapid transition to equilibrium, then there is no role for policy to influence the path of the economy, except perhaps to try to improve the efficiency of production on the supply side in order to shift the *LRAS* curve to the right. On the other hand, if the economy can become caught in equilibrium below the full capacity level of output, then there may be scope for the authorities to tackle this by stimulating aggregate demand.

Wage and price flexibility

An important ingredient of the adjustment to equilibrium is the flexibility of prices and wages. In product markets, it is the price that brings about adjustment to equilibrium, whereas it is the adjustment of wages that brings about equilibrium in labour markets. Translating this into a macroeconomic context, the vertical *LRAS* curve of the new classical economists rests upon flexibility of wages and prices at the microeconomic level. Keynesians, on the other hand, argued that this might not be the case. In particular, they argued that wages would be inflexible downwards. In response to a fall in demand, firms wanting to reduce output by hiring fewer workers at lower wages would face resistance from unions to wage cuts. This would hinder the process of adjustment towards equilibrium. At the microeconomic level, this would show up in labour markets, where there would be disequilibrium unemployment.

The role of expectations

Expectations also play an important part in the process of adjustment towards equilibrium. Decisions are taken by firms and by households on the basis of their expectations about the future course of the economy. The more rapidly and accurately expectations are formed, the more

Exercise 15.1

Sketch a diagram showing a labour market, and analyse the effect of a fall in demand. Show how unemployment could be caused if the wage rate does not adjust downwards.

When considering the differences between the approaches to macroeconomic policy in the context of the *AD/AS* model, always remember these three key sources of contention:

- the elasticity of aggregate supply
- the flexibility of wages and prices
- the role and nature of expectations

Summary

- There have been many debates between macroeconomists about how the economy works, and in particular how it adjusts towards equilibrium.
- The main cause of differences in viewpoints has been differing assumptions about the shape of aggregate supply, the flexibility of wages and prices, and the way in which economic agents form expectations.
- These differences have implications for the design of macroeconomic policy.

rapid is the adjustment to equilibrium. Under new classical assumptions, economic agents rapidly form accurate expectations, so that adjustment to equilibrium is almost instantaneous.

This was seen in the earlier discussion of the Phillips curve, where expectations were seen to influence the position of the short-run Phillips curve. If expectations about inflation adjust slowly, then there may be divergence from the natural rate of unemployment in the short run, but in the long run the economy will return to the natural rate. The new classical economists would argue that expectations will adjust rapidly, so that the natural rate is reached quickly.

Expectations may also be important in influencing firms' willingness to undertake investment. This has been used to maintain stability in the overall price level. If inflation is high and unpredictable, this may deter firms from investing, as they will have an uncertain or pessimistic view of the future course of the economy. This argument was influential in making low inflation the core target of macroeconomic policy in the 1970s, as will be discussed later in the chapter.

Evaluation

How significant are these differences in assumptions? It turns out that they are highly significant because of the very different implications they have for macroeconomic policy, and for the degree to which the government should seek to intervene in order to influence the path of the macroeconomy. The assumptions also affect the form that intervention might take.

The way in which theory and policy interact has tended to be influenced by political considerations and political ideology. In general terms, left-wing parties have tended to favour intervention in order to affect income distribution and to expand public sector provision of services. On the other hand, political parties on the right have tended to favour a less hands-on approach, and have thus been more likely to favour the new classical approach, which suggests that the macroeconomy will find its own way to equilibrium, and will do so in the relatively short term.

The evolution of macroeconomic thinking and the approach to policy

Looking back in time, it is clear that different theoretical views about the macroeconomy have influenced the design of policy in different periods. In turn, the perceived effectiveness of policies has influenced the development of theoretical ideas. This section of the chapter tracks how macroeconomic thinking and policy design have evolved over time.

In order to set the scene, it is helpful to look back at the performance of the UK economy, and how this has changed over time, starting with unemployment. Figure 15.1 shows the unemployment rate since 1920. Notice that there have been changes in the way in which unemployment has been defined and measured over this time period, so the data are indicative rather than precisely measured. Nonetheless, the overall picture is useful in illustrating the changing fortunes of the economy.

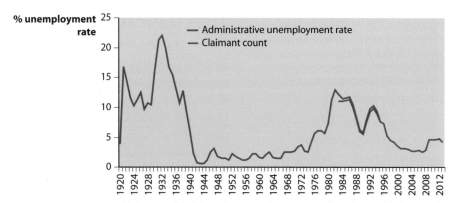

Sources: Administrative unemployment rate from *Labour Market Trends*, January 1996; claimant count from ONS, *Labour Market Statistics*

Figure 15.1 The unemployment rate in the UK since 1920

As the UK emerged from the First World War, unemployment was low, but it rose sharply in 1921, falling back to about 10% for most of the 1920s. The Great Depression saw a large rise in unemployment in 1930, reaching 22% in 1932. This overall rate for the country as a whole disguises the even higher unemployment rates in some parts of the country.

With the outbreak of the Second World War, unemployment fell to below 1% as conscription drew large numbers into the armed forces. At the end of the war, unemployment increased (to just over 3% in 1947), but then it remained between 1.3 and 2.6% during the 1950s and 1960s.

The 1970s saw unemployment rise again, reaching 6% in 1977 before increasing again during the Thatcher years, peaking at 13% in 1982. After 1993 unemployment fell steadily, rising again in 2009 during the financial crisis.

Figure 15.2 shows the path followed by inflation over the same period.

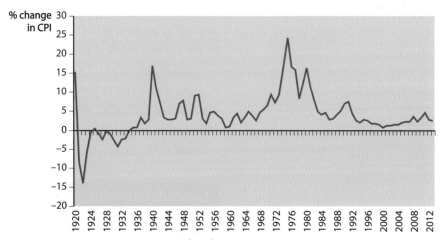

Source: Hills, S., Thomas, R. and Dimsdale, N. (2015) 'Three Centuries of Data — Version 2.1', Bank of England

Figure 15.2 The rate of change in consumer prices since 1920

The UK economy experienced a period of deflation during the 1920s, but from 1935 onwards inflation has been positive. There were some years of high inflation — for example, at the beginning and some years after the end of the Second World War.

Inflation accelerated towards the end of the 1960s and peaked at the time of the first oil price crisis in 1973/74. The 1990s and early 2000s were a period of relatively stable prices, with inflation mainly between 1 and 2%, before it rose again in the late 2000s.

The classical view

The circular flow model (which was introduced in Book 1, Chapter 13) describes a world in which there are injections and withdrawals into and out of the system. Injections occur in the form of investment, government expenditure and export earnings. Withdrawals happen because of saving, taxes and imports. Equilibrium is where planned withdrawals equal planned injections.

In a classical world-view, savings would equal investment. Firms would need funds for investment, and would borrow from households, who would save, doing so in quest of a return on those savings, so the rate of interest would bring saving and investment into equilibrium. Imports would come into line with exports because with the currency being backed by gold, it would not be possible to run either a surplus or a deficit without accumulating gold reserves or running them down. Overall equilibrium, with withdrawals equal to injections, could thus only be achieved if the government ran a balanced budget with taxes equal to expenditure.

The quantity theory of money

The overall price level comes to be determined through the mechanism of the quantity theory of money. To explain this requires a new concept, that of the **velocity of circulation**. If the money stock is defined as the quantity of money (notes and coins) in circulation in the economy, the velocity of circulation is defined as the speed with which that money stock changes hands. It is defined as the volume of transactions divided by the money stock.

In practice, the volume of transactions is seen as being represented by nominal income, which is the level of real income (Y) multiplied by the average price level (P). If V is the velocity of circulation, and M is the size of the money stock, then the following equation holds:

$V = PY/M$

Notice that this is just a definition, sometimes known as the Fisher equation of exchange, after the American economist Irving Fisher. Multiplying both sides of the equation by M gives:

$MV = PY$

> ### Key term
>
> **velocity of circulation (V)** the rate at which money changes hands; the volume of transactions divided by money stock

> ### Quantitative skills 15.1
>
> #### Theories and definitions
>
> It is important to realise that this is still based on a definition. This is significant because a definition is just a statement about the relationship between the variables that are included. As such, it is no more than a statement that always holds true. It only becomes a theory if we introduce some assumptions, which is what is done in the next paragraph.

In a classical world, the velocity of circulation (V) would be constant — or at least would be stable over time. Furthermore, real output would always tend rapidly towards the natural rate. These assumptions together with the $MV = PY$ equation provide us with a direct link between money (M) and the overall price level (P). This relationship suggests that prices can only increase persistently if money stock itself increases persistently, and that money (and prices) have no effect on real output.

How can we interpret this in terms of aggregate demand and aggregate supply? If the money supply increases, then firms and households in the economy find they have excess cash balances — that is, for the given price level they have stronger purchasing power than they had anticipated. Their impulse will thus be to increase spending, which will cause the aggregate demand curve to move to the right. They will probably also save some of the excess, which will tend to result in lower interest rates — which then reinforces the increase in aggregate demand. However, as the AD curve moves to the right, the equilibrium price level will rise, and return the economy to equilibrium.

If money supply continues to increase, the process repeats itself, with price then rising persistently. One danger of this is that people get so accustomed to the process that they speed up their spending decisions, and this accelerates the whole process.

To summarise, the analysis suggests that although a price rise can be triggered on either the supply side or the demand side of the macroeconomy, persistent inflation can arise only through persistent excessive growth in the money stock, which can be seen in terms of persistent movements of the aggregate demand curve.

The Great Depression

At the time that the Great Depression of the 1930s hit the economy, the classical view of the world held sway. The main focus of economic analysis was on microeconomics, and the way that prices (and wages) would bring about equilibrium. When unemployment rose so dramatically in the aftermath of the stock market crashes of 1929, how should the government respond? After all, the prevailing view was that the government should balance its budget and allow markets to adjust. In other words, if there is unemployment, it must be because wages are too high and need to fall. Wage cuts would take the labour market back to equilibrium.

So, in the face of rising unemployment and poverty, the government faced falling tax revenues, but still believed that wage cuts were needed in order to restore the competitiveness of British goods. The depression was thus accompanied by deflation — a period of falling prices, which nonetheless failed to improve competitiveness.

It was in this situation that Keynes produced his *General Theory*, which was the first substantive attempt to think in terms of macroeconomics, and the relationships between economic variables at the aggregate level. The Keynesian argument was that the Depression could have been brought to a more rapid end if the government had stimulated aggregate demand instead of maintaining a balanced budget.

Exercise 15.2

In the equation $MV = PY$, define each of the terms and explain the assumptions that a classical economist would make about each of them. To what extent would you accept these assumptions as describing a modern economy?

Unemployed ship-builders and miners marched from Jarrow to London in October 1936 as a protest against poverty and unemployment in the north-east of England

The Keynesian revolution

The Second World War interrupted the normal course of the economy, but memories of the Great Depression lingered, and Keynes's influence was strong. Keynes had been influential at the Bretton Woods conference held in 1946 in the USA to agree on a set of rules under which international trade would be conducted. As part of the agreement reached at the conference, a fixed exchange rate system was established in which countries agreed to fix their exchange rates in terms of the US dollar. This became known as the Dollar Standard.

The Dollar Standard was significant for policy. Monetary policy needs to be used to maintain the exchange rate, and cannot have an independent use within the domestic economy, as was explained in Book 1, Chapter 17. However, this also makes fiscal policy more powerful in its effects on domestic aggregate demand. With Keynesian ideas coming to the fore, this meant that governments could seek to stabilise the time-path of the economy through discretionary fiscal policy, especially given the existence of the multiplier effect.

Looking back at Figures 15.1 and 15.2, the 1950s and 1960s seemed to be a golden era, with the unemployment rate low by previous standards, and inflation under control. However, this disguises part of the story. The UK economy at this time was growing more slowly than many other developed countries, and was staggering from one balance of payments crisis to the next, a phenomenon that came to be known as 'stop–go'.

This can be interpreted in terms of the need to maintain the exchange rate against the dollar. Attempts to stimulate economic growth by boosting aggregate demand hit problems because increases in real income led to an increase in the demand for imports, forcing the authorities to intervene in support of the exchange rate and slowing the growth rate.

Towards the end of the 1960s, inflation began to accelerate in many countries at the same time. One of the reasons for this can be traced to the link between money supply and prices. This was a period when the USA was involved in the Vietnam War, and was funding it partly by expanding money supply, thus increasing the world supply of dollars. With exchange rates being fixed in terms of dollars, this meant that inflation began to accelerate. An increasing number of countries began to have severe exchange rate problems. Indeed, the UK had to devalue in 1967.

The result was that the fixed Dollar Standard broke down, and was abandoned in the early 1970s. This gave more freedom to governments to use monetary policy for domestic purposes, as they no longer needed to use it to maintain the exchange rate. This in combination with the oil price rises imposed by the OPEC cartel in 1973/74 allowed inflation to take off, as you can see in Figure 15.2. This was fuelled in the UK by the so-called 'Barber boom', when the then Chancellor of the Exchequer, Tony Barber, initiated a monetary expansion in an attempt to keep unemployment from rising.

The monetarist counter-revolution

The 1970s saw the rise of Milton Friedman and the monetarist school, who argued that inflation was 'always and everywhere a monetary phenomenon', and argued for a return to classical ideas. Impetus for these ideas came from the perception that the Keynesian model was not working. A situation of **stagflation** was emerging — where the economy was experiencing both high inflation and high unemployment simultaneously, suggesting that the Phillips curve relationship had broken down.

Monetarist ideas began to influence policy-makers. In 1976, the UK government had to borrow from the International Monetary Fund (IMF) in order to deal with a balance of payments crisis. One of the conditions laid down by the IMF in return for the loan was that the UK should start targeting the growth of money supply in order to prevent inflation from getting out of control. This was the start of a new approach to macroeconomic policy, which focused on monetary policy as the main instrument. Discretionary fiscal policy was seen to have been discredited.

Extension material

Expectations were seen by some economists as important in influencing the effectiveness of fiscal policy. They argued that if it was announced that, for instance, income tax was to be cut, individuals would realise that this could not be permanent, and that taxes would be raised at some point in the future. They would therefore discount the tax change, and not let it affect their behaviour. This was known as *Ricardian equivalence*, after an argument put forward by David Ricardo (1772–1823) some centuries earlier.

The core idea was that monetary policy should be directed at stabilising prices, which would allow markets to fulfil their role in allocating resources. Furthermore, stable and predictable inflation would improve firms' expectations about the future and thus encourage investment. If governments were to intervene, they should do so by looking for ways to stimulate the supply side of the economy: for example, through tax cuts that would improve incentives and stimulate enterprise. New classical economists drew attention to the need for strong microeconomic foundations to underpin macroeconomic analysis.

This ideology suited the political right wing, and during the 1980s was adopted by Ronald Reagan in the USA and Margaret Thatcher in the UK. The new approach to macroeconomic policy coincided with the second oil price crisis of 1979/80, and instead of trying to use expansionary policy to lower unemployment, as Barber had done in the mid-1980s, the approach was to introduce contractionary policies to allow markets to do their job. The result is apparent in Figure 15.1, when unemployment rose to its highest level since the Great Depression.

Meeting up in between

It seemed that neither the extreme Keynesians nor the new classical school (extreme monetarists) had a monopoly on the truth about the macroeconomy. What emerged was a hybrid approach to macroeconomics that combined elements of both extreme positions. It came to be accepted that wages could be a bit sticky in the short run, impeding the adjustment process and allowing unemployment to rise above the natural rate. It came to be recognised that expectations were important in shaping the adjustment process. Furthermore, changes in aggregate demand could affect real output in the short run, but would affect prices in the longer run. This requires an approach to macroeconomic policy that balances the short- and long-run effects. It is also acknowledged that there is a need to coordinate monetary and fiscal policy, recognising their interdependencies.

Inflation targeting was introduced from the late 1990s, giving independence to the central bank to maintain inflation within an acceptable range and improving the credibility of government actions. Arguably, this approach led to one of the most stable macroeconomic periods. The late 1990s and early 2000s saw steady economic growth with low inflation and unemployment.

Globalisation

The process of globalisation will be examined in the next chapter. However, it is pertinent here because the rise of technology in communications and technology led to increasing interconnectedness between economies around the world. This was reinforced by the effects of deregulation, particularly in financial markets. No individual economy can now take decisions about macroeconomic policy without taking into account the global market environment. Within Europe, the establishment of the euro zone brought about even closer coordination of macroeconomic policy between the member nations. When times are good, this benefits everyone, but this period of stability was not to last.

Financial crisis

When countries become so interlinked, it becomes possible that crisis will spread rapidly. There could be contagion effects. If you look back at Figure 13.18, you will see that the recession that hit in 2008/09 not only affected the UK economy, but was widespread across many developed countries. Many commentators were quick to lay the blame for this at the door of macroeconomists for failing to understand how things work. This has led to some reconsideration of the models of, and ways of thinking about, the macroeconomy.

Study tip

Take some time to think about where *you* stand on the spectrum between the new classical and Keynesian schools of thought.

What seems to be emerging from this is a recognition that perhaps too little attention has been paid to the effects of deregulation of financial markets and the impact of technology, which has allowed financial institutions to develop financial instruments that are innovative and profitable but carry risk that has not been fully factored into the design. This will be explored more carefully after the analysis of financial markets in Part 9 of the book.

Summary

- Macroeconomic thinking and macroeconomic policy have evolved together through time, along with developments in the performance of the economy.
- The classical view of the world focused mainly on the adjustment of microeconomic markets, with prices and wages adjusting to equilibrium.
- The quantity theory of money claimed a relationship between the quantity of money in circulation and the price level.
- Policy-makers in the Great Depression relied on markets to adjust through wage cuts, but this was a slow process.
- Keynesians argued that a fiscal stimulus would have allowed a more rapid recovery.
- The period of the Keynesian revolution in the 1950s and 1960s was characterised by low inflation and low unemployment, but a stop–go experience in terms of growth.
- The monetarist counter-revolution re-emphasised the importance of monetary control.
- It came to be recognised that a better balance needed to be achieved between conflicting views in the design of policy.
- Inflation targeting seemed to have ushered in a more stable period, but this was interrupted by the financial crisis.

SECTION
2

MACROECONOMICS

Part 8
The global context

Chapter 16

Globalisation and international trade

The world is becoming increasingly more integrated in many dimensions of economic activity. International flows of factors of production and financial capital have drawn countries closer together and created new interdependencies. There have been good and bad aspects of this process. Increasing trade has opened up new opportunities for some countries, but increased interdependence has created vulnerability, as crisis can also spread more readily between interdependent economies. Multinational firms have come to play an increasing role in global markets, and multilateral organisations such as the World Bank, International Monetary Fund and World Trade Organization have faced new challenges in seeking to oversee the world's economic environment. This chapter focuses on the characteristics and consequences of globalisation.

Learning objectives

After studying this chapter, you should:
- appreciate the importance of international trade and the conditions under which it takes place
- understand the different characteristics of globalisation
- explain the factors that have contributed to the growth of globalisation
- be familiar with the different forms of international capital flows and be able to evaluate their effects
- be able to analyse the impact of multinational corporations
- be able to evaluate the impact of globalisation, particularly the impact of emerging economies on other economies

Prior knowledge needed

International trade was discussed in Book 1, Chapter 16, and the first section of this chapter builds upon that analysis. You may wish to revisit that chapter to remind yourself of the key issues.

The importance of international trade

The central importance of international trade for growth and development has been recognised since the days of Adam Smith and David Ricardo in the eighteenth century. For example, during the Industrial Revolution a key factor was that Britain could bring in raw materials from its colonies for use in manufacturing activity. Today, consumers in the UK are able to buy and consume many goods that simply could not be produced within the domestic economy. From the point of view of economic analysis, Ricardo showed that countries could gain from trade through a process of *specialisation*.

The law of comparative advantage sets out how countries may gain from international trade by specialising in the production of goods (or services) in which they have a comparative advantage — that is, in goods where the opportunity cost of production is relatively low. Trade can be mutually beneficial for countries that trade with each other because of these differences in opportunity cost.

Who gains from international trade?

Specialisation can result in an overall increase in total production. However, one of the fundamental questions of economics in Chapter 1 of Book 1 was 'for whom?' It is *possible* that exchange can take place between countries in such a way that both countries are better off. But whether this will actually happen in practice depends on the prices at which exchange takes place.

In particular, specialisation may bring dangers and risks, as well as benefits. One obvious way in which this may be relevant is that, by specialising, a country allows some sectors to run down. For example, suppose a country came to rely on imported food, and allowed its agricultural sector to waste away. If the country then became involved in a war, or for some other reason was unable to import its food, there would clearly be serious consequences if it could no longer grow its own foodstuffs. For this reason, many countries have in place measures designed to protect their agricultural sectors — or other sectors that are seen to be strategic in nature.

Over-reliance on some commodities may also be risky. For example, the development of artificial substitutes for rubber had an enormous impact on the demand for natural rubber; this was reflected in falls in its price and caused difficulties for countries that had specialised in producing rubber.

The terms of trade

Key term

terms of trade the ratio of export prices to import prices

One of the key factors that determines who gains from international trade is the **terms of trade**, defined simply as the ratio of export prices to import prices.

Suppose that both export and import prices are rising through time, but import prices are rising more rapidly than export prices. This means that the ratio of export to import prices will fall — which in turn means that a country must export a greater volume of its goods in order to acquire the same volume of imports.

Quantitative skills 16.1

Calculating and interpreting the terms of trade

Export and import prices are expressed as index numbers, based on a particular year. Suppose we want to know how the terms of trade have changed in October 2014 relative to 2000. This can be done using the data in Table 16.1, which shows price indexes for exports and imports based on 2000 = 100.

Table 16.1

Date	Price index of exports	Price index of imports
2000	72.1	74.4
October 2014	94.8	95.7

Source: ONS

First calculate the price index number for October 2014 based on 2000 = 100. The rebased price index for exports is 100 × 94.8 / 72.1 = 131.5. For the price of imports, the index is 128.6 (check this calculation to make sure you understand how to do it). These calculations show that prices of both exported and imported goods have risen over the period.

The terms of trade represent the relative price change over the period, so for October 2014 we calculate the ratio of the price of exports to the price of imports. This is normally expressed as a percentage (i.e. as an index number), so the calculation is 100 × 131.5/128.6 = 102.3. The terms of trade increased by 2.3% between 2000 and October 2014. This indicates that the same volume of exports will purchase a greater volume of imports than in 2000.

A fall in the terms of trade indicates that the same volume of exports will purchase a smaller volume of imports than before. A downward movement in the terms of trade is thus unfavourable for an economy. Figure 16.1 shows the terms of trade for the UK economy since 1963. The substantial fall that is seen in 1973 and 1974 is due to the adverse oil price shock that occurred at that time. However, it would seem from this figure that the terms of trade have remained fairly constant since the early 1980s, even through the financial crisis.

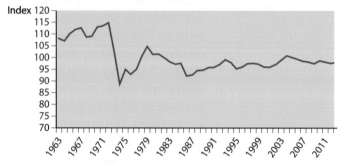

Figure 16.1 The UK terms of trade, 1963–2013 (2005 = 100)

Source: based on data from ONS

The terms of trade are calculated purely with respect to prices, and take no account of changing volumes of trade. In other words, a deterioration in the terms of trade does not necessarily mean that an economy is worse off, so long as the volume of trade is increasing sufficiently rapidly.

Extension material

The terms of trade described in the text are known more formally as the *net barter* terms of trade. As noted, the net barter terms of trade relate solely to the relative prices of exports and imports, so do not take into account changes in the volume of exports and imports. The *income* terms of trade take the volume of trade into account, being defined as the value of a country's exports divided by the price of imports. In other words, this measures the purchasing power of a country's exports in terms of the price of its imports. It is possible for all countries to experience an increase in the income terms of trade simultaneously.

In recent years, concerns have been raised about the effect of changes in the terms of trade for less developed countries (LDCs). One problem faced by LDCs that export primary products is that they are each too small as individual exporters to be able to influence the world prices of their products. They must accept the prices that are set in world commodity markets.

Short-run volatility

In the case of agricultural goods, demand tends to be relatively stable over time, but supply can be volatile, varying with weather and climatic conditions from season to season. Figure 16.2 shows a typical market in two periods. In period 1 the global harvest of this commodity is poor, with supply given by S_1: equilibrium is achieved with price at P_1 and quantity traded at Q_1. In period 2 the global harvest is high at S_2, so that prices plummet to P_2 and quantity traded rises to Q_2.

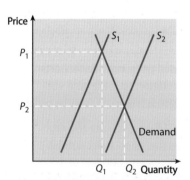

Figure 16.2 Volatility in supply

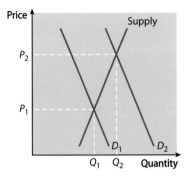

Figure 16.3 Volatility in demand

Notice that in this case the movement of prices is relatively strong compared with the variation in quantity. This reflects the price elasticity of demand, which is expected to be relatively inelastic for many primary products. From the consumers' point of view, the demand for foodstuffs and other agricultural goods will tend to be inelastic, as demand will not be expected to respond strongly to changes in prices.

For many minerals and raw materials, however, the picture is different. For such commodities, supply tends to be stable over time, but demand fluctuates with the economic cycle in developed countries, which are the importers of raw materials. Figure 16.3 illustrates this. At the trough of the economic cycle, demand is low, at D_1, and so the equilibrium price will also be low, at P_1. At the peak of the cycle, demand is more buoyant, at D_2, and price is relatively high, at P_2.

From an individual country's point of view, the result is the same: the country faces volatility in the prices of its exports. From this perspective it does not matter whether the instability arises from the supply side of the market or from the demand side. The problem is that prices can rise and fall quite independently of conditions within the domestic economy.

Instability of prices also means instability of export revenues, so if the country is relying on export earnings to fund its development path, to import capital equipment or to meet its debt repayments, such volatility in earnings can constitute a severe problem: for example, if export earnings fall such that a country is unable to meet its commitments to repaying debt.

Long-run deterioration

The nature of the demand for primary products may be expected to influence the long-run path of relative prices. In particular, the income elasticity of demand is an important consideration. As real incomes rise in the developed countries, the demand for agricultural goods can be expected to rise relatively slowly. Ernst Engel (1821–1896) pointed out that at relatively high income levels, the proportion of expenditure devoted to foodstuffs tends to fall and the demand for luxury goods rises. This suggests that the demand for agricultural goods shifts relatively slowly through time.

In the case of raw materials, there have been advances in the development of artificial substitutes for many commodities used in manufacturing. Furthermore, technology has changed over time, improving the efficiency with which inputs can be converted into outputs. This has weakened the demand for raw materials produced by LDCs.

Furthermore, if some LDCs are successful in boosting output of these goods, there will be an increase in supply over time. Figure 16.4 shows the result of such an increase. Suppose that the market begins with demand at D_0 and supply at S_0. Market equilibrium results in a price of P_0 and quantity of Q_0. As time goes by, demand moves to the right a little to D_1, and supply shifts to S_1. The result is a fall in the price of the commodity to P_1.

It is thus clear that, not only may LDCs experience short-run volatility in prices, but the terms of trade may also deteriorate in the long run.

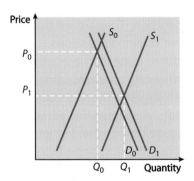

Figure 16.4 Long-term movements of demand and supply

Study tip

You might have thought that the demand and supply model was only useful in microeconomics, but notice that it can be helpful in other contexts also.

Pattern of comparative advantage

In the light of these twin problems, it is perhaps no surprise that many LDCs see themselves as trapped by their pattern of comparative advantage, rather than being in a position to exploit it. They are therefore reluctant to continue in such a state of dependency on primary products, but the process of diversification into a wide range of products has been difficult to achieve.

A potential change in this pattern was seen in 2007 and 2008, with food prices rising rapidly. These included the prices of some staple commodities such as maize and rice. The net effect of this on LDCs was not clear. Countries in a position to export these commodities would benefit from the rise in prices — that is, an increase in their terms of trade. However, there are many LDCs that need to import these staple commodities and for them the terms of trade deteriorated. These trends were interrupted by the onset of recession in many developed countries in 2008.

The degree to which a country or region engages in trade depends upon several factors. One important influence is the extent to which a country has the resources needed to trade — in other words, whether it can produce the sorts of goods that other countries wish to buy. However, it also depends upon the policy stance adopted by a country. Some countries have been very open to international trade. For example, a number of countries in South East Asia built success in economic growth on the basis of promoting exports. In contrast, there are countries such as India that in the past were less eager to trade, and introduced policies that hindered their engagement with trade.

In the 1930s, two Swedish economists, Eli Heckscher and Bertil Ohlin, argued that a country's comparative advantage would depend crucially on its relative endowments of factors of production. They argued that the optimal techniques for producing different commodities varied. Some commodities are most efficiently produced using labour-intensive techniques, whereas others could be more efficiently produced using relatively capital-intensive methods. This then suggests that if a country has abundant labour but scarce capital, its natural comparative advantage would lie in the production of goods that require little capital but lots of labour. In contrast, a country with access to capital but facing a labour shortage would tend to have a comparative advantage in capital-intensive goods or services.

Labour- or land-intensive techniques

Under these arguments, it would seem to make sense for LDCs to specialise in labour- or land-intensive activities such as agriculture or other primary production. Countries like the UK or the USA could then specialise in more capital-intensive activities such as manufacturing activity or financial services. By and large, this describes the way in which the pattern of world trade developed. Whether it is good for countries to rely on their pattern of natural comparative advantage is a different matter — for example, in the light of the changing patterns of relative prices reflected in the evolution of the terms of trade over time. This may suggest that there may be potential for countries to seek to alter the pattern of their comparative advantage by diversifying their economies

China's exports are highly competitive in global markets

and developing new specialisms in the face of changing patterns of global consumer demand. This is not an easy path for an economy to travel, and it may be tempting to turn instead to a more inward-looking protectionist strategy. We will return to this aspect of the topic in Chapter 17.

Countries in South East Asia, such as Hong Kong, Singapore and Taiwan, encouraged the structure of their economies to change over time, switching away from labour-intensive activities as their access to capital goods improved over time. Their success then induced changes in the structure of activity in more developed countries as the availability of imported manufactured goods allowed the expansion of service sector activity. In more recent years, China's economy has been undergoing even faster structural change, with the rapid expansion of the manufacturing sector, supported by an exchange rate policy that has made its exports highly competitive in global markets.

Summary

- Specialisation opens up the possibility of gains from trade.
- The theory of comparative advantage shows that even if one country has an absolute advantage in the production of goods and services, trade may still increase total output if each country specialises in the production of goods and services in which it has a comparative advantage.
- Who gains from specialisation and trade depends crucially on the prices at which exchange takes place.
- The terms of trade are measured as the ratio of export prices to import prices.
- When the terms of trade deteriorate for a country, it needs to export a greater volume of goods to be able to maintain the same volume of imports.
- The terms of trade have tended to be volatile in the short run, and to deteriorate over the longer term for countries that rely heavily on non-fuel primary production.
- The pattern of comparative advantage that characterises a country may depend upon the relative endowments of its factors of production.
- There is a choice to be made between seeking to exploit this natural comparative advantage, or diversifying the economy in an attempt to develop new specialisms.

Globalisation

Key term

globalisation a process by
which the world's economies
are becoming more closely
integrated

Globalisation is a process by which the world's economies are becoming more closely integrated. It has been characterised by a significant increase in the mobility of factors of production between countries, and increased flows of goods, services, capital, knowledge and people across international borders.

The process of globalisation accelerated due to a number of factors. An important influence arose from the advances in the technology of transport and communication, which enabled firms to begin to fragment their production process across different locations around the world. However, also crucial to the process was the reduction of trade barriers and the deregulation of financial markets.

This whole process has led to changes in the pattern of trade between countries — for example, as the UK has become more closely integrated with the rest of Europe, there has been an increase in the share of UK trade that is with the rest of Europe, although the USA also remains a significant trading partner.

The law of comparative advantage helps to explain these changes in the pattern of trade. Indeed, globalisation may be seen as a process that enables countries to enhance the way in which their comparative advantage can be exploited. In some cases, it may enable countries to develop new specialisations, and thus alter the pattern of their comparative advantage.

From the point of view of economic analysis, it would seem likely that this process of globalisation, and the increasing use of comparative advantage, would be welcomed by countries around the world. However, it seems that this is not a universal view. Countries often seem reluctant to open their economies fully to international trade, and have tended to intervene to try to protect their domestic producers from what is perceived as excessive competition from foreign firms. In evaluating the benefits and costs of globalisation, there are other issues to be taken into consideration.

External shocks

One of the issues concerning a more closely integrated global economy is the question of how robust the global economy will be to shocks. In other words, globalisation may be fine when the world economy is booming, as all nations may be able to share in the success. But if the global economy goes into recession, will all nations suffer the consequences? There are a number of situations that might cause the global economy to take a downturn.

Oil prices

Oil prices seem to provide one possible threat. In the past, sudden changes in oil prices have caused widespread disruption — for example, in 1973/74 and in 1979/80.

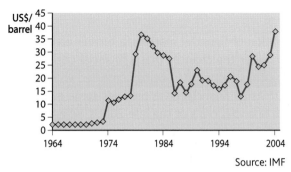

Figure 16.5 The price of oil, 1964–2004

Source: IMF

Figure 16.5 shows the historical time path of the price of oil from 1964 to 2004, measured in US dollars. In 1973/74 the sudden increase in the price of oil took most people by surprise. Oil prices had been steady for several years, and many economies had become dependent upon oil as an energy source, not only for running cars but for other uses such as domestic central heating. The sudden increases in the price in 1973/74 and again in 1979/80 caused widespread problems because demand in the short run was highly inelastic, and oil-importing countries faced sudden deficits on their balance of payments current accounts. However, in time people switched away from oil for heating, firms developed more energy-efficient cars, and demand was able to adjust.

Arguably, national economies in the 2000s should have been less vulnerable to changes in the price of oil than they were in 1973. However, the movements in oil prices in the late 2000s caused some consternation. Figure 16.6 shows monthly oil prices from the beginning of 2000. The earlier price rises in 1973/74 and 1979/80 had been primarily supply-side changes, caused by disruptions to supply following the actions of the OPEC cartel. In the 2000s, part of the upward pressure on price that is visible in the figure came from demand, with China's demand for oil being especially strong. There were also fears about the security of supplies from parts of the Middle East in the aftermath of the Iraq war, and with instability in Iran. In the event, the pressures of falling demand as the global recession began to unfold brought the price of oil tumbling. However, it was not long before oil prices began to creep up again, as some economies began to recover (and China and India continued to expand), and supplies from parts of the Middle East were disrupted — from Libya in particular.

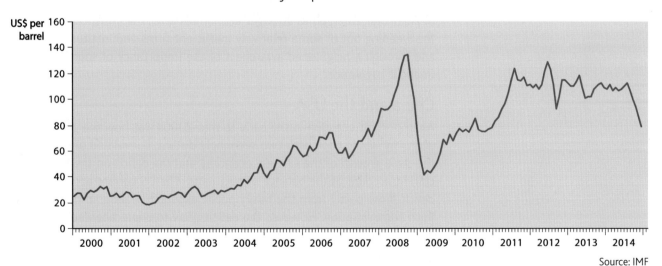

Source: IMF

Figure 16.6 The price of oil since 2000

Financial crises

Given the increasing integration of financial markets, a further concern is whether globalisation increases the chances that a financial crisis will spread rapidly between countries, rather than being contained within a country or region. The 1997 Asian financial crisis provides some evidence on this issue, as well as the financial crisis of the late 2000s, where contagion was seen to affect many economies.

The Asian crisis

The Asian crisis began in Thailand and South Korea. Both countries had been the recipients of large flows of foreign direct investment (FDI). In the case of Thailand, a significant part of this had been investment in property, rather than productive investment. The Thai currency (the baht) came under speculative pressure early in 1997, and eventually the authorities had to allow a devaluation. This sparked a crisis of confidence in the region, and foreign investors began to withdraw funds, not only from Thailand but from other countries too. As far as globalisation was concerned, the key questions were how far the crisis would spread, and how long it would last.

In the event, five countries bore the main burden of the crisis: Indonesia, Malaysia, the Philippines, South Korea and Thailand. Beyond this grouping there were some knock-on effects because of trade linkages, but arguably these were not too severe, and were probably dominated by other events taking place in the period. At the time of the crisis, Indonesia and the Philippines had been at a somewhat lower stage of development than the other countries involved, and thus suffered more deeply in terms of recession. However, with the benefit of hindsight, it seems that the region showed resilience in recovering from the crisis. Indeed, it can be argued that South Korea and Thailand in particular emerged as stronger economies after the crisis, through the weeding out of some relatively inefficient firms and institutions, and through a heightened awareness of the importance of sound financial regulation.

China and the USA

An important question in the early to mid-2000s was how the global economy would cope with two seemingly distant, but related phenomena: the rapid growth of the Chinese economy and the deficit on the US current account of the balance of payments. The US current account deficit arose partly from the heavy public expenditure programme of the Bush administration. However, the deficit grew to unprecedented levels partly through the actions of China and other East Asian economies that had chosen to peg their currencies to the US dollar. Effectively, this meant that those economies were buying US government securities as a way of maintaining their currencies against the dollar, thereby keeping US interest rates relatively low and allowing the US public to borrow to finance high consumer spending. Who gains from this situation? The USA was able to spend, and China was able to sell, fuelling its rapid rate of economic growth.

The credit crunch

Another example of the dangers of close interdependence began to unfold in 2007/08, when the so-called 'credit crunch' began to bite, and commercial banks in several countries found themselves in severe financial crisis. This followed a period in which relatively low interest rates had allowed a bubble of borrowing. When house prices began to slide, many banks in several countries found that they had overextended themselves, and had to cut back on lending, in some cases threatening their viability. This affected a number of countries simultaneously, and the financial crisis began to affect the real economy, leading to a recession. This was a recession that affected countries all around the globe, because of the new interconnectedness of economies. It became apparent that no single country could tackle the problem alone, as measures taken to support the banks in one economy had rapid knock-on effects elsewhere. Once this was realised, coordinated action was taken, and in October 2008 the central banks of several countries reduced their bank rates together. This was followed by action aiming to salvage the situation and avoid a full-blooded recession.

By early 2009, the UK economy was officially in recession, the bank rate had been driven down to an unprecedented 0.5%, and the Bank of England was introducing quantitative easing to try to stimulate the economy. One of the problems was that the commercial banks had become reluctant to lend, so firms that wanted to invest were finding it difficult to obtain funds. Attempts were made to coordinate the efforts of governments of key countries around the world — for example, at the G20 Summit held in London in April 2009. As time went by and the recession deepened, a number of countries in the euro zone faced crises with the level of public debt. This affected Ireland, Greece and Portugal in particular, all of which needed bailouts. The danger in the early 2010s was that these problems would spread to larger countries such as Italy and Spain.

Overseas assistance and foreign direct investment

The changing pattern of financial flows between countries has been a feature of the globalisation era, especially (but not only) insofar as they have affected developing countries. Figure 16.7 shows the pattern of key financial flows to low-income countries since 1990. Note that personal remittances will be discussed in Chapter 19.

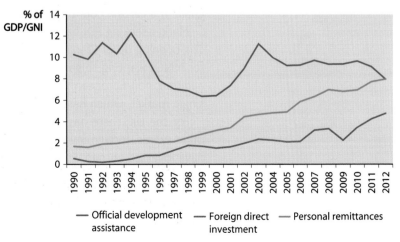

Note: ODA is % of GNI; FDI and remittances are % of GDP. Source: World Bank

Figure 16.7 Financial flows to low-income countries, 1990–2012

Overseas aid

Official development assistance (ODA) is popularly known as foreign aid. It is clear from Figure 16.7 that this has fluctuated relative to GNI during this period, falling in the second half of the 1990s, but recovering subsequently. This was discussed in Chapter 11.

A contentious issue is whether ODA should be channelled to those countries most in need of it, or focused on those countries best equipped to make good use of the funding. If humanitarian motives are uppermost, then you would expect there to be a strong relationship between flows of overseas assistance and average income levels. However, if other motives are important, this relationship might be less apparent. For example, there may sometimes be foreign policy objectives that influence the direction of flows of aid.

Following the Millennium Summit, the flows of overseas aid increased as a result of the agreement to grant debt forgiveness to heavily indebted poor countries. This did enable some less developed countries to make some progress towards achieving the Millennium Development Goals, although the financial crisis and widespread recession that followed have created new difficulties.

Foreign direct investment

An important aspect of globalisation has been the spread of **foreign direct investment (FDI)** by **multinational corporations (MNCs)**. UNCTAD has identified three main reasons for such activity:
1 market seeking
2 resource seeking
3 efficiency seeking

Some MNCs may engage in FDI because they want to sell their products within a particular market, and find it preferable to produce within the market rather than elsewhere: such FDI is *market seeking*. Second, MNCs may undertake investment in a country in order to take advantage of some key resource. This might be a natural resource such as oil or natural gas, or a labour force with certain skills, or simply be cheap unskilled labour: such FDI is *resource seeking*. Third, MNCs may simply review their options globally, and decide that they can produce most efficiently in a particular location. This might entail locating just part of their production chain in a certain country. Such FDI is *efficiency seeking*.

Market-seeking FDI has been important in some regions in particular. The opening up of China to foreign investment has proved a magnet for MNCs wanting to gain access to this large and growing market. In addition, non-European firms have been keen to gain entry to the EU's single market, which has encouraged substantial flows of FDI into Europe.

For the UK, there has been a two-way flow of direct investment. In other words, foreign investors have invested in the UK, and UK investors have invested abroad. Figure 16.8 shows the inward and outward flows, expressed as a percentage of GDP. Both inward and outward flows peaked in 2000, a year in which outward direct investment reached more than 16% of GDP. This reflected intense merger and acquisition activity at that time. The largest outward acquisitions were by Vodafone Airtouch, which invested in Mannesmann AG to the tune of £100 billion, and BP Amoco plc, which purchased the Atlantic Richfield Company for a reported £18 billion. After 2000, merger and acquisition activity slowed down, partly following the terrorist attacks in September 2001. Figure 16.8 shows that it was some time before FDI activity began to pick up again. You can also see how the flows were affected by the financial crisis of the late 2000s and the recession that followed.

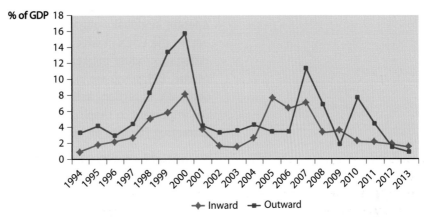

Figure 16.8 UK foreign direct investment, 1994–2013

FDI can have positive and negative effects on the host country. On the positive side, it is hoped that FDI will bring potential gains in employment, tax revenue, capital and technology, with consequent beneficial impact on economic growth. It may also be possible for domestic firms to learn about new technology or work processes that will have spillover effects on productivity. On the other hand, some domestic firms may be competed out of their markets.

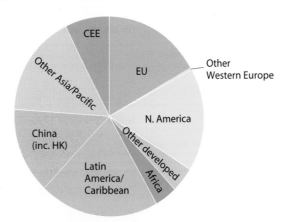

Source: UNCTAD, *World Investment Report*, 2014
Figure 16.9 Destination of global FDI inflows, 2013

The direction of FDI flows is important. Figure 16.9 shows that significant shares of global FDI inflows are into developed economies — especially into the EU and North America. There are also significant flows of FDI into other regions, notably into China. It is perhaps no surprise that FDI has been attractive to many LDCs, given their need to attract funds for investment, and their wish to upgrade their domestic production. This entails encouraging foreign MNCs to set up part of their production in an LDC.

In evaluating the potential impact of MNCs operating in LDCs, it is important to consider the characteristics of such companies. Many operate on a large scale, often having an annual turnover that exceeds the less developed country's GDP. They tend to have their origins in the developed countries, although some LDCs are now beginning to develop their own MNCs.

MNCs are in business to make profits, and it can be assumed that their motivation is to maximise global after-tax profits. While they may operate in globally oligopolistic markets, they may have monopoly power within the LDCs in which they locate. They operate in a wide variety of different product markets — some are in primary production (Geest, Del Monte, BP), some are in manufacturing (General Motors, Mitsubishi) and some are in tertiary activity (Walmart, McDonald's). These characteristics are important in shaping the analysis of the likely benefits and costs of attracting FDI into an LDC.

Potential benefits

Perhaps the prime motivation for LDCs in attracting FDI inflows is the injection they provide into the circular flow. In addition to providing *investment*, MNCs are likely to supply *capital* and *technology*, thereby helping to remedy the LDCs' limited capacity to produce capital goods. They may also assist with the development of the country's human capital, by providing training and skills development for the workers they employ, together with management expertise and entrepreneurial skills, all of which may be lacking in the LDC.

LDCs may also hope that the MNC will provide much needed modern-sector *jobs for local workers*. Given the rate of migration to urban areas, such employment could be invaluable to the LDC, where employment cannot keep up with the rapid growth of the labour force.

The LDC government may also expect to be able to collect *tax revenues*, both directly from the MNC in the form of a tax on profits, and indirectly from taxes on the workers' employment incomes. Moreover, the MNC will export its products, and thus generate a flow of foreign exchange for the LDC.

In time, there may also be *spillover effects*. As local workers learn new skills and gain management expertise and knowledge about technology, they may be able to benefit local firms if at some stage the workers leave the MNC and take up jobs with local companies — or use their new-found knowledge to start their own businesses. These externality effects can be significant in some cases.

Potential costs

In evaluating the potential benefits of FDI, however, LDCs may need to temper their enthusiasm a little, as there may be costs associated with attracting MNCs to locate within their borders. This would certainly be the case if the anti-globalisation protesters are to be believed, as they have accused the MNCs of exploiting their strength and market power, the effect of which can be to damage the LDCs in various ways.

In examining such costs, it is important to be objective and to try to reach a balanced view of the matter. Some of the accusations made by the critics of globalisation may have been overstated; on the other hand, it is also important to remember that MNCs are profit-making firms and not humanitarian organisations seeking to promote justice and equality.

A first point to note is that, because most MNCs originate in more developed countries, they tend to use technology that suits the conditions with which they are familiar. In many cases, this will tend to be relatively *capital intensive*, which may not be wholly appropriate for LDC factor endowments. One upshot of this is that the employment effects may not be substantial, or may be limited to relatively low-skilled jobs.

It is dangerous to generalise here. The sort of technology that MNCs tend to use may be entirely suitable for a country like Singapore, which has progressed to the stage where it needs hi-tech capital-intensive activity to match its well-trained and disciplined workforce. However, such technology would not be appropriate in much of sub-Saharan Africa. MNCs are surely aware of such considerations when taking decisions about where to locate. A decision to set up production in China may be partly market oriented, but efficiency considerations will also affect the choice of technology.

An important consideration is whether the MNC will make use of local labour. It might hire local unskilled labour, but use expatriate skilled workers and managers. This would tend to reduce the employment and spillover effects of the MNC presence. Another possibility is that the MNC may pay wages that are higher than necessary in order to maintain a good public image, and to attract the best local workers. This is fine for the workers lucky enough to be employed at a high wage, but it can make life difficult for local firms if they cannot hold on to their best workers.

In addition, the LDC government's desire for *tax revenue* may not be fully met. In seeking to attract MNCs to locate within their borders, LDCs may find that they need to offer tax holidays or concessions as a 'carrot'. This will clearly limit the tax revenue benefits that the LDC will receive. It is also possible that MNCs can manipulate their balance sheets in order to minimise their tax liability. A high proportion of the transactions undertaken by an MNC are internal to the firm. Thus, it may be possible to set prices for internal transactions which ensure that profits are taken in the locations with the lowest tax. This process is known as *transfer pricing*. It is not strictly legal, but is difficult to monitor.

As far as the *foreign exchange earnings* are concerned, a key issue is whether the MNC will recycle its surplus within the LDC or repatriate its profits to its shareholders elsewhere in the world. If the latter is the case, this will limit the extent to which the LDC will benefit from the increase in exports. However, at least the MNC will be able to market its products internationally, and if the country becomes better known as a result then, again, there may be spillovers for local firms. Gaining credibility and the knowledge to sell in the global market is problematic for LDCs, and this is one area in which there may be definite benefits from the MNC presence.

The onset of recession in the late 2000s highlighted the potential vulnerability that may come from closer integration with the global economy. It is one thing to share in the benefits from increased trade when global demand is buoyant, and quite another to find that recession begins to spread more rapidly between countries. Naturally, it was the most open economies such as China that were among the first to suffer.

A local oil worker at a BP plant in Algeria

The LDC should also be aware that the MNC may use its *market power* within the country to maximise profits. Local competitors will find it difficult to compete, and the MNC may be able to restrict output and raise price. In addition, some MNCs have been accused of taking advantage of more lax environmental regulations, polluting the environment to keep their costs low. The actions of the anti-globalisation protesters in this area may have influenced MNCs to clean up their act somewhat.

Finally, MNCs tend to locate in urban areas in LDCs — unless they are purely resource seeking, in which case they may be forced to locate near the supply of whatever natural resource they are seeking. Locating in the urban areas may increase the *rural–urban inequality* discussed earlier, and encourage an even greater rate of migration.

Given the need to evaluate the benefits and costs of FDI flows, it is important that LDC governments can negotiate good deals with the MNCs. For example, countries such as Indonesia have negotiated conditions on the proportion of local workers who will be employed by the MNC after a period of, say, 5 years. This helps to ensure that the benefits are not entirely dissipated. Of course, it helps if the LDC has some key resource that the MNC cannot readily acquire elsewhere. There is some recent evidence that high levels of human capital help to attract FDI flows, which may help to explain why East Asia and China have been recipients of more FDI inflows than countries in sub-Saharan Africa.

Summary

- Globalisation is a process whereby countries have become increasingly interconnected.
- Official development assistance (ODA) comprises grants and concessional funding provided from the OECD countries to LDCs.
- The countries most in need of ODA may not be in a position to use it effectively.
- In some cases, the direction of ODA flows is influenced by the political interests of the donor countries.
- Multinational corporations (MNCs) are companies whose production activities are carried out in more than one country.
- Foreign direct investment (FDI) by MNCs is one way in which an LDC may be able to attract external resources.
- MNCs may be motivated by markets, resources or cost effectiveness.
- LDCs hope to benefit from FDI in a wide range of ways, including capital, technology, employment, human capital, tax revenues and foreign exchange. There may also be spillover effects.
- However, MNCs may operate in ways that do not maximise these benefits for the LDCs.

The emerging economies

Industrialisation and economic growth began in Britain and other countries in Western Europe and North America, and by the 1960s there was a divide between those countries that had gone through the development and growth process and those that had not. Since the 1960s, relatively few countries have managed to bridge the gap in living standards.

There was a group of countries that became known as the *newly industrialised countries (NICs)* that made the transition. These included some countries in South East Asia, such as Singapore, South Korea, Taiwan and Hong Kong, and some Latin American countries, although the latter group fell foul of hyperinflation, which interrupted their progress.

More recently, some other countries have accelerated in terms of economic growth and human development; they have become known as the **emerging economies**. This group has included the so-called *BRIC countries* (Brazil, Russia, India and China), and a less-defined group including Thailand, Malaysia, Turkey and South Africa, among others.

The BRIC countries

In the early 2000s, a group of countries were identified as experiencing rapid economic growth and closing the gap on the developed economies. The BRIC economies were originally just a set of countries identified as having some characteristics in common. However, they began forming a political group and having summit meetings, and in 2011 they invited South Africa to join them. At this point in time, the BRICs accounted for about 18% of world GDP and 15% of world trade, and contained about 40% of the world's population. If economic growth continues at current rates, the group will gain increasing economic and political influence relative to the G7.

Figure 16.10 shows economic growth in the original four BRIC countries since 1999, with the growth rate for the world as a whole to provide context. The consistency and rapidity of growth during the 2000s reveals why these countries were singled out for attention, although Brazil was perhaps rather less successful in terms of its growth rates. What makes this performance more startling is the size of these economies, both in population and in the size of GDP. The achievements of the economies of China and India are especially impressive, in each case starting from a relatively low base — and for these two economies, the growth seemed relatively robust in the face of the global recession. China in particular has shown very little sign of slowing down. However, the factors underlying the growth performance were different in each case, as these economies are all at very different stages in terms of average incomes and display different characteristics, both politically and economically.

Key term

emerging economies economies that have experienced rapid economic growth with some industrialisation and characteristics of developed markets

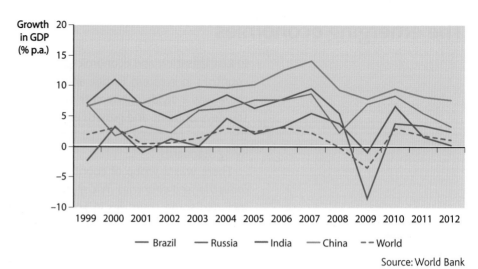

Source: World Bank

Figure 16.10 Growth in the BRIC countries since 1999

These countries, together with some other rapid-growth economies, have had a significant impact on the global economy, most obviously in the case of China, which in 2014 overtook the USA as the world's biggest economy. This is based on GDP in PPP$.

The impact on the global economy has been evident in many ways. China's growth was built upon rapid growth of exports, which for at least part of the period was bolstered by China's exchange rate, maintained at a level that made China's exports highly competitive overseas. A number of the Asian emerging economies also accumulated reserves of US Treasury securities during the 2000s, which had the effect of allowing US interest rates to be lower than they would otherwise have been. This in turn encouraged consumer borrowing, and may have contributed to the financial crisis. Of course, China also needed to import goods that it needed to fuel its production process, with a consequent impact on commodity prices in global markets. The net effect is quite difficult to evaluate, but it could be argued that without China's continuing growth through the period of recession following the financial crisis, the slowdown would have been longer-lived.

Summary
- A number of economies have begun to close the gap on the developed countries.
- These emerging economies include the BRIC countries, which have worked together as a political pressure group as well as enjoying economic success.
- China in particular has shown unprecedentedly high economic growth, and on one measure has now overtaken the USA as the world's biggest economy.
- The success of these economies has had significant impact on other developed and developing countries.

Case study 16.1

More than just exports

The UK imports a great many products, from Audi cars to Hollywood blockbusters, from other European countries and overseas. At the same time, companies based in the UK, from Vauxhall to the BBC, sell their products to customers abroad.

As the 2008 Nobel prize-winning economist Paul Krugman argued in an interview to the BBC, international trade matters as it helps firms to specialise and produce in large quantities. At the same time, it expands everyone's choice. Indeed, if you walk down the cookie aisle in a UK supermarket you will see that it has cookies from Denmark, Britain and the United States, as people enjoy variety. This, of course, applies to both exports and imports: the BBC exports the *Sherlock Holmes* series to Europe and the USA, while BBC4 has taken to showing Scandinavian and other European subtitled crime drama; Cadbury exports chocolate to the USA and Germany, while British supermarkets import Milka from Germany and Belgian Godiva chocolate.

International trade in goods is an important and integral part of any economy. As well as material goods, firms may trade in services such as banking and consultancy, invest directly in other companies abroad or contract a foreign company to produce a specific good exclusively for them. Business people understand the importance of these various international activities, while governments often focus on exports of goods. But why do governments focus on firms' export activities?

One reason is the ease of observation – income statements submitted by companies will detail revenues from domestic and foreign sources separately. Exports are simply revenues from abroad. However, observing other types of involvement in international markets, such as investments and outsourcing, is substantially more difficult.

Internationalisation

A recent survey of European firms allowed researchers to look into firms' international activities in seven European countries, including the UK. One observation is that it is very common for European manufacturing firms to have contacts with firms beyond country borders. Almost 80% of firms with at least ten employees engage in some form of international activity.

Exporting is the most frequent mode of internationalisation, with about two-thirds of firms

The BBC exports the *Sherlock Holmes* series to Europe

shipping some products abroad. However, many other modes are also popular. About half the firms import directly — that is, they do not just buy foreign-made goods from an intermediary. Working with foreign customers based on contracts is quite widespread, as a quarter of firms have outsourced some of their production, using foreign inputs made specifically for them. Almost 40% of firms provide outsourcing for other firms. Foreign ownership is not rare, as about 10% of firms own or are owned by foreign firms. So, while exports are important, firms are likely to get involved in several modes of internationalisation at once.

Some of the most competitive companies are engaged in several modes of internationalisation. Consider Armstrong, a specialist mid-sized company making acoustic and metal ceilings in the UK. This company makes metal and glass ceilings for theatres, shopping malls and tube stations, and exports them worldwide. However, to be globally competitive, it uses a large amount of tools, materials and semi-finished products made in other countries. Part of the labour-intensive work is contracted out to eastern Europe. Moreover, it is part of a global network owned by a US global player designing and manufacturing floors and ceilings.

Often, several modes of internationalisation are interrelated, with one activity leading to another. For instance, when Kraft took over Cadbury, it started to produce Oreo biscuits, previously imported into the UK, at a plant in Sheffield and then exported the biscuits to other countries.

Case study 16.1 (continued)

International activities are found to be related to overall firm performance: companies that are tied into global business are likely to be more efficient and do better in their home market. In some cases, this is the result of learning from foreign business practices. However, it is often the case that a higher level of performance has been achieved before starting to trade: due to fixed trade costs, only the most productive firms may be competitive on export markets.

Source: adapted from Gábor Békés, 'More than just exports', *Economic Review*, November 2013

Follow-up question

Discuss the range of ways in which firms engage in internationalisation, and whether this activity yields net benefits to economies.

Chapter 17

Trade policies and negotiations

The economic landscape of Europe since the Second World War has been shaped by the move towards ever-closer economic integration. The UK has been part of this, although at times a seemingly reluctant participant. The economic arguments in favour of closer economic integration are partly based on notions of comparative advantage and the potential gains of allowing freer trade. However, there are other pertinent issues to be taken into consideration in evaluating the costs and benefits of closer integration. Such integration also has political ramifications that can affect an individual country's attitude towards its potential partners.

Two major steps towards economic integration have taken place in the period since 1990. On 1 January 1993, the Single European Market (SEM) came into operation. Then, on 1 January 2002, 12 European countries adopted the euro as their common currency. The expansion of the SEM in 2004 to incorporate ten new members was a further significant development; two further countries joined in 2007. This chapter highlights these developments and assesses their impact on the economic performance of the UK, referring to relevant areas of economic analysis that help in analysing the costs and benefits of closer economic integration. Finally, there is an evaluation of the work of the World Trade Organization.

Prior knowledge needed

No prior knowledge is needed for this chapter.

Learning objectives

After studying this chapter, you should:

- be aware of the ways in which protectionist policies have been implemented
- be able to evaluate the case for and against protectionism
- be aware of the different forms that economic integration may take: free trade areas, customs unions, common markets and economic and monetary union
- know the features of these alternative forms of integration and understand the distinction between them
- understand the significance of the Single European Market (SEM)
- be able to evaluate the costs and benefits of membership of a single currency area
- be aware of the role and effectiveness of monetary and fiscal policy within a single currency area
- be able to evaluate the operations of the World Trade Organization

Protectionism

The previous chapter analysed the potential gains from international trade and outlined some of the issues that arise. It is clear that the international context is important in seeking to manage an economy, with the need to maintain stability and encourage economic growth. This may be seen as challenging for some countries in the context of an increasingly integrated global economy, where national governments may feel that they are no longer in control of their own destiny. It may also be that some governments, seeking to encourage diversification in their economies, may see a need to provide a period of protection for their newly developing sectors while they learn the business and become competitive. For these and other reasons, many governments have looked for ways in which they can provide protection for domestic economic activities.

When recession began to threaten in 2008, there was strong lobbying from pressure groups in the USA and elsewhere in favour of introducing protectionist measures. Indeed, in the lead-up to the G20 Summit in April 2009, the World Bank reported that 17 members of that group had taken a total of 47 trade-restricting steps in the previous months. However, the drive towards globalisation had created a more integrated global economy, in which many firms relied on a global supply chain. With the production process fragmented between different parts of the world, the dangers of protectionism become more severe, and the possibilities of rapid contagion from a crisis become acute.

Tariffs

A policy instrument commonly used in the past to give protection to domestic producers is a **tariff**. Tariff rates in the developed countries have been considerably reduced in the period since the Second World War, but nonetheless are still in place.

Figure 17.1 shows how a tariff is expected to operate. D represents the domestic demand for a commodity, and S_{dom} shows how much domestic producers are prepared to supply at any given price. The price at which the good can be imported from world markets is given by P_w. If dealing with a global market, it is reasonable to assume that the supply at the world price is perfectly elastic. So, in the absence of a tariff, domestic demand is given by D_0, of which S_0 is supplied within the domestic economy and the remainder ($D_0 - S_0$) is imported. If the government wishes to protect this industry within the domestic economy, it needs to find a way of restricting imports and encouraging home producers to expand their capacity.

When a tariff is imposed, the domestic price rises to $P_w + T$, where T is the amount of the tariff. This has two key effects. One is to reduce the demand for the good from D_0 to D_1; the second is to encourage domestic producers to expand their output of this good from S_0 to S_1. As a consequence, imports fall substantially (to $D_1 - S_1$). On the face of it, the policy has achieved its objective. Furthermore, the government has been able to raise some tax revenue (given by the green rectangle).

However, not all the effects of the tariff are favourable for the economy. Consumers are certainly worse off, as they have to pay a higher price for the good; they therefore consume less, and there is a loss of

Key term

tariff a tax imposed on imported goods

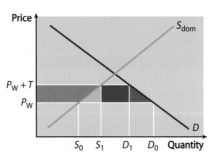

Figure 17.1 The effects of a tariff

Synoptic link

Notice that the notions of consumer and producer surplus turn up again here. These were first discussed in Book 1, Chapters 3 and 4.

Exercise 17.1

Figure 17.1 showed the effects of a tariff.

If a country decides to remove the tariff, identify the effects on:

a consumers of the good

b producers of the good

c the government

Key term

voluntary export restraint (VER) an agreement by a country to limit its exports to another country to a given quantity (quota)

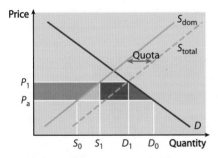

Figure 17.2 The effects of a quota

Study tip

Notice that the diagram for a quota is very like the diagram for a tariff. Make sure you do not confuse the two, as they differ in terms of who gains and who loses from the measure.

consumer surplus. Some of what was formerly consumer surplus has been redistributed to others in society. The government has gained the tariff revenue, as mentioned. In addition, producers gain some additional producer surplus, shown by the dark-blue area. There is also a deadweight loss to society, represented by the red and pale-blue triangles. In other words, society is worse off overall as a result of the imposition of the tariff.

Effectively, the government is subsidising inefficient local producers, and forcing domestic consumers to pay a price that is above that of similar goods imported from abroad.

Some would try to defend this policy on the grounds that it allows the country to protect an industry, thus saving jobs that would otherwise be lost. However, this goes against the theory of comparative advantage, and forces society to incur the deadweight loss. In the longer term it may delay structural change. For an economy to develop new specialisations and new sources of comparative advantage, there needs to be a transitional process in which old industries contract and new ones emerge. Although this process may be painful, it is necessary in the long run if the economy is to remain competitive. Furthermore, the protection that firms enjoy which allows them to reap economic rents from the tariff may foster complacency and an inward-looking attitude. This is likely to lead to X-inefficiency, and an inability to compete in the global market.

Even worse is the situation that develops where nations respond to tariffs raised by competitors by putting up tariffs of their own. This has the effect of further reducing the trade between countries, and everyone ends up worse off, as the gains from trade are sacrificed.

Quotas and non-tariff barriers

An alternative policy that a country may adopt is to limit the imports of a commodity to a given volume. For example, a country may come to an agreement with another country that only a certain quantity of imports will be accepted by the importing country. Such arrangements are sometimes known as **voluntary export restraints (VERs)**.

Figure 17.2 illustrates the effects of a quota. D represents the domestic demand for this commodity, and S_{dom} is the quantity that domestic producers are prepared to supply at any given price. Suppose that, without any agreement, producers from country A would be prepared to supply any amount of the product at a price P_a. If the product is sold at this price, D_0 represents domestic demand, of which S_0 is supplied by domestic producers and the remainder ($D_0 - S_0$) is imported from country A.

By imposing a quota, total supply is now given by S_{total}, which is domestic supply plus the quota of imports allowed into the economy from country A. The market equilibrium price rises to P_1 and demand falls to D_1, of which S_1 is supplied by domestic producers and the remainder is the agreed quota of imports.

Figure 17.2 shows who gains and who loses by this policy. Domestic producers gain by being able to sell at the higher price, so (as in the case of the tariff) they receive additional surplus given by the dark-blue area. Furthermore, the producers exporting from country A also gain, receiving the green rectangle (which, in the case of the tariff, was tax revenue received by the government). As in the case of the tariff, the two triangles (red and pale blue) represent the loss of welfare suffered by the importing country.

Such an arrangement effectively subsidises the foreign producers by allowing them to charge a higher price than they would have been prepared to accept. Furthermore, although domestic producers are encouraged to produce more, the protection offered to them is likely to lead to X-inefficiency and weak attitudes towards competition.

There are a number of examples of such agreements, especially in the textile industry. For example, for a long time the USA and China had agreements on quotas for a range of textile products. Ninety-one such quotas expired at the end of 2004 as part of China's accession to the World Trade Organization. As you might expect, this led to extensive lobbying by producers in the USA, especially during the run-up to the 2004 presidential election. Trade unions in the USA supported the producers, arguing that 350,000 jobs had been lost since the expiry of earlier quota agreements in 2002. In the case of three of these earlier agreements, some restraint had been reinstated for bras, dressing gowns and knitted fabrics. Producers in other countries, such as Sri Lanka, Bangladesh, Nepal, Indonesia, Morocco, Tunisia and Turkey, were lobbying for the quotas to remain, regarding China as a major potential competitor. However, for the USA at least, it can be argued that the removal of the quotas would allow domestic consumers to benefit from lower prices, and would allow US textile workers to be released for employment in higher-productivity sectors, where the USA maintains a competitive advantage.

There are other ways in which trade can be hampered, one example being the use of what are known as **non-tariff barriers** (NTBs). These often comprise rules and regulations that control the standard of products that can be sold in a country. It is difficult to quantify the importance of such measures, but the frequency with which disputes arise at the World Trade Organization (WTO) suggests that they have had significant effects on trade.

Exercise 17.2

Evaluate the case for and against protectionism. You may find it helpful to review some of the trade disputes that have been raised recently at the World Trade Organization (WTO), which has a role as international arbitrator for complaints about the conduct of international trade. You will find information about these at the WTO website: **www.wto.org**

Key term

non-tariff barrier an obstacle to free trade other than a tariff (e.g. quality standards imposed on imported products)

The USA has tried to curtail the growth of the highly competitive Chinese textile industry through the use of import quotas

Summary
- There has often been a tendency for governments to intervene to inhibit trade by the use of protectionist measures.
- Such measures include tariffs, quotas and the imposition of regulations.
- The use of such measures entails the sacrifice of potential gains from trade, but there may be circumstances in which countries may feel justified in using them.
- The validity of these arguments is open to debate.

Economic integration

Economies are becoming more interdependent over time. One aspect of this process deserves close attention: namely, the growing formal integration of economies in regional groupings. This has been a gradual process, but it has accelerated as the technology of transport and communications has been transformed and as markets have been deregulated — especially financial markets; a process which has allowed the increased free movement of financial capital between countries.

There are many examples of such regional trade agreements. The European Union is perhaps one of the most prominent — and one of the furthest advanced — but there are also examples in the Americas (NAFTA, MERCOSUR), Asia (ASEAN, APEC), Africa (COMESA) and elsewhere. These agreements are at varying stages in the integration process. In addition, there has been a proliferation of regional trade agreements. More than 400 arrangements covering trade in goods and services have been notified to the World Trade Organization since its formation.

Regional trade integration can take a variety of forms, representing differing degrees of closeness. The underlying motivation for integration is to allow trading partners to take advantage of the potential gains from international trade, as illustrated by the law of comparative advantage. By reducing the barriers to trade, specialisation can be encouraged, and there should be potential gains from the process. In practice, there may be other economic and political forces at work that affect the nature of the gains, and the extent to which integration will be possible — and beneficial.

Free trade areas

One level of integration is the formation of a so-called **free trade area**. Before the UK joined the European Community in 1973, it was part of the European Free Trade Area (EFTA), together with other countries in Europe that had not joined the Community. The original countries were Austria, Denmark, Norway, Portugal, Sweden, Switzerland and the UK. Finland, Iceland and Liechtenstein joined later, but some EFTA members left in order to join the EU, leaving just Iceland, Liechtenstein, Norway and Switzerland as members of EFTA in the early years of the twenty-first century.

Key term

free trade area a group of countries that agree to remove tariffs, quotas and other restrictions on trade between the member countries, but have no agreement on a common barrier against non-members

The notion of a free trade area is that countries within the area agree to remove internal tariff and quota restrictions on trade between them, while still allowing member countries to impose their own pattern of tariffs and quotas on non-members. The lack of a common external tariff wall may cause problems within the member countries. If one country has lower tariffs than the rest, the natural tendency will be for imports into the area to be channelled through that country, with goods then being resold to other member countries. This may distort the pattern of trade and cause unnecessary transaction costs associated with trading activity. It is worth noting that free trade areas are normally concerned with enabling free trade in goods and do not cover the movement of labour.

In spite of these problems, a free trade area does allow member countries to increase their degree of specialisation, and may bring gains. EFTA is not the only example of such an arrangement. In South East Asia, the Association of Southeast Asian Nations (ASEAN) began to create a free trade area in 1993. This involved six nations (Brunei, Indonesia, Malaysia, the Philippines, Singapore and Thailand). The group was later expanded to include Cambodia, Laos, Myanmar and Vietnam. Progress towards eliminating tariffs in this group has been relatively slow, but intense competition from the rapidly growing Chinese economy provides a strong motivation for accelerating the process.

Another major trading group operating a free trade area is the North American Free Trade Association (NAFTA), which covers the USA, Canada and Mexico. The agreement was signed in 1992 and launched in 1994, and has led to an expansion of trade between those countries. Unlike in Europe, there is as yet no stated intention that NAFTA should evolve into anything more than a free trade area.

Customs unions

Key terms

customs union a group of countries that agree to remove restrictions on trade between the member countries, and set a common set of restrictions (including tariffs) against non-member states

trade creation the replacement of more expensive domestic production or imports with cheaper output from a partner within the trading bloc

A **customs union** is one notch up from a free trade area, in the sense that in addition to eliminating tariffs and quotas between the member nations, a common external tariff wall is set up against non-member nations. Again, the prime reason for establishing a customs union is to encourage trade between the member nations.

Such increased trade is beneficial when there is **trade creation**. This is where the formation of the customs union allows countries to specialise more, and thus to exploit their comparative advantage. The larger market for the goods means that more economies of scale may be available, and the lower prices that result generate additional trade between the member nations. These lower prices arise partly from the exploitation of comparative advantage, but also from the removal of tariffs between the member nations.

Figure 17.3 illustrates the effects of trade creation. It shows the demand and supply of a good in a certain country that joins a customs union. Before joining the union, the price of the good is T, which includes a tariff element. Domestic demand is D_0, of which S_0 comes from domestic producers, and the remainder is imported. When the country joins the customs union, the tariff is removed and the domestic price falls to P. Consumers benefit from additional consumer surplus, given by the area $PTBG$. However, notice that not all of this is pure gain to the country. The area $PTAC$ was formerly part of producer surplus, so there has been

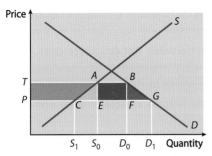

Figure 17.3 The effects of trade creation

Key term

trade diversion the replacement of cheaper imported goods by goods from a less efficient trading partner within a bloc

a redistribution from domestic firms to consumers. *ABFE* was formerly tariff revenue collected by the government, so this represents effectively a redistribution from government to consumers. The area *ACE* is a net gain for the country, as this represents resources that were previously used up in the production of the good, but which can now be used for other purposes. The area *BFG* also represents a welfare gain to the country.

However, it is also important to be aware that becoming a member of a customs union may alter the pattern of trading relationships. A country that is part of a customs union will be more inclined to trade with other members of the union because of the agreement between them, and because of the absence of internal tariffs. However, given the common external tariff, it is quite possible that members of the union are not the most efficient producers on the global stage. So there may be a situation of **trade diversion**. This occurs where a member country of a customs union imports goods from other members *instead* of from more efficient producers elsewhere in the world. This may mean that there is no net increase in trade, but simply a diversion from an external source to a new source within the union. In this situation, there are not necessarily the same gains from trade to be made.

Figure 17.4 helps to show the effects of trade diversion. Here, D represents the demand curve for a commodity that is initially imported from a country outside the customs union. It is assumed that the supply of the good from the non-member is perfectly elastic, as shown by S_n. However, the importing country imposes a tariff of the amount T, so the quantity imported is given by Q_n, and the price charged is $P_n + T$.

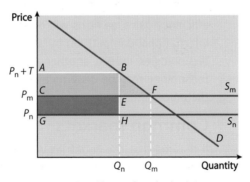

Figure 17.4 The effects of trade diversion

After the importing country joins the customs union, the tariff is removed, but the good is now imported from a less efficient producer within the union. The supply from this member country is assumed to be elastic at S_m, so the new price is P_m and the quantity is Q_m.

In examining the welfare effects, there are two issues to consider. First, notice that consumer surplus has increased by the area *ABFC*. However, this is not pure gain to the economy because, in the original position, the government was collecting tariff revenue of the amount *ABHG*. In other words, the increase in consumer surplus comes partly as a pure gain (the triangle *BFE*), but partly at the expense of the government (*ABEC*). This is not all, because the area *CEHG* was also formerly part of tariff revenue, but now is a payment by domestic consumers to producers in the other (member) country. This means that whether the country is better or worse off depends upon the relative size of the areas *BFE* (which is a gain) and *CEHG* (which is a loss).

There are some further disadvantages of customs unions. Certainly, the transactions costs involved in administering the union cannot be ignored, and where there are traditional rivalries between nations there may be political sensitivities to overcome. This may impede the free working of the union, especially if some member nations are more committed to the union than others, or if some countries have close ties with non-member states.

It is also possible that a geographical concentration of economic activity will emerge over time within the union. This may result where firms want to locate near the centre of the area in order to minimise transportation costs. Alternatively, it may be that all firms will want to locate near the richest part of the market. Over time, this could mean that firms tend to concentrate in certain geographical areas, while the countries that are more remote, or which have smaller populations or lower average incomes, become peripheral to the centre of activity. In other words, over time, there may be growing inequality between regions within the union.

These disadvantages must be balanced against the benefits. For example, it may be that it is the smaller countries in the union that have the most to gain from tapping economies of scale that would not be accessible to them if they were confined to selling only within their domestic markets.

In addition to these internal economies of scale, there may be external economies of scale that emerge over time as the transport and communications infrastructure within the union improves. Furthermore, opening up domestic markets to more intense competition may induce efficiency gains, as firms will only be able to survive in the face of international competition by adopting best practice techniques and technologies. Indeed, another advantage of a customs union is that technology may be disseminated amongst firms operating within the union.

Common markets

It may be that the countries within a customs union wish to move to closer integration, by extending the degree of cooperation between the member nations. A **common market** adds to the features of a customs union by harmonising some aspects of the economic environment between them. In a pure common market, this would entail adopting common tax rates across the member states, and a common framework for the laws and regulations that provide the environment for production, employment and trade. A common market would also allow for the free movement of factors of production between the member nations, especially in terms of labour and capital (land is less mobile by its nature). Given the importance of the public sector in a modern economy, a common market would also set common procurement policies across member governments, so that individual governments did not favour their own domestic firms when purchasing goods and services. The Single European Market (discussed below) has encompassed most of these features, although tax rates have not been harmonised across the countries that are included.

Economic and monetary union

An alternative form of integration is where countries choose to share a common currency, but without the degree of cooperation that is involved with a free trade area or common market. Such an arrangement is known as a **monetary union** or a *currency union*. Full **economic and monetary union** combines the common market arrangements with a shared currency (or permanently fixed exchange rates between the member countries). This requires member states to follow a common monetary policy, and it is also seen as desirable to harmonise other aspects of macroeconomic policy across the union.

The adoption of permanently fixed exchange rates is a contentious aspect of proposals for economic and monetary union, as governments are no longer able to use monetary policy for internal domestic purposes. This is because monetary variables become subservient to the need to maintain the exchange rate, and it is not possible to set independent targets for the rate of interest or money supply if the government has to maintain the value of the currency on the foreign exchange market. This is all very well if all countries in the union are following a similar economic cycle, but if one country becomes poorly synchronised with the others, there may be major problems.

For example, it could be that the union as a whole is enjoying a boom, and setting interest rates accordingly. For an individual member country suffering a recession, this could mean deepening and prolonging the recession, as it would not be possible to relax interest rates in order to allow aggregate demand to recover.

A successful economic and monetary union therefore requires careful policy coordination across the member nations. Notice that economic and monetary union involves fixed exchange rates between the member countries, but does not necessarily entail the adoption of a common currency, although this may follow at some stage.

Structural change

A feature that all of these forms of integration have in common is that they involve the removal of barriers to trade amongst member countries. It is important to be aware that this will not be perceived as a good thing by all the parties involved. In order to benefit from increased specialisation and trade, countries need to allow the pattern of their production to change. The benefits to the expanding sectors are apparent, but it is also the case that industries that formerly enjoyed protection from competition will become exposed to competition, and will need to decline in order to allow resources to be transferred into the expanding sectors. This can be a painful process for firms that need to close down, or move into new markets, and for workers who may need to undergo retraining before they are ready for employment in the newly expanding parts of the economy.

An especially contentious area of debate in the UK concerns the structural change that has taken place in recent decades, in which manufacturing activity has declined and financial services have expanded. This seems to reflect the changing pattern of the UK's comparative advantage, in which banking, finance and insurance have become a major strength of the economy, whereas the manufacturing sector has found it more difficult to compete with the host of new entrants into this market from elsewhere in the world.

Summary

- Economic integration can take a variety of forms, of differing degrees of closeness.
- A free trade area is where a group of countries agree to remove restrictions on trade between them, but without having a common external tariff.
- A customs union is a free trade area with an agreed common set of restrictions on trade with non-members.
- A customs union can entail trade creation, in which member countries benefit from increased trade and specialisation.
- However, there may also be trade diversion, in which countries divert their trading activity from external trade partners to countries within the union.
- Trade diversion does not always bring gains, as the producers within the union are not necessarily more efficient than external producers.
- A common market is a customs union in which the member countries also agree to harmonise their policies in a number of key respects.
- Economic and monetary union entails fixed exchange rates between member countries, but not necessarily agreement to adopt a common currency.

The European Union

The European Union is one of the most prominent examples of regional trade integration, and has progressed further than most in evolving towards economic and monetary integration. Figure 17.5 shows the population size of the 28 EU member countries in 2014, and the dates at which they joined.

Bulgaria and Romania had been judged not to be ready to join in 2004, but joined in 2007; Croatia joined in 2013. Negotiations with Turkey began in 2005, but quickly ran into problems. If Turkey were to join, this would add a massive 74 million citizens to the EU.

Notice that the 15 pre-2004 member countries of the EU (the 'EU15') already contained more people than the USA; the combined population of the EU28 member states in 2012 was 510 million, compared with 314 million in the USA.

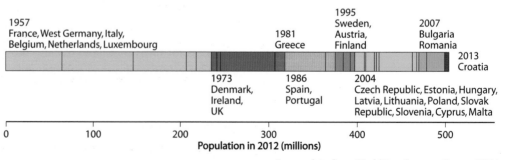

Source: data from *World Development Report*, 2014

Figure 17.5 Population of EU28, 2012

The Single Market package came into effect in 1993, bringing a number of benefits to the EU countries

The Single European Market (SEM)

From the moment of formation of the European Economic Community (EEC) in 1957, the member countries began working towards the creation of a single market in which there would be free movement of goods, services, people and capital. In other words, the idea was to create a *common market* in which there would be no barriers to trade. The EEC was a *customs union* in which internal tariffs and non-tariff barriers were to be removed and a common tariff was to be set against the rest of the world.

A package of measures that came into effect in January 1993 might be seen as the final stages in the evolution of the SEM. The key measures were the removal (or reduction) of border controls and the winding down of non-tariff barriers to trade within the EU. In this way, physical, technical and fiscal barriers were removed. It has also become increasingly easy for people to move around within the EU, with passport and customs checks being abolished at most internal borders. Associated with these measures were a number of expected benefits.

Transaction costs

Tariff barriers between EU countries were abolished under the Treaty of Rome, but a range of non-tariff barriers had built up over the years as countries sought to protect domestic employment. It was expected that the removal of these obstacles to trade, combined with the removal of border controls, would reduce the costs of trade within the EU. However, it is difficult to gauge the significance of these transaction cost savings, as it is not easy to quantify them.

Economies of scale

As trade increases, firms will find that they are operating in a larger market. This should allow them to exploit more fully the economies of large-scale production. From society's point of view, this should lead to a more efficient use of resources, as long as the resulting trade creation effects are stronger than any trade diversion that may take place.

It seems that the nature of technological change in recent years has favoured the growth of large-scale enterprises. Improved transport and communications have contributed to this process. The SEM has enabled firms in Europe to take advantage of these developments.

Intensified competition

Firms will find that they are facing more intense competition within that larger market from firms in other parts of the EU. This then brings up the same arguments that are used to justify privatisation — that intensified competition will cause firms or their managers to seek more efficient production techniques, perhaps through the elimination of X-inefficiencies. This again is beneficial for society as a whole.

From the perspective of individual countries, there has been a divergence of views concerning the large firms that have been created through mergers and acquisitions. In some countries, large firms have been seen as 'national champions'. These have been protected (or even subsidised) by domestic governments, based on the argument that they will then be better prepared to compete in the broader European market. Elsewhere, governments have taken the view that the only way to ensure that domestic firms are lean enough to be competitive in overseas markets is to face intense competition at home, as an inducement to efficiency.

Who gains most from the SEM?

As trade within Europe becomes freer, two groups of countries stand to gain the most. First, the pattern of comparative advantage between countries will be important. Many EU countries are advanced industrial nations, where labour is expensive relative to capital. These countries tend to specialise in manufacturing or capital-intensive service activities, and already have fairly similar structures. It is thus possible that the relatively labour-abundant countries of southern Europe may gain more from closer integration and an expansion of trade. This is because they have a pattern of comparative advantage that is significantly different from existing members. This diversity was reinforced by the new entrants that joined in May 2004.

Second, if the main effect of integration is to remove barriers to trade, the countries with the most to gain may be those that begin with relatively high barriers.

How important is this to the UK?

An important piece of background information is that, over the years, UK trade has become increasingly focused on Europe. This means that the UK depends heavily on trade with other countries in the EU, so successful economic performance cannot be seen in isolation from events in the broader market.

Exercise 17.4

Explain why it might be the relatively labour-intensive countries of southern Europe — and the countries of eastern Europe and the Baltic that joined in 2004, 2007 and 2013 — which stand to gain most from the SEM.

Summary

- The Single Market package came into effect at the beginning of 1993, freeing up trade between participating countries and winding down non-tariff barriers.
- This was expected to encourage trade by lowering transaction costs, enabling firms to reap economies of scale, and enhancing efficiency by stimulating competition between European firms.

The single currency area

The establishment of the SEM was seen by some as an end in itself, but others regarded it as a step towards full monetary integration, in which all member states would adopt a single currency, thereby reducing the transaction costs of international trade even more. However, full monetary union and the adoption of a common currency is about much more than transaction costs and has raised considerable debate, not least because of the political dimension. Critics of closer integration are concerned about the loss of sovereignty by individual countries. This concern is partly an economic one, focusing on the loss of separate currencies and (perhaps more significantly) the loss of control over national economic policy.

The European Monetary System

The foundations for monetary union began to be laid down in 1979, with the launch of the European Monetary System (EMS). One aspect of the EMS was the Exchange Rate Mechanism (ERM), which can be seen as a precursor of the single currency. Those countries that chose to opt into the ERM agreed to maintain their exchange rates within a band of plus or minus 2.25% against the average of their currencies — known as the European Currency Unit (ECU). The UK remained outside the ERM except for a brief flirtation between September 1990 and September 1992. During this period, the UK was operating within a slightly wider (6%) band.

During the period of the EMS/ERM, it was recognised that occasional realignment of currencies might be needed, and in fact there were 11 realignments between 1979 and 1987. However, the conditions under which such realignments were permitted were gradually tightened, so that they became less frequent as time went by.

Another key feature of the EMS period was the removal of capital controls. During the early part of this period, most of the member nations restricted the movement of financial capital across borders. This gave them some scope for using monetary policy independently of other countries. However, it was agreed that such capital controls would be phased out.

The Delors Plan, issued in 1989, set out proposals for creating European economic and monetary union (EMU), together with plans for a single currency and a European central bank. It was crucial to establish a European central bank because, with a single currency, a central bank is needed to administer monetary policy throughout the EU.

Treaty of Maastricht

The next major step was the Maastricht Treaty, signed in 1992, which created the European Union (EU). This treaty encompassed not only economic issues, such as the introduction of the single currency, but also aspects of social policy, steps towards creating a common foreign, security and defence policy, and the development of a notion of European 'citizenship'. It came into force on 1 November 1993.

It was considered that, if a single currency was to be established, the participating nations would need to have converged in their economic characteristics. If the countries were too diverse in their economic conditions, the transition to a single currency would be costly. For example, if they had very different inflation rates, interest rates or levels of outstanding government debt, the tensions of union might be too great to sustain. Strong countries would be dragged down, and weak countries would be unable to cope. The Maastricht Treaty therefore set out the *convergence criteria* by which countries would be eligible to join the single currency area. These criteria covered aspects of both monetary and fiscal policy.

Monetary policy

This is obviously important, as monetary union entails the centralisation of monetary policy within the EU. If there is to be a single currency and a single central bank to control interest rates or money supply, the monetary conditions of the economies concerned need to be reasonably close before union takes place. It was thus important to evaluate whether countries were sufficiently close to be able to join with minimal tension.

Inflation

Could countries with widely different inflation rates successfully join in a monetary union? One view is that it would be unreasonable to expect a country with 10% or 20% inflation to join a monetary union along with a country experiencing inflation at just 1%. An alternative view is that it is equally unreasonable to expect a country to cure its inflation before joining a union when one of the alleged benefits of joining is that it will cure inflation by enforcing financial discipline and removing discretion over monetary policy from individual states. However, the first criterion specified by the treaty was that countries joining the union should be experiencing low and similar inflation rates — defined as inflation no more than 1.5% above the average of the three countries in the EMS with the lowest rate.

Interest and exchange rates

Given that financial capital tends to follow high interest rates, it is argued that diversity of interest rates before union may be undesirable, as this would imply instability of capital movements. Similarly, it has been argued that a period of exchange rate stability before union would be some indication that countries have been following mutually consistent policies, and would indicate that union is plausible.

The criteria set out in the treaty required that long-term interest rates be no more than 2% above the average of the three EMS countries with the lowest rate, and that each joining country should have been in the narrow band of the ERM for a period of 2 years without the need for realignment.

Fiscal policy

Should there also be conformity in fiscal stance between countries? Would there be severe problems if countries embarked upon union and policy coordination in conditions in which unemployment rates differed markedly? These are separate but related questions. If unemployment is high, this will be connected (via social security payments) with the fiscal stance adopted by the government — as judged in terms of the government budget deficit.

The reason why unemployment rates are relevant is that there may need to be fiscal transfers between member states in order to reduce the differentials. This will clearly be politically significant in the context of a monetary union, and is an issue that will affect the long-term viability of the union. However, although unemployment rates are potentially important for this reason, the convergence criteria did not refer to unemployment directly. Instead, the criteria included a reference to fiscal policy. In practice, the divergence in unemployment rates was substantial.

Two areas are critical in judging the distance between countries in terms of fiscal policy. First, there is the question of the short-term fiscal stance, which can be measured by the budget deficit. Second, it is important to consider some indication of a longer-term commitment to stability in fiscal policy, in terms of achieving sustainable levels of outstanding government debt. Thus, the treaty required that the budget deficit be no larger than 3% of GDP, and that the national debt be no more than 60% of GDP.

Economic and monetary union

The final stage of the transition towards the single currency was European economic and monetary union (EMU). Under EMU, exchange rates between participating countries were permanently locked together: in other words, no further realignments were allowed. Furthermore, the financial markets of the countries were integrated, with the European Central Bank setting a common interest rate across the union. This was achieved in 1999.

Formation of the euro area

In the event, 11 countries were judged to have met the Maastricht criteria (Belgium, Germany, Spain, France, Ireland, Italy, Luxembourg, the Netherlands, Austria, Portugal and Finland). Together with Greece, these countries formed the single currency area, which came into operation on 1 January 2002. Slovenia joined the euro zone in 2007, followed by Cyprus and Malta in 2008, Slovakia in 2009, Estonia in 2011 and Latvia in 2014.

Euro notes and coins began to circulate in the euro zone in 2002

Costs and benefits of a single currency

Some of the arguments for and against a single currency area such as the euro zone are similar to those used in evaluating a fixed exchange rate system against a flexible one. This is because a common currency is effectively creating an area in which exchange rates between member nations are fixed for ever, even if that common currency varies relative to the rest of the world. The question of whether such an arrangement is beneficial overall for the member states rests on an evaluation of the benefits and costs of joining together. An *optimal currency area* occurs when a group of countries are better off with a single currency.

Benefits

The main benefits of a single currency area come in the form of a *monetary efficiency gain*, which has the effect of encouraging more trade between member countries. The hope is that this will bring further gains from exploiting comparative advantage between countries and enabling firms to reap the benefits of economies of scale.

The efficiency gain comes from two main sources. First, there are gains from reducing *transaction costs*, if there is no longer a need to convert from one currency into another. Second, there are gains from the *reduction in uncertainty*, in the sense that there is no longer a need to forecast future movements in exchange rates — at least between participating countries. This is similar to the gains from a fixed exchange rate system, but it goes further, as there is no longer a risk of occasional devaluation or revaluation of currencies.

The extent to which these gains are significant will depend upon the degree of integration between the participating nations. If most of the trade that takes place is between the participants, the gains will clearly be much more significant than if member nations are also trading extensively with countries outside the single currency area.

Costs

The costs come in the conduct and effectiveness of policy. Within the single currency area, individual countries can no longer have recourse to monetary policy in order to stabilise the macro economy. As with the fixed exchange rate system, one key question then is how well individual economies are able to adjust to external shocks. Thus, it is important for each economy to have flexibility. In addition, individual countries have to be aware that, once in the single currency area, it is impossible to use monetary policy to smooth out fluctuations in output and employment.

In this context, it is very important that the economic cycles of participating economies are well synchronised. If one economy is out of phase with the rest, it may find itself facing an inappropriate policy situation. For example, suppose that most of the countries within the euro zone are in the boom phase of the economic cycle, and are wanting to raise the interest rate in order to control aggregate demand: if one country within the zone is in recession, then the last thing it will want is rising interest rates, as this will deepen the recession and delay recovery. These arguments came to the fore during the recession of the late 2000s.

> ## Exercise 17.5
>
> Use an *AD/AS* diagram to analyse the problems that could arise if a country that is part of a single currency area enters a period of recession at a time when other countries in the union are in a boom.

Evaluation

Paul Krugman suggested a helpful way of using cost–benefit analysis to evaluate these aspects of a single currency area. He argued that both the costs and the benefits from a single currency area will vary with the degree to which member countries are integrated. Thus the benefits from joining such a currency area would rise as the closeness of integration increased, whereas the costs would fall.

Figure 17.6 illustrates the balance between costs and benefits. For countries that are not very closely integrated (that is, if 'integration' is less than t^*), the costs from joining the union exceed the benefits, so it would not be in the country's interest to join. However, as the degree of integration increases, so the benefits increase, and the costs decrease, so for any country beyond t^*, the benefits exceed the costs, and it is thus worth joining.

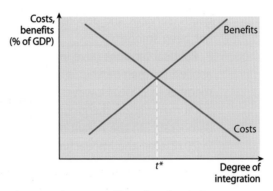

Figure 17.6 Costs and benefits of a single currency area

For an individual country considering whether or not to join the euro area, a first step is to reach a judgement on whether the country is to the left or to the right of t^*. There may be other issues to consider in addition to the costs and benefits, but unless the country has at least reached t^*, it could be argued that entry into the union should not be considered.

One way of viewing the situation is that the costs are mainly macroeconomic, but the benefits are microeconomic. This complicates the evaluation process. Some research published in 2006 argued that most of the boost to trade within the euro area occurred during the initial period, and would not continue to build up over time. It was also suggested that the EU countries that decided not to join the euro (the UK, Sweden and Denmark) gained almost as much as the countries that had joined.

The experience of some European countries during and in the aftermath of the financial crisis has cast doubt on whether the euro zone could be viewed as an optimal currency area. In particular, some countries faced problems because they could not pursue independent monetary or fiscal policies.

From a UK perspective, the debate has shifted substantially. There was a time when the key issue was whether the UK should join the euro, and the 1997 Labour government went to great lengths to set out the conditions that would need to be met for this to be seen as the best way forward. This debate has now been supplanted by views expressed by some pressure groups that not only should the UK not join the euro, but it should withdraw entirely from the EU, in spite of the importance of trade with Europe in terms of both exports and imports.

Exercise 17.6

Identify the costs and benefits that would be associated with the UK's entry into the euro single currency group of countries, and discuss whether you believe that the UK should join if conditions favour it. Do you consider that the UK should remain in the EU?

Other regional trade agreements

There are many other examples of regional trade agreements that have been negotiated around the world, some of which are now well established. These have influenced the pattern of global trade, although it has been argued that the strengthening of regional groupings of countries may inhibit the development of freer global trade — especially, of course, where these agreements involved setting common tariffs against countries outside the blocs.

MERCOSUR ('the common market of the south')

Mercosur is South America's largest trading bloc. it was established in 1991 with four member states — Argentina, Brazil, Paraguay and Uruguay. A treaty signed in 1994 formalised the agreement as a customs union. The aim of the agreement is to promote the free movement of goods, services and people among the member states, but progress has not been smooth.

Political tensions have impeded progress of the agreement. Venezuela applied for membership in 2004 and was accepted as an associate member in 2006. However, Paraguay objected to Venezuela becoming a full member on the grounds that the country was not sufficiently democratic. In the meantime, Paraguay was suspended from membership in 2012 after the impeachment of the president and, during the period of suspension, Venezuela was admitted to full membership. Paraguay finally accepted Venezuela's membership towards the end of 2013, and returned from suspension under a new president. Bolivia was expected to be admitted as a full member in 2015.

There have also been some disputes around trade. For example, in 1999 Argentina imposed restrictions on some imported products from Brazil, and Brazil responded by imposing its own barriers to trade. More recently, Mercosur member nations agreed to raise their external tariffs on imports to 35% on certain products.

These difficulties in encouraging more liberal trade illustrate the importance of political factors in achieving gains from trade.

In 2013, the EU accounted for 20% of Mercosur's total trade, and Mercosur was the EU's sixth largest export market. The EU imports mainly agricultural products and raw materials from Mercosur and mainly exports manufactured goods and chemicals. In addition, the EU exports commercial services to Mercosur and is the biggest foreign investor in the region. Negotiations have been under way for a trade agreement between the EU and Mercosur.

The Association of Southeast Asian Nations (ASEAN)

ASEAN was established in 1967 as an agreement between Indonesia, Malaysia, the Philippines, Singapore and Thailand. These nations were later joined by Brunei Darussalam in 1984, Vietnam in 1995, Lao PDR and Myanmar (Burma) in 1997 and Cambodia in 1999. By 2006, ASEAN nations included 560 million people. The original aim of the association was partly economic (to promote economic growth, social progress and cultural development), but also to promote regional peace and stability.

These original aims were bolstered in 1992 by the launch of AFTA (the ASEAN Free Trade Area), which set out to eliminate tariff and non-tariff barriers among the member nations. A longer-term aim is to move towards an East Asian Free Trade Area that would also include China, Japan and the Republic of Korea. Negotiations towards this have begun — indeed regular summit meetings of ASEAN+3 have been taking place since the mid-1990s. Another objective of ASEAN is to move towards closer economic integration, and 2007 saw the signing of a declaration announcing moves towards establishing the ASEAN Economic Community (AEC).

Summary

- The first step towards monetary union was the launch of the European Monetary System (EMS) in 1979.
- An important part of this was the Exchange Rate Mechanism (ERM), under which participating countries (which did not include the UK) agreed to keep their currencies within a narrow band (plus or minus 2.25%) against the average of their currencies.
- The Maastricht Treaty created the European Union (EU), and set out the route towards closer integration.
- The treaty also set out the convergence criteria, to be used to judge which countries were ready to join in monetary union. These criteria covered financial and fiscal aspects.
- Twelve countries adopted the euro as their common currency in January 2002.
- The main benefit of a common currency area is that it encourages trade by reducing transaction costs and reducing foreign exchange risk.
- However, the downside is that individual countries have less autonomy in controlling their macroeconomies. Adjusting to external shocks and smoothing short-term fluctuations in output and employment become more difficult with a common monetary policy that may not always be set in ways that are appropriate for all participating countries.
- There are many other examples of regional trade agreements that have reached various stages of integration, such as NAFTA and ASEAN.

Exercise 17.7

Discuss the costs and benefits that need to be taken into account in evaluating the effects of a regional trade agreement.

Globalisation and the WTO evaluated

The economic arguments in favour of allowing freer trade are strong, in the sense that there are potential gains to be made from countries specialising in the production of goods and services in which they have a comparative advantage. Globalisation facilitates and accelerates this process. And yet, there have sometimes been violent protests against globalisation, directed in particular at the WTO, whose meeting at Seattle in 1999 ended in chaos following demonstrations in the streets.

Tension has always been present during moves towards freer trade. Even if the economic arguments appear to be compelling, nations are cautious about opening up to free trade. In particular, there has been concern about jobs in the domestic economy. This is partly because there are transitional costs involved in liberalising trade, as some economic activities must contract to allow others to expand. Vested interests can then lead to lobbying and political pressure, as was apparent in the USA in the early part of the twenty-first century. There is also the question of whether globalisation will allow recession to spread more quickly between countries.

In many ways, the WTO gets caught in the middle. It has responsibility for encouraging moves towards free trade, and thus comes under pressure from nations that want to keep some degree of protection because they are unwilling to undergo the transitional costs of structural change. The WTO thus has the unpalatable job of protecting countries from themselves, enforcing short-term costs in the interests of long-term gains.

The Doha Agenda

In 2000, new talks started covering agriculture and services. The fourth WTO Ministerial Conference in Doha in November 2001 incorporated these discussions into a broader work programme, the Doha Development Agenda. The WTO website indicates that this agenda includes:

> ...work on non-agricultural tariffs, trade and environment, WTO rules such as anti-dumping and subsidies, investment, competition policy, trade facilitation, transparency in government procurement, intellectual property, and a range of issues raised by developing countries.

Progress on the Doha agenda has been far from smooth. This is partly because agriculture is an especially contentious area, with the USA, the EU and Japan having large-scale policies in place to support their agricultural sectors. In the case of the EU's Single Market, some moves have been made towards reforming the Common Agricultural Policy, but progress has not been as rapid as developing countries would like — remembering that agriculture is especially important for many of the less developed countries. Reluctance on the part of the rich nations to provide concessions in these key areas, combined with determination on the part of LDCs to make genuine progress, results in a seeming deadlock.

The so-called 'Bali package' of measures was agreed in 2013, amidst great optimism amongst ministers, but the crucial issues surrounding agriculture remained, and the future of the Doha round remains uncertain.

Anti-globalisation protests

The anti-globalisation protests are based on rather different arguments. One concern is that economic growth can proceed only at some cost to the environment. It has been argued that, by fragmenting the production process across countries, the cost to the environment is high. This is partly because the need to transport goods around the world uses up valuable resources. It is also argued that nations have an incentive to lower their environmental standards in order to attract MNCs by enabling low-cost production. This is not so much an argument against globalisation as an argument that an international agency is required to monitor global environmental standards.

It has also been suggested that it is the rich countries of the world that stand to gain most from increasing global trade, as they have the market power to ensure that trading conditions work in their favour.

Activists protest against the WTO in Bali in 2013

Again, the WTO may have a role here in monitoring the conditions under which trade takes place. At the end of the day, trade allows an overall increase in global production and more choice for consumers. The challenge is to ensure that these gains are equitably distributed, and that the environment can be conserved.

Summary

- Globalisation is a process by which the world's economies have become more closely integrated.
- This has enabled greater exploitation of comparative advantage.
- Although closer integration may bring benefits in terms of increased global production and trade, it may also create vulnerability by allowing adverse shocks (e.g. oil price changes or financial crises) to spread more rapidly between countries.
- However, the integrated global economy may turn out to be more resilient in reacting to adverse circumstances.
- Globalisation facilitates and accelerates the process by which gains from trade may be tapped.
- However, the transitional costs for individual economies in terms of the need for structural change have encouraged politicians to turn to protectionist measures.
- Critics of globalisation have pointed to the environmental costs of rapid global economic growth and the expansion of trade, and have argued that it is rich countries and multinational corporations that gain the most, rather than less developed countries.

Free trade and protectionism

Some early economic thinkers such as Adam Smith and David Ricardo drew attention to the possible benefits that nations could derive from engaging in international trade. These arguments were developed from notions of specialisation and division of labour, and Ricardo's law of comparative advantage. In spite of these potential economic gains, nations have always been tempted to introduce protectionist measures that interfere with free trade.

Specialisation

The arguments in favour of free trade stem from the observation that if countries specialise in the production of goods (or services) in which they have a comparative advantage, then it is possible for overall economic welfare to be increased through engaging in international trade. At the heart of this is the issue that countries face different patterns of potential specialisation — in other words, differing opportunity costs in the production of goods. For example, an industrialised country is likely to have a comparative advantage in the production of manufactured goods relative to agricultural commodities, whereas a less developed country may have a comparative advantage in agricultural goods. Another way of putting this is that the opportunity cost of producing agricultural goods is higher for the industrial country than for the less developed country. Because of this, if each country specialises in producing the good in which it has a comparative advantage, total production of the goods can be increased.

One very important point to notice is that it cannot be guaranteed that both countries will actually be better off with trade. Some of the critics of globalisation have argued that many less developed countries today find themselves in a position in which they are encouraged to open up to more trade — but then find that the gains are being pre-empted by others.

Trade liberalisation

One of the hopes for a trade liberalisation policy is that resources may be released from inefficient domestic production into more productive employment in the export sector. For many less developed countries, it may turn out that the export sector is unable to expand, so that the only effect of liberalisation is to release workers and other resources into unemployment.

Another political or strategic issue arises in this situation. Suppose that a country agrees to specialise completely in producing manufactures at the expense of agricultural goods, and then finds itself unable to engage in trade because of a war? How does it then feed its people? Following two world wars, many European countries in the 1950s may have seen this possibility as a real threat, and felt that maintaining some form of protection of their agricultural sectors was strategically crucial. This was one of the stated motivations behind the development of Europe's Common Agricultural Policy (CAP), which remains one of the world's prime examples of a protectionist policy.

Globalisation

Globalisation has given an added impetus to world trade, but has also highlighted problem areas. The rapid rise of China's economy and its success in export activity has been seen as threatening by some, and a protectionist lobby in the USA put trade policy on the US election agenda. The developed countries are eager to persuade developing countries to open up their economies to services and manufactured goods, but a sticking point has been the reluctance of the developed countries to reduce their high farm subsidies, which make it difficult for developing countries to market the produce in which they have a natural comparative advantage. If an agreement is to be reached, it is likely that concessions will be needed on both sides.

Follow-up questions

a Explain the difference between absolute advantage and comparative advantage. Which of these notions gives rise to the potential gains from trade?

b Discuss why these gains may not always be shared equally among the trading partners.

c Examine the arguments for and against the use of tariffs.

Case study 17.2

The North American Free Trade Agreement (NAFTA)

NAFTA is a trilateral agreement between the USA, Canada and Mexico that was launched on 1 January 1994, with the aim of removing tariff barriers between the countries. These provisions were fully implemented on 1 January 2008. Although NAFTA is primarily about trade in goods and services between the three countries, there are also side agreements dealing with environmental and labour issues.

The US Department of Agriculture claims that NAFTA is 'one of the most successful trade agreements in history', having stimulated 'significant increases in agricultural trade and investment' between the three member countries.

Whether all partners have gained equally remains an open question. There is a strong protectionist lobby in the USA that has argued that jobs have been lost as a result of the agreement. Some commentators in Mexico have argued that NAFTA has damaged Mexico's agricultural sector, as it has faced subsidised imports from the USA. Labour issues have also been highly contentious, and the proposal from the USA to erect new fences to stem the flow of migrants from Mexico into the USA has provoked substantial debate.

It is important to treat these arguments with great care, as there are sensitive political issues that can sometimes override economic analysis. The law of comparative advantage suggests that there are potential gains from engaging in trade, but the process of liberalising trade entails short-run costs.

These may be expected to be transitional, especially for economic activities that are forced into decline in the face of expanding imports from partner countries. The existence of these costs should not prevent trade liberalisation if the long-term gains are sufficient to overcome the costs eventually. There must be a balancing of the costs against the benefits.

Follow-up questions

a What do you think might have motivated the members of NAFTA to join together in a free trade agreement?

b Which countries do you think would have most to gain from NAFTA?

c What factors would you need to take into account in evaluating the potential benefits of trade liberalisation in the context of an agreement such as NAFTA?

SECTION
2

MACROECONOMICS

Part 9
The financial sector

Chapter 18

The financial sector and the real economy

This chapter explores the role of the financial sector in the economy. It has often been argued that the quantity of money in the economy — and its rate of growth — are crucial in influencing the rate of inflation, and hence the overall performance of the economy. However, it has also been noted that money stock is difficult to define, measure, monitor and control. This chapter explains why this is the case, setting out the various sources of money and credit creation in a modern economy. It also discusses the main theories that seek to explain the importance of money in the macroeconomy. Finally, it outlines the role of the banking sector and the patterns of lending and borrowing.

Learning objectives

After studying this chapter, you should:

- appreciate the importance of the financial sector in the macroeconomy
- be familiar with the sources of money in the economy — in particular, noting the actions of commercial banks, the government, and the stock and bond markets, and the impact of international financial transactions
- be aware of the determinants of the demand for money
- understand the way in which interest rates are determined in different money markets
- be familiar with the liquidity preference theory and the loanable funds approach
- be able to evaluate the role of the financial sector in the real economy

Prior knowledge needed

No prior knowledge is needed for this chapter.

Money in the modern economy

Money plays an important role in the modern economy. However, Chapter 14 noted that the monetary authorities find it difficult to measure and monitor the amount of money in the economy — let alone trying to control it directly. Why should this be? Part of the explanation is that there are many sources of money in a modern, open economy. In other words, it is not simply a question of measuring, monitoring and controlling the quantity of banknotes and coins in circulation.

This partly stems from the functions of money, which were discussed back in Chapter 1 of Book 1. Money performs four key roles — as a medium of exchange, a store of value, a unit of account and a standard of deferred payment.

Gold has long been considered a form of money

In order to fulfil these functions, money needs to have certain characteristics:

- *portability*: money must be easy to carry
- *divisibility*: money needs to be readily divided into small parts in order to undertake transactions
- *acceptability*: money must be generally acceptable if it is to act as a medium of exchange
- *scarcity*: money cannot be in unlimited supply, nor should it be able to be counterfeited
- *durability*: money needs to be able to withstand wear and tear in use
- *stability in value*: the value of money must remain reasonably stable over time if it is to act as a store of value

Many commodities have acted as money at various times in various circumstances. For example, cigarettes acted as money in prisoner of war camps during the Second World War. In parts of West Africa, slaves were used as money in historical periods — slaves were portable, but were neither divisible nor durable.

It may be possible to measure and monitor the quantity of legal money such as cash and banknotes, but other assets may also fulfil the functions of money, such as bank deposits and other financial assets. This helps to explain why it is difficult to measure and monitor the amount of money in the economy. These other assets have varying degrees of **liquidity**.

Cash and banknotes are the most liquid assets, as they can be used for transactions directly. Current (chequing) accounts are almost as liquid, but although savings accounts in banks may also be quite quickly converted to cash, there may be a time delay or a cost involved. Shares or government bonds are much less liquid, as it takes time to convert them into cash. Nonetheless, they are several types of asset that can be regarded as being near-money. The central bank can control the quantities of some of these assets, but not all.

The commercial banks and credit creation

The operations of commercial banks can influence the quantity of money. Banks accept deposits from their customers, and issue loans. The way in which they undertake lending has an impact on the quantity of money.

Study tip

Notice that it is bank deposits that count as money, not the cheques drawn on them.

Key term

liquidity the extent to which an asset can be converted in the short term and without the holder incurring a cost

Study tip

Remember that Chapter 14 drew a distinction between *narrow money* and *broad money*. Check back if you cannot recall the difference.

The credit creation multiplier

Think first of all about the way in which the money supply is created. You might think that this is simply a question of controlling the amount of notes and coin issued by the central bank. However, because there are many different assets that act as near-money in a modern economy, the real picture is more complicated. The actions of the commercial banks also have implications for the size of money supply.

One of the reasons why it is difficult for a central bank to control the supply of money is the way that the commercial banks are able to create credit. Consider the way that commercial banks operate. They accept deposits from customers, and supply them with banking services. However, they also provide loans — and this is how they make profits. Suppose that the government undertakes a piece of expenditure, and finances it by issuing money. The firms receiving the payment from the government are likely to bank the money they receive, so bank deposits increase. From the perspective of the commercial banks, they know that it is unlikely that all their customers will want to withdraw their money simultaneously, so they will lend out some of the additional deposits to borrowers, who are likely to undertake expenditure on goods or services. As their expenditures work their way back into the banking system, the commercial banks will find that they can lend out even more, and so the process continues. In other words, an increase in the amount of money in the economy has a multiplied effect on the amount of credit created by the banks. This process is known as the **credit multiplier**.

Consider an arithmetic example illustrated in Figure 18.1. Suppose that the commercial banks always act such as to hold 10% of their assets in liquid form — that is, as cash in the tills. If an extra £100 is lodged as deposits, the commercial banks will add £10 to the cash in tills, and lend out the remaining £90. When that £90 finds its way back into the hands of the bank, it will keep £9 as cash, and lend out the remaining £81. And so on. The process will stop when the bank is back to a cash ratio of 10%. The original extra £100 will have been converted into £100 in cash, and £900 in loans!

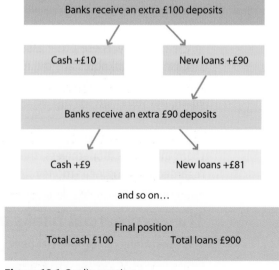

Figure 18.1 Credit creation

Key term

credit multiplier a process by which an increase in money supply can have a multiplied effect on the amount of credit in an economy

The value of the multiplier is given by 1 divided by the cash ratio that the commercial banks decide to hold. The smaller is this ratio, the larger is the credit multiplier. If the commercial banks want to hold only 5% of their assets in the form of cash, then the credit multiplier will be 1/0.05 = 20.

The significance of this relationship is that changes in the supply of cash have a multiplied impact on the amount of credit in the economy. This makes monetary control through money supply a highly imprecise business, especially if the central bank does not know exactly what the commercial banks' desired liquidity ratio is. In the past, one way that the monetary authorities tried to control money supply was to impose requirements on the proportion of assets that banks held in liquid form. However, this is also imprecise, as banks need not hold exactly the proportion required, in order to give themselves some leeway in the short run. This method of control was abandoned long ago, although the commercial banks are required to keep a small portion of their assets as cash at the Bank of England. This is purely for operational reasons.

> ### Exercise 18.1
>
> Suppose that the commercial banks in a country follow a rule such that they always aim to hold one-tenth of their assets in liquid form (i.e. as cash). Calculate the total increase in bank lending that would follow if government action leads to an extra £200 being lodged as bank deposits. Explain your answer.

Summary

- Money plays an important role in the macroeconomy, fulfilling functions as a medium of exchange, a store of value and a standard of deferred payment.
- There are several different sorts of assets that have the necessary characteristics to achieve these functions.
- Money supply is difficult to measure or control because money can be generated from a range of sources.
- Commercial banks can influence money supply through their lending policy via the credit multiplier.

The determination of interest rates

Chapter 14 introduced the idea that the equilibrium interest rate could be seen as being determined by the intersection of the demand for and the supply of money. This now needs to be explored more closely.

The demand for money

There are three key motives for holding money: for transactions, as a precaution and for speculative reasons (see the next page). Between them they determine the demand for money.

The opportunity cost of holding money

It is important to notice that the decision to hold money balances carries an opportunity cost. If a firm or household chooses to hold money, it forgoes the possibility of using the money to purchase some other financial asset, such as a bond, that would yield a rate of return.

This means that the interest rate can be regarded as the opportunity cost of holding money: put another way, it is the price of holding money. At high rates of interest, people can be expected to hold less money, as the opportunity cost of doing so is high.

The transactions demand for money

The first motive for holding money is clear — people and firms will hold money in order to undertake transactions. This is related to the need to use money when buying goods and services, and is closely associated with the functions of money as a medium of exchange and a unit of account. The demand for money for this purpose will probably be determined by the level of income, because it is the level of income that will determine how many transactions people and firms will wish to undertake. The rate of interest (the opportunity cost of holding money) may be less important than income in this instance.

The precautionary demand for money

People and firms may also hold money for precautionary reasons. They may wish to have liquid assets available in order to guard against a sudden need to cover an emergency payment, or to take advantage of a spending opportunity at some point in the future. The opportunity cost of holding money may come into play here, as if the return on financial assets is high, people may be less inclined to hold money in a relatively liquid form.

The speculative demand for money

The rate of interest may affect the demand for money through another route. If share (or bond) prices are low (and the rate of interest paid is therefore high), then the opportunity cost of holding money is high, and people and firms will tend to hold shares. On the other hand, when the interest rate is low, and share prices are high, people will be more likely to hold money. This effect will be especially strong when people and firms see share prices as being unreasonably high, so that they expect them to fall. In this case, they may speculate by selling bonds in order to hold money, in anticipation of taking advantage of future expected falls in the price of bonds.

Liquidity preference

If the interest rate may be regarded as being the opportunity cost of holding money, it can be argued that economic agents, whether households or firms, will display a demand for money, arising from the functions that money fulfils in a modern economy. This theory of **liquidity preference**, as it is known, was noted by Keynes in his *General Theory*. Figure 18.2 (which reproduces Figure 14.8) illustrates what is implied for the money market. If the rate of interest is the opportunity cost of money, then it is expected that the demand for money will be lower when the rate of interest rate is relatively high, as the opportunity cost of holding money is high. People will be more reluctant to forgo the rate of return that has to be sacrificed by holding money. When the rate of interest is relatively low, this will be less of a concern, so the demand for money will be relatively high. This suggests that the money demand curve (*MD*) will be downward sloping. If money supply is fixed at *M** in Figure 18.2, then the money market will be in equilibrium at the rate of interest *r**.

Key term

liquidity preference a theory that suggests that people will desire to hold money as an asset

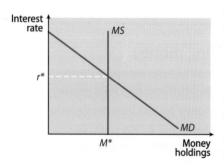

Figure 18.2 The demand for money

The existence of this relationship means that the monetary authorities have to be aware of the need to maintain (or allow) equilibrium in the money market. Interest rates and money supply cannot be fixed independently. This is a clear constraint on the use of monetary policy. An important question is the extent to which the demand for money is stable. If money demand were to be volatile, moving around from one time period to the next, then it would be virtually impossible for the monetary authorities to have any precise control over the market. The situation is further complicated by the way that interest rates influence behaviour. The degree to which the demand for money is sensitive to the rate of interest will also be important. This will be reflected in the shape of the *MD* curve. Notice that because the level of income is also important in determining money demand, this will affect the *position* of the *MD* curve in the diagram. An increase in income will lead to a rightward shift in money demand, as people and firms will require larger money holdings when incomes are higher.

The market for loanable funds

Although the rate of interest can be interpreted as being the opportunity cost of holding money, this is not the only way of viewing it. From a firm's point of view, it may be seen as the cost of borrowing. For example, suppose that a firm is considering undertaking an investment project. The rate of interest represents the cost of borrowing the funds needed in order to finance the investment. The higher the rate of interest is, the less will investment projects be seen as being profitable. If the firm is intending to finance its investment from past profits, the interest rate is still pertinent, as it then represents the return that the firm could obtain by purchasing a financial asset instead of undertaking the investment. Either way, the rate of interest is important in the decision-making process.

The rate of interest is also important to households, to whom it may represent the return on saving. Households may be encouraged to save more if the return on their saving is relatively high, whereas when the rate of interest is low, the incentive to save is correspondingly low. Within the circular flow of income, expenditure and output, it is the flow of saving from households that enables firms to find the funds needed to fund their investment expenditure. It is now apparent that the rate of interest may play an important role in bringing together these flows.

This is shown in Figure 18.3. The investment schedule is shown as downward sloping, because firms will find more investment projects to be worthwhile when the rate of interest rate is low. The savings schedule is shown to be upward sloping because a higher rate of interest is expected to encourage households to supply more saving. In other words, the supply of loanable funds will be higher when the rate of interest rate is relatively high.

Exercise 18.2

Analyse the effect on the rate of interest if there is an increase in the supply of money in an economy. Use a diagram such as Figure 18.2 as a starting point.

Key term

market for loanable funds the notion that households will be influenced by the rate of interest in making saving decisions, which will then determine the quantity of loanable funds available for firms to borrow for investment

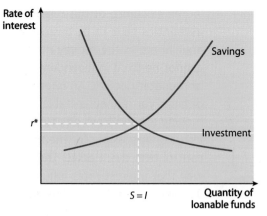

Rate of
interest

Savings

r^*

Investment

$S = I$

Quantity of
loanable funds

Figure 18.3 The market for loanable funds

Keynes believed that this could lead to instability in financial markets.
He argued that investment and saving would be relatively insensitive
to the rate of interest, such that the schedules in Figure 18.3 would
be relatively steep. Investment would depend more crucially on firms'
expectations about the future demand for their products, which could
be volatile, moving the investment schedule around and thus leading to
instability in the rate of interest. Keynes thus came to the conclusion
that governments should manage aggregate demand in order to stabilise
the economy.

Summary

- People and firms within the economy choose to hold money for
  certain purposes.
- The demand for money reflects transactions, precautionary and
  speculative motivations.
- The rate of interest can be regarded as the opportunity cost of
  holding money.
- Keynes developed liquidity preference theory, showing how the
  demand for money would be related to the rate of interest.
- It has been argued that both investment and saving depend upon the
  rate of interest.
- The rate of interest is important in determining equilibrium of saving
  and investment within the market for loanable funds.

Money and inflation

Why should the quantity of money or credit in circulation be so
important? Recall the quantity theory of money, which was introduced
in Chapter 15. This quantity theory relationship suggests that prices can
only increase persistently if money stock itself increases persistently, or if
money stock persistently grows more rapidly than real output.

How can we interpret this in terms of aggregate demand and aggregate
supply? If the money supply increases, then firms and households in the
economy find they have excess cash balances — that is, for the given price
level they have stronger purchasing power than they had anticipated. Their

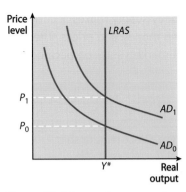

Figure 18.4 A monetary expansion

impulse will thus be to increase spending, which will cause the aggregate demand curve to move to the right. They will probably also save some of the excess, which will tend to result in lower interest rates — which then reinforces the increase in aggregate demand. However, as the AD curve moves to the right, the equilibrium price level will rise, and return the economy to equilibrium.

Figure 18.4 illustrates this in the case of a monetarist long-run aggregate supply — recall that the AS curve would be vertical at the full employment level under monetarist assumptions. If aggregate demand begins at AD_0, and then shifts to AD_1, the figure shows that price increases from P_0 to P_1, but real output remains unchanged at Y^*.

If money supply continues to increase, the process repeats itself, with price then rising persistently. One danger of this is that people get so accustomed to the process that they speed up their spending decisions, and this accelerates the whole process. Inflation could then accelerate out of control.

To summarise, the analysis suggests that persistent inflation can only arise through persistent excessive growth in the money stock, which can be seen in terms of persistent movements of the aggregate demand curve.

Quantitative skills 18.1

Real and nominal interest rates

It is worth being aware that when there is inflation in an economy, there is an important distinction between nominal and real interest rates. The stated rate of return on a financial asset represents the nominal return. For example, if you invest £100 now at an annual fixed rate of 5%, you expect to receive £105 in a year's time. However, if inflation has been proceeding at 2% per annum over that year, the value of your investment has been eroded by that 2% increase in prices. The *real rate of interest* is thus the net return after allowing for inflation. This can be approximated as the difference between the nominal rate and the inflation rate. In the above example, the real rate of interest would be 5 − 2 = 3%.

Exercise 18.4

Sketch an AD/AS diagram with a Keynesian shape for aggregate supply. Discuss the extent to which this produces different results from those outlined above.

Evaluation

How significant is the quantity theory relationship in understanding the operation of the macroeconomy?

Remember that the equation of exchange is a definition, and only becomes a theory if some assumptions are made. The strength of the theory therefore rests on the validity of those assumptions — namely, that the velocity of circulation is constant and that real output would always tend to the natural rate. This goes back to the debate between the monetarist and Keynesian schools. The former — especially those of the new classical following — argued that the economy would always return to equilibrium rapidly. The stability of the velocity of circulation is closely related to the stability of the demand for money relationship, and the monetarists thought this would be stable — if it existed at all. The Keynesians, on the other hand, did not believe that the economy would always return to equilibrium, and thought that the demand for money (and hence the velocity of circulation) could be quite volatile. Under these assumptions, the direct relationship between money and the price level would be broken.

Either way, the difficulty of identifying money supply makes it difficult to explore the real-world relationship between money and prices. The rapidity of technological progress in financial markets has complicated things even more.

Summary

- The quantity theory suggests that there is a direct relationship between money and the overall price level.
- Persistent inflation can only occur if money supply persistently grows more rapidly than real incomes.
- The validity of the quantity theory relationship depends upon the validity of the underpinning assumptions.

The financial sector and the macroeconomy

The macroeconomy depends heavily on the financial sector to operate effectively. Lending and borrowing underpin the way in which the economy works: firms need to borrow in order to finance their investment, and households borrow for their spending. Insurance markets and pension funds are key features of the financial landscape. The process of globalisation enhances the importance of having an efficient foreign exchange market.

The credit crunch and financial crisis highlighted the importance of an effective financial sector for the real macroeconomy, given its impact on economic growth and unemployment. To understand how this came about, it is necessary to explore the ways in which the banking sector has developed over time, against a backdrop of deregulation and innovation in types of financial asset.

Financial institutions

Financial institutions provide the key link between borrowers and lenders and are often referred to as **financial intermediaries**. This term covers banks, building societies and a range of other specialist institutions that provide financial services. Traditionally, the banking sector has been seen as being divided into two main sectors, made up of the **retail banks** and the **wholesale banks**.

The retail banks include the high-street banks that provide banking services to households and small firms, accepting deposits and making loans, mainly on a relatively small scale, and providing a distributed branch banking service. Wholesale banks operate on a larger scale, taking deposits and making loans to companies and other banks. These include the investment banks and other specialist financial institutions. Building societies in the past were distinct institutions providing a specific service, accepting deposits from a range of small depositors and making long-term loans for house purchase, with the property acting as collateral on the debt.

One of the developments of recent years has been the blurring of these distinctions. Deregulation has allowed most building societies to rebrand themselves as retail banks, and the high-street banks have diversified into wholesale banking, becoming **universal banks**, operating in large-scale

financial intermediaries institutions such as banks and building societies that channel funds from lenders to borrowers
retail banks banks that provide high-street services to depositors
wholesale banks banks that deal with companies and other banks on a large scale
universal banks banks that operate in both retail and wholesale markets

High-street banks have diversified into wholesale banking, becoming universal banks

lending and investment as well as fulfilling their traditional high-street functions. The growth of internet banking has allowed them to reduce the extent of their branch banking networks, thus reducing costs.

Banks operate in order to make profits. They take deposits and make loans, making profit from the return on the loans that they make. The more loans they make, the more profit, but this must be balanced against the need to carry enough liquid assets to meet the demands of depositors who wish to withdraw funds for use in transactions. There is thus a trade-off that the banks need to get right, between making loans and holding enough liquidity to service their customers. The **liquidity ratio** is the ratio of liquid assets to total assets.

In the short run, banks can borrow from each other in order to maintain their liquidity ratio. Such **interbank lending** takes place at a rate of interest that depends upon the amount of liquidity in the market and on the period over which the loan is required. The average rate of interest on loans made in the London interbank market is known as the **LIBOR**, which is set daily. Under normal circumstances, such lending ensures that banks have sufficient liquidity on a day-by-day basis, but problems emerged during the financial crisis.

Another way of accommodating a short-run shortage of funds is to sell financial assets to the central bank (or to other banks), then repurchase them at an agreed date — perhaps two weeks later. These sale and repurchase agreements are known as **repos**, and act like a loan.

Forms of borrowing

Borrowing takes place for various reasons and takes different forms. The nature and characteristics of the borrowing determine the conditions under which borrowing takes place, including the rate of interest to be charged.

The mortgage market is an important form of borrowing. Mortgages are long-term loans taken out for house purchase, in which the loan is secured against the value of the property. If the borrower defaults on the loan, the lender takes the property in lieu of the debt. The size of the loan is partly based on the lender's assessment of the ability of the borrower to maintain payments over the life of the loan. This may be related to the income and expected income of the borrower, but also to the expectation that house prices will rise in the future. Borrowing may also take place without such collateral to cover default. Such unsecured borrowing will carry a higher rate of interest. In recent years, there has been an increase in very short-run loans to provide households with funds to tide them over until the next pay-day. Such pay-day lending comes at a very high rate of interest.

Another form of borrowing comes in the form of overdrafts, an arrangement whereby a bank's customer can spend more than is covered by current deposits at a pre-announced rate of interest. Such borrowing is limited to an amount agreed in advance. Credit cards also allow borrowers to incur debt, and allow ready payment for everyday transactions.

Figure 18.5 shows selected interest rates, before and after the financial crisis, all measured in per cent per annum at the end of the month shown.

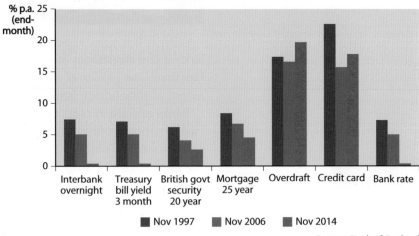

Source: Bank of England

Figure 18.5 Selected interest rates in the UK

The interest rates shown reveal substantial variation. This can be explained with reference to some key characteristics of the form of borrowing to which they relate, particularly the risk involved with lending. The security and length of the loan contribute to the risk. It would be expected that lending with no collateral would carry a risk premium, as the cost of default is high for the borrower. It is also the case that risk may be higher for a long-term loan because of the uncertainty attached to the future. This may be balanced by the nature of collateral — for example, in the case of mortgage lending, where the asset providing the collateral is expected to appreciate in value over time. This was especially true in periods when house prices were rising at a fast rate.

The figure shows that unsecured loans, such as overdrafts and credit cards, carry significantly higher interest rates than the secured loans such as mortgages, or government securities, which may be perceived as much less risky.

Financial instruments

Synoptic link

Notice, however, that when firms are owned by a large and fragmented number of shareholders, the managers who run the firm may not face great accountability, thus giving rise to the principal–agent problem, as was discussed in Chapter 2.

Shares, bonds and certificates

The development of new financial instruments in recent decades has had a major influence on the way in which financial markets operate. Shares are issued by firms in need of finance. Shareholders become part-owners of the company, and may receive dividends from the profits made by the firm. Those holding a large portion of a firm's shares can have a major say in how the firm operates.

When the government needs to borrow, it can do so by issuing bonds. A bond is a financial asset that pays a fixed amount each year and also carries a fixed value payable at a fixed date in the future when the bond matures. Bonds can be bought and sold, and the price of the bond varies with the market valuation at any point in time. The price of a bond varies inversely with the rate of interest.

Certificates of deposit (CDs) are one way in which a financial institution can extend its borrowing. These are certificates issued by banks to customers in return for deposits for a fixed term. For example, a large firm may agree to deposit a sum of money for a fixed period, receiving a CD in return. The CD can be sold on in the secondary market, so if the firm needs liquid funds, it can obtain them in spite of having agreed to the long-term deposit. From the bank's point of view, it knows it does not have to repay the deposit until a fixed point in the future.

Securitisation

Banks have also found ways of selling some of their assets to other financial institutions. For example, suppose a bank has a stock of assets in the form of residential mortgages that generate a regular cash flow. It is possible for the bank to bundle these together and sell them on. This process is known as **securitisation**. This is a device that effectively turns future cash flows into a bond.

One effect of this is that banks find that they need not maintain such a high liquidity ratio in order to meet their obligations, and can thus expand their lending. This is what happened in the lead-up to the financial crisis of the late 2000s. Securitisation altered the balance of bank assets, with a higher proportion now being in the form of bonds rather than equity/shares. There is a key difference between the two, because firms can suspend dividends in a hard year, but the return on bonds has to be paid. It also turned out that some of the securitisation that had taken place had involved assets and cash flows that were less secure and more risky than had been thought — for example, the so-called sub-prime mortgage market, where some households began to default on their debts.

This sowed the seeds of the financial crisis, when some banks began to have difficulty in meeting their obligations. Furthermore, with the banks holding lower liquidity ratios, the interbank lending system also came under pressure. In the UK, the government had to step in to bail out banks that were in difficulties.

Key term

securitisation a process whereby future cash flows are converted into marketable securities

As public debt rose, the government cut back on spending at the same time that banks were cutting down on lending. In this way, the crisis spread to the real sector of the economy. Recession was here. Chapter 20 will explore the way in which the Bank of England responded to the situation.

The impact was also felt through the stock market, where falling share prices put pressure on insurance and pension funds. It also became apparent that it is not only the liquidity ratio that is important. Partly through securitisation, banks were holding a wider variety of financial assets, carrying varying amounts of risk. Their ability to meet all demands from their depositors and to cover loan defaults would depend upon a bank's capital relative to its current liabilities and assets (weighted by the risk). This is measured by the **capital adequacy ratio**, defined as the ratio of a bank's capital to the value of its risk-weighted assets.

Key term

capital adequacy ratio the ratio of a bank's capital to its current liabilities and risk-weighted assets

Extension material

Recall the credit creation multiplier. This showed that when a bank finds it has an increase in deposits, it can create credit through its lending, and that increase in credit will be multiplied through successive rounds of borrowing. This also applies if a bank considers that its capital adequacy ratio is lower than it needs to be. As banks expanded into ever more inventive types of asset, the capital adequacy ratio became more difficult to monitor. In any case, the banks were becoming more confident in their ability to reap higher profits into the future. When the bubble burst, the danger was that banks would retreat, and stop lending. This would then set the credit creation multiplier into reverse, compounding the problem.

Exercise 18.5

Discuss what effect the rise of internet banking would have on the financial system.

Summary

- Financial institutions provide the key link between borrowers and lenders.
- The banking sectors cover retail and wholesale banking, but the distinction has become blurred over time.
- Banks aim to make profits, and face a trade-off between making loans and retaining sufficient liquidity to service their customers.
- Short-term liquidity requirements are managed through the interbank market.
- Borrowing takes a variety of forms.
- Interest rates payable on loans reflect risk and security.
- New financial instruments developed in recent decades through securitisation have increased the importance of the secondary market.
- Some banks found themselves in difficulties for a variety of reasons.

Chapter 19

The financial sector in developing and emerging economies

For developing and emerging economies, the need to be able to raise finance for investment and for development projects is paramount. The lack of a fully functioning stock market or extensive networks of branch banks acts as a constraint on the development process, especially in rural areas where many households face a struggle for survival. This chapter explores the importance of savings and investment for economic growth and human development, and how access to finance can be accomplished.

Learning objectives

After studying this chapter, you should:

- understand the importance of saving and investment for less developed countries
- be familiar with the Harrod–Domar model of economic growth
- be able to explain what is meant by microfinance, and why it is important
- be aware of the extent to which international financial markets have influenced flows of capital into and out of emerging and developing economies
- be able to evaluate the impact of public and private sector debt on developing and emerging economies
- be familiar with the role of the financial sector in promoting economic development
- be able to explain what is meant by remittances and their importance to economies

Prior knowledge needed

No prior knowledge is needed for this chapter.

Saving and investment

For developing and emerging economies, a high priority is to enable economic growth to take place. Resources are needed to tackle poverty and provide the physical and social infrastructure required for human development. One way of viewing economic growth is as a shift in aggregate supply. This suggests that the focus must be on investment, which is necessary to enable an increase in productive capacity. If investment is to take place, then saving is also necessary in order to provide the finance for investment.

Harrod–Domar model a model of economic growth that emphasises the importance of savings and investment

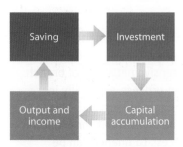

Figure 19.1 The Harrod–Domar process of economic development

Saving → Investment → Capital accumulation → Output and income → Saving

Study tip

This is quite a useful schematic diagram describing the process of economic growth, as long as you remember all the ways in which it may fail to work smoothly.

This idea is supported by the **Harrod–Domar model** of economic growth, which first appeared in separate articles by Roy Harrod in the UK and Evsey Domar in the USA in 1939. This model was to become significant in influencing LDCs' attitudes towards the process of economic growth. It was developed in an attempt to determine how equilibrium could be achieved in a growing economy.

The basic finding of the model was that an economy can remain in equilibrium through time only if it grows at a particular rate. This unique *stable growth path* depends on the *savings ratio* and the *productivity of capital*. Any deviation from this path will cause the economy to become unstable. This finding emphasised the importance of savings in the process of economic growth, and led to the conclusion that a country seeking economic growth must first increase its flow of savings.

Figure 19.1 illustrates the process that leads to growth in a Harrod–Domar world. Savings are crucial in enabling investment to be undertaken — always remembering that some investment will have to be used to replace existing capital that has worn out. Investment then enables capital to accumulate and technology to be improved. The accumulation of capital leads to an increase in output and incomes, which leads to a further flow of savings, and the cycle begins again. This figure highlights a number of problems that may prevent the Harrod–Domar process from being effective for LDCs.

Generating a flow of savings in an LDC may be problematic. When incomes are low, households may have to devote most of their resources to consumption, and so there may be a lack of savings. Nonetheless, some savings have proved possible. For example, in the early 1960s South Korea had an average income level that was not too different from that of countries like Sudan and Afghanistan, but it managed to build up the savings rate during that decade.

Setting aside the problem of low savings for the moment, what happens next?

Extension material

The algebra of the Harrod–Domar model

The algebra of the Harrod–Domar model can be revealing.

Suppose there is a closed economy with no government. If there is equilibrium in the goods market, then planned saving (S) equals planned investment (I):

$$S = I$$

Assume that there is no depreciation, so investment results in capital accumulation (ΔK, where Δ means 'change in'):

$$I = \Delta K$$

Assume also that the capital–output ratio (k) remains constant over time. Then:

$$k = \Delta K/\Delta Y$$

where Y is income and/or output.

If savings are a proportion (s) of income, then for equilibrium to be maintained:

$$sY = \Delta K = k\Delta Y$$

Rearranging, this implies that the growth rate of output ($\Delta Y/Y$) must be equal to s/k.

This then provides a simple rule. If a government wishes to achieve a growth rate of, say, 5%, and knows that the capital–output ratio is 3, then the saving ratio needs to be $3 \times 5 = 15\%$. However, although this is a simple rule, it is deceptive. There are many reasons why it is not enough to generate a flow of saving and then sit back and wait for results, especially in the context of less developed countries.

Will savings lead to investment and the accumulation of capital?

If a flow of savings can be generated, the next important step is to transform the savings into investment. This is the process by which the sacrifice of current consumption leads to an increase in productive capacity in the future.

Some important preconditions must be met if savings are to be transformed into investment. First, there must be a way for potential borrowers to get access to the funds. In developed countries this takes place through the medium of financial markets. For example, it may be that households save by putting their money into a savings account at the bank; then with this money the bank can make loans to entrepreneurs, enabling them to undertake investment.

In many LDCs, however, financial markets are undeveloped, so it is much more difficult for funds to be recycled in this way. For example, a study conducted in 1997 by the Bank of Uganda found that almost 30% of households interviewed in rural Ugandan villages had undertaken savings at some time. However, almost none of these had done so through formal financial institutions, which did not reach into the rural areas. Instead, the saving that took place tended to be in the form of fixed assets, or money kept under the bed. Such savings cannot readily be transformed into productive investment. The lack of branch banking may thus be an impediment to the process of economic growth.

In addition, governments in some periods have made matters worse by holding down interest rates in the hope of encouraging firms to borrow. The idea here is that a low interest rate means a low cost of borrowing, which should make borrowing more attractive. However, this ignores the fact that, if interest rates are very low, there is little incentive to save because the return on saving is so low. In this case, firms may wish to invest but may not be able to obtain the funds to do so. This argument reflects the analysis of loanable funds introduced in Chapter 18.

The other prerequisite for savings to be converted into investment is that there must be entrepreneurs with the ability to identify investment possibilities, the skill to carry them through and the willingness to bear the risk. Such entrepreneurs are in limited supply in many LDCs.

During the 1950s, Hong Kong, one of the so-called *tiger economies*, benefited from a wave of immigrant entrepreneurs, especially from Shanghai, who provided the impetus for rapid development. In Singapore the entrepreneurship came primarily from the government, and from multinational corporations which were encouraged to become established in the country. Singapore and South Korea also adopted policies that ensured a steady flow of savings. Gross savings in Singapore amounted to almost half of GDP in 2012.

Will investment lead to higher output and income?

For investment to be productive in terms of raising output and incomes in the economy, some further conditions need to be met. In particular, it is crucial for firms to have access to physical capital, which will raise production capacity. Given their limited capability of producing capital goods, many LDCs have to rely on capital imported from the more developed countries. This may be beneficial in terms of upgrading home technology, but such equipment can be imported only if the country has earned the foreign exchange to pay for it. One of the most pressing problems for many LDCs is that they face a **foreign exchange gap** — in other words, they find it difficult to earn sufficient foreign exchange with which to purchase crucial imports required in order to allow manufacturing activity to expand. In order to do this, physical capital is needed, together with key inputs to the production process. Indeed, many LDCs need to import food and medical supplies in order to develop their human capital. A shortage of foreign exchange may therefore make it difficult for the country to accumulate capital.

During their main development phase, the emerging economies of East Asia were all very open to international trade, and focused on promoting exports in order to earn the foreign exchange needed to import capital goods. This strategy worked very effectively, and the economies were able to widen their access to capital and move to higher value-added activities as they developed their capabilities. China followed a similar strategy more recently.

The importance of human capital

If the capital *can* be obtained, there is then a need for the skilled labour with which to operate the capital goods. Human capital, in the form of skilled, healthy and well-trained workers, is as important as physical capital if investment is to be productive.

Key term

foreign exchange gap a situation in which an LDC is unable to import the goods that it needs for development because of a shortage of foreign exchange

In principle, it might be thought that today's LDCs have an advantage over the countries that developed in earlier periods. In particular, they can learn from earlier mistakes, and import technology that has already been developed, rather than having to develop it anew. This suggests that a *convergence* process should be going on, whereby LDCs are able to adopt technology that has already been produced, and thereby grow more rapidly and begin to close the gap with the more developed countries.

However, by and large this has not been happening, and a lack of human capital has been suggested as one of the key reasons for the failure. This underlines the importance of education in laying the foundations for economic growth as well as contributing directly to the quality of life.

The education systems of the tiger economies had been well established, either through the British colonial legacy (in the case of Singapore and Hong Kong) or through past Japanese occupation periods (in Taiwan and South Korea). In all of these countries, education received high priority, and cultural influences encouraged a high demand for education. The tiger economies thus benefited from having highly skilled and well-disciplined labour forces that were able to make effective use of the capital goods that had been acquired.

Harrod–Domar and external resources

Figure 19.2 extends the earlier schematic presentation of the process underlying the Harrod–Domar model of economic growth. This has been amended to underline the importance of access to technology and human capital.

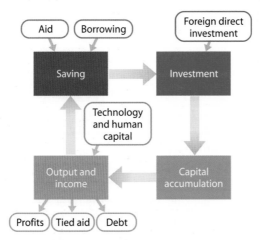

Figure 19.2 The Harrod–Domar process of economic development augmented

The discussion above has emphasised the difficulty of mobilising domestic savings, both in generating a sufficient flow of savings and in translating such savings into productive investment.

The question arises as to whether an LDC could supplement its domestic savings with a flow of funds from abroad. Figure 19.2 identifies three possible injections into the Harrod–Domar process. First, it might be possible to attract flows of overseas assistance from higher-income countries. Second, perhaps the amount of investment could be augmented directly by persuading multinational corporations to engage in foreign direct investment. Third, the LDC might be able to borrow on international capital markets to finance its domestic investment. The tiger economies took full advantage of these external sources of funds.

However, it is worth noting that each of these ways of attracting external resources has a downside associated with it. As far as overseas assistance is concerned, in the past such flows have been seen by some donor countries as part of trade policy, and have brought less benefit to LDCs than had been hoped. In the case of the multinational corporations, there is a tendency for the profits to be repatriated out of the LDC, rather than recycled into the economy. Finally, international borrowing has to be repaid at some future date, and many LDCs have found themselves burdened by debt that they can ill afford to repay.

Summary

- Although development is a broader concept than economic growth, growth is a key ingredient of development.
- The Harrod–Domar model of economic growth highlights the importance of savings, and of transforming savings into productive investment.
- However, where markets are underdeveloped, this transformation may be impeded.
- Human capital is also a critical ingredient of economic growth.
- If resources cannot be generated within the domestic economy, a country may need to have recourse to external sources of funding.

Microfinance

For many LDCs, a particular problem has been the provision of finance for small (but important) projects in rural areas of LDCs. Where a large portion of the population live in the rural areas, the difficulty of raising funds for investment has been an impediment to improving agricultural productivity — in spite of the significance of this sector in many LDCs.

There are elements of market failure in rural credit markets. In particular, there is an information failure. In the absence of branch banking, people in the rural areas do not have access to the formal financial sector. The commercial banks based in the urban areas do not have the information needed to be able to assess loan applications for rural projects. Furthermore, property rights are not secure, so it may be difficult to provide collateral against loans, when ownership of land cannot be proved.

This means that many people in the rural areas are forced to depend upon informal markets for credit, borrowing from local moneylenders or merchants at high, sometimes punitive, interest rates. The rates of interest in the informal sector tend to be much higher than are available in the formal sector, partly because of the risk premium, with it being difficult to assess the probability of default. In addition, local moneylenders may have monopoly power as people in a village may not be able to access other sources of finance.

Attempts have been made to remedy this situation through **microfinance** schemes. This approach was pioneered by the Grameen Bank, which was founded in Bangladesh in 1976. The bank made small-scale loans to groups of women who otherwise would have had no access to credit, and each group was made corporately responsible for paying back the loan. The scheme has claimed great success, both in terms of the constructive use of the funds in getting small-scale projects off the ground and in terms of high pay-back rates.

The Grameen Bank

In 1974 a severe famine afflicted Bangladesh, and a flood of starving people converged on the capital city, Dhaka. Muhammad Yunus was an economics professor at Chittagong University. He tells how he was struck by the extreme contrast between the neat and abstract economic theories that he was teaching, and the plight of those surviving in bare poverty, or suffering and dying in the famine.

He also tells how he decided to study the problem at first hand, taking his students on field trips into villages near to the campus. On one of these visits they interviewed a woman who was struggling to make a living by making bamboo stools. For each stool that she made, she had to borrow the equivalent of 15p for the raw materials. Once she had paid back the loan, at interest rates of up to 10% per week, her profit margin was just 1p. The woman was never able to escape from her situation because she was trapped by the need to borrow, and the need to pay back at such punitive rates of interest. Her story was by no means unique, and Yunus was keen to find a way of enabling women like her to have access to credit on conditions that would allow them to escape from poverty. He began experimenting by lending out some of his own money to groups in need.

Muhammad Yunus launched the Grameen Bank experiment in 1976. The idea was to provide credit for small-scale income-generating activities. Loans would be provided without the need for collateral, with borrowers being required to form themselves into groups of five with joint responsibility for the repayments. The acceptance of this joint responsibility and the lack of collateral helped to minimise the transaction costs of making and monitoring the loans.

On any criteria, the project proved an enormous success. The repayment record has been impressive, although the Grameen Bank charges interest rates close to those in the formal commercial sector, which are much lower than those of the informal moneylenders. Since the initial launch of the bank, lending has been channelled primarily to women borrowers, who are seen to invest more carefully and to repay more reliably — and to be most in need.

By the end of May 1998 more than $2.4 billion had been loaned by Grameen Bank, including more than 2 million loans for milch cows, nearly 100,000 for rickshaws, 57,000 for sewing machines and many more for processing, agriculture, trading, shop keeping, peddling and other activities. Grameen-type credit programmes are now operating in 59 countries in Africa, Asia, the Americas, Europe and Papua New Guinea. By 2009, more than $8.7 billion had been loaned by Grameen, covering 83,458 villages.

As for the impact of Grameen loans in economic terms, the loans are seen to have generated new employment, to have reduced the number of days workers are inactive, and to have raised income, food consumption and living conditions of Grameen Bank members — not to mention their social impact on the lives of millions of women.

Muhammad Yunus and the Grameen Bank were awarded the Nobel peace prize in 2006.

ROSCAS

Other schemes have involved groups of households coming together to pool their savings in order to accumulate enough funds to launch small projects. Members of the group take it in turns to use these joint savings, paying the loan back in order for the next person to have a turn. These are known as *rotating savings and credit schemes* (ROSCAS), and they have had some success in providing credit on a small scale. In spite of assisting some successful enterprises, however, such schemes have been found to be less sustainable than Grameen-style arrangements, and have tended to be used to obtain consumer durable goods rather than for productive investment and innovation.

Suppose that 12 individuals are saving for a bicycle (a key form of transport in many developing countries). A bicycle costs $130, and each individual saves $10 per month. Simple arithmetic indicates that it would take 13 months for enough funds to have accumulated for the 12 individuals to buy their bicycles. Suppose that the 12 people agree to work together. First, they explain to the bicycle dealer that there is a guaranteed order for 12 bicycles, and they negotiate a discount of $10 per bicycle. They then meet at the end of each month, and each pays $10 into the fund. At the end of the first month, there are sufficient funds for one person to buy a bicycle — usually chosen by a lottery. As a result, even the last person in turn gets the bicycle earlier because of the discount they negotiated. Of course, without the discount, one unfortunate person would have to wait the full period, but clearly this is a very efficient way of making use of small amounts of savings. With more people, or higher contributions, the funds can be used for more substantial projects. Administration costs are minimal, but the schemes do rely on trust, such that the first person to win the lottery does not then stop making payments.

In the absence of such schemes, households may be forced to borrow from local moneylenders, often at very high rates of interest. For example, the Bank of Uganda survey mentioned earlier found that households were paying rates between 0% (when borrowing from family members) and 500%. In part this may reflect a high risk of the borrower's defaulting, but it may also reflect the ability of local moneylenders to use market power. The absence of insurance markets may also deter borrowing for productive investment, especially in rural areas.

There is limited arbitrage between the formal and informal sectors, and institutions in the formal sector may find it difficult to gain information that they would need to make loans available.

How successful has the microfinance movement been? The Grameen Bank has provided finance to many people in many parts of the world. Attempts to replicate the Grameen model have also had some success, but in many cases have struggled to be sustainable in funding terms, needing support from governments or non-governmental organisations (NGOs).

Exercise 19.1

Identify ways in which market failure has caused problems in the provision of small-scale credit for projects in LDCs.

Summary

- The provision of credit in LDCs is problematic, especially in rural areas.
- This is partly due to forms of market failure.
- Microfinance is one way in which attempts have been made to provide credit for small projects in LDCs.
- The Grameen Bank in Bangladesh pioneered such schemes, using group-lending schemes focusing on women.
- Other schemes have included rotating savings and credit schemes.
- In the absence of access to formal credit arrangements, the informal market operates, charging high interest rates relative to the formal sector.

International financial flows

Chapter 16 discussed how foreign direct investment and overseas assistance could provide a flow of resources to augment domestic resources. It was seen that neither could be relied upon to guarantee economic growth and development. A further option for LDCs is to borrow the funds needed for development. This may be on concessional terms from the World Bank or the International Monetary Fund (IMF), or on a commercial basis from international financial markets.

As with other forms of external finance, problems have arisen for some LDCs that have tried to borrow internationally. These problems first became apparent in the early 1980s, when Mexico announced that it could not meet its debt repayment commitments. But the stock of outstanding debt has been a major issue for many LDCs, especially in sub-Saharan Africa.

The origins of this date back to the time of the first oil price crisis in 1973/74, when oil prices were suddenly raised by a substantial percentage. For many oil-importing countries, this posed a major problem, as the demand for oil was relatively inelastic, so the increase in the price of oil led immediately to a deficit on the current account of the balance of payments. Borrowing from the International Monetary Fund was one solution, as offering help with short-run balance of payments problems is exactly the role that the IMF was designed to fulfil. However, IMF loans come with strings attached, so many LDCs in the late 1970s looked elsewhere for funds, borrowing from commercial sources. Such loans were often on variable interest rate terms. In the 1980s, oil prices rose again. Furthermore, interest rates rose worldwide when governments in North America and Western Europe adopted strict monetary policies. This created problems for many LDCs that had borrowed heavily — especially those that had not perhaps used the funds as wisely as they might have. Some countries in Latin America threatened to default on their loans, and various plans had to be devised to salvage the financial system.

The problems of debt have proved a major obstacle to development in many countries. Latin American countries were affected strongly, as they had borrowed large amounts in US dollar terms. Countries in sub-Saharan Africa had borrowed less in money terms, but accumulated debts that were substantial relative to GDP or exports. They thus found that a high share of their export revenues was being used to make payments on past debts, and so these revenues were not available for promoting development at home. The problem reached a point at which it was clear that the debt burdens of many LDCs were unsustainable, and the World Bank launched an initiative to tackle the problem.

A number of plans (including the Baker and Brady Plans) were introduced to safeguard the international financial system, but from the LDCs' viewpoint these entailed mainly a *rescheduling* of existing debt: in other words, they were given longer to pay. A consequence was that debt levels continued to grow.

The problems were made worse because in some countries the borrowed funds were not used wisely. Development through borrowing is sustainable only if the funds are used to enable exports to grow, so that the funds can be repaid. When they do not lead to increased export earnings, repayment problems will inevitably result.

A key issue here is the quality of governance in some LDCs. Where the political environment is unstable, and the ruling government knows that its hold on power is fragile, there is little incentive to embark on the long-term investment in infrastructure that could benefit the country. Instead, the temptation is to use the funds available for projects that have short-run impact that might help to maintain the government's political position, or to make the most of being in power and siphon off the funds for personal use by government officials.

The Heavily Indebted Poor Countries (HIPC) Initiative

In spite of the poor track record of some LDCs, it became clear that the debt position of many countries in sub-Saharan Africa was unsustainable, and that this was a serious obstacle to development. In the run-up to the new millennium, much pressure was put on the governments

Synoptic link

The concept of moral hazard was introduced in Book 1, Chapter 8, in the context of the insurance market.

Key term

HIPC Initiative an initiative launched in 1995 to provide debt relief for heavily indebted poor countries

of the advanced countries to take action. For many years, the World Bank was reluctant to consider debt forgiveness. One of the reasons for this concerns moral hazard. It is argued that if a country expects to be forgiven its debt, it will have no incentive to behave responsibly. Furthermore, a country that has been forgiven its debt may have no incentive to be more responsible in the future — and other countries too will have less of an incentive to pay off their debts.

Nonetheless, the response to the debt problem was the **HIPC Initiative**, which allowed for debt forgiveness on condition that the country demonstrated a commitment to 'good' policies over a period of time. The HIPC Initiative was first launched in 1995, but the conditions were so restrictive that few countries were able to benefit. Thus, a number of pressure groups, including Jubilee 2000, lobbied the World Bank to allow the initiative to be more accessible. The original HIPC measures required countries to follow the policy package for a period of 6 years before they would qualify for any debt relief.

The HIPC policy package incorporated four main steps:

1 successful implementation of policies to enhance economic growth (the World Bank's model of market-friendly growth was discussed in Chapter 11)
2 development of a Poverty Reduction Strategy Paper (PRSP)
3 encouragement of private enterprise
4 diversification of the export base

In July 2005 government leaders from the G8 countries met at a summit meeting in Gleneagles. At this meeting the countries present pledged to cancel the debt of the world's most indebted countries — which effectively meant those countries that had qualified under the HIPC initiative.

Figure 19.3 presents some data about this. It can be seen that in 1990 the debt position for many of these countries had been serious indeed. For example, in the case of Uganda, in 1990 more than 80% of the value of exports of goods and services was needed just to service the outstanding debt. For a country with limited resources, this leaves little surplus to use for promoting development. The encouraging aspect of Figure 19.3 is that for most of these countries the situation was much improved in 2012. A major problem with heavy levels of debt is that countries are forced to use precious foreign exchange in repayment of debt, rather than in tackling problems in the domestic economy.

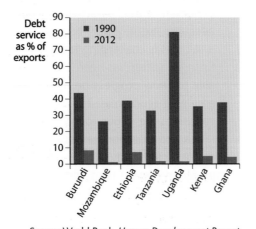

Source: World Bank, *Human Development Report*

Figure 19.3 Debt servicing in sub-Saharan Africa

What is not entirely clear is the extent to which improvements in debt service levels can be attributed to the HIPC Initiative. A number of commentators have pointed out that it is not only the HIPC countries that witnessed a reduction in debt service levels during the period.

Personal remittances

Looking back at Figure 16.7, the other important source of external financial flows into low-income countries shown in the figure is personal remittances. These have shown a steady increase throughout the period since 1990. Personal remittances here are defined as personal transfers and compensation of employees. In other words, this includes current transfers in cash or in kind to residents of an economy from non-residents, together with incomes of workers who are employed in an economy in which they are not residents. For example, a worker may take a job abroad, but send part of the earnings back to the family in the home country.

The steady increase in such remittances may reflect the effects of globalisation, with more workers being more able to migrate to work abroad and more people being forced to migrate as a result of violence and conflict in the home economy. The World Bank has estimated that more than 215 million people live outside the country of their birth.

Evaluation of the financial sector in development

The Harrod–Domar approach suggests that saving and investment are crucial ingredients for a strategy to promote economic growth and human development. If funds cannot be raised domestically, then an injection of funds from abroad will be necessary, in the form of foreign direct investment, overseas assistance or borrowing on international financial markets.

Whichever approach is adopted, the financial sector is vital as a way of channelling the resources to where they are needed. This needs to be accomplished in a way that addresses areas of market failure. Rural credit markets may need specific attention, but funds also need to be provided for improvements in physical and social infrastructure that will then enable markets to operate effectively. In other words, funds are needed for physical infrastructure such as road and communication links, market facilities and so on. In addition, it is important to be able to invest in human capital, by providing education and healthcare and ensuring adequate nutrition for the population.

All this is challenging for LDCs with limited resources. Where the financial sector has been able to work effectively, countries have been able to show progress on many fronts. This has been evident in the emerging economies. The economies that entered a period of rapid growth in the 1960s found ways of mobilising funds. For example, both Korea and Singapore laid the foundations for rapid growth by finding ways of encouraging saving, the funds from which were then channelled into productive investment and infrastructure. More recently, China's success in mobilising foreign direct investment has been one of the key factors in enabling growth.

In sub-Saharan Africa economic growth has been more elusive. Financial markets have not developed to the same extent as in East Asia, nor

Mobile phones give people in rural areas access to market information

have stock markets flourished. Such funds as have been generated — for example, through overseas assistance or international borrowing — have not always been used effectively.

However, there are some encouraging signs for countries in sub-Saharan Africa. Some countries were able to maintain some momentum of growth through the period of global recession, and have made progress in alleviating poverty (although there is still a long way to go).

Some progress has also been made in the financial sector, from what may be a surprising source. The use of mobile phones has expanded in many African countries. This has given people in rural areas access to market information, so that they can make better judgements about what is a fair price for their produce. Mobile phone technology has also provided a way of handling transactions previously denied because of lack of access to the formal financial sector. This is in spite of the fact that relatively few people may own their own mobile phone. Entrepreneurs in some villages make a living from renting out their mobile phones or undertaking transactions.

However, to what extent is the relative performance of emerging and less developed countries due to differences in the performance of the financial sector? The emerging economies had other factors working in their favour. The East Asian economies that developed in the 1960s and 1970s all had good social infrastructure to begin with, in the form of education and healthcare sectors that provided the foundations for developing human resources. They also developed in a period that favoured world trade, and where some of the advanced economies were moving towards a service orientation, leaving gaps for newly industrialising nations to fill. In the later wave, China had vast resources and a plentiful supply of labour to be mobilised. It was also able to channel funds into investment and maintain the competitiveness of its exports.

On this basis, the evidence seems to suggest that an effective financial sector is a necessary condition for economic growth and human development to take place, as it enables funds to be channelled to where they are needed. However, this may not be a sufficient condition to guarantee that success will be achieved.

Exercise 19.4

Analyse the importance of the financial sector for economic growth and human development.

Summary

● One way for LDCs to obtain external funds is through borrowing.
● Loans provided by the World Bank and the IMF have conditions attached that are not always palatable for LDCs.
● Many LDCs have borrowed in the past, but have then been unable to meet the repayments.
● In some cases this was because the funds were not well used.
● Debts built up to an unsustainable level and actions were taken to allow debt forgiveness.
● The HIPC Initiative contributed to large reductions in the debt burden for many LDCs.
● Personal remittances have become increasingly important for LDCs with the increase in migration between countries.

Case study 19.1

Uganda and debt relief

Uganda is a landlocked country in East Africa. It was the first country to qualify for debt relief under the HIPC Initiative and illustrates some of the key issues.

The country gained independence from the UK in 1962, and was governed initially by Milton Obote. There was some political instability in the early years, although GDP per capita remained fairly constant. Obote stayed in power partly by using the army to carry out a coup against his own government. Then in 1971 he was overthrown by Idi Amin, who ruled through military power. During this period the Ugandan economy essentially collapsed, as you can see in Figure 19.4, which shows the time-path of Uganda's real GDP per capita. This was partly the result of Amin's expulsion of all Asian Ugandans, who

had run the country's limited manufacturing industry and distribution sector. He also killed an estimated 300,000 people during his time in power.

Amin was illiterate and allowed no written instructions, which impeded the bureaucracy. In 1978 he invaded Tanzania, but the Tanzanian army, with the help of exiled Ugandans, fought back and took Kampala in 1979. Elections were held in 1980, and Milton Obote came back to power, albeit under allegations of election fixing. Obote's second period was characterised by civil war and lasted until a coup by Tito Okello in 1985. The Okello regime lasted only until 1986 when the current president, Yoweri Museveni, took over, bringing some stability and economic recovery.

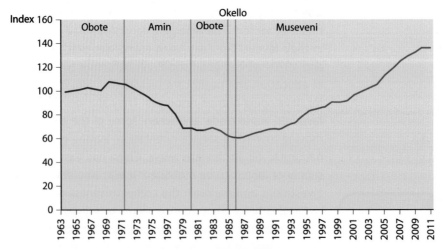

Sources: data from 1982 are from the World Bank; earlier data are from Ugandan sources

Figure 19.4 Real GDP per capita in Uganda (1963 = 100)

Case study 19.1 (continued)

In terms of the HIPC requirements, Uganda did everything expected of it. It established a strong record of sound macroeconomic policies and structural adjustment reforms. It produced its Poverty Reduction Strategy Paper (PRSP) and tried to implement it. The plan included a drive for universal primary education initiated in 1997, supported by $75 million from the World Bank. Figure 19.5 shows the time-path of Uganda's stock of external debt relative to gross national income. The dramatic fall shown in the later years may reflect the effect of the HIPC debt relief.

I visited Uganda in November 1997 to undertake a survey in the rural areas. Even at this early stage in the new policy, some of the effects of the HIPC Initiative were evident. In some cases, children had been held back from attending school in anticipation of the new measures. In other cases, some older children had returned to school — there were several 13-year-olds in the first year of primary education, and 'children' of up to 19 years old enrolled in primary education.

However, although the debt burden has lessened, and in spite of rapid growth during the 1990s (Uganda was one of the fastest-growing economies in the world in this period), the country remains poor.

A number of factors seem to have affected Uganda's situation. First, the international price of coffee fell to unanticipated low levels. With Uganda continuing to rely heavily on coffee for export earnings, this was a major setback. Efforts have been made to bring about greater diversification, and this has shown some results. However, the IMF also concedes that 'further cooperation of the international community is needed to help remove the barriers to trade'. There is a major issue lurking here: it is all very well persuading LDCs to stimulate and diversify their exports, but if they cannot find buyers, the impact will be limited.

In addition, some countries have not conceded the debt relief that is due under the agreements — another indication that international cooperation is crucial in enabling the HIPC measures to become effective.

There is some further evidence that one of the reasons for the persistence of poverty in the rural areas, in spite of Uganda's macroeconomic success, was the lack of integration of these rural areas into national markets. In part this is a result of poor infrastructure — poor roads, lack of market facilities and poor information about national trading conditions.

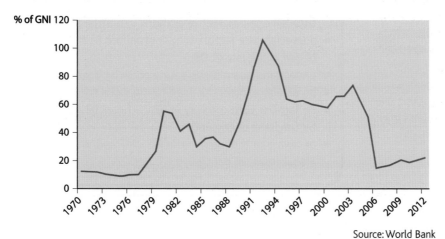

Source: World Bank

Figure 19.5 Uganda's external debt stock

Follow-up question

Discuss the importance of political stability in shaping the development process.

Chapter 20

The central bank and financial regulation

This final chapter explores the role of the central bank in the financial system, looking at the functions of the central bank, and the measures it has available to carry out those functions. Of particular importance are the provision of liquidity to the banking system and the role of an independent central bank in meeting targets set by the government. The need for regulation is examined, together with the way in which changes in the regulatory framework may have contributed to the crisis and its resolution.

Prior knowledge needed

Notice that this chapter builds upon material presented in earlier chapters, especially Chapters 14, 18 and 19. The instruments and operation of monetary policy were introduced in Book 1, Chapter 15.

The functions of the central bank

Key term

central bank the banker to the government, performing a range of functions, which may include issue of coins and banknotes, acting as banker to commercial banks and regulating the financial system

All developed and most developing countries have a **central bank** that fulfils a range of roles, including having the responsibility for issuing currency (banknotes and coins). For example, the UK has the Bank of England to act as the country's central bank. Being the body responsible for issuing notes and coins, the central bank has some direct impact on the quantity of money in circulation in the country. However, this does not mean that it has complete control over the total stock of money, as has been explained in earlier chapters.

The central bank in the UK is the Bank of England

The central bank has other important roles to fulfil. The central bank acts as banker to the government, and may manage the government's programme of borrowing and the country's foreign exchange reserves. Furthermore, the central bank may act as a banker for the commercial banks and other financial institutions that operate in the economy. In addition, the central bank may act as the regulator of the financial system, monitoring the behaviour of the commercial banks and financial institutions. In some countries, the central bank has independent authority delegated from the government to pursue targets for inflation through the setting of interest rates or to promote growth and development. However, not all central banks perform all of these various functions.

The Bank of England operates in sterling money markets — known as the Sterling Monetary Framework (SMF). The Bank's responsibilities include ensuring an adequate supply of liquidity to the SMF participants — that is, the banks and other financial institutions that operate in sterling money markets.

In less developed countries, the central bank may have an important role in establishing and consolidating the domestic financial system in order to build confidence in the currency and financial institutions. It is worth being aware that in parts of sub-Saharan Africa, less than 20% of households have an account with a financial institution. This is not only because of the lack of bank branches (although this is clearly important), but is partly due to a lack of confidence in financial institutions. There may also be a developmental role in ensuring that credit can be made available for key development priorities.

In some cases, the central bank may be given responsibility for roles that support other objectives of the government. An example here would be the State Bank of Pakistan, which also has a responsibility for the 'Islamisation' of the banking system, to recognise the importance to the country of developing Islamic forms of financial instrument.

Islamic banking

The key difference between banking as it is known in Western countries and Islamic banking is that Islam prohibits the use of interest (or usury, as it is known). This means that Islamic banks cannot charge interest on loans or pay interest on savings. Gambling is also prohibited.

A variety of financial instruments have been developed to allow banks to lend to firms or to households without charging interest. For example, a bank may agree a profit-sharing deal with a firm. The bank lends to the firm and then shares in the profits of the project. An alternative is a cost-plus-margin agreement. The bank purchases a given property at an agreed price, and immediately sells it to the buyer, stating the cost plus profit margin. The property is then treated as a commodity sold for money rather than an interest-based loan. The client pays in agreed termly instalments.

The core activities of the Bank of England, the UK's central bank, include acting as banker to the government and financial institutions, managing the country's exchange reserves and supply of currency, and regulating the financial system. These have strong implications for the supply of money and credit in the economy.

Issuing notes and coin

The issuing of notes and coin has long been a core function of the Bank of England, although it does not have a monopoly in the UK, only in England and Wales. Commercial banks in Scotland and Northern Ireland can also issue banknotes, but the issue is regulated by the Bank of England. It is important to control the issue of banknotes in order to make sure that demands are met without leading to inflation. However, issuing notes and coin does not mean exercising control of the money supply because of the wide variety of other financial assets that are near-money.

Banker to the government

The Bank of England acts as banker to the government, in the sense that tax revenues and items of government expenditure are handled by the Bank, as are items of government borrowing and lending. In the past, the Bank of England also had responsibility for managing government debt by issuing Treasury Bills, but this was transferred to the Debt Management Office (an executive office within the Treasury) when the Bank was given independence to control the interest rate in order to meet the inflation target.

Banker to the commercial banks

The commercial banks and other SMF participants hold deposits at the Bank of England in the form of reserve balances and cash ratio deposits. The reserve balances are used as a stock of liquid assets, but also fulfil a clearing role, in the sense that they are used to equalise any imbalance in transactions between the major banks on a day-by-day basis. In normal times, the Bank agrees an average level of overnight reserves that SMF participants expect to require in the month ahead. If any institution holds reserves out of their agreed range, this attracts a charge. In other words, if a bank needs to borrow beyond its agreed average reserve level, it must pay a rate that is above the bank rate. Deposits above the agreed average are remunerated below bank rate. This encourages institutions to meet their requirements in the interbank market, which helps to keep the interbank rate close to the bank rate.

Managing the exchange rate

The Bank of England manages the UK's gold and foreign currency reserves on behalf of the Treasury. However, interventions have been rare in recent years, with the pound being allowed to find its own level in the foreign exchange market.

Monetary and financial stability

Apart from the functions outlined above, the Bank's main mission is 'to promote the good of the people of the United Kingdom by maintaining monetary and financial stability'. **Monetary stability** is interpreted in terms of stability in prices (relative to the government's inflation target). **Financial stability** means an efficient flow of funds in the economy and confidence in UK financial institutions.

The efficient flow of funds requires that there is sufficient liquidity in the economy. In other words, there must be enough liquidity for the financial institutions to conduct their business. The traditional way in which this was done was by the Bank acting as the **lender of last resort**, being prepared to lend to banks if they could not obtain the funds that they needed elsewhere, albeit at a penalty rate. Although this was traditionally seen as a key role, events during the financial crisis made it untenable.

Inflation targeting

In 1997 a significant change in the conduct of monetary policy was introduced by the incoming Labour administration. The Bank of England was given independent responsibility to set interest rates in order to achieve the stated inflation target set by the government. This represented a major change by taking discretion for monetary policy away from the government. This was discussed in Chapter 14, where it was pointed out that an important motivation for this change was to increase the credibility of government policy, in the sense that it could no longer try to use short-run policy measures to create a 'feel-good' factor in the economy. Instead, it was declaring a pre-commitment to controlling inflation, which it hoped would improve expectations about the future course of the macroeconomy.

The **Monetary Policy Committee (MPC)** has as its primary responsibility the maintenance of monetary stability by meeting the inflation target. However, it also has as a secondary responsibility, as meeting the target for inflation is subject to supporting the economic policy of the government, including the objectives for economic growth and employment. In other words, the MPC cannot pursue the inflation target if this excessively endangers growth or employment.

The challenge of the period of inflation targeting has thus been to balance the needs of monetary stability (meeting the inflation target) with ensuring financial stability (by ensuring the efficient and adequate provision of liquidity).

The advantage of having an independent central bank to pursue the inflation target is that it reinforces the credibility of the government's commitment to monetary stability, but the danger is that this could be pursued at the expense of the government's target for economic growth.

Study tip

Be clear about the core activities of the Bank of England and their relative importance for financial markets.

Key terms

monetary stability a situation in which there is stability in prices relative to the government's inflation target

financial stability is present when there is an efficient flow of funds in the economy and confidence in financial institutions

lender of last resort the role of the central bank in guaranteeing sufficient liquidity is available in the monetary system

Monetary Policy Committee (MPC) the body within the Bank of England responsible for the conduct of monetary policy

Study tip

Make sure that you are familiar with the way in which a change in bank rate eventually feeds through to affect aggregate demand and the rate of inflation.

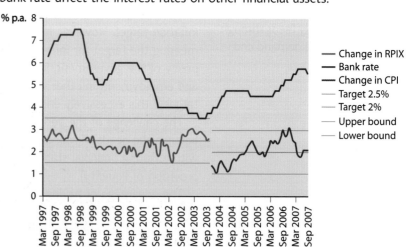

Summary

- The central bank of a country fulfils a number of important roles within the financial system to create monetary and financial stability.
- The central bank takes responsibility for issuing notes and coins — or at least for controlling the quantity in circulation.
- It may act as banker to the government and to other financial institutions.
- It also has a role in regulating the foreign exchange market.
- It may manage the government's debt position.
- In some countries, the central bank has been given independent responsibility for meeting the government's target — for example, the Bank of England has responsibility for meeting the inflation target.

Policy measures available to the Bank of England

There have been significant changes to the operations of the Bank of England in response to the introduction of inflation targeting and the financial crisis that began in the late 2000s. The crisis highlighted the need for closer monitoring of the financial system in order to ensure financial stability.

The pre-crisis period, 1997–2007

In 1997, the incoming Labour government delegated to the Bank of England the responsibility for meeting its inflation target. Specifically, the Bank was to keep inflation within 1 percentage point of the target, which was initially set at 2.5%, as measured by the retail price index (RPI). From January 2004, the target was reset in terms of the consumer price index (CPI), with its rate of change falling within 1 percentage point of 2%. The performance relative to the target from 1997 to 2007 is shown in Figure 20.1.

In the pre-crisis period, the Bank targeted inflation by using the interest rate. As was explained in Chapter 18, there are many different interest rates on financial assets, varying with the degree of risk associated with the asset, the length of loans and so on. However, they are interconnected, so the Bank can influence the rates of interest by changing the rate that it charges on short-term loans to domestic banks. This is known as **bank rate**. You can see how this moved around in Figure 20.1. These changes in bank rate affect the interest rates on other financial assets.

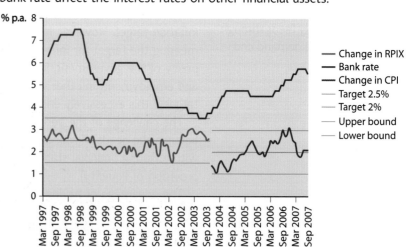

Sources: ONS, Bank of England

Figure 20.1 UK interest rates and the inflation target, 1997–2007

Key term

open market operations
intervention by the central bank to influence short-run interest rates by buying or selling securities

Exercise 20.2

Suppose there was excessive liquidity in the economy. Explain how open market operations would be used to deal with the situation.

Rates of interest also move around in response to market conditions, and the Bank of England can intervene to make sure that short-run interest rates are kept in line with bank rate. It does this by using **open market operations**, buying or selling securities in order to influence short-run interest rates.

Suppose there is a shortage of liquidity in the financial system. Financial institutions will need to borrow in order to improve their liquidity position. This puts upward pressure on interest rates, so there is a danger that interest rates will move out of line with bank rate. The Bank of England can intervene to prevent this by providing liquidity in the system by buying securities (Treasury bills or gilts) in the open market. Conversely, if there is excess liquidity in the system, interest rates may tend to fall, and the Bank can prevent this by selling securities in the open market.

This was a period in which policy appeared to be working effectively. Inflation remained within the specified 1 percentage point of its target, apart from one month when it dipped to 1.9% (April 2000), and one month when it rose to 3.1% (March 2007). Economic growth was steady during this period, and there were no obvious problems with liquidity.

Monetary policy from 2008

This period of stability was not to last. Figure 20.2 shows bank rate and inflation (measured by the percentage change in the CPI) from the beginning of 2008. You can see that the pattern here is very different from that in the period 1997–2007. Inflation moved out of its target range, and bank rate plummeted to an all-time low.

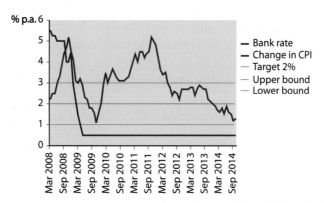

Sources: ONS, Bank of England

Figure 20.2 UK interest rates and the inflation target, 2008–14

During 2008, inflation accelerated. This partly reflected increases in food and commodity prices world-wide. The Monetary Policy Committee took the view that this acceleration would not persist. Economic growth was expected to slow, and inflation was expected to move back below 2% per annum. Rather than increasing bank rate in order to put downward pressure on aggregate demand and inflation, the MPC reduced bank rate in August in anticipation of falling growth and inflation. In the following months, the financial crisis began to unfold.

Even in 2007, it was becoming clear that a number of banks were facing difficulties, having expanded their borrowing substantially relative to their capital base. The response was to reduce lending, sell assets and look for new capital. Borrowing against property was one of the root causes of the problem, as the expectation that house prices would continue to rise had encouraged mortgage lending. When house prices in the USA stalled in 2005/06, defaults began to rise, putting pressure on lenders. The failure of some institutions prompted fears of recession, and one of the side-effects of globalisation was that financial markets were interconnected across national boundaries.

A problem with bank failures is the effect they have on confidence in the financial system. As the crisis developed, it was perceived that some of the banks that were in danger were 'too large' to be allowed to fail. The demise of a large financial institution would have such an effect on expectations that the whole financial system might be called into question. Hence the moves by the UK and other governments to bail out banks that were in difficulties, in spite of the effect that this had on public finances (see Figure 14.3).

Quantitative easing

In the UK, the crisis showed up in the interbank market, where a shortage of liquidity put upward pressure on the interbank rate. By March 2009, bank rate had been reduced to 0.5%, and could not feasibly be taken any lower. The Bank of England suspended the reserves averaging regime at this point in time, as it could no longer be effective. Instead, it introduced **quantitative easing**, a policy under which it created central bank reserves, which were used to purchase high-quality financial assets in order to provide additional liquidity. This was financed by creating electronic money, and allowed the Bank to continue to influence credit and interest rates.

This is essentially a way of increasing money supply. The foundations for this had been set in January 2009 by establishing the Asset Purchase Facility (APF), a subsidiary company of the Bank of England that carries out the necessary transactions. By the end of 2014, the APF had purchased £375 billion of assets by the creation of central bank reserves. The level of quantitative easing is decided by the MPC as a joint decision with that on bank rate.

The problem faced by the Bank in this situation was that the rate of inflation had to be kept under control, but at the same time, the reluctance of banks to lend would affect investment and the growth of the real economy, which was heading into recession. Expectations were weak, threatening to prolong the recession. The UK was not alone in facing this combination of circumstances, and other central banks were adopting similar strategies to deal with the growing crisis.

Figure 20.3 shows the extent to which some other countries were following a common path for economic growth. Having badged the financial turmoil as being the worst since the 1930s, governments were anxious to avoid a repetition of the mass unemployment that had happened then. This was avoided, but you can see in the figure that the recovery was not rapid. It is difficult to disentangle the extent to which the recovery was a consequence of the policy stance adopted by the government and the Bank of England.

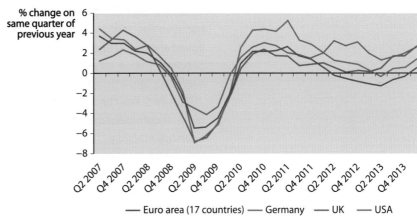

% change on same quarter of previous year

—— Euro area (17 countries) —— Germany —— UK —— USA

Source: OECD

Figure 20.3 Annual growth rate of GDP, 2007–13 (quarterly data)

Financial regulation

Key terms

microprudential regulation financial regulation intended to set standards and supervise financial institutions at the level of the individual firm

macroprudential regulation financial regulation intended to mitigate the risk of the financial system as a whole

Prudential Regulation Authority (PRA) the decision-making body in the Bank of England responsible for microprudential regulation of deposit-takers, insurers and major investment firms

Financial Policy Committee (FPC) the decision-making body of the Bank of England responsible for macroprudential regulation

Financial Conduct Authority (FCA) a body separate from the Bank of England responsible for conduct regulation of financial services firms

A commonly held view was that one of the key factors leading to the crisis had been the inadequate regulation of financial institutions, which had allowed banks to build up portfolios of lending that carried risk beyond what could be covered by their capital. One way of viewing this is that, although central banks such as the Bank of England had structures to enable them to achieve monetary stability, the regulatory framework had not allowed the same degree of control over financial stability.

A new regulatory framework came into operation in April 2013 to try to remedy this situation, and to avoid repetition of the financial crisis in the future. Two new statutory decision-making bodies were created that are part of the Bank of England. The **Prudential Regulation Authority (PRA)** is responsible for **microprudential regulation**, working at the level of the individual firm to promote the safeness and soundness of deposit-takers, insurers and major investment firms. The **Financial Policy Committee (FPC)** became responsible for **macroprudential regulation**:

> *responsible for identifying, monitoring and taking action to remove or reduce systemic risks with a view to protecting and enhancing the resilience of the UK financial system. And, subject to that, supporting the economic policy of the Government, including its objectives for growth and employment.*

'Changes to the Bank of England', *Bank of England Quarterly Bulletin*, 2013 Q1

In addition, the **Financial Conduct Authority (FCA)** will be responsible for ensuring that relevant markets function well, and has responsibility for financial services firms that are not supervised by the PRA, including asset managers, hedge funds, many broker-dealers and independent financial advisers.

The intention of these arrangements is to improve the resilience and stability of the financial system by filling a perceived regulatory gap that had allowed the seeds of the crisis to develop. Other countries, including the USA and the EU, have also established new bodies to perform similar tasks. This is crucial given the interconnectedness of financial markets following globalisation.

Notice that the FPC has primary responsibility for financial stability, but (like the MPC) it also has secondary responsibility for supporting the government's economic policy. This means that it must keep a balance between taking steps to stabilise the financial system and facilitating economic growth and employment.

The FPC has the power to make recommendations. For example, it can make recommendations to the PRA and FCA to take action to safeguard financial stability. The PRA and FCA need to comply, or to explain why this is not seen as appropriate. The FPC can also use the *countercyclical capital buffer,* under which banks, building societies and large investment firms can be required to hold additional loss-absorbing capital. The FPC can also impose *sectoral capital requirements*, under which firms need to meet additional capital requirements where the FPC perceives a risk to the stability of the financial system as a whole. A further power held by the FPC concerns the scope of regulation: in other words, it can recommend changes to the boundary between regulated and non-regulated activities.

The aim of these measures is to reduce the likelihood of future financial crises by monitoring activity more closely and having early warning of where problems may be building up. The FPC and PRA between them can then take action to mitigate the risks of a crisis. Given the impact of globalisation, it is recognised that there is also a need for international coordination of financial regulation. This is discussed in the next section.

Evaluation

The financial crisis highlighted the importance of the financial system for the real economy. Monetary stability is important because low and predictable inflation helps economic agents to form expectations about the future. This encourages firms to invest and allows households to plan their consumption. This in turn can promote economic growth and improvements in the standard of living. However, the crisis demonstrated that financial stability is also crucial, as this enables the flow of funds needed for firms to finance their investment.

The period before the crisis was characterised by monetary stability, with the inflation target being met, and economic growth proceeding at a steady rate. However, the inadequacy of regulation led to a build-up of pressure which finally erupted in financial instability. This disrupted the financial system and had spillover effects for the real economy, resulting in recession and rising unemployment.

The main manifestations of this were in the failure of liquidity. The interbank market was unable to deliver the liquidity that was needed, and the Bank of England's role as lender of last resort could not be sustained with bank rate at 0.5%. In this situation, the Bank resorted to expansion of the money supply through the process of quantitative easing to supply liquidity whilst still keeping inflation within its target range.

The need for financial stability was tackled by the creation of new decision-making bodies with the responsibility for maintaining financial stability through enhanced regulation of the financial system and by monitoring developments in financial markets.

Be clear in your mind about the distinction between monetary stability (low and predictable inflation) and financial stability (the efficient flow of liquidity). You should also be aware of the primary and secondary objectives of the Bank of England in terms of both monetary and financial stability.

In seeking to maintain its primary objectives of both monetary and financial stability, the Bank needs also to maintain balance with its secondary objective of supporting the government's overall macroeconomic policy stance. This is no mean feat when the need to bail out failing banks has left a legacy of high public debt.

Summary
- There have been significant changes to the operations of the Bank of England since the financial crisis.
- The Bank had been given independent responsibility for the conduct of monetary policy in 1997 with a brief to meet the government's inflation target.
- This was to be accomplished through the Monetary Policy Committee (MPC) setting bank rate.
- By setting bank rate, the rates of interest in other segments of the money market would also be affected.
- Open market operations were used to keep short-term interest rates in line with bank rate.
- In the financial crisis, banks faced shortages of liquidity and the interbank market could not cope.
- With bank rate at the lowest level that could be sustained, quantitative easing was introduced to supply liquidity to the financial sector.
- The crisis highlighted the need for greater regulation to maintain financial stability.

The international context

Along with globalisation has come the need to provide coordination of financial markets across countries. Deregulation increased the interconnectedness of financial markets, and the runaway advances in technology and the internet allowed financial transactions to take place smoothly and instantaneously. This improved the efficiency with which markets could operate, but also heightened the possibility for contagion — in other words, it increased the probability that crises could spread rapidly between countries.

There are three key organisations that contribute to international coordination of financial markets and regulation: the Bank for International Settlements (BIS), the International Monetary Fund (IMF) and the World Bank. Each fulfils a specific function in the global financial system. The BIS was established in 1930 and acts as a banker to central banks. It has also played a key role in financial regulation by brokering international agreements.

At the end of the Second World War in 1945, a conference was held at Bretton Woods, New Hampshire, USA, to establish a system of fixed exchange rates. This became known as the Dollar Standard, as countries agreed to fix their currencies relative to the US dollar. John Maynard Keynes was an influential delegate at the conference. In addition to establishing the exchange rate system that operated until the early 1970s, the conference set up the IMF and World Bank to help to oversee aspects of the international financial system. A third organisation took responsibility for the conduct of international trade. This was the General Agreement on Tariffs and Trade, which was the precursor of the World Trade Organization, which was discussed in Chapter 17.

The Bank for International Settlements

The **Bank for International Settlements (BIS)** was originally set up in 1930 to settle the then-controversial issue of the reparation payments imposed on Germany at the end of the First World War. The onset of the Great Depression changed the focus, which switched to activities involving technical cooperation between central banks. The Bretton Woods conference called for the abolition of the BIS on the grounds that it would be rendered redundant by the IMF and World Bank. However, instead it refocused on European monetary and financial issues, becoming a forum for European monetary cooperation.

After the collapse of the Dollar Standard in the early 1970s, the need for international cooperation in the operation of financial markets became apparent, and in 1982 G10 central bankers created the Basel Committee on Banking Supervision, which was to play a key role in financial regulation. The debt crisis that affected a number of Latin American countries in the early 1980s highlighted the need to have measures in place to provide regulation and avoid the possibility of sovereign default — that is, where nations fail to meet their obligations in international debt.

The Basel Committee established a credit risk measurement framework that became a globally accepted standard. This has since been refined, the latest agreement being the Basel III agreement, which specifies internationally agreed capital adequacy requirements for banks. These are administered by central banks, so in the UK these Basel III capital requirements are built into the Bank of England's regulatory framework. The requirements are being phased in, and are due to be complete by 2019. This gradual phasing in of the new regulations is intended to avoid slowing the recovery.

In this way, it is hoped that the likelihood of financial instability spreading across countries will be reduced, as central banks will be imposing similar regulations on their respective financial systems.

The International Monetary Fund

The International Monetary Fund (IMF) was set up with a specific brief to offer short-term assistance to countries experiencing balance of payments problems. Thus, if a country were running a deficit on the current account, it could borrow from the IMF in order to finance the deficit. However, the IMF would insist that, as a condition of granting the loan, the country put in place policies to deal with the deficit — typically, restrictive monetary and fiscal policies.

This role was especially important during the period of the Dollar Standard, when countries were agreeing to fix their exchange rates relative to the US dollar. Loans from the IMF could be used to avoid having to go through the devaluation of a currency. The transition to floating exchange rates in the early 1970s was significant in altering the role of the IMF. However, the IMF was still called upon to help countries to support their currencies — for example, Iceland took an IMF loan in 2008 to stabilise the krona.

Key term

Bank for International Settlements (BIS) an institution that acts as a bank for central banks and sets standards for regulation of banks that are accepted globally

Christine Lagarde, managing director of the IMF, speaking in 2014

In the world of the twenty-first century, the IMF continues to play an important role in maintaining the stability of the interconnected global financial system. In particular, it has provided loans to prevent sovereign default. An example is the loan provided to Greece in 2010 (which is discussed in Case study 20.1 at the end of this chapter). The IMF has also provided loans to governments needing to bail out private banks that had become insolvent because of exposure to risky loans. Recent examples include loans to the governments of Ireland, Latvia and Hungary.

The World Bank

The International Bank for Reconstruction and Development was the second institution established under the Bretton Woods agreement. It soon became known as the World Bank. The role of the World Bank is to provide longer-term funding for projects that will promote development. Much of this funding is provided at commercial interest rates, as the role of the bank was seen to be the channelling of finance to projects that normal commercial banks would perceive as being too risky. However, some concessional lending is also made through the International Development Association (IDA), which is part of the World Bank.

The role of the World Bank is especially important for less developed countries (LDCs), where internal financial markets are undeveloped or dysfunctional. The World Bank has a presence in most LDCs, being involved in a variety of projects to promote development and alleviate poverty. It has also undertaken research into ways of improving access to finance for people and firms in LDCs. Access to finance can be a substantial impediment for firms in LDCs wanting to expand, and for households in need of small loans to improve their income-earning potential. This was discussed in Chapter 19.

Evaluation

Globalisation has increased the interdependence of countries. This allows people around the world to share in economic success and gain mutual advantage through trade. However, it also allows financial crisis to spread more rapidly, and there is a need for international cooperation in regulating financial markets to reduce the likelihood of financial problems occurring.

The BIS, IMF and World Bank have contributed by providing a global framework within which financial markets can be coordinated, and common regulations agreed. However, this has not been enough to prevent crises from occurring, such as the Asian financial crisis of 1997 and the global credit crunch of the late 2000s. In earlier years, the debt crisis of the 1980s gave warning that serious problems could occur when markets are not carefully monitored.

At the time of the 1980s debt crises, there was much criticism that the steps taken in response, such as the rescheduling of the debt of LDCs, were designed to safeguard the global financial system, but not designed to provide a permanent remedy to LDC debt. It was only with the HIPC Initiative that the World Bank agreed to allow debt forgiveness for LDCs — and even then under strict conditions. This may have impeded the development of some countries, especially in sub-Saharan Africa, where debt was putting such a strain on their resources. It is encouraging that some progress has now been made towards promoting growth and development in LDCs, and that measures are now being put in place to improve the stability of the global financial system in the future.

Summary

- The process of globalisation has brought with it the need to coordinate the regulation and operation of financial markets around the world.
- The financial crisis of the late 2000s showed how rapidly a crisis could spread through global markets.
- Three organisations contribute to international coordination in financial markets.
- The Bank for International Settlements has produced standards for the conduct of financial markets that are accepted internationally.
- The IMF has moved on from its traditional role in providing loans for balance of payments purposes, and has made loans to prevent sovereign default.
- The IMF has also made loans available for national governments to avoid the failure of banks.
- The World Bank provides funds for key projects to promote human and economic development in less developed countries.

Case study 20.1

The bailout of Greece in 2010

In May 2010 the EU and the IMF announced a €110 billion bailout loan for Greece. Traditionally, the IMF made loans to help a country to overcome a balance of payments problem or to stabilise its currency. But does that apply to this example?

In this case there was only one reason for the IMF to lend money to Greece and that was to prevent a Greek sovereign default. Prior to the credit crunch, highly indebted governments could borrow cheaply. Governments such as the one in Greece took advantage of low borrowing costs by using debt to finance better public services. The recession that followed the crash of 2008 dented confidence. This led to an increase in the cost of borrowing. In Greece, the government debt servicing costs climbed, which created an even bigger fiscal deficit. The government was in a debt spiral, and a Greek sovereign default seemed imminent.

So, this was not a bailout for the people of Greece. Ordinary Greeks did not receive their share of the loan to blow recklessly on imported German BMWs. Instead, the money borrowed was used by the Greek government to pay its bondholders. These bondholders were French and German banks. According to research carried out by the Bank for International Settlements at the end of 2010, 96% of Greek government bonds were held by European banks. German banks alone held €22.7 billion of Greek debt. The Greek 'rescue package' was really designed to save the German and French banking system, which would have collapsed in the event of a Greek sovereign default. Most of the money lent to Greece spent no time in Greece; instead it was paid straight to French and German bankers.

A protester in front of the Greek parliament — the bailout was used by the Greek government to pay its bondholders

Follow-up question

Discuss why it is so important to prevent sovereign default by a country such as Greece.

Macroeconomics key terms

absolute poverty the situation of a household whose income is insufficient to purchase the minimum bundle of goods and services needed for survival

accelerator a theory by which the level of investment depends upon the change in real output

aggregate demand curve (AD) a curve showing the relationship between the level of aggregate demand in an economy and the overall price level; it shows planned expenditure at any given overall price level

automatic stabilisers a process by which government expenditure and revenue vary with the economic cycle, thereby helping to stabilise the economy without any conscious intervention from government

Bank for International Settlements (BIS) an institution that acts as a bank for central banks and sets standards for regulation of banks that are accepted globally

bank rate the rate of interest charged by the Bank of England on short-term loans to other banks

broad money (M4) M0 plus sterling wholesale and retail deposits with monetary financial institutions such as banks and building societies

capital adequacy ratio the ratio of a bank's capital to its current liabilities and risk-weighted assets

central bank the banker to the government, performing a range of functions, which may include issue of coins and banknotes, acting as banker to commercial banks and regulating the financial system

common market a set of trading arrangements in which a group of countries remove barriers to trade among them, adopt a common set of barriers against external trade, establish common tax rates and laws regulating economic activity, allow free movement of factors of production between members and have common public sector procurement policies

credit multiplier a process by which an increase in money supply can have a multiplied effect on the amount of credit in an economy

crowding in a process by which a decrease in government expenditure 'crowds in' private sector activity by lowering the cost of borrowing

crowding out a process by which an increase in government expenditure 'crowds out' private sector activity by raising the cost of borrowing

customs union a group of countries that agree to remove restrictions on trade between the member countries, and set a common set of restrictions (including tariffs) against non-member states

development a process by which real per capita incomes are increased and the inhabitants of a country are able to benefit from improved living conditions, i.e. lower poverty and enhanced standards of education, health, nutrition and other essentials of life

direct tax a tax levied directly on income

economic and monetary union a set of trading arrangements the same as for a common market, but in addition having a common currency (or permanently fixed exchange rates between the member countries) and a common monetary policy

economic cycle a phenomenon whereby GDP fluctuates around its underlying trend, following a regular pattern

emerging economies economies that have experienced rapid economic growth with some industrialisation and characteristics of developed markets

exchange rate the price of one currency in terms of another

Financial Conduct Authority (FCA) a body separate from the Bank of England responsible for conduct regulation of financial services firms

financial intermediaries institutions such as banks and building societies that channel funds from lenders to borrowers

Financial Policy Committee (FPC) the decision-making body of the Bank of England responsible for macroprudential regulation

financial stability is present when there is an efficient flow of funds in the economy and confidence in financial institutions

fiscal policy decisions made by the government on its expenditure, taxation and borrowing

foreign direct investment (FDI) investment undertaken in one country by companies based in other countries

foreign exchange gap a situation in which an LDC is unable to import the goods that it needs for development because of a shortage of foreign exchange

free trade area a group of countries that agree to remove tariffs, quotas and other restrictions on trade between the member countries, but have no agreement on a common barrier against non-members

General Agreement on Tariffs and Trade (GATT) precursor of the WTO, GATT organised a series of 'rounds' of tariff reductions

Gini index a measure of the degree of inequality in a society

globalisation a process by which the world's economies are becoming more closely integrated

GNI per capita GDP plus net income from abroad, expressed as an average per person

Golden Rule of fiscal policy a rule stating that, over the economic cycle, net government borrowing will be for investment only, and not for current spending

Harrod–Domar model a model of economic growth that emphasises the importance of savings and investment

HIPC Initiative an initiative launched in 1995 to provide debt relief for heavily indebted poor countries

Human Development Index a composite indicator of the level of a country's development, varying between 0 and 1

indirect tax a tax on expenditure, e.g. VAT

inflation targeting an approach to monetary policy in which the central bank is given independence to set interest rates in order to meet an inflation target

interbank lending borrowing and lending between banks to manage their liquidity and other requirements for short-term funds

International Monetary Fund (IMF) a multilateral institution that acts as a bank for central banks and sets standards for regulation of banks that are accepted globally

Keynesian school a group of economists who believed that the macroeconomy could settle in an equilibrium that was below the full employment level

lender of last resort the role of the central bank in guaranteeing sufficient liquidity is available in the monetary system

LIBOR the average rate of interest on interbank lending in the London interbank market

liquidity the extent to which an asset can be converted in the short term and without the holder incurring a cost

liquidity preference a theory that suggests that people will desire to hold money as an asset

liquidity ratio the ratio of liquid assets to total assets

liquidity trap a situation in an economy when interest rates can fall no further, and monetary policy cannot influence aggregate demand

long-run aggregate supply curve (LRAS) a curve that shows the amount of real output that will be supplied in the economy in the long run at any given overall price level

long-run economic growth an increase in the productive capacity of the economy

Lorenz curve a graphical way of depicting the distribution of income within a country

macroprudential regulation financial regulation intended to mitigate the risk of the financial system as a whole

marginal propensity to withdraw the sum of the marginal propensities to save, tax and import; it is the proportion of additional income that is withdrawn from the circular flow

marginal tax rate tax on additional income, defined as the change in tax payments divided by the change in taxable income

market for loanable funds the notion that households will be influenced by the rate of interest in making saving decisions, which will then determine the quantity of loanable funds available for firms to borrow for investment

microfinance schemes that provide finance for small-scale projects in LDCs

microprudential regulation financial regulation intended to set standards and supervise financial institutions at the level of the individual firm

Millennium Development Goals (MDGs) targets set for each less developed country, reflecting a range of development objectives to be monitored each year to evaluate progress

monetary policy decisions made by the government (or the central bank on its behalf) regarding monetary variables such as money supply and interest rates

Monetary Policy Committee (MPC) the body within the Bank of England responsible for the conduct of monetary policy

monetary stability a situation in which there is stability in prices relative to the government's inflation target

monetary transmission mechanism the channel by which monetary policy affects aggregate demand

monetary union a situation in which countries adopt a common currency

money stock the quantity of money that is in circulation in the economy

multinational corporation (MNC) a company whose production activities are carried out in more than one country

multiplier the ratio of a change in equilibrium real income to the autonomous change that brought it about; it is calculated as 1 divided by the marginal propensity to withdraw

narrow money (M0) notes and coins in circulation and as commercial banks' deposits at the Bank of England

natural rate of unemployment the equilibrium full employment level of unemployment

new classical (monetarist) school a group of economists who believed that the macroeconomy always adjusts rapidly to the full employment level of output; they also argued that monetary policy should be the prime instrument for stabilising the economy

non-accelerating inflation rate of unemployment (NAIRU) the rate of unemployment in an economy that is consistent with a constant rate of inflation; equivalent to the natural rate of unemployment

non-tariff barrier an obstacle to free trade other than a tariff (e.g. quality standards imposed on imported products)

official development assistance (ODA) aid provided to LDCs by countries in the OECD

open market operations intervention by the central bank to influence short-run interest rates by buying or selling securities

output gap the difference between actual GDP and its trend value

Phillips curve an empirical relationship suggesting that there is a trade-off between unemployment and inflation

primary production production using natural resources, including the extraction of raw materials and the growing of crops

progressive tax a tax in which the marginal rate rises with income

Prudential Regulation Authority (PRA) the decision-making body in the Bank of England responsible for microprudential regulation of deposit-takers, insurers and major investment irms

quantitative easing a process by which liquidity in the economy is increased when the central bank purchases assets from the commercial banks

recession a situation in which an economy's real GDP falls in two consecutive quarters

regressive tax a tax bearing more heavily on the relatively poorer members of society

relative poverty a situation in which household income falls below 50% of median adjusted household income

repo a sale and repurchase agreement, whereby one financial institution sells a financial asset to another with an agreement to buy it back at an agreed future date

retail banks banks that provide high-street services to depositors

secondary production the production of manufactured goods

securitisation a process whereby future cash flows are converted into marketable securities

short-run aggregate supply curve (SAS) a curve showing how much output firms are prepared to supply in the short run at any given overall price level

short-run economic growth an increase in GDP as the economy moves towards capacity output

stages of economic growth a process described by economic historian Walt Rostow, which set out five stages through which he claimed that all developing countries would pass

stagflation a situation describing an economy in which both unemployment and inflation are high at the same time

tariff a tax imposed on imported goods

terms of trade the ratio of export prices to import prices

tertiary production the production of the service sector; may include the quaternary sector, which includes production based on information technology and information products

trade creation the replacement of more expensive domestic production or imports with cheaper output from a partner within the trading bloc

trade diversion the replacement of cheaper imported goods by goods from a less efficient trading partner within a bloc

universal banks banks that operate in both retail and wholesale markets

velocity of circulation (V) the rate at which money changes hands; the volume of transactions divided by money stock

voluntary export restraint (VER) an agreement by a country to limit its exports to another country to a given quantity (quota)

wholesale banks banks that deal with companies and other banks on a large scale

World Bank a multilateral organisation that provides financing for long-term development projects

World Trade Organization (WTO) multilateral body responsible for overseeing the conduct of international trade

Macroeconomics practice questions

Part 5: Macroeconomic policy and performance

1 GNI per capita is a common way of comparing average income levels across countries. Which of the following is **not** a disadvantage of this measure?

  A The conversion process from local currency units into US dollars may give a misleading view of the purchasing power of income in different countries.

  B GNI per capita focuses on the measurement of material goods and services.

  C It is difficult to capture economic activity that takes place in the informal sector.

  D GNI data are widely understood and available for most countries in the world.

2 Which of the following indicators is **not** used in calculating the human development index?

  A GNI per capita in PPP$

  B Percentage of people living on less than $1.25 per person per day

  C Expected years of schooling

  D Life expectancy at birth

3 Which of the following statements about overseas assistance is true?

  A Since 1974, most advanced countries have delivered on their promise to devote 0.7% of their GDP to providing overseas assistance to developing countries.

  B The direction of flows of overseas assistance is never influenced by political self-interest of donor countries.

  C Debt relief has been provided to many of the most indebted countries, which is not included as part of overseas assistance.

  D In a number of less developed countries, debt relief has released funds for the relief of poverty and for the improvement of human capital and social infrastructure.

4 **a** Explain what is meant by economic and human development.

  b To what extent does the human development index capture the key dimensions of human development?

  c Discuss alternative indicators that could help to evaluate a country's level of development.

5 **a** Examine factors that influence the level of income inequality in a country of your choice.

  b Assess the impact of inequality on economic growth and on economic development.

6 **Poverty in India**

It has been estimated that, despite rapid economic growth in recent years, 450 million Indians are living in absolute poverty. Meanwhile, inequality is growing rapidly: the top 10% earned 12 times as much as the bottom 10% in 2012, compared to 6 times in 1992. Indeed, India is fourth in a world league table of the greatest number of billionaires: there were 61 at the last count, who have a combined wealth of $250 billion. The growth of capitalism has resulted in India's 100 richest people owning assets equivalent to 25% of the GDP.

Growth rates of 8–9% over an extended period have helped to create a large middle class who provide a large market for cars and white goods. However, problems have been created through significant urbanisation and the exploitation of the environment.

  a Distinguish between absolute poverty and relative poverty.

  b Explain how inequality may be measured. Illustrate your answer with an appropriate diagram.

  c To what extent is inequality necessary for the operation of a market economy?

  d Examine the view that poverty is a major constraint on economic development.

  e Assess problems that might arise when a country such as India experiences a period of rapid economic growth.

7 Referring to relevant examples, discuss the view that dependence on primary products is the most significant constraint on economic development.

8 An important aspect of a country's economy is the structure of its economic activity. Identify each of the following as being primary, secondary, tertiary or quaternary.

	Primary	Secondary	Tertiary	Quaternary
Economic activity such as transport, communication, distribution and other services				
The sector in which raw materials are transformed into goods, including manufacturing activity				
Activity that involves the extraction of minerals and other raw materials and the growing of crops				
Hi-tech industry, information technology, scientific research and other information products				

Part 6: Aggregate demand and aggregate supply

1 Which of the following statements about macroeconomic equilibrium is true?

  A The Keynesian school of economists argued that the economy would always converge on an equilibrium level of output and the natural rate of unemployment at full employment.

  B Economists in the Keynesian school believed that the economy could not settle in a macroeconomic equilibrium that was below the full employment level.

  C Long-run aggregate supply is vertical according to the monetarist view.

  D According to the monetarist school, an increase in aggregate demand will lead to a higher price level and an increase in real output.

2 Which **one** of the following does **not** help to explain why the aggregate demand curve slopes downwards?

  A When the overall level of prices is relatively low, the purchasing power of income is relatively high.

  B When prices are relatively low, this raises the real value of households' wealth.

  C When prices are relatively low, government expenditure will tend to be relatively high.

  D When prices are relatively low compared with the rest of the world, the international competitiveness of domestic goods will be strong.

3 Which of the following statements is true?

  A The aggregate demand curve shows planned expenditure at any given overall price level.

  B There is no difference between short-run and long-run aggregate supply.

  C The aggregate supply curve can be derived by adding up the supply curves from individual markets in the economy.

  D An important influence on the position of the aggregate demand curve is the availability and effectiveness of factors of production.

4 Which of the following describes the change in macroeconomic equilibrium in the short run if there is an increase in aggregate demand?

A An increase in the overall price level and an increase in real output
B An increase in the overall price level and a decrease in real output
C A decrease in the overall price level and an increase in real output
D A decrease in the overall price level and a decrease in real output

5 Which of the following describes the change in macroeconomic equilibrium in the short run if there is a decrease in aggregate supply?

A An increase in the overall price level and an increase in real output
B An increase in the overall price level and a decrease in real output
C A decrease in the overall price level and an increase in real output
D A decrease in the overall price level and a decrease in real output

6 Under monetarist assumptions, what would be the effect on macroeconomic equilibrium of an increase in money supply?

A An increase in real output and an increase in the overall price level
B A decrease in real output and an increase in the overall price level
C No change in real output or the price level
D No change in real output but an increase in the overall price level

7 The Phillips curve shows a relationship between:

A Unemployment and the price level
B Employment and the price level
C Unemployment and inflation
D Inflation and aggregate demand

8 Which of the curves in Figure 1 shows a typical Phillips curve?

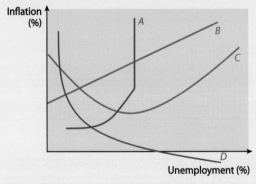

Figure 1 Unemployment and inflation

A Curve A
B Curve B
C Curve C
D Curve D

9 Which of the following statements is true?

A The Phillips curve was based on observation of data over a period of ten years.
B Rapid inflation in the domestic economy relative to the rest of the world is likely to result in a loss of international competitiveness.
C When price expectations are taken into account, the Phillips curve can be seen to become horizontal.
D The combination of high unemployment and low inflation in a number of economies in the 1970s suggested that the Phillips curve had disappeared.

Part 7: The application of policy instruments

1 Which of the following statements about the objectives of macroeconomic policy is true?

  A The macroeconomic policies needed to tackle the range of macroeconomic problems that may be faced by an economy rarely have conflicting effects.

  B Low inflation is seen as an objective because it can help to create an environment in which economic growth can be encouraged.

  C High unemployment is a key objective of macroeconomic policy because it increases the productive potential of the economy.

  D The pursuit of long-run economic growth should be given priority over other objectives, including the need to attain environmental sustainability.

2 Which of the following is **not** a fiscal policy measure?

  A An increase in indirect taxes

  B An increase in government expenditure on infrastructure

  C An increase in interest rates designed to influence aggregate demand

  D A reduction in income tax rates

3 Which of the following statements about monetary policy is true?

  A Monetary policy entails the use of monetary variables such as money supply, the interest rate and the government budget to influence aggregate supply.

  B The two key monetary policy instruments are money supply and the interest rate, but these cannot be set independently of each other — and the exchange rate must also be taken into account.

  C Monetary policy to reduce inflation entails reducing the interest rate in order to reduce the pressure coming from aggregate demand.

  D Money supply is normally the preferred instrument of monetary policy because it is easier to control than the interest rate.

Part 8: The global context

1 Which of the following defines the terms of trade?

  A The ratio of import prices to export prices

  B The ratio of export prices to import prices

  C Export prices multiplied by import prices

  D Export prices minus import prices

2 Which of the following statements is true?

  A If a country's export prices rise by more than import prices, then the terms of trade will deteriorate.

  B If a country's terms of trade deteriorate, the country must export a greater volume of its goods in order to acquire the same volume of imports.

  C The prices of agricultural goods tend to be volatile because world demand for such goods is unstable.

  D There has been a long-run tendency for non-fuel primary product prices to rise relative to the prices of manufactured goods.

3 Which of the following statements is true?

  A A free trade area entails a common external tariff against imports from non-member countries.

  B A feature of economic and monetary union is always the adoption of a common currency.

  C Trade diversion is the replacement of cheaper imported goods by goods from a more efficient trading partner within the bloc.

  D Trade creation is the replacement of more expensive domestic production or imports with cheaper output from a producer within the trading bloc.

4 a Assess the view that transnational companies are the most important cause of globalisation.

  b Evaluate the benefits of globalisation to a country of your choice.

5 a For over 40 years the value of world trade has been growing more quickly than the growth rate of world GDP. Examine the reasons that might explain this trend.

   b Assess the disadvantages of an increase in trade liberalisation to a country of your choice.

6 a Examine the economic effects of the growth of trading blocs on the global economy.

   b Evaluate the likely economic effects on the global economy of an increase in protectionism by developed countries.

7 a Examine the role of the World Trade Organization in world trade.

   b Evaluate the reasons why a country might wish to restrict free trade.

Part 9: The financial sector

1 Which of the following would be seen as the **most** liquid form of asset?

   A Savings accounts in banks

   B Wholesale deposits with banks

   C Notes and coin

   D Treasury bills

2 Money performs four key roles in the economy. Which of the following is **not** one of these?

   A Medium of exchange

   B Outlet for government borrowing

   C Unit of account

   D Standard of deferred payment

3 Suppose that the commercial banks in a country follow a rule such that they always aim to hold 5% of their assets in liquid form. What would be the total increase in bank lending if government action led to an extra $100 being lodged as bank deposits?

   A $180

   B $200

   C $1,800

   D $2,000

4 Which of the following statements is true?

   A The prime determinant of the transactions demand for money is the interest rate.

   B Liquidity preference is a theory that suggests that people will desire to hold money as an asset.

   C Interest rates and money supply can be fixed independently.

   D In most countries, the monetary authorities prefer to target the money supply rather than interest rates because it is easier to control.

5 Suppose that the market for loanable funds is initially in equilibrium, but the government decides to enforce an interest rate ceiling in order to encourage firms to invest more. Which of the following is likely to happen?

   A Firms will borrow more in order to invest more.

   B Households will save more and firms will invest more.

   C The supply of loanable funds will increase, enabling firms to invest more.

   D Households will save less, there will be a shortage of loanable funds, and investment will fall.

6 a Many countries have experienced a rise in their national debt since 2008. Assess factors that could explain this trend, referring to examples of countries in your answer.

   b Discuss the view that governments should take measures to engineer a reduction in their national debt as quickly as possible.

7 a Assess reasons why many countries have experienced a slow rate of economic growth since the financial crisis.

   b Discuss the effectiveness of monetary policy as a means of increasing the rate of economic growth in a country of your choice.

8 a Distinguish between monetary and financial stability.

   b Explain the measures used by the Bank of England to achieve monetary and financial stability.

Index

Page numbers in **bold** refer to **key term definitions**.